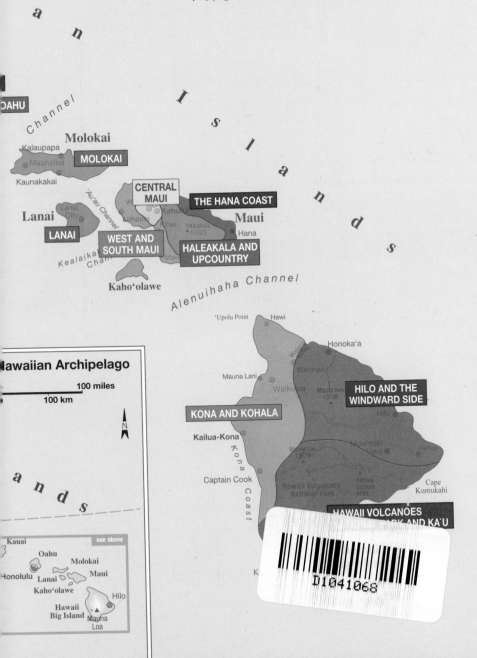

PACIFIC OCEAN

OAHU

Channel

Molokai

Kalaupapa

MOLOKAI

Maunaloa

Kaunakakai

CENTRAL MAUI

THE HANA COAST

'Au'au Channel

Maui

Lanai

Lanai City

Lahaina

Kahului

Kihei

Haleakala
10023

Hana

LANAI

WEST AND SOUTH MAUI

HALEAKALA AND UPCOUNTRY

Kealaika...
Channel

Kaho'olawe

Alenuihaha Channel

'Upolu Point   Hawi

Honoka'a

Waimea

Mauna Lani   Waimea

Waikoloa

Mauna Kea
13796

HILO AND THE WINDWARD SIDE

KONA AND KOHALA

Kailua-Kona

Hilo

Kona Coast

Mauna Loa
13679

Mountain View

Pahoa

Captain Cook

Hawaii Volcanoes
National Park

Kilauea
Caldera
4091

Cape Kumukahi

HAWAII VOLCANOES NATIONAL PARK AND KA'U

Hawaiian Archipelago

100 miles

100 km

N

n d s

Kauai

see above

Oahu

Molokai

Honolulu

Lanai

Maui

Kaho'olawe

Hilo

Hawaii
Big Island

Mauna Loa

Contents

Introduction

The Best of Hawaii.....................4
Aloha...17
Volcanic Isles............................19

History

Decisive Dates...........................26
Beginnings: Ancient Hawaii....29
Arrival of Captain Cook............37
The Hawaiian Monarchy..........41
Modern Hawaii.........................49

Features

Hawaii's People........................59
Outdoor Activities....................71
Music and Hula........................77
An Eclectic Cuisine..................87
Hawaii on Screen.....................93

Insights

PHOTO FEATURES

Ancient Ways and Places........68
Lei..84
Disappearing Flora and
    Fauna...................................198
A State of Fire in the
    Pacific Ocean.....................254

MINI FEATURES

Hawaiian Gods.........................35
Traditional Beliefs....................60
The Lu'au..................................91

Duke Kahanamoku................130
Surfing.....................................157
The Leeward Islands.............165
Humpback Whales.................178
Ni'ihau....................................277

Places

Introduction............................103
Oahu..107
Honolulu..................................111
Waikiki.....................................123
Greater Honolulu...................135
Southeast Oahu......................144
Windward Oahu......................149
North Shore............................154
Central Oahu and the
    Wai'anae Coast.................159
Maui...169
Central Maui...........................173
West and South Maui.............176
Haleakala and Upcountry......185
The Hana Coast......................191
Molokai....................................203
Lanai..214
Hawaii: The Big Island..........221
Kona and Kohala....................225
Hilo and The Windward Side.237
Hawaii Volcanoes National
    Park and Ka'u....................247
Kauai..259
North and West Kauai..........263
South and East Kauai..........271

Travel Tips

TRANSPORTATION
Getting there...........................**280**
Getting around.......................**281**

ACCOMMODATIONS
Choosing a hotel....................**284**
Oahu...**286**
Maui **288**
Molokai **290**
Lanai **290**
Hawaii (Big Island).................**291**
Kauai.......................................**293**

EATING OUT
Choosing a restaurant...........**294**
Oahu...**295**
Maui **296**
Molokai **297**
Lanai **297**
Hawaii (Big Island).................**298**
Kauai.......................................**299**

ACTIVITIES
The Arts..................................**300**
Children's activities...............**301**
Festivals.................................**302**
Nightlife..................................**304**
Shopping................................**305**

Sightseeing tours **308**
Sports.....................................**308**

A – Z
Admission charges...............**310**
Animals **310**
Budgeting for your trip..........**310**
Children..................................**310**
Climate and weather.............**311**
Crime and safety **311**
Customs regulations **311**
Disabled travelers **311**
Emergencies..........................**312**
Embassies and consulates...**312**
Electricity **312**
Gay and lesbian travelers **312**
Health and medical care......**312**
Internet **312**
Maps **312**
Media **312**
Money **313**
Opening hours **313**
Postal services **313**
Public holidays......................**313**
Tax **313**
Telephones **313**
Time zone..............................**314**
Tipping....................................**314**
Tourist information **314**

Tour operators **314**
Visas and passports.............**314**
Weights and measures.........**314**
What to bring **314**
What to wear..........................**314**

LANGUAGE
Background **315**

FURTHER READING
Non-fiction **317**
Fiction **317**

Maps
Hawaiian Islands **104**
Oahu...**108**
Honolulu Center **116**
Waikiki....................................**126**
Honolulu **132**
Maui **170**
Lahaina **179**
Molokai **206**
Lanai **214**
Hawaii (Big Island).................**222**
Hilo..**240**
Kilauea Volcano.....................**248**
Kauai and Ni'ihau..................**260**
Inside front cover Hawaii
Inside back cover Honolulu

THE BEST OF HAWAII: TOP ATTRACTIONS

Hawaii's epic volcanic landscape, scenic highways, and idyllic beaches are the main draw for many visitors, but the islands' historical sights are just as fascinating.

△ **Hawaii Volcanoes National Park**. There aren't many places on Earth where you can see new land being born. That – and the omnipresent evidence of lava flows from years past – is what makes this destination on Hawaii Island a must-see. See page 247.

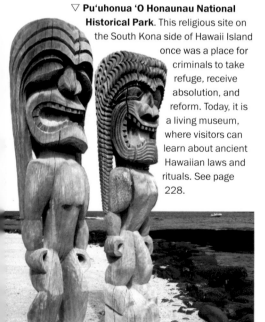

▽ **Pu'uhonua 'O Honaunau National Historical Park**. This religious site on the South Kona side of Hawaii Island once was a place for criminals to take refuge, receive absolution, and reform. Today, it is a living museum, where visitors can learn about ancient Hawaiian laws and rituals. See page 228.

△ **Na Pali Coast**. The lush coastline on the North Shore of Kauai is arguably one of the most picturesque spots in all of Hawaii. Take a boat trip from Hanalei to see the 4,000ft (1,220-meter) cliffs from the water, or hike the hamstring-straining 11-mile (18km) Kalalau Trail for a closer look. See page 265.

▽ **Surfing**. Legends are born (and crushed) on the North Shore of Oahu, where winter brings some of the biggest waves in all of Hawaii. See page 157.

△ **Waikiki Beach**. Sun-drenched sand meets busy metropolis on Honolulu's iconic Waikiki Beach, where high-rise hotels tower over some of the most pristine oceanfront property in Hawaii. See page 123.

▷ **USS Arizona Memorial**. As President Franklin Roosevelt predicted, December 7, 1941, the day the Japanese attacked the US military at Pearl Harbor, has "lived in infamy." Today, visitors to the Oahu site can pay respects to soldiers who lost lives in the attack at the floating memorial over one of the sunken carriers. See page 142.

▽ **Bernice Pauahi Bishop Museum**. This museum, on the outskirts of downtown Honolulu, contains the most comprehensive and mind-boggling collection of art and artifacts from pre-contact Hawaii. See page 135.

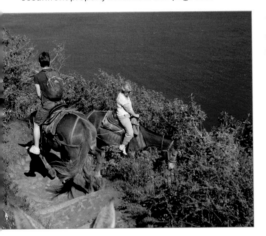

△ **Kalaupapa National Historic Park**. Few visitors to Hawaii make the trek to Molokai, but this national park, famous for its history as a colony for those suffering from Hansen's Disease, is worth the extra effort. See page 206.

▽ **Hana Highway**. It's about 45 miles from Paia to Hana along the world-famous Hana Highway on Maui, and every turn brings new sights to see. Be sure to stop and get out to experience some of the dozens of waterfalls along the way. See page 191.

△ **Whale-watching**. Ka'anapali Beach is Maui's most famous white-sand stretch, but also happens to be one of the best places on Earth to watch humpback whales from shore. See page 180.

THE BEST OF HAWAII: EDITOR'S CHOICE

Stunning landscapes straight from your dreams of a South Seas paradise, ravishing golden beaches, fascinating historical sites, dynamic resorts, and charming 19th-century towns...here, at a glance, are our top picks for a fabulous visit.

Sliding Sands Trail, Haleakala National Park.

MAJOR HIGHLIGHTS

Na Pali Coast, Kauai. Familiar from many a Hollywood movie, the pleated, towering cliffs of Kauai's North Shore are mythic in scale. See page 265.

Diamond Head, Oahu. This dormant volcanic tuff named for the crystals in its soil sits just beyond the soft sands of Waikiki Beach; an invitation to exploration. See page 144.

Haleakala, Maui. The crumbling, multi-colored sands in the summit caldera of Maui's highest volcano serve as a haven for rare species. See page 188.

Kilauea, Hawaii Island. Watch new land burst into life, literally at your feet, as the world's most active volcano makes the Big Island even bigger, day by day. See page 247.

BEST SURFING SITES

Honolua Bay, Maui. Beautifully located bay at the top of verdant West Maui, blessed with dependably towering waves. See page 181.

Honoli'i Bay, Hawaii Island. A lovely spot on the windward side of the Big Island, where Hilo's best surfers battle with fierce surf. See page 240.

Hanalei Bay, Kauai. This huge curving bay, in view of the Na Pali cliffs, is the spiritual home to Kauai's surfing community. See page 264.

Sunset Beach, Oahu. The regular site for several major world championships, Oahu's North Shore attracts the world's premier surfers every winter. Novices beware. See page 308.

Waimea Bay, Oahu. Probably the world's most famous surfing venue, with the biggest rideable waves you will ever see anywhere in the world. Extremely dangerous in winter. See page 154.

Na Pali coastline.

Surfing in the waters off Maui.

Inside the 'Imiloa Astronomy Center.

BEST WALKS

Kalalau Trail, Kauai. This legendary hike along Kauai's Na Pali cliffs offers Hawaii's most breathtaking scenery. See page 266.
Sliding Sands Trail, Maui. An unforgettable hike through the extraordinary moonscape at the summit of Maui's mighty Haleakala volcano. See page 189.

Alaka'i Swamp Trail, Kauai. The only way to explore the eerie rainforest swamplands with stupendous ocean views along the way. See page 267.
Koko Head Trail, Oahu. Not for novices, the hike to the top of Koko Head includes more than 1,000 steps. See page 146.

Hiking in the Na Pali Coast State Wilderness Park.

BEST MUSEUMS AND GALLERIES

Bishop Museum, Honolulu, Oahu. For anyone interested in Hawaii and its Polynesian heritage, the Bishop Museum is the best place to start. See page 135.
'Imiloa Astronomy Center, Hilo, Hawaii Island. A fascinating, hands-on museum that explores the links between modern astronomers and ancient Hawaiian beliefs. See page 239.
Honolulu Museum of Art, Honolulu, Oahu.

This sophisticated gallery houses a globe-spanning collection of artistic treasures. See page 117.
Polynesian Cultural Center, La'ie, Oahu. One part history museum, one part live entertainment venue, the PCC boasts the best lu'aus in Hawaii. See page 152.
Whaling Center, Ka'anapali, Maui. An enlightening introduction to the part Hawaii played in the whaling industry. See page 180

Kailua Beach, Oahu.

BEST BEACHES

Kailua Beach, Oahu. Tempting turquoise waters lap Oahu's Windward Shore. Ideal for kayaking. See page 149.
Papohaku Beach, Moloka. The perfect spot for swimming and beach-combing. See page 210.

Ka'anapali Beach, Maui. Hawaii's best family beach is great for relaxing with the kids. See page 180.
Waikiki Beach, Oahu. Warm waters and gentle waves make this Hawaii's most famous beach. See page 123.

Windsurfing at Ho'okipa.

BEST HISTORIC SITES

Pearl Harbor, Oahu. A sombre memorial to the "date which will live in infamy," Hawaii's finest harbor hauntingly evokes the surprise Japanese attack of 1941. See page 141.

Pu'uhonua O Honaunau, South Kona, Hawaii Island. A beautiful spot in its own right, this so-called "place of refuge" was once a royal precinct, and is still adorned with fearsome carved images. See page 228.

Kealakekua Bay, South Kona, Hawaii Island. A stark white obelisk marks the precise location where Captain Cook lost his life in 1779. See page 228.

Pi'lanihale Heiau, Hana, Maui. The largest ancient temple in all Polynesia, a multi-tiered oceanfront pyramid on Maui's ravishing Hana coast. See page 194.

Pu'ukohola Heiau, South Kohala, Hawaii Island. The "war temple" where Kamehameha the Great performed human sacrifices before he conquered all the islands, still dominates the Kohala shoreline. See page 231.

'Iolani Palace, Honolulu, Oahu. Built in 1882, this imposing palace in the heart of Honolulu served as a prison for Hawaii's last queen, after her kingdom was overthrown. See page 111.

'Iolani Palace, Honolulu.

BEST OCEAN ACTIVITIES

Windsurfing at Ho'okipa, Maui. Crowds of spectators gather on the hillsides to watch the amazing feats at the planet's premier destination for top-class windsurfers. See page 186.

Snorkeling at Hanauma Bay, Oahu. Shoals of iridescent fish congregate in this gorgeous nature preserve; a volcanic crater that's a short ride out from Waikiki. See page 146.

Diving at Molokini. The crystal-clear waters, a few miles off South Maui, attract boat-loads of divers daily. See page 183.

Whale-watching off Maui. Every winter, the shallow waters that separate Maui from Lanai and Molokai are teeming with migratory humpback whales. See page 178.

Kayaking in Kailua Bay, Oahu. There's no better place to paddle a rented kayak than in the beautiful shallow waters off Oahu's finest beach. See page 149.

BEST SMALL TOWNS

Hanapepe, Kauai. Loop off Kauai's circle-island highway to while away an hour or two in this delightful little village, with its fading antique stores and swinging rope-bridge. See page 275.

Hawi, Hawaii Island. Hidden at the quiet northernmost tip of the Big Island, Hawi makes a great half-way stopping point on a tour of the lovely North Kohala district. See page 234.

Lanai City, Lanai. Once the pineapple capital of the world, this former plantation town, with its pretty gardens and simple cafés, is unlike any city you've ever seen.

See page 216.

Hale'iwa, Oahu. The only town on Oahu's North Shore is a laidback hangout for surfers and backpackers, with quirky stores, galleries, and wholefood restaurants on all sides. See page 155.

Makawao, Maui. This one-horse town still evokes the days when Maui's verdant Upcountry was home to the Hispanic cowboys known as *paniolos*. See page 186.

Kaunakakai, Molokai. Molokai's sleepy little capital is the perfect place to hang out for a lazy afternoon of simply "talking story". See page 204.

The beautiful 'Akaka Falls.

HAWAII'S NATURAL WONDERS

'Akaka Falls, Hawaii Island. This towering, majestic waterfall is reached by a short hike deep into the rainforest of the Big Island's Hamakua coast. See page 240.

Nu'uanu Pali Lookout, Oahu. Travelers crossing the Ko'olau Mountains are suddenly confronted by the vast sweeping cliffs that line the Windward Coast. See page 139.

'Iao Needle, Maui. An abrupt, velvet-coated pinnacle buried deep in the West Maui Mountains. See page 175.

Waimea Canyon, Kauai. This deep chasm is slowly splitting Kauai in two, and glows green, gold, and red as the sun crosses the sky. See page 267.

Garden of the Gods, Lanai. These eerie red badlands are more like something you'd find in the Wild West than in lush Hawaii. See page 217.

Halawa Valley, Molokai. This magnificent valley was home to some of Hawaii's earliest Polynesian settlers. See page 209.

Storefronts in Makawao, Maui.

MONEY-SAVING TIPS

Inter-island travel Hawaii's various airlines are constantly in fare-cutting competition to attract inter-island passengers. Check their websites for current rates, rather than booking your flights between the islands as part of your trans-Pacific itinerary.

Getting around On Oahu's excellent public bus network, TheBus, fares are much cheaper, and the range of routes served is much wider, than on the various overpriced "trolley" services that operate in Waikiki. You can even travel around the entire island for just $2.50. Public transportation is less helpful on other islands, but rental car specials are available every season.

Cheap eating Visitors to every island can save enormously on inflated prices by dining at farmers' markets, or in the food courts at major shopping centers. "Local" restaurants operated by Hawaii's various immigrant groups offer more varied cuisine at bargain prices.

Adventuring on land and sea Access to beaches and the ocean is always free and unrestricted. Bring your own surfing or snorkeling equipment, or rent it cheaply on the islands. Similarly, most of Hawaii's very best hiking trails, such as on the volcanoes of Maui and Hawaii Island, are clearly marked routes in national and state parks.

One man and his dog at 'Ehukai
Beach Park, home of the Banzai
Pipeline, Oahu.

The Milky Way from Mauna Kea Observatory on Big Island.

Kailua Beach, Oahu.

ALOHA

On the six major, freely visitable islands of
Hawaii, spectacular scenery, colorful history,
and modern comforts add up to paradise.

*Waterfalls near the Hana
Highway, Maui.*

Smack in the middle of the Pacific Ocean, the eight
major inhabited islands of the Hawaiian archipelago
rise from the sea like oases out of a desert. In reality,
they are giant volcanoes – one of which is still active, by the
way. But for many, including the Polynesians who discovered
them hundreds of years ago, the islands represent paradise
– a tropical wonderland that almost is too beautiful to com-
prehend. Secluded beaches, fragrant rainforests, mountains
that soar above the mists, fiery sunsets silhouetting majestic
waving palm trees, and waterfalls shimmering like silvery ribbons in valleys unmarred by human footsteps: these are the attributes that have made
Hawaii one of the most alluring destinations on Earth.

But physical beauty is only the beginning for Hawaii is rich
in culture and history as well. Native Hawaiians have perhaps
the most celebrated past; it's difficult to explore these rocks
without hearing about their legends and creation myth once
or twice. (Their language, with its tricky-to-master glottal
stop (see page 316), is omnipresent too.) In modern history,
the islands of Hawaii also have become home to an amaz-
ingly diverse gathering of peoples from all over the world.
These cultures have grown together, creating a new, distinctly
Hawaiian take on food, fashion, and art.

*A wiliwili tree blooms by the
windy road to Hana, Maui.*

Today, Hawaii's economy is driven in large part by tourism. Nearly eight million people visited the islands in 2012,
pumping more than $14 billion into the state. While Oahu,
the island with the state's largest city (Honolulu), draws the greatest crowds,
other islands, such as Maui, Kauai, and Hawaii Island (which many also call
"The Big Island"), have experienced significant traffic in the last decade, as
well. Lanai and Molokai receive the fewest visitors, and Niʻihau, the westernmost island, is open only to native Hawaiians. Kahoʻolawe isn't open to visitors at all. Think of the eight islands like siblings from the same family; while
each has a distinct personality, all are very much part of the same whole.

No matter how you experience Hawaii, you will be touched by Hawaii's
spirit of *aloha*. Translated, the word *aloha* breaks down as *alo*, to face, and *ha*,
the breath of life. It is the spiritual glue that binds the islands' population,
whatever the ethnic or cultural background. At the same time, it is perhaps
the best way to describe the locals' perspective on visitors from afar: welcoming, inviting, and eager to share.

Sunrise over Haleakala National Park, Maui.

VOLCANIC ISLES

Technically, the Hawaiian Islands are volcanoes
rising out of the sea; what is visible is just the
tops of these hulking landmasses that have
emerged from the ocean floor.

It's difficult to think about things in geologic time; because most of us are only here for around three quarters of a century (if we're lucky), pondering the past in the context of so many years can boggle the mind. Nevertheless, this type of long-term perspective is critical for understanding how the islands of Hawaii came to be, because each and every one of the islands is – or once was – a volcano that rose from the depths of the sea and weathered over time.

Consider recent lava flows at Kilauea, the active volcano on Hawaii Island. Every week the lava oozed from the Earth and dropped into the sea, the island grew another few inches. Over hundreds of thousands of years, this is how the entire archipelago was born – a necklace of volcanoes in the middle of the Pacific Ocean.

Scientists believe it all began about 28 million years ago, when lava from the fiery interior of the Earth rumbled and surged, blasting through a jagged vent 15,000ft (4,600 meters) below the ocean's surface. A fraction of an inch at a time – 2 to 3ins (5 to 8cm) a year – the Pacific Plate of the Earth's crust crept northwest, rafting the volcano that had formed away from the hot spot and allowing a new sea mount to build under the water. A number of islands broke the ocean's surface, grew, and then eroded away into atolls, while at the same time newer islands formed. Eons later, a line of subterranean mountains, some rising to 15,000ft (4,600 meters) above sea level, stretched majestically in a row across 1,600 miles (2,500km) of the Pacific Ocean, from Hawaii Island to Kure Atoll, far to the northwest.

After these cataclysmic geologic events, biology took over. Over the centuries, floating seeds, fish, and marine larvae drifted to the islands on ocean currents. Winds carried fern spores,

Na Pali Coast State Wilderness Park, Kauai.

tiny seeds, and insects. Birds, sometimes full of fertile eggs or viable seeds, landed here, often propelled by storm winds. These isolated colonists adapted to suit their environment, making them unique, or endemic, to Hawaii. Over time, they have interacted with other non-native species (many brought by man) to populate an ecosystem that is now uniquely Hawaiian.

Hawaii's shield volcanoes

More than 10,000 years from now, we may write about Hawaii having nine major islands. Some 30 miles (50km) southeast of Hawaii Island's southernmost point, far beneath the surface of the ocean, a new island – Lo'ihi – is forming over a hot spot in the Earth's crust. Such eruptions, which begin on the ocean bottom, are the first stage in building Hawaii's broad shield volcanoes; the name derives from their supposed resemblance to the shields of ancient warriors, lying on the ground. Each volcano slowly grows as a thin layer of lava covers earlier layers. Underwater, lava hardens into pumice – light rocks full of gas bubbles – and pillow lava, or rock hummocks with rounded, smoother shapes.

Lo'ihi is predicted to jut from the ocean as a new sheer-sided, cliff-rimmed island some tens of thousands of years from now. Depending on the forces of nature – or on the whim of the volcano

> With its 132 islands, atolls, reefs, and shoals, Hawaii has the fourth-greatest length of coastline in the United States.

when it erupts, producing a fluid flow that hardens to smooth, ropy lava. 'A 'a, on the other hand, hardens to rough, chunky, and sharp lava.

Eventually, the tops of the volcanoes collapse, creating wide depressions known as calderas. On Hawaii Island, Kilauea (which is currently erupting) and Mauna Loa both have calderas.

Carlsmith Beach Park, Hilo, Big Island.

goddess Pele – it may eventually connect with Hawaii above sea level, making Hawaii Island even bigger.

When seamounts break the ocean's surface, the lava erupts in fiery fountains, flowing from craters and rifts in the mountain's sides. Five such seamount volcanoes formed Hawaii Island: Kilauea, Mauna Loa, Hualalai (all have been active within the past 200 years), Mauna Kea, and Kohala, the oldest volcano on Hawaii Island. Basaltic lava from ancient and more recent eruptions is the most common rock in the Hawaiian chain. A drive around the Volcano area and Ka'u reveals two types of hardened lava: *paho'eho 'e* and *'a 'a*. Both have the same chemical composition. *Paho'eho 'e*, because it retains more gas, is hotter

When lava from these active volcanoes reaches the sea, you can witness the awesome process of island creation.

Hot lava pouring into the ocean turns shore waters into churning cauldrons, giving rise to towers of steam and cloud build-up. Sulfur dioxide released by active calderas combines with rain from these clouds, falling as dilute sulfuric acid. Chlorine gas freed from boiling sea water mixes with the sulfur, giving the area a chemical odor. It's a primordial scene not to be missed, but it can be dangerous.

The life cycle of an island

Once the volcano-building stops, other forces take over. Wind and sun eat away at the land, surf carves the coastlines, and rain cuts valleys and ridges into the new mountains. Volcanic rocks break down and gradually turn into soil. Plants arrive, then animals. Eventually, humans take over. What was once just a hot spot on the ocean floor is now fertile, life-supporting land.

Like the creatures that populate them, islands become middle-aged, grow old, and die. This aging process is visible in the Hawaiian Island chain. After new islands form, coral reefs start growing at the edges, circling the island like underwater *lei* (garlands). As an island erodes

islands in a circular shape. Kure, at the northwest end of the Hawaiian chain, is such an atoll. Molokini, a popular snorkeling spot between Maui and Kahoʻolawe, is another.

Forces of erosion have turned gentle slopes similar to those found on Mauna Loa into breathtaking ridges like those of Kauai's Na Pali coast. The towering North Shore cliffs of Molokai are the tallest ocean cliffs in the world, rising nearly 2,000ft (600 meters) above the sea. Sandy beaches, rocky shores, and crater-shaped bays line other coastal areas throughout the state.

On the Sliding Sands Trail in Haleakala National Park, Maui.

and sinks toward the northwest with the shifting tectonic plate, the coral grows upward, searching for the sunshine so it can survive. Reefs growing on the outskirts of middle-aged islands like Maui, Molokai, Lanai, Oahu, and Kauai are called fringing reefs. The fringing reef associated with Hawaii Island is only now just beginning to be formed.

As the Pacific Plate continues to sink, lagoons tend to appear between the reef and its island. These barrier reefs can be seen in some of the older Hawaiian islands of the northwest chain. Eventually, the island in the center vanishes underwater, creating an atoll – a coral reef enclosing a lagoon. The coral reef rises above the ocean unevenly, forming numerous low

Climate

Ecosystems in Hawaii are many and varied, depending not only on the location of the islands on the Earth's surface, but also on the topography of the land and the amount of wind, rain, and sunshine in each area.

Because Hawaii is in the sub-tropics, seasonal differences are slight. Temperatures are relatively stable, varying from an average of 80°F (25°C) around the coastal areas in winter months to 88°F (31°C) in the summer. At higher elevations, the difference increases. On the same latitude as Mexico City, Hong Kong, and Cairo, Hawaii's longest day is 13 hours and 20 minutes compared to Seattle's 16 hours; the shortest day is 10 hours and 50 minutes, while

Seattle's is 8 hours and 20 minutes.

Rainfall in the islands is most sparse in leeward areas – central mountains drain the northeasterly trade winds – and atop the highest mountains of Hawaii Island. The average annual rainfall ranges from less than 10ins (25cm) to more than 430ins (10 meters).

Weather develops as the trade winds carrying clouds across the ocean ascend the mountains and the air is cooled. Condensation causes rainfall on the windward side of the mountain ranges, leaving little moisture to fall as the depleted winds pass over the leeward side of

communities in Hawaii, which are named according to elevation, moisture, and vegetation. Within each of these, the plants and animals interact with one another and their environment to form ecosystems. In some areas, preserves – rainforests or shifting sand dunes that might hide traces of former lives, the bones of extinct birds, or ancient Hawaiian burial grounds – have been set aside. In these ecosystems, native species are protected.

A wetland is one kind of ecosystem. The term wetland refers to areas where water dominates the environment and its plants and animals. Wet-

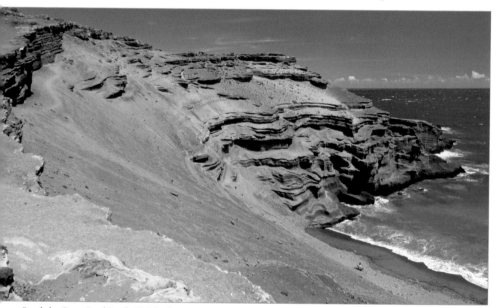

Papakolea Green Sand Beach, Big Island.

each island. The climates of the islands mimic climates of much larger continents, with tropical rainforests, grasslands, deserts, and even areas of tundra represented on a smaller scale.

Ecosystems of Hawaii

Narrow bands around each island where land and ocean meet are called coastal vegetation zones. Here, hundreds of plant and animal species live, each having adapted in its own way to this unique environment. There has been human settlement in coastal zones for so long that it is difficult to find a place that hasn't been altered by human activity.

However, even with so much human influence, researchers recognize 150 different plant

lands can contain salty, brackish (salt and fresh), or fresh water, and can be up to 6ft (2 meters) deep. Anything deeper is a lake. Hawaii's bogs, estuaries, swamps, and streams contain and nurture unique scenery, plant life and bird life that's well worth checking out. Luckily, much of what remains undeveloped is preserved as parkland, as are Hawaii's remaining wetlands and mountainous interior. Land use issues are a hot item in today's Hawaii.

Forests contain dozens of ecosystems. Hawaii's forests are divided into dryland, medium-wet, and rainforests. Before humans came to Hawaii, dryland forests covered the leeward side of the larger islands and nearly all of Lanai and Kaho'olawe.

Ancient Hawaiians cleared much of this land for agriculture; later settlers finished the job. Today, dryland forests are rare. Researchers believe that in the past, the islands were wetter, with extensive dryland forests producing and holding moisture.

Medium-wet forests, growing between 2,000 and 9,000ft (600 and 2,700 meters), have the largest number of native tree species of all ecosystems in Hawaii, including the rainforests, which grow in the elevation zone just above the medium-wet forests. Hawaii's rainforests receive at least 100ins (254cm) of rain per year. During the winter, clouds often engulf these forests, producing thick, cool mists. The two native trees seen most often in both types of forests are *koa* and *'ohi'a lehua*, which support Hawaii's famous forest birds, the honeycreepers and their relatives.

Above the forests are alpine zones where few plants grow. Some desert-type plants like Hawaii's famous silverswords thrive in these high, dry, alpine areas, along with some insects. In some of these alpine areas, on Hawaii Island's Mauna Loa and Maui's Haleakala, for example, snow sometimes falls in winter.

Plants and animals

The Hawaiian Islands began as barren lava rock, thousands of miles from the nearest land. Today the islands are lush with plants and teem with animal life; some of these are native, but most have been introduced by people.

Hawaii's native species are the plants and animals that managed to establish themselves without human interference. This colonizing of the islands was a slow process. If today's Hawaiian

Common Hawaiian plants like coconut palms, bananas, sugar cane, and breadfruit were actually early imports.

islands are between 1 million (Hawaii Island) and 7 million (Kauai) years old, then only one plant needed to establish itself every 15,000 years to account for today's mix of native plants. The best places to see these plants and animals are in Hawaii's national parks, wildlife refuges, and the state's marine conservation districts, where all reef-life is protected from fishing.

Most marine life encountered is native, or endemic, except for several species of snappers,

imported by the state from Tahiti in the 1950s as game fish. All sea turtles in Hawaii are native, and are endangered and protected by law. It is illegal to ride or chase these harmless creatures.

Hawaii's only native land mammal is the hoary bat. Because of their night-time habits and secretive natures, bats are extremely difficult to find, even for researchers.

Native marine mammals include whales, dolphins, and monk seals. These are also protected by federal laws. Perhaps the greatest success story is that of the humpback whale, which once was endangered but now is thought to be thriv-

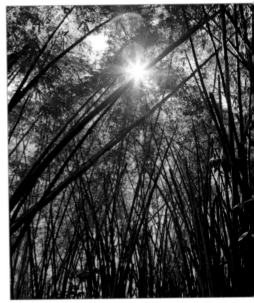

Bamboo forest, Na Pali Coast State Wilderness Park, Kauai.

ing to the point where researchers are considering removing it from the endangered species list. On the flipside, with only about 1,300 of them left, Hawaiian monk seals are in extreme danger of extinction. If you see one resting on a beach, which is normal behavior for them, back off quietly and consider it a lucky day.

Only a few of the flowers and trees along Hawaii's highways are native. Seven kinds of hibiscus are native, but with 200 species of hibiscus in the world and more than 5,000 hybrids, the ones you see are often not Hawaii originals. Pandanus, also called screwpine or *hala*, are roadside native trees. *Koa* (popular for furniture) and *'ohi'a lehua* are native trees common to parks and preserves. Since many of their seeds float, beach plants are often native, including beach morning glories and beach *naupaka*, or thick green bushes with white flowers.

Introduced species

By AD 500, Polynesians had brought with them the plants and animals they needed to live in their new home. Although keeping these species alive through such voyages was a tricky business, the immigrants managed to shuttle at least 27 kinds of plants and several kinds of animals – some wanted, some not – to Hawaii.

Even though this happened centuries ago, these

and the nuts themselves are polished to make necklaces and bracelets. It's easy to spot the abundant *kukui* trees in a forest: their leaves, which look as if they've been dusted with flour, are very pale next to others.

Sugar cane is another introduced Polynesian plant. Ancient Hawaiians used it as a sweetener, for food during famines, and as medicine. The leaves were used for hats and thatching. For decades, sugar cane was Hawaii's leading crop. It is still grown today; one acre (0.5 hectare) of land yields more than 11 tons (9,900kg) of cane, giving Hawaii the highest yield per acre in

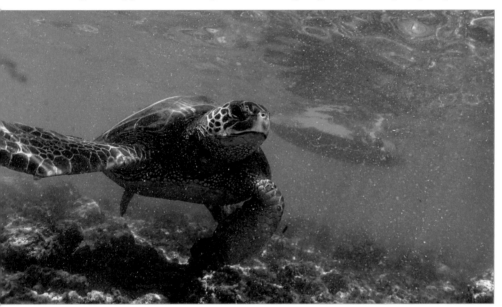

Green turtle at Carlsmith Beach, Hilo, Big Island.

species are considered alien because humans had a hand in their introduction. As a result, a few plants and animals that many might think of as native to Hawaii are actually aliens, introduced by those early settlers. Some common plants on this list are coconut palms, bananas, bamboo, ginger, breadfruit, taro, sweet potatoes, yams, mountain apples, and bottle gourds.

Candlenut trees, called *kukui* in Hawaiian, were also introduced, but this is still Hawaii's official state tree, partially due to the fact that the nut had so many uses in early Hawaii. The meat could be burned for light or ground up for seasoning food. The nut itself was used for body adornment. *Kukui* products are still common: the oil from the nuts is used in cosmetics,

the agricultural world. In recent years a number of corporations (and wealthy individuals) have tried to burn sugar cane as an alternative energy source, but potential environmental ramifications have hindered widespread adoption of these efforts. Generally speaking, high overhead and steady competition from other sweeteners have caused a dramatic and continuing decline in the Hawaiian sugar cane industry overall.

The post-contact onslaught

Hawaii's landscape changed forever when the first Polynesian explorers landed with their plants and animals, but that was only the beginning. Since Cook's arrival, plants and animals have streamed into the islands from all over the world. Today, many of these are more common than native or Polynesian-introduced species.

As these aliens often out-compete or eat native species, the flood of introductions is causing the extinction of many endemic plants and animals. Hawaii has the dubious distinction of having more endangered plant and animal species than any other American state. This can be attributed partly to its isolation, as a lack of natural enemies allowed more species to adapt and survive here than elsewhere.

Obviously, introduced species aren't all bad. Exotic plants provide Hawaii with stunning

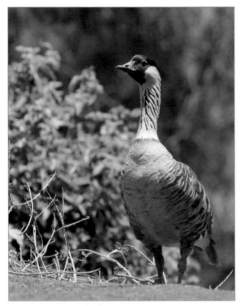

Nene goose on Big Island.

HAWAIIAN GOOSE

One of the most famous animal stories in Hawaii is that of the *nene*, or the Hawaiian Goose. Believed to have descended from the Canada Goose, the official state bird is endemic to Hawaii and is believed to have first landed on Hawaii 500,000 years ago. By the mid-1900s, the *nene* was once endangered due to hunting and predation (by mongooses and other critters). State-led conservation efforts in the last 20 years have succeeded in rehabilitating the species significantly, but it is still considered the rarest goose on Earth. The animals can be spotted in the wild on Hawaii Island and Maui; there also is a healthy population at the Honolulu Zoo.

flower *lei*, sweet-smelling gardens, and highways lined with color, which comes from bougainvilleas and plumerias, native to tropical America. Other common aliens are ironwood and silk oaks from Australia, banyan trees from Asia, and Cook's pines from the South Pacific Cook Islands. Orchid growers, especially on Hawaii Island, have made Hawaii world-famous for orchid hybrids. Hawaii has just three native orchids, a minute number compared to the 30,000 species that make up the entire family.

Many food plants associated with Hawaii are foreign, including coffee (Africa), pineapples (Brazil), mangos (India), papaya (tropical America), and lychee (China).

Many alien animals, however, are not welcome: pigs, goats, sheep, and wild cats have all caused environmental disasters. Mongooses, for example, were imported by sugar growers to eat rats, but preferred native birds and their eggs. It was realized too late that mongooses hunt during the day, while rats are active at night. Only Kauai remains mongoose-free, and it therefore holds the largest population of birds.

Some non-native creatures, such as mynah birds and red-crested cardinals, are welcome, but state officials guard against pests such as snakes, particularly the brown tree snake from Guam, which has virtually extinguished avian life there. (The snakes hitchhike in the wheel wells of commercial and military aircraft flying to Hawaii from Guam.) Strict laws have been largely successful: outside the zoo, only a few illegal snakes have been found. However, there is growing concern about the brown tree snake.

Finally, perhaps the most egregious evidence of humans impacting upon the marine ecosystem off the shores of the Hawaiian Islands is the Great Pacific Garbage Patch. This is a constantly spinning mass of marine debris in the North Pacific; much of the debris is plastic that cannot always be seen by the naked eye. Apart from the obvious threats to birds, sea mammals, and turtles from plastic bags and packaging, tiny pieces of plastic can block sunlight from reaching plankton and algae below. These both play a crucial part in the food web; if their numbers dwindle this will have a knock-on effect on their predators, their predators' predators and so on. Unless humans pay more attention to how they dispose of their waste, the Great Pacific Garbage Patch will keep growing every year with potentially disastrous consequences.

DECISIVE DATES

150,000 BC
Diamond Head forms through crack in the emerged reef of Oahu.

AD 200–500
First settlers arrive in Hawaii, probably from the Marquesas Islands.

800–1200
Polynesian pioneers arrive, this time from Tahiti.

c.1750
Kamehameha (the Great) born on Hawaii Island's northernmost point.

The modern era

1778
Captain James Cook encounters Hawaiian Islands, and names them Sandwich Islands, after his patron, the Earl of Sandwich.

1779
Cook killed in a skirmish with Hawaiians.

1790–1
Kamehameha I begins

"The Death of Captain James Cook, 14 February 1779" by Johann Zoffany (1794).

unification of the Hawaiian Islands by conquering Maui and Lanai.

1812
Sandalwood trade booms.

1819
Kamehameha I dies in Kailua, on Hawaii Island. His son, Liholiho, becomes Kamehameha II, and paves way for the introduction of Christianity in the islands by abolishing the ancient *kapu* system.

Western influences

1820
The first contingent of Protestant missionaries arrives in Hawaii. The kingdom's capital and royal court are moved to Lahaina, on Maui.

1825
Whaling industry begins 40-year boom.

1835
First Hawaiian sugar plantation established at Koloa, Kauai.

King Lunalilo.

1842
Kawaiahaʻo Church dedicated in Honolulu.

1845
Hawaii's capital moved back to Honolulu from Lahaina. First legislature in Hawaii convenes. King announces plans for constitutional government.

1848
Kamehameha III enacts Great Mahele, dividing land among the crown, chiefs and commoners.

1852
The king unveils new constitution.

1869
"Big Five" company Alexander & Baldwin founded.

1872
Kamehameha V dies, ending the dynasty. He leaves no heir.

1873
Lunalilo elected king.

1874
After Lunalilo dies, Kalakaua is elected king. New monarch visits Washington, DC, to push for a reciprocity treaty with US.

1878
Thousands of immigrant plantation workers arrive, primarily from Portugal and Asia.

1887
Kalakaua signs Bayonet Constitution, which limits his power.

1889
Robert Wilcox leads unsuccessful revolt against opponents of the king.

1891
Kalakaua dies in San Francisco. His sister, Lili'uokalani, is named queen.

End of the monarchy

1893
Anti-royalists launch successful coup. Self-proclaimed provisional government is established.

1894
Provisional government declares itself to be the Republic of Hawaii.

1895
Supporters of Lili'uokalani stage a counter coup, but are defeated.

1898
President William McKinley signs legislation to annexe Hawaii.

1900
Hawaii becomes territory of the United States.

Construction of naval base at Pearl Harbor begins.

1902
First transpacific telegraphic cable linking Hawaii and California is laid.

1903
Prince Jonah Kuhio Kalaniana'ole begins term as Hawaii's delegate to Congress.

1912
Hawaii's premier surfer, Duke Kahanamoku, wins Olympic gold medal in swimming.

1917
Queen Lili'uokalani dies.

1922
James Dole's Hawaiian Pineapple Company buys island of Lanai.

1929
Inter-Island Airways (now Hawaiian Airlines) starts passenger service between islands.

1936
Pan American Airways launches transpacific passenger service to Hawaii.

Linda Lingle.

1941
Japanese fighter planes bomb Pearl Harbor, propelling the United States into World War II.

Statehood

1959
Hawaii becomes 50th state.

1986
Hawaii's first ethnic Hawaiian governor, John Waihe'e, takes office.

1990s
Resort development takes off along Oahu's Waikiki Beach, and on Maui, Kauai, and Hawaii Island.

2002
Former Maui mayor Linda Lingle, a Republican, becomes Hawaii's first female governor. She is re-elected in 2006.

2006
Del Monte ceases operating in Hawaii, leaving Dole as the island's only pineapple producer.

2008
Barack Obama, a native of Hawaii, elected President of the United States. He is re-elected in 2012.

2011
Opening of Aulani in Oahu's Ko 'Olina resort area signifies Disney's entry into Hawaiian resort market.

2012
Larry Ellison, CEO of Oracle Corporation, buys 98 percent of the island of Lanai for a reported $600 million.

2013
State legislature legalizes same-sex marriage.

Waikoloa petroglyph field, Big Island.

BEGINNINGS: ANCIENT HAWAII

Thousands of centuries passed after the Hawaiian
Islands' creation before the first life took root.
People, however, arrived just 15 or so centuries ago.

The Hawaiian Islands have existed for millions of years: culturally, however, they are relative newcomers to the modern world as humans arrived only 1,500 years ago. Those first humans, ancient seafaring Polynesians from the Marquesas and the other islands around Tahiti (more than 2,000 miles south of Hawaii), came en masse, probably in search of a better life.

These island people made the journey in seaworthy, double-hulled canoes embellished with *'aumakua* – carved images of their family gods. In the years that have followed, researchers have not been able to pinpoint specifically what prompted them to make the trip, or why they went in the direction they did. Perhaps they followed the migrating speckled plover, which headed north every spring. As for why they came, some have postulated that they may have been seeking refuge from persecution and conquering enemies, escaping the pressures of overpopulation, or simply following curiosity about what lay beyond the horizon.

These islanders – who represented nearly 1,000 islands overall – were but the last chapter of an island-hopping migration of peoples that had begun thousands of years earlier, probably in Southeast Asia. By AD 400, Marquesan canoes had sailed as far east as Easter Island, 2,500 miles (4,000km) away. In time they also reached New Zealand and Hawaii; recently archeologists have even found proof that they reached the Americas, albeit too late to have any significant cultural input.

In the stars

The first Polynesians to reach Hawaii, located in latitudes high above the familiar stars, had not just ventured into the unknown, but

A helmeted, tattooed warrior in a feather cape, drawn by a French artist in 1819.

had, in the words of contemporary American author and ecologist Kenneth Brower, literally "left their universe." Instead of relying on navigational instruments and charts using latitude and longitude and the tools upon which European sailors had come to rely, they used an internal navigation system programmed by intuition, knowledge, and experience. The Polynesian navigator counted on an eclectic mix of information and clues gained from studying the behavior of birds, dolphins, and the colors of the ocean and the clouds.

Most obvious, of course, were the stars. The early Polynesians did not use just one star, or even a dozen stars. They used hundreds of stars that were woven into a memorized tapestry of mnemonic chants that detailed hundreds of known course settings throughout the Pacific.

Based on observational and astronomical data accumulated over the years, it seems that Polynesians made the incredible 2,000-mile (3,200km) journey to Hawaii by fixing on two key stars – Sirius and Arcturus. Astronomers at the Bishop Museum in Honolulu note that "Sirius, the brightest star in the sky, passed almost directly over Tahiti and Raiatea (also called Hawa'iti). The present position of Sirius

Discovery of Hawaii

The first discoverers and settlers of Hawaii are believed to have arrived sometime between AD 200 and 500. Evidence of Marquesan landfalls in Hawaii has been confirmed by carbon dating, and by comparison of fishhooks and adzes found in Hawaiian and Marquesan sites dating from around the same period. These new Hawaiians lived in isolation for several centuries, but sometime between 800 and 1200, other Polynesians arrived from Tahiti. Some researchers believe there were only a few voyages between Tahiti and Hawaii.

Priests row across Kealakekua Bay for rituals surrounding first contact with Westerners, sketched by an artist with Captain Cook.

with respect to the equator has changed very little from that of the days of Polynesian voyaging. Arcturus, called Hokule'a by the Hawaiians and noted for its bright redness off the Big Dipper's handle, presently passes over the northern end of the island of Hawaii. At the time of the great voyaging it passed over the island of Kauai.

Some of the most skilled Polynesian navigators did not use the stars at all. Perhaps because their boats were considerably smaller than the large European sailing ships, the Polynesians "felt" the ocean more, sensing its subtle moods and messages. They felt the ocean, literally, in the direction of swells and the subtle interference of waves reflected off distant islands.

VOYAGES OF THE HOKULE'A

In the constellation Boötes, the star Arcturus is a zenith star for Hawaii, meaning that it passes directly overhead daily. In Hawaiian, the star is called *Hokule'a* – star of gladness. In the 1970s, a Polynesian-style voyaging canoe was built to recreate the journeys of ancient Polynesians to Hawaii. It was named *Hokule'a*. Since then, *Hokule'a* has made several successful voyages between Hawaii and southern Polynesia. *Hokule'a* was joined in the 1990s on expeditions by a sister canoe, *Hawai'iloa*. When not out exploring, *Hokule'a* is berthed at Honolulu's Polynesian Voyaging Society, and is expected to sail around the world in 2014.

Others argue there were numerous voyages over a period of two centuries.

Scholars have speculated that this second wave of Polynesians subjugated the earlier Marquesans as slaves, or perhaps drove them farther north in the Hawaiian chain until they were completely eliminated. When the Tahitian migration ended, the newcomers lived in isolation for several centuries, developing into the Hawaiian culture that would later greet Captain Cook.

Conquered Marquesans may have been the *manahune*, or *menehune*, mentioned in

A gourd helmet with foliage and tapa (bark cloth) strip decoration.

early Hawaiian and Tahitian chants. The term *manahune* was used derisively in the Tahitian homeland to refer to slaves or plebeian castes, but its meaning changed through the centuries to mean, probably sarcastically, the mysterious gnomes supposed in Hawaiian folklore to inhabit remote corners of the islands. (The little gnomes have become quite a large part of modern Hawaiian folklore, especially on Kauai.)

"Offspring of Tahiti"

The Marquesans and Tahitians brought with them a similar language, as well as foods, myths, traditions, and gods. It was the Tahitian, however, who is credited with bequeathing the name "Hawaii," which was first given to the largest of the islands, now commonly called Hawaii Island, and later to the complete chain of islands. As the Polynesian bard Kamahualele chanted centuries ago, "Behold Hawaii, an island, a people/The people of Hawaii are the offspring of Tahiti."

Sir Peter Buck, the eminent half-Maori ethnologist who once served as the Bishop Museum's director, explained the origin of the word Hawaii in his book, *Vikings of the Pacific*, published in 1938. He noted that in ancient times "the headquarters of the Polynesian main body was established in the largest island of the leeward group of Tahiti, named Havai'i after an ancient homeland."

As Tahiti-based fleets set out to settle the Society Islands, Samoa, Tonga, Fiji, Hawaii, and New Zealand, they established colonies often named after their home island. Dialectal differences resulted in today's place name variations. An even more persuasive Hawaii–Tahiti relationship is exemplified by the ancient name of a channel located south of Maui, between the islands of Lanai and Kaho'olawe. The channel's Hawaiian name is Kealaikahiki. By substituting the letter *k* in the word with *t*, the word *te-ala-i-tahiti* is formed, which translates as "the pathway to Tahiti," or "the pathway to foreign lands."

Ancient ways

Most of what we know of ancient Hawaiian life is from poetic oral traditions, known as *mele*. In these *mele*, the Hawaiians' *kupuna*, or ancestors, passed on to their descendants all they knew of their history. Various aspects of life, from the trivial to the momentous, were reported in this unwritten literature, which consisted of family genealogies, myths, and day-to-day accounts of human experiences.

Other insights about early Hawaii come from the initial observations made by foreign explorers such as James Cook, George Vancouver, and Otto von Kotzebue. Additionally, there are the important memoirs of early Hawaiian scholars, notably John Papa Ii (1800–70), Samuel Kamakau (1815–76), Kepelino Keauokalani (1830–78), and David Malo (1793–1853).

Another source has been the antiquities and folklore collected by Abraham Fornander (1812–87), a surveyor, editor, and judge.

Fornander, who was married to a Hawaiian woman, spoke and wrote the Hawaiian language fluently. He wrote a history of the islands entitled *An Account of the Polynesian Race: Its Origins and Migrations*. He also collected and translated many Hawaiian chants into English. According to these chroniclers, the people of Hawaii developed one of the most complex non-technological cultures ever encountered by early Europeans.

Early Hawaiian culture operated within systematic laws known as *kapu*, the Hawaiian version of the Tahitian word *tapu*, from which

marked by tattoos on their foreheads, and they were summarily conscripted as sacrificial victims by the priestly *kahuna*.

Under this hierarchy, the tightly circumscribed *kapu* and bloodlines could not be crossed. A typical penalty for a *kapu* violation was execution by stoning, clubbing, or strangulation; violators might also be buried or burned alive. Sometimes a *kapu*-breaker was singled out as a convenient sacrificial victim for a god, but usually he was sacrificed as a lesson to others. The Hawaiian historian David Malo wrote that a person could be put to death

Articles of ceremony from early Hawaii.

the word "taboo" originates. At the time of the first contact with Europeans, Hawaiian society was feudal and defined mostly by territory, with two or three *mo'i*, or kings, contending for control of each island. Ranking below the kings were hereditary groups of *ali'i*, or nobles. The *ali'i* were supported by *kahuna*, a prestigious group including priests, healers, and astrologers. Lower down was a class of craftsmen and artists, *kanaka wale*, who made the canoes, calabashes, and *lei* (garlands). This class also included fishermen and hula dancers. The labor and working class, *maka'ainana* or commoners, worked the land. At the very bottom were the social outcasts, the slaves or *kauwa maoli*. Sometimes the unfortunate *kauwa* were

for allowing his shadow to fall upon the house of a chief, or for passing through that chief's stockade or doorway, or for entering the house before changing his *malo* (loincloth). He also could be executed because he appeared before the chief with his head smeared by mud. Other common *kapu* declared that women could not eat pork, coconuts, bananas, and shark meat, nor could they eat with men.

Certain seasons were established for the gathering or catching of scarce plants or animals for food, probably as conservation measures. Sometimes sporting chiefs declared certain surfing-spots *kapu* for their own exclusive use. Some *kapu* were implemented by Machiavellian chiefs, priests or influential court retainers under the guise of religion, or to tyrannically oppress a person or group of people. Many of the laws, however, were simply to protect resources and assure social stability.

Kapu violators had a place where they could seek sanctuary, whatever their crime. These places of refuge, called *pu'uhonua*, had to be reached by the transgressor before he was caught. The odds, of course, were against the transgressor. A good example of a *pu'uhonua* is located on a lava promontory at *Pu'uhonua* O Honaunau National Histori-

lava stones. In ancient times, they housed *kapa*-covered oracle towers, sacrificial platform-altars, carved stone and wooden sculptures, images of gods made of thatch and feathers, sacred stones, rough-hewn monoliths, groupings of wood and stone sub-temple structures, and often a disposal pit for decayed human, animal, or plant offerings.

The most complex temples were those built by Hawaiian chiefs to initiate a war. These *heiau waikaua* (war temples), also called *luakini*, were kept spiritually "alive" by periodic human sacrifices. Only *ali'i* were allowed access to the

An 1873 engraving of female surfers.

cal Park, on Hawaii Island's Kona coast. This *kapu* system affected every aspect of Hawaiian life, from birth to death, until it was abolished in 1819 by King Kamehameha II. But until its abolition, *kapu* protected the powers of Hawaiian kings.

Worship

Hawaiians generally worshiped privately and at small shrines they built in their homes or outdoors, but the focal points of most major religious observances were large open-air temples known as *heiau*. Ruins of these *heiau* can be seen throughout Hawaii. In most cases, what remains today are rudimentary platforms, terraces and walls made of large river-rounded

heiau. Once it had been decided to wage war, and appropriate sacrifices had been made to Ku, the war god, the high chief would call for his *kilo lani* (astrologer) to determine the most auspicious day to do battle. Exceptional power might be elicited from the gods by sacrificing an enemy chief at the *luakini*.

War and arts

Given the generally clannish and feudalistic structure of ancient Hawaiian society, wars were frequent. Periodic and courtly sham battles were held between friendly chiefs to keep young warriors prepped and alert. This system of forearming and forewarning was reminiscent of European days of chivalry.

The ritual aspects of Hawaiian wars quickly gave way to brutality. There might be some opening decorum, gladiator-style, in which two renowned warriors would fight to the death in front of opposing armies. But more often than not, the two armies would meet on an impromptu or chosen battleground, usually during daylight hours and following an exchange of verbal taunts and insults, commence battle.

Common Hawaiian weapons included spears up to 18ft (5 meters) in length, shorter javelins, assorted daggers (some lined with shark teeth),

Admiring a temple's carved deities.

stone-headed clubs, serrated shark tooth clubs, a variety of carved wood and stone weapons, slingshots, strangling cords, and any and all objects (rocks, boulders, branches) that could be spontaneously introduced into the fray by resourceful warriors.

But life in ancient times was not an endless cycle of war-making, oppression, and workaday drudgery. Hawaiians developed unique forms of recreation, including such diversions as kite-flying, puppet theater and staged dances, numerous games of skill and chance, archery, toboganing on *holua* sleds that were raced down specially prepared hillside runways, and surfing, known as *he'e nalu* or "wave sliding."

> *A chief's feather cloak could require some 450,000 feathers plucked from an estimated 80,000 birds.*

The Hawaiians also created the most exquisite variety of fine artwork and personal adornments found anywhere in Polynesia. Wood and stone sculpture was graphic and bold, while Hawaii's delicate featherwork is still considered to be the finest example of this art to be found. James Cook, in describing Hawaiian featherwork, observed that "the surface might be compared to the thickest and richest velvet." His lieutenant, James King, suggested that the "feathered cloak and helmet… in point of beauty and magnificence, is perhaps nearly equal to that of any nation in the world."

It would be impossible today to duplicate one of these cloaks, because most of the birds whose feathers were plucked for use have since become extinct. In old Hawaii, the king commissioned specially selected groups of royal feather-pluckers who stalked and snared their preferred prey with nets and long sticky wands. Most of the birds were released after the desired feathers had been removed.

Hawaiian *kapa*, the soft bark-cloth fashioned from paper mulberry, also represents a major artistic achievement. Strips of bark were soaked, then beaten until smooth and paper-thin. The cloth was then decorated by bamboo stamps with intricate designs carved on them, inked by dyes made from the leaves, bark, fruit, and roots of various native plants.

Perhaps the most diverse art practiced was in the form of necklaces, headbands, and anklets made of flowers, nuts, seeds, shells, ivory, teeth, turtle shells, and human hair. Tattooing, too, was popular, often as an expression of mourning. Both men and women tattooed their bodies with a variety of bright designs: some were of a topical nature, but there were also repetitious, geometric motifs. These tattoos were created with small sharp needles made of fish and bird bones, or shells.

Tattooing was condemned by the missionaries and had largely disappeared until the late 1980s, when it was revived as an art form and as a way of asserting native Hawaiian identity.

Hawaiian Gods

Polynesians brought with them to Hawaii steadfast belief in four major gods; around these deities belief in all other higher beings revolves.

From their South Pacific homelands, early Polynesian seafarers brought north with them the foods that had sustained them back home. By doing so, they also brought to Hawaii the great gods of Polynesia: Kane, Ku, Lono, and Kanaloa.

Polynesian gods were never distant and abstract. Rather, they moved through the waters and on the earth, and they could take on many forms, including plants. For instance, by bringing taro, one of the god Kane's forms, to Hawaii, the Polynesians carried with them Kane himself. Kane, the supreme god, was the procreator, the ancestor of all chiefs and commoners, the male power who dwells in eternity – the god of sunlight, fresh water, and forests. Kane was not fond of human sacrifices. An owl was one of his assumed forms.

Hawaiians prayed to Ku for rain and growth, and for successful fishing and sorcery, but he was best known as a patron god of war. Resplendent images of Ku, whose combative title was "The Island Snatcher," were carried on the war canoes of Kamehameha the Great. According to oral traditions, these fearsome images – wrought of red *i'wi* feathers embellished with mother-of-pearl eyes and mouths of jagged dog teeth – would utter dreadful cries during battle.

Lono was a god of thunder (*lono* means "resounding"), clouds, winds, the sea, agriculture, and fertility, but his personage could assume dozens of forms, including a fish or a man-dog being. Hawaiians never appealed to benevolent Lono with human sacrifices. Most notably, he was honored during the annual *makahiki* harvest festivals of November, December, and January, when his image was carried by chiefly retainers on their tribute-and-tax-collecting tours of the islands. It was during *makahiki* that Captain James Cook's arrival on Hawaii Island was greeted joyously by Hawaiians gathered at Kealakekua Bay. Some theorize the Hawaiians mistook his visit for the prophesied return of Lono.

Kanaloa, lord of the ocean and the ocean winds, was often embodied in the octopus and squid, but also in other natural things, such as the banana. He was a companion of Kane, and according to some, the two traveled together, "moving about the land and opening spring and water holes for the benefit of men."

Hierarchy of deities

Coming to Polynesia from distant, unknown places, these four gods had been created before all other gods. They created the universe from the earth, symbolized as a calabash. By tossing the calabash's cover skyward, the sky, sun, and moon were formed. Seeds in the calabash became stars. The pantheon of Hawaiian deities is extensive, including the lesser specialized gods, such as Pele, the volcano goddess, and Laka, goddess of hula.

Wooden image of Kakailimoku, the war god.

For the contemporary traveler to Hawaii, Pele is the best known of the lesser gods. As the fire goddess, she is responsible for the current eruptions of Kilauea. A common misconception is that Pele created the Hawaiian Islands. The islands had already surfaced when Pele, driven by wanderlust, arrived from Tahiti in a great canoe provided by the god of sharks. From Ni'ihau, she traveled down the island chain looking for a suitable home, which was within active volcanoes. On Hawaii Island, she sought out the reigning fire god, Aila'au, hoping to settle in with him. But he had heard of her awesome power and the blazing firepits she dug. As she approached Kilauea, he ran away, leaving her to build a soaring palace of fire that endures in legend and in periodic eruptions on Hawaii Island to this day.

ARRIVAL OF CAPTAIN COOK

Captain James Cook was noted for his sensitivity to the cultures he encountered during his global explorations. Still, after his arrival, Hawaii changed immensely.

Hawaii's modern era began in 1778, amid excitement and terror, when Hawaiians on the island of Oahu saw two strange, white-winged objects moving at sea. These "floating islands," as the Hawaiians were to describe them, were the British ships HMS *Resolution* and HMS *Discovery*, commanded by Captain James Cook.

One of a kind

En route from the South Pacific to the north – and, it was hoped, an elusive Northwest Passage – Cook and his crew, which included an astronomer and artist assigned to the expedition by the British Admiralty, had accidentally become the first known non-Polynesians to land on the Hawaiian Islands. It was a formidable find, the last significant land on Earth to be found by Europeans. In his ship's log, Cook later suggested that finding Hawaii was "in many respects the most important discovery made by Europeans throughout the extent of the Pacific Ocean." Cook marveled at the existence of the Polynesian settlements: "How shall we account for this nation spreading itself so far over this vast ocean…?" Cook named these isles the Sandwich Islands, in honor of Cook's patron, the Earl of Sandwich, First Lord of the Admiralty.

Oahu was the first island to be sighted, but Cook passed by and continued on to the northeast, making landfall on January 21, 1778 at Waimea, on Kauai's west coast, after a long search for safe anchorage. After five days of replenishment and sightseeing, strong winds at night blew his ships away from Kauai toward the smaller island of Ni'ihau. There, Cook's men received salt and yams from the islanders in exchange for goats, pigs, and the seeds of melons, pumpkins, and onions. Western flora and fauna were thus introduced.

The British navigator James Cook.

WERE THE SPANISH FIRST?

Spanish ships may have landed in Hawaii up to two centuries before Cook. Historians point to artifacts, including a chart of the northern Pacific that marked the track of the round trip between the Philippines and Acapulco taken from a captured Spanish galleon by the British in 1742. The map showed islands in approximately the same latitude as Hawaii. Also, feather cloaks and helmets – not found elsewhere in Polynesia – with a Spanish look and usually of red and yellow, the royal colors of Spain, were found in Hawaii. Furthermore, early Western visitors reported island residents with distinctly Caucasian features.

Also introduced, against Cook's explicitly posted orders, were syphilis, gonorrhea, and other European diseases. All too aware of the effects of introduced diseases on indigenous peoples, Cook had told his men clearly that no Hawaiian women were to be allowed on board the ships, nor any person "having or suspected of having the venereal disease or any symptoms thereof, shall lie with any woman" under threat of severe lashing at the ship's masthead.

Thomas Edgar, master of the *Discovery*, said his men employed every devious scheme possible to get women on board the ships, even "dressing them up as men." But he noted also that the Hawaiian women "used all arts to entice them into their houses and even went so far as to endeavour to draw them in by force."

The return visit

In February, Cook left Hawaii to continue his search for the Northwest Passage, taking his two ships far above the Arctic Circle. As winter again approached, Cook returned to Hawaii, sighting Maui in November. For two months, the *Discovery* and *Resolution* charted the islands, first Maui, then Hawaii Island. Coming around

Engraving showing Cook receiving an offering.

THE HAOLE ARRIVE

Many Hawaiian scholars have opined about the day that Captain James Cook first arrived in Hawaii. According to Samuel M. Kamakau, a 19th-century Hawaiian author and historian, "The ship was first sighted from Waialua and Wai'anae (on Oahu) sailing for the north. It anchored at night at Waimea, on the island of Kauai. A man named Moapu and his companions who were fishing with heavy lines saw this strange thing move by and saw the lights… they hurried ashore and hastened to tell Ka'eo and the other chiefs of Kauai about this strange apparition. The next morning the ship lay outside Ka'ahe at Waimea. Chiefs and commoners saw the wonderful sight and marveled at it. Some were terrified

and shrieked with fear. The valley of Waimea rang with the shouts of the excited people as they saw the boat with its masts and sails shaped like a gigantic stingray. One asked another, 'What are those branching things?' and the other answered, 'They are trees moving on the sea.' A certain *kahuna* named Kuohu declared, 'That can be nothing else than the *heiau* of Lono, the tower of Keolewa, and the place of sacrifice at the altar.' The excitement became more intense…"

Some say natives, who had gathered to honor the god Lono were so convinced that he would return during the festival held in his honor, that they considered Cook to be the god immediately.

Hawaii Island's southern tip from the east, Cook anchored along the Kona coast in a bay called Kealakekua, the "pathway of the god." It was exactly one year since his first landfall in Kauai.

If Cook was impressed a year earlier by the way Hawaiians on Kauai had prostrated themselves in his presence, he must have been even more impressed by his reception at Kealakekua Bay; Cook's second coming was monumental. He arrived at a propitious time: the *makahiki* celebration, an annual tribute to the god Lonoi-kamakahiki – and some researchers believe that Cook's auspicious arrival was identified by the Hawaiians as Lono's return. Consequently, Cook was afforded the greatest welcome ever accorded a mortal in Hawaii.

One of Cook's lieutenants estimated that 10,000 Hawaiians turned out in canoes, on surfboards, swimming in the bay, and waiting on shore to greet the return of Lono. Cook wrote, "I have nowhere in this sea seen such a number of people assembled in one place; besides those in the canoes, all the shore of the bay was covered with people, and hundreds were swimming about the ship like shoals of fish." John Ledyard, an American adventurer who had signed on board the *Resolution* as corporal of the marines, reported later that two officers counted from 2,500 to 3,500 canoes afloat in Kealakekua's waters. Ledyard and others also described unusual white *kapa* (bark cloth) banners held aloft on crossbars – an ancient symbol of Lono – which resembled the ships' masts and sails. Ledyard wrote that when Cook went onshore, the masses of Hawaiians "all bowed and covered their faces with their hands until he was passed."

There were extravagant ceremonies held in Cook's honor, including one at a sacred temple, or *heiau*. Cook and his men tried their best to please the Hawaiians with tours of their ships, a flute and violin concert, and a fireworks display. All the while, Cook readied his ships for a voyage to Asia, and after two weeks, they set sail. But three days later, just off Hawaii Island's North Shore, a fierce winter storm damaged the *Resolution's* foremast. Cook returned to Kealakekua to make essential repairs.

Death of Cook

Cook now found that the *makahiki* festival at Kealakekua was finished, and because of a *kapu* put on Kealakekua Bay by King Kalaniopu'u, the area was nearly deserted. Those Hawaiians who remained were not as generous in their tribute, and in fact were surprised that a god's property could be badly damaged within his own domain. The Hawaiians grew increasingly bold, taking objects from the ships that pleased their fancy, particularly items made of metal. When they seized the *Discovery's* cutter, Cook went ashore with nine marines to take Kalaniopu'u hostage in exchange for return of the boat, a strategy that had worked before on other Pacific islands. A violent scuffle broke out, and a group of more than 200 Hawaiian warriors attacked Cook's landing party, five of whom escaped, but four

Bewohner der Sandwich-Inseln.

Image of the islands' inhabitants, by Karl Joseph Brodtmann.

others, as well as Cook himself, died. The British ships fired on the Hawaiians, who retreated.

Two delegations of concerned Hawaiians later returned parts of Cook's body "cut to pieces and all burnt," wrote James King, Cook's second lieutenant. One bundle of Cook's bones, wrapped in fine *kapa* and a cloak made of black and white feathers, included "the captain's hands, the scalp, the skull, wanting the lower jaw, thigh bones and arm bone; the hands only had flesh on them, and were cut in holes, and salt crammed in; the leg bones, lower jaw and feet." Cook's remains were buried at Kealakekua Bay, and in February 1779, the *Discovery* and *Resolution* set sail, passing Maui, Molokai and Oahu before anchoring again briefly at Waimea, on Kauai.

Portrait of Queen Lili'uokalani, 1891.

THE HAWAIIAN MONARCHY

The monarchy of Hawaii began with Kamehameha the Great, who united the Hawaiian Islands. It ended with the overthrow of Queen Lili'uokalani.

All told, Hawaii had eight main monarchs between 1795 and Hawaii's designation as an American territory in 1900.

Kamehameha I (1795–1819)

Often mentioned in the logs and diaries of visiting ships' captains and merchants was Kamehameha, which means "the lonely one." A distinguished warrior and one of King Kalaniopu'u's nephews and subordinate chiefs, Kamehameha (pronounced *ka may-ha may-ha*) had impressed Cook at Kealakekua Bay. Kamehameha was a careful observer of the *haole* (Caucasians). He had been wounded by a gun on the beach when Cook was killed, and it was evident to Kamehameha that one man with a small brass cannon could have a great advantage over several warriors with clubs and spears. By 1789, Kamehameha's own large double canoe was carrying a swivel gun mounted on a platform strapped across the hulls.

A 10-year civil war involving Kamehameha and others erupted on Hawaii Island in 1782. When the timing seemed astrologically and militarily propitious, Kamehameha conquered Maui and Lanai in 1790, then fought to keep Maui again a few years later. Perhaps his toughest battle was against Keoua, his chief Hawaii Island rival. Kamehameha took no chances against Keoua. He built the immense Pu'u Kohala *heiau* (temple) to his war god near Kawaihae in Kohala – it still stands – and invited Keoua to meet him there. When he arrived, Kamehameha had him killed. Kamehameha was now king of all of Hawaii Island. He recaptured Maui, then Molokai. In the meantime, civil war had erupted on Oahu, and Kamehameha took advantage of the disorder to land his fleet there, at the foot of Diamond Head in 1795. In a display

One of the few paintings made of Kamehameha while he was alive.

of military strength, his warriors drove Oahu's defenders into Nu'uanu Valley and over the edge of Nu'uanu Pali, a precipitous cliff. With Oahu's conquest, and the ritual sacrifice of its king, Kalanikupule, to Kamehameha's war god, Kamehameha became monarch of all of Hawaii, except Kauai and Ni'ihau, more than 70 miles (110km) west of Oahu.

In both 1796 and 1809, Kamehameha assembled invasion fleets destined for Kauai and Ni'ihau. In 1810, Kauai's king peacefully yielded his throne. The islands thus finally became united under a single ruler, Kamehameha the Great.

Although Kamehameha retained the traditional ways, such as the *kapu*, he also learned from the Europeans whose ships he supplied with provisions. Hawaii's sandalwood proved a lucrative trade for Kamehameha, and he directed commoners by the thousands to harvest it for shipment to Asia. Exports continued until there were no more sandalwood trees in the islands..

Kamehameha the Great died after a long illness in 1819, at his royal compound Kamaka Honu – the Eye of the Turtle – in what is now Kailua on Hawaii Island. He was about 63 years old. So that nobody could defile them or use their powerful *mana* (spirit), Kamehameha's

Queen Ka'ahumanu with a servant.

bones were hidden in a still-secret location somewhere on the Kona coast.

Kamehameha II (1819–24)

Kamehameha's son and successor, Liholiho, was not a strong and commanding ruler like his father. But Ka'ahumanu, the favorite of Kamehameha the Great's many wives, was intelligent, fearless, and powerful. Upon Kamehameha's death, she made it clear to Liholiho that it was his father's wish that she be the *kuhina nui*, the joint ruler or queen regent of Hawaii.

One of Ka'ahumanu's first actions was to abolish the ancient *kapu* system. Urged on by Ka'ahumanu, Liholiho sat down with his mother, Keopuolani, and Ka'ahumanu at a feast,

violating the *kapu* that prohibited men and women from eating together. Ka'ahumanu and Liholiho then ordered that all the *heiau* and carved wooden idols be destroyed. The social and cultural shock to Hawaiians was enormous, leaving an overwhelming spiritual vacuum.

The vacuum didn't last long. The first party of New England missionaries arrived in 1820 aboard the American brig *Thaddeus*, ready to fill the religious void. Had the timing of the *kapu* collapse and the arrival of Christian missionaries not been so coincidental, the history of Hawaii could have been very different.

Although Ka'ahumanu and Liholiho had reservations about these overdressed *haole*, they let the American missionaries preach at Kailua-Kona and Honolulu for a one-year trial. The missionaries never left, and their descendants garnered land and power.

The English had retained an interest in Hawaii since Cook's first contact, and in 1822 Liholiho received a gift from King George IV: a small schooner named the *Prince Regent*. Delighted, Liholiho left Hawaii the next year on a British whaling ship to visit King George and negotiate a treaty. Liholiho and his entourage were royally feted in London, but before he could meet with King George, he and his queen, Kamamalu, caught the measles and died. Liholiho designated his younger brother Kauikeaouli as his logical successor.

Kamehameha III (1825–54)

The early years of Kauikeaouli – Kamehameha III – would better be called the reign of Ka'ahumanu, since Kauikeaouli was only 10

CIVILIZED MISSIONARIES

Reverend Hiram Bingham, whose grandson was credited with "discovering" Machu Picchu for the Western world, led the first group of Christian missionaries to Hawaii and wrote of his followers' impressions: "The appearance of destitution, degradation, and barbarism among the chattering, and almost naked savages, whose heads and feet, and much of their sunburnt skins were bare, was appalling. Some of our number, with gushing tears, turned away from the spectacle. Others, with firmer nerve, continued their gaze, but were ready to exclaim, 'Can these be human beings? Can such things be civilized?'"

years old when his brother died. As *kuhina nui*, Ka'ahumanu exerted a strong influence on both the boy king and the Hawaiian people, most of whom were still disoriented and adrift after the demise of the *kapu* system.

Half a year after Liholiho left on his ill-fated trip to England, Ka'ahumanu had announced a system of civil laws obviously based on the Congregationalist missionaries' teachings. In fact, the Congregationalists had cultivated considerable spiritual and political influence over Ka'ahumanu, eventually converting her to Christianity. Ka'ahumanu became one of the Congregationalists' most enthusiastic converts. Another convert to Christianity was an *ali'i* peer, the Hawaii Island high chiefess Kapi'olani.

In 1824, Kapi'olani (not to be confused with her niece and namesake, the future Queen Kapi'olani) hiked to the mouth of Halema'uma'u in the Kilauea caldera on Hawaii Island. There, at the edge of the fire goddess Pele's domain, Kapi'olani defiantly renounced her. She lived to tell the tale, and at the Hilo Congregationalist mission, 90 impressed Hawaiians instantly became new converts.

Encouraged by the royal support, missionaries built churches and schools throughout the islands. Even more, as "messengers of Jehovah," the missionaries used their court influence to veil Hawaiians with everything Puritan. Bare skin on women in any degree – much less nudity – was condemned, and women were draped in dresses mostly ill-suited to the tropics. The ancient and sacred hula, which combined dance and poetry, was outlawed as lewd and lascivious.

Equally high on the agenda was putting the Hawaiian language into Romanized script. The missionaries' intent in doing so was evangelical, no doubt, but teaching Hawaiians to read and write gave them a new tool with which to communicate their own histories and thought. This was especially important as the missionaries had suppressed traditional storytelling methods like the hula.

When Ka'ahumanu died in 1832, Kamehameha III took full control of the government in a reign noted for a couple of frivolous early years of horseracing, gambling, drinking, and dancing. His half-sister, Kina'u, the *kuhina nui* successor to Ka'ahumanu, managed state matters during his bouts with the bottle. The missionaries continued to consolidate power, accepting government appointments.

In the mid-1820s, just as the sandalwood trees had all but disappeared in the islands, whaling became Hawaii's major source of revenue, with Honolulu and Lahaina among the Pacific's most important ports. Whaling kept Hawaii's economy above water for over 30 years. At its peak in 1846, 429 ships were anchored in Maui's Lahaina Harbor.

The missionaries, of course, protested the extracurricular activities of sailors on liberty. Attempts by the missionaries to quench liquor and prostitution were not well received, and the homes of several preachers in Lahaina were

Hawaii's royal coat-of-arms engraved on the Queen's piano in Washington Place, Honolulu.

bombarded with cannon by angry sailors from aboard the safety of anchored ships.

Perhaps Kamehameha III's most significant act was an edict issued in 1848, which became known as the Great Mahele. Under subtle pressure from missionary advisers and businessmen, the king divided Hawaii's land ownership – previously the pleasure of the royalty – among the monarchy, government, and common people, thus allowing ordinary Hawaiians to own property for the first time.

Two years later, foreigners also were permitted land ownership. Within a few years, the *haole* had accumulated large estates; by 1886, about two-thirds of all government lands sold had been bought by resident *haole*. Hawaiians, unfamiliar with land ownership, had done little to thwart the foreigners' acquisitions.

By the late 1850s, whales had been hunted nearly to extinction, petroleum and coal were replacing whale oil, and the United States was sinking into a civil war. The boom days of the Hawaiian Islands were over.

Hawaii's business and political interests turned from whaling to a new commodity, sugar. During California's gold rush in 1849, a handful of small sugar planters in Hawaii had made great profits when Kaleponi – California – turned to Hawaii for its sugar supply. Sugar's

today descends from those early immigrant laborers.

Before the 30-year reign of Kamehameha III was over, the king had established a supreme court, an upper house of royalty, and a lower house of elected representatives. Kamehameha III had no children and named a nephew, Alexander Liholiho, as his successor.

Kamehameha IV (1855–63)

Alexander Liholiho – the grandson of Kamehameha the Great – had a certain dislike for America, and during his short reign, he was to

View of Honolulu from the harbor, c.1854.

potential looked sweet, especially for those with the land under the cane. Whereas whaling had been mostly a merchants' boom, sugar would be a land barons' boom. But sugar plantations are labor intensive, and the local pool of laborers was small. More pragmatically, Hawaiians saw little appeal in the low-paying, backbreaking work of harvesting sugar cane, especially as the islands offered plenty of traditional foods.

For sugar to become a major industry, thousands of laborers needed to be imported. The first group of 293 Chinese arrived in 1852, followed over the decades by Japanese, Portuguese, Filipinos, Norwegians, Germans, Koreans, Puerto Ricans, Spaniards, and Russians. A significant percentage of Hawaii's ethnic mix

shift Hawaii closer to the British Empire both in spirit and in policy. Educated by Americans at an elite royal school, Kamehameha IV and a brother had visited Europe and America in 1849 and 1850. Their experiences in Europe, especially England, were enjoyable and enriching. Their experiences in America were not.

Today, Alexander Liholiho is remembered for his concern for Hawaiians. One surviving legacy is the Queen's Medical Center, established by him and his wife, Queen Emma, in 1859 to care for sick and destitute Hawaiians, many of whom were still suffering from introduced European diseases.

In 1863, after the death of his son, Kamehameha IV died (at age 29) during an asthma attack.

Kamehameha V (1863–72)

A believer in the strong, autocratic style of Kamehameha the Great, Lot Kamehameha, an elder brother of Kamehameha IV, refused to take an oath to uphold the liberal constitution of 1852. He believed that it weakened the powers of the Hawaiian monarchy, making it vulnerable to overthrow by non-royalists, a forethought that later turned out to be true.

In 1864, Lot Kamehameha declared a special convention to revise the constitution. This convention accomplished nothing, so the king then offered a new constitution that abolished

Kamehameha V.

the matriarchal office of *kuhina nui*, set up a one-chamber legislature for nobles and elected representatives, and decreed that persons born after 1840 be required to pass literacy tests and meet certain property qualifications before being allowed to vote or serve in the legislature. His act was in effect a bloodless but effective coup d'état. This strengthening of the monarchy led to increasing resentment among non-royalists – mostly foreign businessmen – and added fuel to the fire that would later bring down the monarchy.

A bachelor, Lot left no heir and named no successor. When he died at the age of 42, the 77-year-long dynasty of Kamehameha the Great at last ended.

> *A train conductor in New York mistook the future Kamehameha IV for a servant and ordered him out of the railroad car. That memory of America lingered long.*

William Lunalilo (1873–4)

Under the constitution of 1864, the legislative assembly unanimously elected Prince Lunalilo as king in 1873. It was a popular decision with the Hawaiians, who had already voted for him a week before. As popular as Lunalilo – or Prince Bill – was with the people, he was ineffective in leadership and was thought to have a drinking problem. Thirteen months later he died without an heir. The kingdom's legislative assembly once again went about the sticky business of electing a new sovereign.

Kalakaua (1874–91)

There were two contenders for the throne: David Kalakaua, who had lost to Lunalilo in the previous election, and Queen Emma, widow of Kamehameha IV. After a spirited campaign, the assembly handily elected Kalakaua as king of Hawaii in 1874. Kalakaua's ancestors had been high chiefs on Hawaii Island.

Ruling with a flourish and style that earned him the nickname "the Merrie Monarch," Kalakaua ignored the calls for annexation by the US and devoted his energy to fashioning his kingship in the courtly tradition of European monarchs. He built himself the magnificent 'Iolani Palace; became the first monarch to circumnavigate the globe; and presented gala horse races, grand balls, and old-style Hawaiian feasts. During his reign, Kalakaua openly clashed with educators and Christians about restoring Hawaii's rapidly disappearing cultural traditions.

In 1874, the same year he ascended the throne, Kalakaua traveled to Washington, DC, hoping to negotiate a reciprocity treaty with the US. He and his entourage were grandly received by President Ulysses S. Grant and a joint session of Congress. Newspaper reporters described the state banquets arranged for Kalakaua as the most lavish ever seen in the nation's capital. Kalakaua subsequently received strong personal support from Grant.

By the following year, the US Senate approved a treaty giving Hawaii "favored nation" duty concessions and thus eliminating tariffs on sugar.

While the treaty was a triumph for the new king, it also gave America a lock on the islands, presaging its future interest in Pearl Harbor as a military base, and preventing Kalakaua from using Hawaii's location to gain concessions from Britain or France.

Perhaps most importantly for Hawaii's immediate future, the treaty gave the sugar growers increased economic confidence and security. And, as would later become clear, the agreement gave the growers disproportionate political and social leverage, eventually weakening the Hawaiian monarchy's power.

armed followers loyal to the kingdom swashbuckled their way past the King's Guards and occupied 'Iolani Palace. But Wilcox's coup d'état failed miserably. Within hours, he and the other revolutionaries were flushed out with rifle fire and crude dynamite bombs laced with twentypenny metal spikes. Seven of his men were dead and another 12 wounded.

For the remainder of his reign, Kalakaua was, for the most part, a figurehead monarch. In 1891, while visiting California in an effort to restore his failing health, Kalakaua died in a San Francisco hotel suite. Before leaving Hawaii, Kalakaua

Coronation of Kalakaua in Honolulu.

A string of scandals began to taint Kalakaua's reign, much to the self-righteous delight of the foreign business community. In 1887, an armed insurrection led by a *haole* political group called the Hawaiian League forced Kalakaua to accept a new so-called "Bayonet Constitution" that seriously constrained his powers. This new constitution required that voters own at least $3,000-worth of property or have an income of at least $600 a year, requirements that effectively eliminated most Hawaiians from the political franchise. Power conclusively shifted to Hawaii's land-owning and predominantly white minority.

Two years later, a fiery part-Hawaiian revolutionary named Robert Wilcox staged a counter coup against the businessmen. He and about 150

had appointed his sister, Princess Lydia Kamakaeha Lili'uokalani, heir to the throne, as regent during his absence. She became Hawaii's first and only reigning queen.

Lili'uokalani (1891–3)

Lili'uokalani was a staunch royalist. Right from the start, she made it clear that she planned to restore monarchical power and the rights of native Hawaiian people. Weary of the plodding cabinet government created by the Bayonet Constitution of 1887, she announced in 1893 that she would issue a new constitution placing power firmly back in the hands of the monarchy.

Pro-annexation, anti-royalist forces planned to overthrow the monarchy and support

Queen Emma's backers protested at Kalakaua's selection, and a free-for-all fight took place inside and outside the courthouse.

annexation negotiations with the United States. In January 1893, they launched their revolt after first enlisting John B. Stevens, the US minister in Hawaii. An ardent supporter of the pro-annexation movement, Stevens ordered the landing of Marines from the visiting gunship USS *Boston*, ostensibly to protect American lives and prop-

King Kalakaua, Hawaii's last king.

erty – but without authorization from Washington. That afternoon, some 160 armed Marines positioned artillery pieces and Gatling guns at strategic points in Honolulu, and by the next day, "without the drawing of a sword or the firing of a shot," a self-proclaimed government led by Sanford Dole was in power. Lili'uokalani had no choice but to abdicate her throne.

She believed that the American government, learning of the coup, would reinstate the monarchy. She was right – sort of. Unlike his predecessor, newly elected President Grover Cleveland did not support the coup, and he dispatched a special investigator to Honolulu to investigate. The investigator arrived in Hawaii to find American flags flying above Hawaii's public buildings.

He ordered the flags to be taken down and the Marines withdrawn. He reported to Cleveland that "a great wrong has been done to the Hawaiians." Cleveland sent a message to Congress stating that the unauthorized use of American troops in Hawaii was "an act of war against a peaceful nation." Congress, lobbied by the sugar interests, disagreed.

In 1894, the provisional government established itself as the Republic of Hawaii. Sanford Dole was named president. President Cleveland sent a representative to Hawaii seeking the reinstatement of Queen Lili'uokalani, but Dole and his cabinet refused to step down. Lili'uokalani and her supporters planned a counter-coup, to be led by the indefatigable Robert Wilcox. The government arrested the royalists, including Queen Lili'uokalani. She denied guilt, but bombs and arms were found in her Washington Place garden. She was placed under house arrest and a week later she gave up the throne. She was found guilty of treason and sentenced to five years of hard labor and fined $5,000. The penalties were never enforced, but she remained imprisoned at 'Iolani Palace until later that year.

In November 1897, Cleveland lost the US presidential election to William McKinley, and in 1898 McKinley signed annexation papers. Two years later, Hawaii was an American territory. Sanford Dole was its first territorial governor. Lili'uokalani and Dole publicly reconciled in 1911 at the opening of the Pearl Harbor naval base. In 1917, during World War I, Hawaii's last monarch raised the American flag over Washington Place for the very first time. Seven months later, she died at the age of 79.

HISTORICAL HINDSIGHT

In the 1890s, right around the time Hawaii achieved statehood, two different leaders had two similar perspectives of Hawaii. First, President Grover Cleveland wrote in his memoirs: "Hawaii is ours. As I look back upon… this miserable business and as I contemplate the means used to complete the outrage, I am ashamed of the whole affair." Next, Queen Lili'uokalani wrote in her memoirs: "Overawed by the power of the United States… the people of the Islands have no voice in determining their future, but are virtually relegated to the condition of the aboriginals of the American continent."

MODERN HAWAII

First it was sugar that defined Hawaii's economy.
Pineapples came along and helped out, as did the
military. Now, tourism is the state's financial anchor.

At the start of the 20th century, it looked as though the schemes of the business and land barons had finally come to pass. Hawaii became an American territory in 1900; the governor and judges were now appointed by the American president. Sugar was soon joined by a new commodity, pineapples, when James Dole (a relative of Sanford Dole) began marketing Hawaii-grown pineapples successfully on the US mainland. Hawaii would soon become the world's major supplier of the fruit.

The rise of sugar

With Sanford Dole leading the territorial government, just about all of the new territory's banking, commerce, and transportation remained under the continuing control of five large *haole* corporations built largely on sugar: Castle and Cooke, Alexander and Baldwin, C. Brewer, Theo H. Davies, and American Factors (now called Amfac). By intention and default, the so-called "Big Five" controlled Hawaii's politics and government.

Sanford Ballard Dole, c.1900.

Sugar's future remained of paramount importance. Because it was now part of the US, Hawaii was classified a domestic producer and thus no longer subject to import tariffs. Greater profits could be anticipated, and the plantations could grow. But expansion of the sugar plantations required yet more labor, and the companies had to import more workers to do the job.

Before, as an independent kingdom and republic, there had been no restrictions on immigration to Hawaii, and so the sugar barons had brought in tens of thousands of workers from Asia, first from China and then from Japan. Later, workers came from Portugal, Puerto Rico, Korea, and the Philippines. But now, as an American territory, immigration quotas were determined in Washington. Immigration from Asia was curtailed. With their traditional labor sources evaporating, Hawaii's sugar plantations were nevertheless in luck with a new source: the Philippines, under the American flag since 1898.

At this time, Hawaii was very much a Republican territory, governed by an entrenched oligarchy of businessmen intent on preserving their power. Hawaii was a place of well-defined social hierarchies. White men owned the plantations and held supervisory positions, while immigrant laborers ranked low. The first generation of immigrant laborers, indentured and mostly from Asia, buttressed this rigid plantation hierarchy.

The new Americans

As Hawaii swaggered into the 20th century, something happened that had not been anticipated at all. Those first-generation Chinese, Japanese, and Filipinos who had worked hard and quietly on the plantations decided to stay in Hawaii after their labor contracts ended. They had children, and these plantation babies were by birth American citizens. Unlike their parents, they were not foreigners, nor were they newcomers, nor strangers in a strange land. Hawaii was their home.

As this second generation of Asian immigrants grew up, the power of the Big Five

World War II

Early on Sunday morning, December 7, 1941, two waves of Japanese aircraft – 360 planes in all – dropped below cloud cover and attacked every major military installation on Oahu. The surprise attack devastated the US Pacific fleet: 2,323 Americans were killed while Japanese casualties numbered fewer than 100. Most of the ships in the harbor were severely damaged if not sunk. Some 68 Oahu residents were killed or injured. Japanese submarines sank cargo and passenger vessels in local waters. They also surfaced to shell Hilo, Nawiliwili, and Kahului harbors.

Pineapples and plantation workers, c.1910.

Japan had been expanding its control in Asia. Now the Pacific was next, including Pearl Harbor, home of the US Pacific fleet since 1908.

corporations, Republican politicians, and missionary landowners was challenged, their footing further undermined by an economic depression that boosted the confidence of labor movements. In 1935, 10 years after a violent strike by cane laborers in Hanapepe, Kauai, left many Filipino workers dead, legislation passed by the US Congress made it legal for workers to organize into unions and engage in collective bargaining.

The same day as the attack on Oahu, President Franklin Roosevelt declared war on Japan. Later in the morning, Hawaii was placed under martial law. The state remained under martial law until 1944, during which time military courts completely replaced all civilian jurisdiction in Hawaii. The US Supreme Court ruled after the war that this was an unconstitutional move.

At the beginning of the war, the largest ethnic group in Hawaii were the *nisei*, of Japanese ancestry. On the mainland, Americans of Japanese ancestry (AJAs) were confined in desert internment camps, a policy that was entirely racial and not substantiated by claims of national security. (Americans of German and

Italian ancestry were, in contrast, left alone.)

In Hawaii, the *nisei* were far too prominent to be confined, not only because they were a majority percentage of Hawaii's population, but also because they were a major thread in Hawaii's social and cultural fabric.

Eventually, AJAs of military age were permitted to enlist in the army; after the war, returning home to Hawaii, many AJAs used veterans' benefits to pay for college, turning later to law and politics and becoming the core of another shift in Hawaii's structure.

After the war, a succession of workers' strikes

Push for statehood

Between 1903 and 1957, 22 bills addressing statehood for Hawaii failed Congressional votes in Washington. Unlike mainland areas annexed as territories, there had been no provisions in Hawaii's territorial legislation for eventual statehood. And in any case, territorial status had suited the sugar interests just fine.

But in 1934, Congress had given Hawaii's sugar barons a kick in the *'okole* (buttocks) by grouping Hawaii along with foreign producers of sugar. Exports to the mainland plummeted. Statehood would be necessary to sustain Hawaii

US Navy battleships being attacked at Pearl Harbor.

established unions among Hawaii's major political and economic forces. They solidified their power in 1952 with a six-month work freeze on Hawaii's docks that nearly devastated the territory's economy, which was almost completely dependent on shipping. Hawaii's business and political *ancien régime*, however, were sore and sour losers, accusing the unions of being part of the Marxist plague. However, the Republican Party, which had been entrenched since well before anyone alive could remember, was knocked out of power in 1954 by a decidedly different incoming group of territorial legislators – half of whom were AJAs – and who were supported by labor unions.

as a leading sugar producer. The Big Five and other interests pushed for statehood and eventually overcame Congressional reluctance. It has been suggested that southern congressmen were against admitting Hawaii as a state dominated by non-Caucasians.

A deal was finally struck linking Hawaii and Alaska for statehood, and in 1959 Hawaii became the 50th American state. Statehood was ratified by Hawaii's voters by 17 to 1. Only the precinct of Ni'ihau, the privately owned island off Kauai, peopled by native Hawaiians, voted against it. Statehood was one of those historical pivots, like Cook's visit and the overthrow of Lili'uokalani, that irrevocably changed Hawaii's destiny and direction.

At the time of statehood, the tallest building in Hawaii was the 10-story-high Aloha Tower, and Waikiki was peppered here and there with just a few hotels. Defense and agriculture, primarily sugar and pineapples, were Hawaii's two main sources of revenue.

That same year, a regular commercial jet service was inaugurated by Qantas between Australia, Hawaii, and San Francisco, cutting travel time to California from nine propeller hours to less than five hours by jet. A few months later Pan Am connected Honolulu with the Pacific Coast and Tokyo, Japan.

> *In the 1950s, Hawaii's activist unions were accused of being revolutionary tools of an unproven Communist conspiracy.*

The commercial jet's ability to maintain a constant turnover of visitors made mass tourism a very promising enterprise. The jets brought an increasing numbers of visitors, and the once-stately, low-rise Waikiki hotels soon found themselves surrounded, and dwarfed, by bigger and taller hotels.

John Burns, Delores Martin, Henry Jackson and Governor William Quinn celebrate Hawaiian statehood.

HAWAII BY AIR

Air transport between islands arrived in 1929, when Inter-Island Airways, now Hawaiian Airlines, connected the islands with amphibious aircraft. Five years later, the new airline began regular inter-island mail routes. The first flight between Hawaii and another destination beyond the chain had almost been completed four years earlier when a US Navy seaplane coming from California ran out of fuel 300 miles (480km) from Hawaii. Just two years later, the first civilian flight to reach the islands similarly ran out of fuel, and crashed into a mesquite tree on Molokai.

A more reliable air connection with the US mainland was established on an April morning in 1935, when a 19-ton Pan Am Clipper landed at the fleet air base in Pearl Harbor, completing an "exploratory" flight from San Francisco that took 19 hours and 48 minutes.

Seven months later, a second Pan Am aircraft touched down with a cargo of mail, then continued an island-hopping route to Manila, creating the first Pacific air connection between North America and Asia. Less than a year later, the *Hawaii Clipper* skimmed across Pearl Harbor's waters with a cargo of seven paying passengers – a new kind of tourist with money to spend.

In the neighboring islands, too, agricultural land was converted into resort developments, especially on Maui and Kauai. On Hawaii Island, vacation resorts were built on barren lava. Former sugar-plantation workers became hotel employees.

Hawaii's urban center since the end of whaling, Honolulu simply exploded as new mainlanders and businesses arrived. Some peripheral neighborhoods expanded in population by up to 600 percent. And in the areas where it couldn't spread out, Honolulu shot upwards in wall to wall office buildings and

Asian investment

In the 1980s, Hawaii's tourism entered a period of unparalleled expansion, fueled in part by the triumph of plastic money over cash. Additionally, an influx of Asian capital, mostly from the over-heating Japanese economy, prompted a building boom that extended beyond Waikiki to the Neighbor Islands. Huge "fantasy resorts," developed to suit upscale tastes, became the new paradigm. Designed to keep visitors and therefore money on the property, the resorts themselves, not Hawaii, became the destination.

Honolulu in the 1950s.

high-rise condos. Small, quiet rural towns around Honolulu, such as Kailua, Kaneʻohe, Mililani, Hawaii Kai, Makakilo, turned into bedroom communities for Honolulu-bound commuters.

In the early 1980s, tourism overtook government and military spending in economic importance. Agriculture, meanwhile, slipped to a distant third. Some of the lost agricultural revenues were replaced by the exponential growth of *pakalolo*, or marijuana, cultivation, which illegally flourished in Hawaii's forests, sugar cane fields and backyards. Since then, an aggressive eradication effort, involving aerial herbicide spraying, has cut production substantially.

By the late 1980s, Japanese investors had injected $15 billion into Hawaii's economy. The Japanese bought heavily into hotels and resorts, acquiring 30 percent of all hotel rooms in Hawaii, and 70 percent of those that cost over $100 a day. There was some backlash against such a concentration of foreign ownership. But the Japanese kept the hotels under American management – thus successfully deflecting the worries of labor unions and local residents – and spent tens of millions of dollars to upgrade tired hotel properties. Throughout the islands, hotel standards increased.

While immense profits were made in the 1980s by some Hawaii residents with upscale property to sell, many others were pushed out of their homes and neighborhoods where families had lived for generations. When low-income retired people started being evicted from apartments they had rented for years, Hawaii's welcome of the yen wavered.

The infusion of yen into Hawaii finally skidded to a halt in the early 1990s, when the over-leveraged Japanese investors lost their shirts as Japan's stock markets and real estate markets crashed. The subsequent downturn in Hawaii saw property values plummet, thereby aggravating economic instability.

Pineapple field on Oahu.

Land issues

Today about half of Hawaii is owned by the state, county, and federal governments. Of the remaining land, three quarters is owned by a collection of fewer than 40 owners, mainly descended from the early Protestant missionary families with names like Bishop, Campbell, and Wilcox. These private landowners collectively own 60 percent of Molokai, and 40 to 50 percent of Oahu, Maui, Hawaii Island, and Kauai. Nearly all of Lanai and Ni'ihau are privately owned by single people or families. Land ownership in Hawaii involves both "fee simple" purchase, whereby the land is included in a real-estate transaction, and leasehold, in which the land is held

for a set period of time, generally ranging from 20 to 50 years. Many of Hawaii's larger hotels have been built on leased land, particularly those on Maui and in Honolulu.

Through the 1970s many private homes and condominiums were also built on leased land, although since that time, the land beneath most of these homes and apartment buildings has been sold to homeowners and converted to fee simple ownership.

The heady swirl of money and resort development during the 1980s rekindled concerns about the land, and about Hawaii's priorities. The state's over-heated real-estate market peaked in the early 1990s and then stagnated, along with the state's economy. The question of land, unfortunately but perhaps inevitably, has the potential to polarize and divide ethnic interests in the islands.

Hawaiian sovereignty

In 1993, the land issue came to the forefront during a four-day centennial remembrance of Queen Lili'uokalani's overthrow. With 'Iolani Palace covered in black bunting, it was certainly not a time of celebration and festivities. Then Governor John Waihe'e, the state's very first governor of Hawaiian ancestry, issued executive orders that only the Hawaiian flag, not the American one, should fly over state office buildings during the four days of remembrance.

There is no dispute that the overthrow of Queen Lili'uokalani was illegal under international law. In fact, the sovereignty of the islands had earlier been recognized by both the United States and the European powers. The immediate events of the overthrow were orchestrated by local businessmen and a representative of the United States whose actions, which included the dispatch of American troops from a visiting ship to sustain the coup, were taken without the authorization of the American president. This was sustained by congressional inaction.

On the centennial of the overthrow of the Hawaiian monarchy in November 1993, the

All of Hawaii's shoreline up to the high-tide mark is public property and must be accessible to the public.

then President Bill Clinton formally apologized on behalf of the US government for its role in the 1893 coup in Hawaii. The joint Congressional resolution that he signed also acknowledged the illegitimacy of the 1898 annexation.

The resurgence of tourism

In 2002, former Maui mayor Linda Lingle was elected as Hawaii's first Republican governor for 40 years, as well as the first-ever woman governor. Although Democrats continue to have overwhelming majorities in both chambers of the state legislature, Lingle was re-elected as governor in 2006 by the largest margin in Hawaiian history.

Lingle earned much of her reputation as a champion of tourism on Maui, helping to spearhead the apparent recovery of Hawaii's tourist industry from its 1990s downturn. However, visitor numbers were dealt a further body blow by the terrorist attacks of September 2001. For a nerve-wracking couple of years, American travelers in particular seemed reluctant to brave the long flight from the mainland. More recently, however, the figures have first matched and then exceeded previous record levels, and Hawaii for the moment seems to be booming once more.

Perhaps the most significant changes have been on Oahu, where Waikiki, which had fallen rather behind the times and become a little seedy, has determinedly set about re-branding itself as a classy, upscale destination. Modern tower-blocks are replacing the small-scale, family-run places that were the

last remaining vestiges of the 1950s and 1960s, with the extravagant Trump International Hotel, at the heart of the Waikiki Beachwalk development, typifying the new era with its emphasis on luxury individually owned condos. All its 464 units sold on the very first day they were made available, for a record-breaking $700 million.

The construction boom has been present on other islands, too. On Maui, both the Wailea and Ka'anapali Beach areas have expanded in recent years; on Hawaii Island, the South Kohala resort area has grown as well. Even on

Souvenirs of US president Barack Obama, who was born in Honolulu.

Lanai, development is picking up; when Larry Ellison bought the island for (a reported) $600 million, he promised to invest another (reported) $500 million in the island's infrastructure. Rumor has it that eventually will mean condominiums.

Perhaps the biggest impact of new resort construction in Hawaii has been reinvestment in some of the islands' older resorts. To compete with the newcomers, more "veteran" properties have consistently upgraded their facilities to remain at the very highest international standard. The best example of these improvements: a 2011 room refresh at the Royal Hawaiian, one of Waikiki Beach's signature hotels.

A HAWAIIAN PRESIDENT

When Barack Obama was elected 44th President of the United States in 2008, he not only became the nation's first-ever African-American president, but also became the nation's first ever president born in the state of Hawaii. Obama was born in Honolulu, and has made many aspects of Hawaiian culture part of his presidential persona. For starters, he has spoken publicly about his love for the sweet snack, shave ice. He also has popularized the "shaka" sign, a greeting popular in Hawaiian surf culture that means, essentially, "Hang Loose." When he visits Oahu, he has been known to frequent the restaurants of Kapahulu on the outskirts of Waikiki.

HAWAII'S PEOPLE

With "natives" originating from as far afield as Asia, Europe, North America, and the South Pacific, Hawaii has an extraordinary ethnic and cultural mix.

The entire United States often is seen as a "melting pot," and Hawaii is perhaps the best representation of this idea. Over the decades, Hawaii has received waves of immigrants from various cultures. Except for the Native Hawaiians, who were here first, and the Caucasians, who came to convert or build business empires, or in later years to settle in "paradise," most of Hawaii's ethnic groups came to work on sugar cane or pineapple plantations and stayed to raise families. According to the 2012 census statistics, which used "self-0defining" categories, Asians make up 38 percent of the state's nearly 1.4 million people, Caucasians follow with about 26 percent, then the Native Hawaiians (or other Pacific Islanders) at about 10 percent. The rest comprise people who identify themselves as having a mixed-race background, or those who identify as Hispanic, Latino, and African-American.

In a glassblower's workshop in the town of Lahaina, Maui.

The Hawaiians

Indigenous Hawaiians are now among the most inconspicuous people walking the streets of Hawaii. In the century following first contact with Europeans, most of Hawaii's native people died from epidemics of introduced diseases: cholera, influenza, mumps, measles, whooping cough, and smallpox. Gonorrhea caused sterility; syphilis resulted in stillbirths.

The statistics astound. Hawaii's aboriginal population had shrunk from an estimated 300,000 at the time of Captain Cook's 1778 visit to about 40,000 in 1893, when the Hawaiian monarchy was overthrown. And many of those 40,000 were *hapa*-Hawaiian, or part-Hawaiian. By the mid-19th century, a hauntingly intangible but real disease killed many more thousands of Hawaiians: sheer

psychological depression. *Na kanaka ku'u wale aku no i ka 'uhane* – The people freely gave up their souls and died.

Given the degree of inter-racial mixing over the past two centuries, it's difficult to know how many full Hawaiians remain. According to state health department estimates, there are approximately 9,000 Hawaiians of unmixed ancestry, fewer than one percent of Hawaii's total population, including military. Those of partial Hawaiian ancestry number roughly 130,000. The most Hawaiian of islands is Ni'ihau, a privately owned island off Kauai's west coast with a population of about 130 – all Hawaiian. Molokai has the next largest percentage of part Hawaiians – about 40 percent

Traditional Beliefs

Tradition is alive and well in Hawaii. Spiritual beliefs inform everyday life and many ancient rituals are still in practice today.

Even though Hawaii has stormed into the 21st century, some of its belief systems are still just as traditional as they were hundreds of years ago; and many of its inhabitants are markedly supersti-

A woodcarver.

tious. In Hawaiian tradition, for instance, the land, or 'aina, is mother. 'Aina literally means "that which feeds." The land doesn't belong to people; Native Hawaiians, or kanaka maoli, as they call themselves, belong to it and are part of it. The kanaka maoli sense of balance requires being in the natural environment. If separated from the land, Hawaiians and their culture tend to drift and lose meaning. The sheltering home, the trees outside, the earth beneath – all are alive and aware.

Hidden messages

The shapes of the clouds, the cries of birds at night, the sounds of waves on the reef – all have messages for the Hawaiian people. Hawaiian tradition involved constant communication with other living beings, with the land, rocks, clouds, sea, and spirits of ancestors.

Preserving cultural traditions

Beyond 'aina, a number of key concepts have evolved as critical aspects of preserving cultural traditions. No. 1 on the list: spiritual power, or Mana. Mana can come from a number of places. One source is rank at birth. Ali'i (royalty) are born with more mana than commoners. Higher-born ali'i have more mana than lesser-born.

The other source is training: a skilled carver, fisherman, chanter, navigator, physician, or dancer gradually acquires this kind of mana, as ability is refined. These skills require long apprenticeship. They also require protection; one's specialized knowledge shouldn't be too readily shared with others lest its power be diminished. Most skills incorporate the notion of Huna – certain confidential, secret aspects of the skill. According to tradition, this requires the understanding of how numerous forces interact, the maintenance of certain kinds of protocol, and the observance of strict forms of behavior.

The right way

At all levels of society, kanaka maoli believe in balance and protocol. Preparing and consuming a meal has to be done in a certain way. Preparations for the treatment of someone who is ill, such as the gathering of la'au lapa'au (medicinal plants), must be completed at a certain time of day with certain rules, prayers, and thoughts. Chants, dances, and rituals have to be conducted impeccably. There is a right way to do everything, and even the smallest daily activity is enmeshed in a web of belief and practice.

Signs and symbols

The chants used in ritual, prayer, and hula, if the words and songs are uttered properly, carry with them considerable power. Hawaiians don't merely petition the gods and hope they'll act; Hawaiians participate by their way of asking. The belief, the ritual, and the result all become one process. And prayers are two-way communications between humans and gods. Responses are received and interpreted in whatever form they may come: patterns in the fire, images in a dream, a sudden gust of wind, a grumble of thunder, a thought that seems to come from nowhere. But of course, nothing comes from nowhere; everything has causes and exists for a reason.

of its population. Lanai, another mostly privately owned island, is next with just under 10 percent.

The Hawaiians have made a comeback, it might be argued, by marrying into other racial groups and thus sustaining some of the blood lines. Equally if not more important is the revival of the Hawaiian culture, nearly extinguished by Protestant missionaries in the 19th century.

A *malihini*, or newcomer, might point out that part-Hawaiians are also part something else, but part-Hawaiians, whatever their other

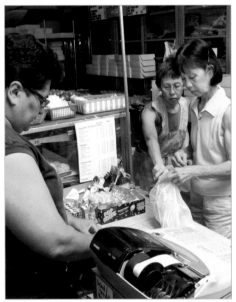

Shopping at the T. Komoda Store & Bakery in Makawao, Maui.

ancestry, almost unanimously think of themselves as Hawaiian first. It's a point of pride, if not of status, to be a *keiki o ka 'aina*, a child of the soil.

Many Hawaiians embrace this pride in a variety of ways. For some, it might be speaking a Hawaiian version of the English language known as pidgin. For others, it might be participating in cultural events such as hula or falsetto contests – both of which harken back to a simpler time in Hawaii's history. Still others staunchly support sovereignty; going so far as to be distrustful of and spiteful toward Caucasians. Granted, most of the biggest divisions between locals and migrants from the

mainland play out in schoolyards. Still, in some communities, there is definitely anti-outsider sentiment that runs deep.

The Chinese

"The ball at the Court House on Thursday night last, given to their majesties the King and Queen by the Chinese merchants of Honolulu and Lahaina, was the most splendid affair of its kind ever held in Honolulu... We have heard but one opinion expressed by those present (which includes all Honolulu and his wife), and that was that the Celestials have outshone the 'outside barbarians' in fete-making for the throne."

According to this newspaper report, the party hosted by Chinese business leaders in 1856 to honor the marriage of King Kamehameha IV and Queen Emma took Honolulu by storm.

At the time of the ball, Hawaii's Chinese community numbered maybe 600 people. It marked the entry of local Chinese into the highest circles of society. The king was so pleased that one of the Chinese sponsors married the foster sister of the future King Kalakaua, later becoming the first and only full-blooded Chinese to be appointed to the Hawaiian royal court.

Hawaii's Chinese didn't always have it so good. In the 1890s, jealous American businessmen, in an attempt to restrict the inroads that enterprising Chinese were making into local commerce, initiated legislation that restricted the freedom of Chinese immigrant laborers. Nevertheless, over the decades the Chinese have become one of Hawaii's most prominent, influential, generous, and financially successful ethnic groups. They and the Japanese represent the biggest players in the Asian immigration boom that Hawaii has experienced since the turn of the millennium.

From the sandalwood trade of the early 1800s, the Chinese were well acquainted with Hawaii, known to them as Tan Heung Shan, or the Country of the Fragrant Tree. The first Chinese laborers arrived here in 1852, about 300 workers from Guangdong and Fujian provinces in southeastern China. Before they left China, they had signed five-year contracts promising them $36 a year, sea passage, food, clothing, and housing.

Many of those first Chinese were intent on finishing their contracts and returning to China with money. Others married local women and, with their savings, set up shops in Honolulu and Lahaina, the boomtowns of the mid-1800s. The Chinese often found a niche in retail, especially as they were not welcome in the sugar industry except as laborers.

Most Chinese who used to live in Honolulu's so-called Chinatown (near the harbor) left Downtown long ago, taking their new-found affluence to other, ritzier, sectors of the community, especially after World War II. But a few persistent old-timers stayed behind, where they still mind Hong Kong-style acupuncture

The Japanese

When Hirohito, the late Emperor of Japan, arrived in Hawaii in 1975, his aircraft landed at Honolulu International Airport from a southeasterly approach, rather than the standard northwesterly. The reason: the emperor's pilots wanted to avoid flying over Pearl Harbor and subjecting him to reminders of the war fought in his name 35 years earlier. Meeting him at the airport was an *aloha* delegation that included three US congressmen of Japanese descent, the recently elected Japanese-American governor of Hawaii, and an

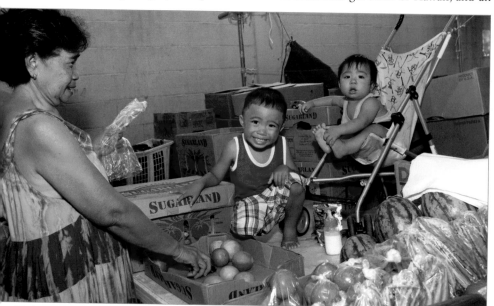

Vendor at Hilo Farmers' Market, on the Big Island.

clinics, market food stalls, noodle factories, and restaurants.

It was in Chinatown where Honolulu schoolmates Ho Fon and Dr Sun Yatsen met to plan a Chinese revolution. Dr Sun Yatsen, considered the father of modern China by both Communist and Nationalist Chinese, founded his original revolutionary group in Honolulu in 1895. That secret society, first known by the Chinese-Hawaiian name Hsing Chung Hui (Revive China Group) was crucial to the future success of China's revolutionary movement against foreign powers. Because Chinese patrons in the islands contributed generous support to Dr Sun's cause, Hawaii became known in some Chinese circles as the cradle of the Chinese republic.

THE REAL CHARLIE CHAN

During the 1910s and 1920s, downtown Honolulu was the turf of Chang Apana, a Hawaiian-Chinese police detective. Known to the local Chinese as Kana Pung, Apana retired in 1932 after 34 years of distinguished service. At his funeral the following year, the Royal Hawaiian Band marched in his cortege. Apana was the inspiration for Charlie Chan, a fictional character from American writer Earl Derr Biggers. In 1925, with the publication of Biggers' novel *House Without a Key*, the whimsical Inspector Chan assumed a place in fictional history. Biggers wrote many installments of *The Adventures of Charlie Chan*.

American of Japanese ancestry, then president of the University of Hawaii.

Along the highway from the airport to Downtown and Waikiki, Hirohito and his entourage rolled past dozens of businesses with Japanese names, fleets of fishing sampans wriggling with fresh tuna for Hawaii's sashimi-crazy households, and opulent Buddhist and Shinto temples and shrines. To say that the Japanese have succeeded in Hawaii is an understatement. From World War II until the present day, their political and social power has been considerable.

This Japanese rise to prominence began with humble origins. It wasn't until 1868, during the first year of Japan's reformist Meiji Era, that an "official" group of immigrants from Japan put into Hawaii. These *gannenmono*, or first-year men, arrived at Honolulu on board the British sailing ship *Scioto*. Carrying three-year laborer contracts, all were quickly assimilated into local plantations, earning about 12 cents a day or, according to one account, about twice what they could make in Japan. By 1885 that income quadrupled to about 50 cents a day.

Strict emigration laws in Japan, however, made it difficult for more Japanese to come to Tenjiku, or the Heavenly Place, as Hawaii also came to be known. A little diplomacy was called for on this matter. So in 1881, King Kalakaua visited Japan on the first leg of a tour around the world. He initiated treaty discussions with the Japanese and actively pursued the Japanese immigration issue until it was given sanction. In 1885, a group of 943 immigrants – 676 men, 159 women, and 108 children – arrived in Honolulu.

Life was often miserable in the plantation camps, but Japanese continued to arrive in ever increasing numbers. By 1900, there were 61,000 Japanese workers and dependants in the islands, or more than twice the number of Hawaiians, Caucasians, or Chinese in Hawaii. Until the mid-1970s, the Japanese remained Hawaii's largest ethnic group.

The Japanese, like nearly all of Hawaii's non-*haole* laborers, suffered from racial and economic prejudices under Hawaii's plantation elite. And when Japan attacked Pearl Harbor, a small number of local Japanese-Americans were forced into internment camps on the mainland. In Hawaii, where Americans of Japanese ancestry (AJAs) made up 40 percent of the population in the early 1940s, internment of all AJAs was out of the question. But under martial law, Japanese language schools and radio stations were shut down; Buddhist, Shinto and Zen temples were closed; and Japanese newspapers were strictly censored. Still, not a single case of Japanese-American disloyalty or sabotage occurred during the war.

Regardless of ethnic background, nearly everyone in Hawaii lives a little bit of the Japanese lifestyle, knowingly or not. Few are the homes where shoes aren't removed before entering, and many are the *kama'aina* (long-time

Baristas give a "shaka" at Grandma's Coffee House in Kula, Maui.

GOING FOR BROKE

Despite internment during the war, second-generation *(nisei)* Japanese-Americans still volunteered by the hundreds for the army. The government finally created an all-*nisei* unit in 1942: the 100th Battalion. A year later, a larger unit was formed: the 442nd Infantry Regiment. Both were sent to Italy in 1944, where they were nicknamed, "Go For Broke."

Fighting in Italy and France, the *nisei* units won seven presidential unit citations and 6,000 individual awards, the most highly decorated unit in the American military during World War II. Their casualty rate was over three times the military's average.

residents) who order sushi or sashimi without thinking twice. All residents of Hawaii are very much at home with things Japanese. The thump of *mochi* pounding or of drums for the Buddhist *bon odori* that honors souls of the dead are common sounds in Hawaii's diverse neighborhoods. Even Spam is most commonly eaten Japanese-style – in a form of sushi known as Spam *musabi*.

The Filipinos

The first Filipinos to call Hawaii home were acrobats and musicians who swept into Hon-

Inside St Francis Church in Kaluapapa, Molokai.

olulu after a performing tour of China and Japan. In true Filipino spirit, they set to work entertaining Oahu's residents for two weeks in 1888 while waiting for their ship to San Francisco.

"The Filipino troupers pleased their Hawaiian audiences, and the spell of Hawaii upon the performers was even more potent: so much so that when sailing time came and their manager refused to pay their salaries until arrival in San Francisco, they returned to their lodgings and took up their abode in Hawaii. Four of the 12 young men found immediate employment in the Royal Hawaiian Band of King Kalakaua."

It is the sugar industry more than anything that gets the credit for making Hawaii the largest Filipino community in the world outside the Philippine archipelago. Immigration of Filipinos as laborers began in 1906 with the arrival of 15 Filipino laborers to work on a sugar plantation. For the next 40 years, Filipinos poured into Hawaii at a pace exceeded only by Japanese.

More than 125,000 Filipinos were recruited by the labor-hungry sugar companies, mostly in northern Ilocos. Of them, however, only 10,000 were women, and another 7,000 children. Not keen on being bachelors, about half of the men returned home to find wives and begin lives anew with money earned in the fields. Most who remained in Hawaii either married women from other ethnic groups or endured an extended if not eternal bachelorhood.

Tired of the plantation hierarchy and inequalities, the Filipinos organized into labor unions. The Filipino Federation and Labor Union, for example, was well organized and actively agitating for employee benefits as early as 1919. And although some of their early labor-management confrontations ended in violence, death, and defeat, *bum-by* (by-and-by), to use a favorite Filipino expression, their tenacity and eventual successes nurtured a collective dignity. Eventually, unions attained legal status and protection.

Filipino celebrations follow Roman Catholic observances, including an exotic candlelight festival held every spring on the Feast Day of Santa Cruz. The biggest annual event is the June Fiesta Filipina, which takes place at various locations throughout the islands. You'll find people in traditional garb enjoying Filipino music and food.

Filipino cuisine hasn't captivated island palates as have the cuisines of Korea, China, Thailand, Vietnam, and Japan. But for complete menus à la Manila or Zamboanga, stroll into one of several eateries around Honolulu and wish the proprietor a sincere *mabuhay* (hello).

The Koreans

"In Hawaii you rarely ever see a group of Koreans, but you see a Korean in every group." This comment by a Honolulu-born Korean businessman is a contemporary comment on Hawaii's highly mobile and adaptable Korean community.

Unlike the more clannish Japanese and Chinese, Hawaii's 20,000-plus Koreans have rapidly fanned out into society; their "out-marriage" rate, for example, has been as high as 80 percent for both men and women, an inter-racial marriage statistic second only to part-Hawaiians. In the United States, Honolulu is second only to Los Angeles in the number of native-born Korean residents. Both long-established and recently immigrated Koreans have capitalized on their verve, ambition, and versatility to achieve business and social successes in Hawaii. Their overall education and income levels, for example, are the highest per capita of any ethnic group in Hawaii. Whether in the land of Morning Calm

of an ancient Korean board game, *changgi*, or Korean chess.

In the islands, probably the most popular nickname for Koreans is *yobo*. Literally, *yobo* means "my dear" and is a way of addressing one's husband or wife. It is also the informal equivalent of "hello" or "hey there," when used to catch one's attention. Early Korean immigrants would address one another as *yobo-seyo*, or simply *yobo*, which is not quite as polite. This term stuck as an island nickname.

Koreans first arrived as laborers in 1903. Over the next two years, more than 7,000 Kore-

At Home Maid Bakery in Wailuku, Maui.

or in Hawaii, Koreans are a down-to-earth lot, who speak their minds and tend to be more direct in their communication than their Asian neighbors. Since Korea was opened to the West, they have been dubbed the Irish of Asia: being highly sociable people, they enjoy a drink or two.

They've adapted well to Hawaii, but many of their traditions elude the younger generation. *Halmoni* (grandmothers) who first came to Hawaii as "picture brides" still try to arrange marital matches in the traditional Korean way, but second- and third-generation children usually have other ideas. The *haraboji* (grandfathers) still gather at community centers to spend long hours deep into clacking rounds

ans, most of them young men (10 for every Korean woman), signed up to work in Hawaii. But in 1905, Korea's emperor cut off all labor emigration after hearing that Korean laborers had been mistreated on hemp plantations in Mexico. Not until the Japanese annexed Korea in 1910 and allowed a thousand Korean "picture brides" to join their "picture grooms" did Korean immigration to Hawaii resume.

After Japan invaded Korea, Hawaii became a source of pro-Korean revolutionary support. In fact, most Korean social societies still in Hawaii began as anti-Japanese and restore-the-homeland groups, and some of them are highly secretive. Dr Syngman Rhee, an American-educated diplomat, turned to Koreans in Hawaii for revolutionary support against the Japanese occupation. After Japan's defeat in World War II, Dr Rhee returned to Korea triumphant as the first president of the Republic of Korea. Following a Korean military coup d'état that deposed him in 1960 at the start of his fourth term, he fled to Hawaii, dying in exile in 1965.

The Samoans

Samoans were later arrivals to the Islands, coming from the six isles that make up the territory of American Samoa, an 80-sq-mile (200-sq-km)

Everything's OK for this couple on the Big Island.

group located about 2,600 miles (4,200km) due southwest of Honolulu.

Some 500 Samoans had trickled into Hawaii after World War I, the majority of them to join a Mormon community based in Laʻie, on Oahu's Windward Shore. In 1952, after Samoan immigration to America was liberalized, a group of 900 Samoan men, women, and children – about half of them Samoan-American navy men and dependants being transferred to Pearl Harbor – boarded a navy transport ship and set off for the Hawaiian Islands. At the time, these emigrants from American Samoa represented 6 percent of American Samoa's total population.

Perhaps out of all the local Asian-Oceanic ethnic groups, Samoans have best retained their traditional cultural touchstones. When a Samoan "community" problem arises, elected chiefs, some of whom represent the various expatriate Samoan clans in Hawaii, call a spe-

> *Samoan Americans have become quite successful in sumo wrestling, especially in Japan. Some have even become Japanese citizens.*

cial council called a *fono*. At these councils, the chiefs establish policy, mediate in the case of intra-Samoan grievances, and, if they feel a Samoan problem requires government attention, draft mutually agreed-upon statements for the appropriate outside individual or agency.

Most Samoan gatherings, however, are of a more celebratory nature: a wedding, or the investiture of a new chief, or Flag Day, an annual holiday that celebrates the raising of the American flag over Eastern Samoa in 1899. As part of this celebration, out come the *kava* cups and the colorful *lava-lava* sarongs and *puletasi* dresses, and the finely woven *lau hala* mats to be spread out on the ground. Joined by expatriates from Tonga, Fiji, Tahiti, and the Marquesas, the Samoans get together in fine *fia-fia* (feasting) fashion – *faʻa Samoa*, the Samoan way.

The Caucasians

As some Hawaiians explain it, their ancestors called the first Europeans *haole* because they could not believe that men with such pale skins and frail bodies could be alive. *Haole*, from *ha*, which means breath or the breath of life, connects with *ole*, which connotes an absence of the breath of life or, more simply, without life. Originally applied to any outsider, *haole* now refers to Caucasians, sometimes with neutral meaning, occasionally with negative meaning. Since the time of Cook, it has been fashionable in Hawaii for both *haole* and non-*haole* to put down *haole*.

For many years, the term was more of a slur than a synonym for Caucasian. *Haoles*, whether a *malihini* (newcomer) or *kamaʻaina* (long-time resident, old-timer), are now one of the fastest-growing ethnic groups in the islands and are vying against residents of Asian descent as the islands' main political force.

Since World War II, most *haole* coming to the islands more or less assimilated into the local lifestyle and rhythms, or at least made an attempt to. In recent years, however, new arrivals sometimes seem more interested in fashioning Hawaii into their own image of a paradise, or at least bringing a West Coast (from where a good percentage originate) attitude with them. It is not a new phenomenon. Since the first Polynesians arrived, every group has brought cultural baggage.

One distinct *haole* group that deserves special mention is the Portuguese, or *Portagee* in the local pidgin dialect, who immigrated in large numbers when Hawaii was still a much more quickly than the Asian immigrants who worked alongside them. By the 1930s, the Portuguese community had a territorial supreme court chief justice, a territorial secretary and an acting governor, and the Catholic vicar apostolic of the Hawaiian Islands.

The Portuguese also introduced a small four-stringed instrument, known as the *braquino* or *cavaghindo* in Portugal, which became the *'ukulele* in Hawaiian. The Hawaiian word *'ukulele* literally means "leaping flea," and the story goes that it came from the nickname of Edward Purvis, an English expatriate who arrived in Hawaii

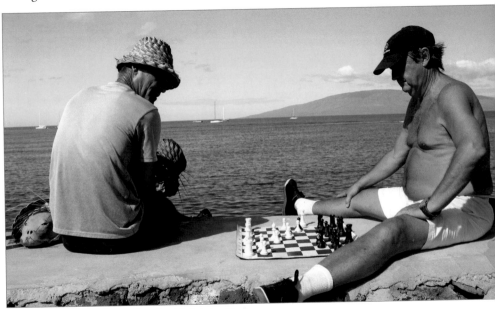

Playing chess by the waterfront on Front Street in Lahaina, Maui.

kingdom, mostly to work in the cane fields. As early as 1872, there were perhaps 400 or so Portuguese in Hawaii, mostly sailors who had left whaling ships for life on land. These Europeans were well received by both Hawaiians and *haole* merchants and planters, so in 1878 the Hawaiian government and sugar barons conducted an official labor recruitment campaign in Portugal's Azores and Madeira islands. Twenty years later, almost 13,000 Portuguese had made the rough voyage to the Hawaiian Islands, which, with their volcanic soils, offered very similar conditions for agriculture.

Many became *luna*, or foremen, on the sugar plantations, gaining a mid-level power foothold in 1879. Purvis made friends with newly arrived Portuguese immigrants, and he soon learned to play the *braquino* with entertaining finesse. Purvis was small in stature and quick with his hands, so his Hawaiian friends nicknamed him *'Ukulele*, the Leaping Flea.

Local Portuguese, although more than two generations removed from the old country, still celebrate Portuguese traditions and religious festivals. A series of post-Easter *festas* are known as the Seven Domingas, or Holy Ghost festivals. During the seven weeks of *festa*, families participate in prayer and celebration. Traditional delicacies are prepared, such as *pao dolce* (sweet bread) and hot fried *malasadas* (a delicious light Portuguese donut).

ANCIENT WAYS AND PLACES

While the Westernization of the Hawaiian islands has been thorough, ancient ways are still available to explore.

The arrival of Europeans in Hawaii sparked a process that sociologists call "dualism," in which two distinct cultures and economies exist simultaneously. While Western processes and values eventually supplanted those of traditional Hawaii, one still may witness the ways and places of old Hawaii even today.

Archeologists, anthropologists, and sociologists have undertaken reconstructions and preservation of sacred temples and villages. Some of these sites: Puʻukohola, Lapakahi, and Puʻuhonua ʻO Honaunau, all on Hawaii Island; Kaneʻaki and Puʻu O Mahuka *heiaus* (temples) on Oahu; Piʻilanihale Heiau, *in the Kahanu Garden* on Maui; and ʻIli ʻili ʻopae Heiau on Molokai.

Life in ancient times

In ancient Hawaii, the *ʻaina*, or land, was considered the property of the gods, held in trust by a chief or king. He allocated land to support the *aliʻi* (royalty), who allowed *makaʻainana* (commoners) to cultivate it. The commoners, protected by the *aliʻi*, turned over food grown to the *aliʻi*.

The land itself was divided into wedge-shaped parcels called *ahupuaʻa*, which usually extended from the coast up into a mountain valley.

Life during these times was satisfactory, but it wasn't especially idyllic. Warfare was common, and commoners had to be careful not to violate *kapu* (see page 32). A person always could find safety in a *puʻuhonua*, a place of refuge. Here, absolution by a *kahuna*, or priest, cleansed transgressions or assured sanctuary.

Carved wooden kiʻi at the Hale o Keawe Heiau (temple), Big Island.

Craftsmen still carve the fearsome sacred images called kiʻi akua.

Polynesian statues of gods in the Honolulu Museum of Art.

Ancient petroglyphs on Lanai.

ROYAL STONES AND PETROGLYPHS

In central Oahu are the birth stones of Kukaniloko, which have been sacred to Hawaiians as far back as the 1100s.

The wives of high-ranking chiefs gave birth on the stones' gently curved surfaces. Attendant chiefs, high priests, and physicians would gather in a ceremony marked by chants and offerings. The *ali'i* child would be named and the umbilical cord – *piko* – would be cut.

Hawaiians would place the severed *piko* in a hole carved into the rock, essentially a simple petroglyph, or *kaha ki'i*. *Piko* were put where *mana*, or spirit, was strong, such as at Kukaniloko. It was hoped that the child might be influenced by the *mana*, and maybe even absorb some of it. Sometimes a representation of the family's *'aumakua* (family or personal god) would be carved into the rock adjacent to the *piko* hole.

On Hawaii Island, the Kona and Kohala districts offer several easily accessible petroglyph sites, such as at Puako. As most of them are at ground level, take extreme care and don't walk on top of them.

Tapa, or cloth made from bark, was used for clothes.

Pu'ukohola Heiau National Historic Site protects the ruins of Pu'ukohola Heiau, a major ancient Hawaiian temple on the Big Island.

Ki'i at the Hale o Keawe Heiau. These fearsome god images or idols were used to protect and impress.

Ziplining with Kolekole Falls in the background, Big Island.

OUTDOOR ACTIVITIES

With countless trails, hundreds of thousands of acres of jungle, miles upon miles of coastline, and great dirt roads, Hawaii is one big playground for outdoor adventure-seekers.

I f you like the outdoors, there's never a shortage of things to do in Hawaii. Hiking, bicycling, surfing, snorkeling, diving, swimming, stand-up paddling, kayaking, outrigger canoeing, wildlife-watching, paragliding, horseback riding, ziplining, deep-sea fishing, and off-roading are just some of the outdoor activities available here.

You can ride a bike down the flanks of a volcano, ride a motorcycle on one of the curviest roads in America, or kitesurf into the teeth of strong trade winds. Because none of the islands is very big, it is possible to wake up early and enjoy two or three of these pastimes in a day. And you can still be home before dinner.

Many visitors come to Hawaii to sip Mai Tais in a chaise lounge near a resort pool. A growing number of other visitors fly to the islands exclusively to enjoy all of the outdoor recreation the islands have to offer. These travelers rarely leave disappointed.

Surfing at Ho'okipa Beach, Maui.

Hiking

To put it simply, Hawaii is a hiker's paradise. Local groups estimate the state boasts more than 3,000 miles (4,828km) of hiking trails. With options ranging from easy to moderate to hard, there is something for everyone.

Some of the trails have reputations that precede them. The 11-mile (18km) Kalalau Trail, for instance, along the Na Pali Coast on Kauai, is considered one of the best backcountry hikes in the United States, and usually requires two or three overnights to get from the trailhead near Ke'e Beach to the Kalalau Valley. Another epic tromp is the trail to Koko Head, on Oahu. It's not the length of this trail that presents a challenge for hikers (it's only 1.5 miles/2.4km long). Instead, it's the elevation gain: the trail includes more than 1,000 steps as it climbs 1,600ft (488 meters).

Elsewhere – and on other islands – hiking is less about the trails themselves and more about the journey. On Maui and Hawaii islands, just about any hike on national park land will be fulfilling. On Molokai, especially in Kalaupapa National Historical Park, hiking (you must go with a guide) is almost always part of an immersive learning experience. On Lanai, in places like the fire-red Garden of the Gods, you can feel as if you are on another planet.

Bicycling

Another great way to experience the Hawaiian countryside: by bike. Once considered an alternative sport, the bicycling community in Hawaii has grown rapidly over the last ten years, and has gotten to the point where most of the major cities and towns have at least one bike shop.

There are benefits to seeing sights via bicycle. For starters, admission to national parks is cheaper, and admission to state parks is free. Second, since all of the islands were volcanoes at one point, most roads have incline, meaning that using a bicycle likely will provide quite a workout. Finally, using a bicycle produces no greenhouse gases, which means that it's the more

Accomplished surfers gravitate toward the best of the "Big Wave" surfing destinations: the North Shore of Oahu and Peahi (or Jaws), on the northern shore of Maui. Amateurs usually opt for calmer spots: Waikiki Beach on Oahu, Poipu Beach on Kauai, Kahalu'u Beach Park near Kailua on Hawaii Island, and off Lahaina on Maui. Surf schools operate in all four of these latter spots; average lessons last 1–2 hours and cost anywhere from $95 to $150. (However, instructors do not guarantee you'll be able to get up on the board after one class!)

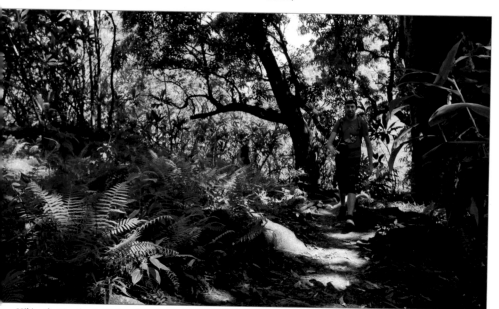

Hiking the Hanakapi'ai Falls trail in the Hanakapi'ai Valley, Kauai.

environmentally friendly choice. One word of caution: the majority of rides must occur alongside automobile traffic, which sometimes can be a problem for families with little children.

For those who prefer to just do downhill on a bike, outfitters near Haleakala National Park, on Maui, run trips during which participants quite literally careen down roads that hug the side of the volcano. Most of these trips are offered just after sunrise and guaranteed to get the adrenaline pumping.

Surf's up

The Hawaiian Islands are considered to be the birthplace of modern surfing, which makes Hawaii a great place to hang ten.

HIKING KAPALUA

Even the ritziest resorts such as the Kapalua Resort, amidst beautiful scenery in the westernmost corner of West Maui, have hiking trails. Here, since the late 1990s, officials have invested big bucks in creating and maintaining a trail system worth exploring. The crown jewel of this network is the grueling 6-mile (10km) Mahana Ridge Trail, which connects the Maunalei Arboretum with D.T. Flemming Beach Park. Kapalua has also built a short boardwalk trail that hugs the coast on resort land. On a clear day, this pathway is a great spot from which to watch the sunset.

There are other ways to get your surf on in Hawaii. Stand-up paddling (paddleboarding), an ancient activity that Polynesian fishermen likely used to spear fish hundreds of years ago, has enjoyed a spike in popularity in recent years, and today is one of the most popular

> In January 2013, Hawaiian pro surfer Garrett McNamara set a world record when he surfed a wave off the coast of Portugal that was roughly 100ft (30 meters) tall.

just about anywhere (provided the seas are calm). Resort areas on Maui, Oahu, Kauai, and Hawaii Island all offer some degree of snorkeling off the beaches right in front of the hotels. For even better experiences, check out Hanauma Bay on Oahu, or hop aboard a charter from Ma'alea Harbor to Molokini, a tiny atoll between Maui and Kaho'olawe.

Snorkeling might be the most common form, but the most popular wildlife-watching activity takes place every winter, when humpback whales migrate to Hawaii from Alaska to mate, and birth and rear their young.

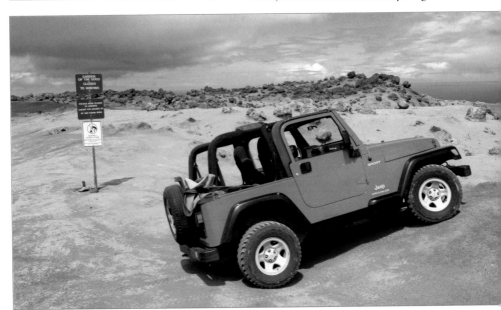

Take a jeep on the 4x4 trail to the Garden of the Gods rock formations, on Lanai.

sports in Hawaii. Other forms of surfing (kitesurfing and windsurfing) are harder to come by but available to thrill-seekers who wish to seek them out. Then, of course, there's bodyboarding, which just about anyone can do on just about any beach with sand and the smallest of waves.

Wildlife-watching

The waters surrounding the Hawaiian Islands teem with life. Naturally, then, Hawaii is a great place to observe some of these creatures and critters in their natural environments.

Perhaps the most common wildlife-watching activity is snorkeling – it's cheap, it's easy, and the water is clear enough to do it

> Whale researchers know humpback whales come to Hawaii to mate and birth their young, but they have never witnessed whales mating or giving birth.

The whale-watching is best in the 'Au'au Channel between Maui and Lanai; on any given day, you might spot 20–30 whales less than five minutes from shore. Two- and four-hour boat trips are available from Lahaina Harbor and Ma'alea Harbor between December and April.

Finally, you've always got to be on the lookout for two of Hawaii's most endangered (and, therefore, most loved) animals: Hawaiian Monk Seals and Hawaiian Green Sea Turtles. These critters can appear on any beach at any time, but they seem to show up with frequency on beaches along the North Shore of Oahu, especially in summer.

Deep-sea fishing

It should come as no surprise that the Hawaiian Islands represent one of the best deep-sea fishing destinations anywhere in the world – after all, the rocks are surrounded by water. – attracting visitors from all over the world.

yourself riding a horse across volcanoes in the middle of the Pacific Ocean. That said, most of the Hawaiian Islands offer a variety of options for horseback riding, and the activity is a great way to get to know the land.

Without question, the best place to ride is Maui, where, in the cowboy town of Makawao, outfitters such as Pi'iholo Ranch lead visitors on two-hour, half-day and full-day excursions a few times every week. Also of note here is the annual rodeo on July 4; the event draws thousands of people from the local community and is fun for everyone,

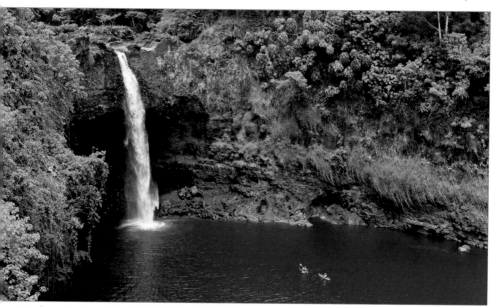

Kayakers at Rainbow Falls, Wailuku River State Park, Big Island.

The best fishing in the islands is from charter trips on which attendants bait your line and help you remove all of the fish you've caught. These sorts of trips leave from just about every major harbor, including Hilo (on Hawaii Island), Ma'alea (on Maui), and others. No experience is necessary for these kinds of outings, but it does come in handy if you know your way around a ship. And if you're a total pro, consider entering the Hawaiian International Billfish Tournament, held every summer on Hawaii Island

Horseback riding

No matter how many times you do it, it is always exhilarating and mind-boggling to find

even those who don't ride.

Horseback riding tours also are available on Hawaii Island, in both the North Kohala and Waimea areas, and on Oahu, at private ranches with lots of land to explore. On Molokai, mules (part horse, part donkey) are a key part of one of the tours you can take to explore Kalaupapa National Historic Park.

Off-roading

Undeveloped and underdeveloped parts of Hawaii offer great terrain on which to go off-roading. In some cases, this means taking a Jeep or 4x4 out for a spin; in other cases, it means climbing aboard a dirt bike and kicking up some dirt.

Perhaps the best place to go off-roading in the Hawaiian archipelago is Lanai. The island offers nearly 400 miles (644km) of dirt roads to explore by Jeep. The dirt road of the Munro Trail climbs up to the 3,370ft (1,027-meter) peak of Lanaihale, where, on a clear day, the view of the open ocean is spectacular.

Two trips from Lanai City also are worth mentioning: the road through the lush Kanepu'u Preserve, on the north side of the island; and the bumpy ride to Shipwreck Beach, from which you can see an oil tanker that ran aground in the 1940s.

Other islands offer off-roading experiences that require ATVs. On Kauai, many of these these tours follow old sugar cane access trails to remote locations that have served as backdrops for major Hollywood movies. On Hawaii Island, ATV tours of the Waipi'o Valley include descending a treacherous dirt road into the valley, and lead participants through lush jungle down below.

Outfitters on all four of the main islands also offer dirt-biking tours. On Maui, some of these outfitters take customers along the "Back Road to Hana," a ride that is bumpy but beautiful. On Hawaii Island, near Hilo, customers can rent bikes (or bring their own) and zip and zoom around a course on the slopes of Mauna Loa.

Other adventure sports

Just about all of the Hawaiian Islands have reefs worth diving to explore. One of the best: Kealakekua Bay, about 40 miles (64km) south of Kailua, on Hawaii Island. Here, calm waters teeming with marine life provide the perfect backdrop to get up-close-and-personal with dozens of different kinds of tropical fish. Within the bay you can also kayak or take a boat ride to the seaside memorial of Captain James Cook, the British Explorer who discovered the Hawaiian Islands in 1778.

Ziplining has become another big draw on the islands, with a number of zipline "parks" sprouting up since 2008. On Maui, Pi'iholo Ranch, the horseback riding outfitter in Makawao, has built a spectacular zipline course. On Kauai, a number of outfitters offer the same sort of amenities; one, near Lihu'e, combines ziplining with inner-tubing down the open-air canals of a former sugar cane plantation.

Kayaking is prevalent around Hawaii, as well. In most cases, visitors are kayaking in the open ocean; because of the elevation associated with most of the rivers in the Hawaiian Islands, it's basically impossible to paddle very far up or down these waterways. When kayaking, the more protected the water, the better. This is what makes paddling near Wailea and Ka'anapali on Maui so popular; especially in the morning, the ocean is as calm as a bathtub.

To experience rougher waters, try outrigger canoeing. In many ways, this sport is quintessentially Hawaiian: it mimics the very same way Polynesians traveled from one island to another,

Tandem paragliding over Kula, Maui.

hundreds of years ago. Hawaiians take their outrigger canoeing very seriously, regularly competing in races that stretch for hundreds of miles. You also can get a taste of outrigger canoeing along Waikiki Beach, or in Lahaina Harbor on Maui.

Finally, paragliding has become a more popular option for visitors to Hawaii in the most recent part of the 21st century. Almost all of these flights happen "in tandem," which means that visitors must go with a guide essentially attached to them at all times. The presence of a stranger doesn't diminish the impact of the experience at all; as beautiful as the Hawaiian Islands are from the ground, they are even more beautiful from above.

Hula lessons at Kualoa Ranch on Oahu.

MUSIC AND HULA

The missionaries nearly erased the ancient forms of music and dance from the islands. Thankfully, they did not succeed.

Few other types of music have girdled the earth more smoothly, more often, and more completely than Hawaiian music, and few musical genres have remained so popular with so many for so long. Say "Hawaiian music" to a banker in Bangkok, an army captain in Amsterdam, or a housewife in Minneapolis, and all get the same romantic, dreamy look. They're thinking of swaying palms and hips, the sultry slack-key guitar, a tremulous falsetto voice, and the sassy plunky-plunkiness of a *'ukulele*.

Hawaii has been described as a melting pot, historically quick to accept whatever comes to its golden shores. Nowhere is this phenomenal rate and degree of cultural assimilation more apparent than in the music.

Musical legends

In ancient times, Hawaiian music sounded simpler, consisting of long, monotonous chants recited either without accompaniment or against a percussive background of drums made from coconut trees, gourds, bamboo rattles and pipes, sticks, and pebble castanets. The ritualistic aspects of the music were complex and played a vital part in daily life and a significant role in religious beliefs and services. Chants, for example, were the means of establishing contact between humans and gods.

In the 1800s, Christian missionaries from New England had an impact on Hawaiian music, too. These devout and dedicated settlers built churches amid the Hawaiian huts, held services, and sang hymns. Hawaiians had never heard melody and four-part harmony before, and they collected by the hundreds outside the small churches to listen to these exotic combinations. Thinking that the

Playing the 'ukulele.

quickest way to a Hawaiian's soul might be through the ears, the missionaries enrolled the Hawaiians in church choirs. Progress was slow; the broader tones required by church hymns were new to Hawaiians, so songs had to be learned by rote as the missionaries sang the hymns, called *himeni* by the Hawaiians, over and over and over again, and the Hawaiians copied as best they could.

Outside influences

Hawaiian music's other most dominant influence came in the form of a single man and reflected a Hawaiian king's wish to be Westernized. King Kamehameha V decided that he wanted a royal band like those in Europe, and so the brisk, mustachioed Heinrich Berger was imported from Germany in 1868 to be bandmaster. Berger, who is known today as the father of Hawaiian music, served as director of the Royal Hawaiian Band from 1872 until 1915. During this time, he conducted more than 32,000 band concerts, arranged more than 1,000 Hawaiian songs, and composed 75 original Hawaiian songs, including several still popular today.

He also reversed the traditional order of the *mele*, or song, by composing the music before the words. Hawaiians began doing the

The Royal Hawaiian Band is still going strong after all these years, appearing in several public concerts each week, notably at noon nearly every Friday at the 'Iolani Palace Coronation Stand (see page 112).

key, and is as uniquely Hawaiian as flamenco is Spanish.

From Madeira came a small, four-stringed instrument called the *braquino*, or *cavaquinho*. It was brought to Hawaii by laborers imported to

Engraving of locals dancing, 1822.

same, and before the 1870s ended, they were composing lyrics and music simultaneously. Heinrich Berger also served as inspiration and teacher for two generations of Hawaiian musicians, some of whom later went on to local, if not national or international, stardom.

Other influences arrived: the guitar, for instance, was brought by early whalers or perhaps by traders from Mexico and California, but not, as is popularly believed, by Mexican cowboys, who arrived later in the early 1830s. In time, the traditional style of playing changed as the Hawaiian musicians loosened their strings, and tunings became whatever the player wished them to be. This style of playing came to be known as *ki ho'alu*, or slack

work in the sugar cane fields, in 1878. As with so much else in Hawaiian musical history, there is disagreement as to how the *braquino* became *'ukulele*, which, in Hawaiian, roughly translates as "jumping flea".

Scholars also continue to argue about who invented the steel guitar. Some say a Hawaiian student discovered the sound in the 1880s when he dropped his pocket knife upon the strings of a guitar, and holding it there with one hand, plucked the strings with the other, moving the steel knife to "slide" the sound.

Others think the inventor once visited India, where he could have seen a stringed instrument, the *gottuvadyam*, played in a similar fashion. While the steel guitar has since been much identified with country-and-western music, it remains the single most identifiable part of the Hawaiian instrumental sound.

Royal inspiration

The descendants of the ancient *ali'i* ruling Hawaii in the final years before annexation to the United States were among the most talented and prolific composers of song that the island culture ever produced. The best known of these was King David Kalakaua, a complex and jovial man whose reign was also an inspiration for a genuine renaissance of music and dance.

ball games and public assemblies. The hula, long suppressed by the Christian missionaries, was revived under his personal direction. Much music is played every year on November 16, Kalakaua's birthday; the state's biggest hula competition also takes place on Hawaii Island every year around that time. His sister, Lili'uokalani played a major part in the history of Hawaiian music, too, composing a song that has been a certifiable "hit" for almost a century: "Aloha 'Oe."

The sound of Hawaiian music changed again after Lili'uokalani's kingdom was made

Henri Berger, at the front, and the Royal Hawaiian Band, 1889.

Hula dancers were popular in vaudeville. They were called "cootch" dancers because many non-native performers adapted the movements lasciviously.

a territory of the United States. This focused mainland interest toward Hawaii, and in 1915 a group of Hawaiian musicians, singers, and dancers were the runaway sensation of the Panama-Pacific International Exposition in San Francisco, sparking a craze that swept North America and spread to Europe.

Kalakaua was a gifted politician, world traveler, and patron of the arts. He promoted the *'ukulele* and steel guitar, and formed his own musical group, entering into competitions with relatives and friends. He collected the legends and myths of Hawaii into a definitive and literate book, and co-wrote with Heinrich Berger Hawaii's national anthem, "Hawaii Pono'i," a song that's still sung at

Even if most of those new songs had little to do with true Hawaiian musical tradition, the influence was immediate and significant. The craze propelled authentic Hawaiian musicians across America for many years. They, in turn, accepted the phony Hawaiian songs to satisfy requests, eventually turning them into Hawaiian "classics." At the same time, they began arranging traditional, more authentic Hawaiian songs with the newly popular jazz beat that they heard everywhere they went.

In Hawaii, the first hotels were going up in Waikiki, and dance bands were formed for the growing number of tourists. Ragtime, jazz, blues, Latin, and foxtrot rhythms were interspersed with Hawaiian themes and English lyrics. The purists were appalled, as always, but by 1930 the *hapa-haole* (halfCaucasian) song was an entrenched and accepted part of Hawaiian music, soon to become a staple on what was eventually the most widely heard radio program in the world. In 1935, Hawaii's music

> Bing Crosby introduced two songs in the 1937 movie Waikiki Wedding. One of them, "Sweet Leilani" won an Oscar, so Hollywood began churning out musical romances.

Paddle," "Days of My Youth," and "I'll Remember You."

The most important figure among those responsible for keeping the flame of traditional Hawaiian music alive during this time was the slack-key guitarist Gabby Pahinui. He

Hula dancers perform at the Kuhio Beach Hula Show in Waikiki, Oahu.

caught the ears of the mainland's West Coast listeners via "Hawaii Calls," a radio program broadcast from under a banyan tree in Waikiki Beach and other exotic locales. Today, many of the more than 300 Hawaiian musicians who were on that radio program are legends of the state's musical past, among them Danny Kaleikini, Alfred Apaka, and Benny Kalama.

Traditional sounds revitalized

The period from 1930 to 1960 is regarded as Hawaiian music's "golden age," as the music of the islands circled the world on television and in radio and film. Crooners such as Kui Lee and Don Ho emerged as top Hawaiian stars, rendering songs such as "One Paddle, Two

made his first solo recording, "Hi'ilawe," in 1947, and in the late 1950s formed the Sons of Hawaii group with 'ukelele virtuoso Eddie Kamae, a keen musicologist who hunted out long-forgotten Hawaiian-language songs from all the islands. In the early 1970s, their reunion album, "The Folk Music of Hawaii," was hugely influential among younger musicians, many of whom began to write their own songs, celebrating the poetic resonance of the Hawaiian language and also addressing contemporary social realities.

During this so-called "Hawaiian renaissance," all the traditional Hawaiian arts experienced a rich revival, as islanders with Hawaiian blood discovered a renewed sense of ethnic awareness and pride. Many were influenced by the cultural changes taking place in the rest of the United States, and some of the Hawaiian music of the era, it has to be said, sounds awfully like Californian-style rock.

However, there was also a great resurgence of interest in the more traditional Hawaiian sounds. As Moe Keale, who also played *'ukulele* with the Sons of Hawaii, put it, "Music is not something you just hear with your ears. It's something you hear with your heart. I can tell when Hawaiian music is being played right, because it makes me cry."

'Ukulele shop on Kalakaua Avenue in Honolulu.

Gabby Pahinui left the Sons in the mid-1970s, and, thanks in part to his collaborations with guitarist Ry Cooder, went on to achieve international acclaim before his premature death in 1980. Meanwhile, new stars were emerging in Hawaii, such as guitarist Keola Beamer, who honed his techniques on an album called "Hawaiian Slack Key in the Real Old Style." Beamer says, "There's power in our music which is drawn from the environment. If you sit and watch a waterfall or listen to the trade winds for a while, you begin to feel a rhythm. You can be far away from Hawaii and hear a song and instantly be transported."

Among other new names on the scene were the Sunday Manoa, who included the Cazimero brothers; Hui Ohana, a trio featuring Ledward and Nedward Ka'apana and Dennis Pava'o; Palani Vaughan; and a young group from Gabby's hometown of Waimanolo, Oahu – the Makaha Sons of Ni'ihau, featuring the brothers Skippy and Israel Kamakawiwo'ole.

By the early 1990s, Hawaiian music was at the forefront of the political struggle for Hawaiian sovereignty. Dennis Pava'o recorded the popular "All Hawaii Stand Together," but it was Israel Kamakawiwo'ole, by then a solo artist and universally known as "Iz," who gave the movement its greatest anthems, in the form of songs like "Hawaii 78." Morbidly obese and plagued by the chronic health problems that had already killed his brother – whose weight is said to have exceeded a phenomenal 1,000lbs (454kg) – but blessed with a voice of astonishing power and delicacy, Iz became a much-loved superstar. He died in 1997, and was honored with a state funeral. His legacy was albums such as "E Ala E," and, especially, "Facing Future," which was still high in the world music charts a decade after his death, while his million-selling medley of "Somewhere Over The Rainbow/What A Wonderful World" has become a staple of Hollywood soundtracks.

Falsetto tradition

Women have always played a crucial role in Hawaiian music. Queen Lili'uokalani composed many of the islands' most enduring classics, while chanter/dancer Edith Kanaka'ole was the 20th-century's greatest repository of the Polynesian heritage. Female vocalists have been especially significant as performers of the unique Hawaiian tradition of falsetto singing, which is characterized by audible breathing for extra effect. Lena Machado, known as "Hawaii's Songbird," championed the form from the 1930s until the 1960s, while Auntie Genoa Keawe, who first recorded in the 1940s and established her own record label, was still performing regularly in Waikiki when she celebrated her 89th birthday in 2007. The latest divas in the genre are Amy Hanaiali'i Gilliom, known for her entertaining live performances with guitarist Willie K, and Molokai's Raiatea Helm. Popular falsetto vocal groups include the trio Na Leo Pilimehana, responsible for albums like "Anthology I" and "Colours," and Na Palapalai. It's worth mentioning too that there have been some fabulous male falsetto singers, such as Bill Lincoln Ali'iloa, and the phenomenal Mahi Beamer.

Hawaiian music today

New generations of young entertainers continue to emerge, sending out Hawaiian vibes to the mainland, Japan, and beyond, combining music with showmanship that draws on early Hawaiian traditions. On stage, composer, chanter, dancer, and singer Keali'i Reichel stands bare-chested, hair streaming about his shoulders, carved bone fishhook nestled at his neck. His body tattoos run from his ankle to disappear under his brief *malo* (loincloth). In the bright spotlight, he sings in sweet, resonant tones, switching from ballads like "Ku'u Pua Kanaka'ole's great-grandson Kaumakaiwa; and the *'ukulele* prodigy Jake Shimabukuro. For details of where to hear live music, see page 305.

Return of hula

There was a time in Hawaiian history when entering a *halau* (hula school) was equivalent to entering a monastery. Today, the hula is both a spiritual and an artistic expression of Hawaiian culture.

Legends say that the goddesses of dance were Laka and Hi'iaka. (If not actually worshipped, both are still revered today.) At first, both men

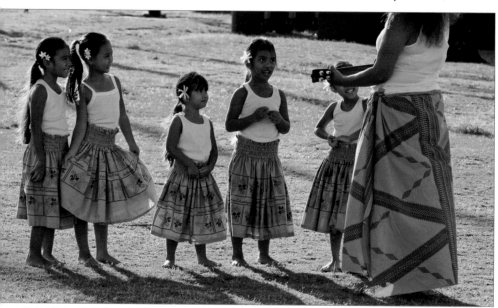

Keiki (children) hula dancers.

Mae 'Ole" (about lasting romance and calming waters), to a poetic chant "Maika'i Ka 'Oiwi O Ka'ala" with *ipu* (gourd) accompaniment.

Singer/songwriter Jack Johnson, who lives on the North Shore of Oahu, attracted a huge following among the surfer set, and now has a mass popular appeal. In recent years, singer-songwriter Bruno Mars has done Hawaii proud; Mars was born and raised in Honolulu and performed in various musical venues there throughout his childhood before moving to Los Angeles. Other names to watch out for these days include Keola Beamer, a slack-key artist from Maui (and cousin of Mahi Beamer); the duo Hapa, who, as their name suggests, consist of a *haole* and a nativeHawaiian; Edith

HITTING THE BIG TIME

Despite centuries of catchy and culturally significant songs, Hawaiian music officially arrived in 2005, when the National Academy of Recording Arts and Sciences started giving out a Grammy award for the Best Hawaiian Music Album of the year. In the first few years, awards were doled out to Charles Brotman, Tia Carrere, George Kohumoku, Jr., and others. Six of the seven Grammy-winning albums were released through the record label Daniel Ho Creations. The Academy retired the award category in 2011; today Hawaiian artists are eligible to win the Best Regional Roots Music category.

and women performed the dance, but only men could perform the hula during temple worship services. It was believed that by pantomiming an action, that action could be controlled in the future. Thus there were many dances for desired events, such as a successful hunt, fertility, or other successes. The hula later engulfed all of Hawaiian society and became many things – teaching tool, popular entertainment, and a basic foundation for *lua*, an art of self-defense promoted by the Hawaiians. As the dance became widespread and society increasingly complicated, wars and governing duties kept the

a symbol of the islanders' newly rediscovered sense of Hawaiian identity.

Hula events

Hawaii's most prestigious hula event is the Merrie Monarch Festival, which pays homage to King David Kalakaua, Hawaii's last king. It has been held every April since 1964 at the Edith Kanaka'ole Stadium in Hilo. The highlight of the week-long festival, which includes a parade and musical celebrations, is the two-day competition of *kahiko*, or ancient hula, and *'auwana* or modern hula.

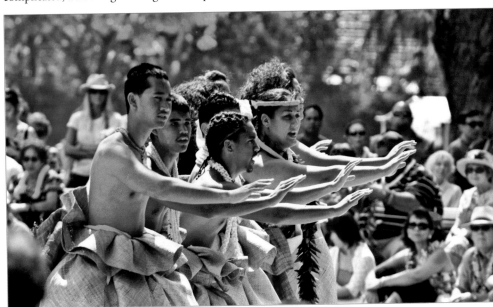

Hula dancers at the May Day festival.

men too busy for the years of training required to be a performer. Thus, the women began to share equally in the performance of the hula.

Hula was banned in the beginning of the 19th century; by the 1850s it had nearly disappeared. Forty years later, by the time King Kalakaua revived the sacred dance, a great deal of the art of hula had already been lost forever.

Today, hula has regained much of its serious heritage. Contemporary students heed ancient ritual religiously, although they are not asked to give up sex in order to be a hula performer, as was true in ancient times. Different *halau* compete fiercely; hula masters, or *kumu hula*, are revered figures. And with the male hula now in a period of rich revival, the dance has become

Every island has its signature hula events. On Oahu, the Queen Lili'uokalani Keiki Hula festival draws 500 children to perform every July, and in the same month, the Prince Lot Hula Festival is played out under the giant monkey pod trees of Moanalua Gardens. At Princeville, Kauai, local entertainers meet mainland musicians at the Prince Albert Hula Festival every May. On Maui, the Na Mele O Maui Song Contest and Hula Festival takes place annually in Ka'anapali, while Molokai's Ka Hula Piko Festival is celebrated each May close to hula's supposed birthplace, near Maunaloa. If you are in Hawaii when any of these events is being celebrated it will be well worth attending.

LEI

Flower necklace *lei* once were sacred symbols, but today are used to convey *aloha* and respect.

Lei, necklaces made from flowers, have a colorful history in Hawaii. In ancient times, *they* were offered to the gods during sacred dances and chants. Today they are draped around the necks of grooms and prom escorts.

Lei are made of flowers, leaves, shells, and paper. There are six basic *lei*-making techniques. If a *lei*-maker uses *wili paukuku*, she is winding roses and begonias in a certain style. *Humuhumu* is a *lei* sewn onto a backing. *Wili* is a *lei* that is wound or twisted, *hili* is braided with leaves, and *haku* is braided with flowers. *Kui* is strung on a thread.

Before needle and thread were introduced to Hawaii, stiff grass blades from the Nuʻuanu Valley were used as needles, and strands of banana bark were utilized as string. For the more elaborate feather *lei* reserved for the royalty of old Hawaii, strips of *olona* bark were twisted into a cord that was flexible and strong.

Prices may range today from less than $5 up to $50 for the fragrant *maile* and multiple strands of *pikake*. Many *lei*, like the woven ginger *lei* or the complex maunaloa orchid *lei*, are intricate works of art. Others, such as a simple plumeria *lei*, can be strung by anyone with a needle and thread.

Makers of lei produce hundreds, if not thousands, of lei daily for the islands' tourism industry. Most common is the plumeria lei.

Rosettes for the winners of the wili-style (a corkscrew-type twi used to make the lei) May Day contest. Competitors need to b able to describe the types of flora used.

The hula, both traditional and modern, uses lei as an important adornment. Often in hula, lei are not made from flowers, but leaves and other parts of flora considered to impart importance.

Leis at the grave of Father Damien at St Philomena Church in Kalawao.

DRAPED BY *ALOHA* AND RESPECT

In Hawaii, a *lei* is a special symbol or gift given as a sign of respect, welcome (or departure), or good feeling. *Lei* are also draped over the statues or images of important people in Hawaii's history.

Each island has its own special material for making *lei*. The delicate orange *'ilima* blossom represents Oahu. Feathery red lehua blossoms from gnarled *'ohi'a* trees symbolize the island of Hawaii. Pink *lokelani* (an introduced Castilian rose) make up Maui's *lei*, while Molokai is adorned by silver-green leaves from the *kukui* tree and decorated with tiny white blossoms.

Oblong leaves and dark berries from the *mokihana* tree are fashioned into a *lei* for Kauai. On Lanai, *lei* are woven from slim strands of *kauna'oa*, an orange, mossy beach vine. Even uninhabited Kaho'olawe has a *lei* from *hinahina*, a beach plant with narrow green leaves and little white flowers. Ni'ihau is the only island not represented by a flower, but by shells: the rare and very tiny *pupu* that are treasured by *kama'aina* as much as valuable gems.

...autiful haku lei, made by twining or braiding foliage into ...ouquet. Nearly any flower or nut can be fashioned into a ...including bougainvillea, ginger, and plumeria with its ...cious scent.

...king leis at a stand in Honolulu.

Lei made of plumeria flowers, of which the yellow and white version is the most common.

AN ECLECTIC CUISINE

With ethnic influences from Polynesia, Asia, Europe, and North America, Hawaii's cuisine is among the world's most eclectic.

Island menus read like a United Nations lunch order: sushi, pasta, crispy *gau gee*, *kim chee*, tortillas, tandoori chicken, Wienerschnitzel, spring rolls – you name it, they eat it in Hawaii. Within a relatively small geographical area, visitors find a universe of dishes served in surroundings both down-home and haute, from casual eateries that serve two scoops of rice for a "plate lunch," to candle-lit corners with chateaubriand and chocolate mousse on the menu.

Food from all over

Hawaii has many to thank for its tasty diversity. Chinese immigrants, for instance, taught islanders that rice goes just as well with eggs at breakfast as it does with lunch and dinner. Supermarkets of all stripes stock supplies of *cilantro*, lemongrass and ginger, and restaurants turn out everything from Mandarin, Sichuan, and Cantonese to Mongolian barbecue and stir-fry. For an energizing assault on the senses, go to a house of *dim sum*, where waitresses load your table with little plates of bite-sized dumplings until hands are held up in surrender.

From the Japanese came the gifts of *shoyu* (soy sauce), *sashimi* (thinly sliced raw fish), and *tempura* (deep-fried vegetables and meats, introduced to Japan from Portugal, actually). Almost every street has a sushi bar for swigging *sake* while chefs with lightning-fast hands fashion edible fantasies out of rice, seafood and *wasabi* (hot green-horseradish). Japanese culinary sensibilities are best summed up by the *bento*, a lunch box with tidy compartments for morsels of chicken, shrimp, pork cutlets, fishcake, pickled plums, rice, and other artful treats.

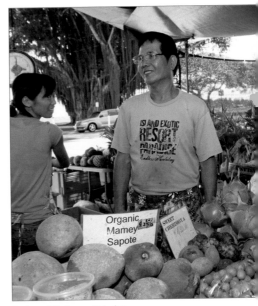

Fruits at Hilo Farmers' Market.

Wafts of garlic and grilled specialties lure hungry diners through the doors of Hawaii's Korean restaurants, which generally assume the form of Formica-tabled eateries. Therein await *kim chee* (pickled vegetables), *kalbi* (marinated short ribs), *jun* (foods fried in an egg batter), and the musical *bi bim bap*, which is a bowl of rice, with vegetables, fried egg, and a sweet sauce.

A more recent influx of people from Thailand has introduced spring rolls, *mee krob* (noodle salad), and a coconut-milk/hot pepper-flavored dish called Evil Jungle Prince, best followed by Thai iced tea with sweetened condensed milk. Vietnamese food – less spicy than Thai – is particularly popular for its *phô*,

A staple of the traditional diet, poi is a thick, viscous paste-like food. It is made from the taro root, light purple in color, and often served in knotted plastic bags.

the 1880s, they lived side-by-side with Hawaiian and Chinese workers in simple, single-walled wooden houses. The Chinese built community cookhouses, the Japanese added mom-and-pop tofu factories. People grew their own *bok choi* and lemongrass in backyards.

a broth with noodles and beef or chicken slices. Portuguese influence makes itself known in *pao dolce* (sweet bread), chorizo (spicy sausage), *vinha d'alhos* (marinated meat), and a robust bean soup, while from the Philippines comes *lumpia* (fried spring rolls),

Celebrating regional cuisine

The most recent take on island food is called Hawaii Regional Cuisine – a variation of what's known elsewhere as Pacific Rim Cuisine or New Australian Cuisine. This movement gained momentum in 1992, when a dozen curious, crea-

Harvesting taro, which grows in paddy fields.

pancit (noodles, vegetables, and pork), *pork guisantes* (pork rump), *bagoong* (fish sauce), and *bitsu bitsu* (sweet potato scones).

Stir into this pot the creativity of classically trained chefs from France, Switzerland, Germany, North America, and Italy who have been imported to work in some of Hawaii's upscale restaurants. The state's continental ideas of the 1970s have evolved into today's more health-conscious cooking, but without too much effort you can still find an authentic veal *scaloppini* or a slab of salmon drenched in dill sauce.

Inevitably, the blending of cooking styles occurred in Hawaii's plantation villages. When Japanese contract laborers were imported in

tive, and congenial chefs began getting together to share their ideas as well as their wish lists for a wider variety of fresh produce and other more varied ingredients. In the kitchens of their own elegant restaurants, their sous-chefs and *garde-mangers* were feasting on interesting, flavorful treats they had learned to make at home.

Alan Wong was one of the 12. He says the diversity of Hawaii's food is inextricably linked to its cultural history: "While I was growing up in Hawaii, my grandfather cooked Chinese and my mother cooked Japanese, but she mingled in flavors of Filipino, Chinese, Japanese, and Hawaiian dishes."

The growth of Hawaii Regional Cuisine has made a difference on Hawaii's culinary scene.

Today, any number of farmers are growing crops to the specifications of chefs who visit the fields and make known what they want for their own restaurants. Tomatoes are vine-ripened; arugula and baby lettuces fill upcountry fields on Maui and the Big Island. Several hotels grow their own fresh herbs, while a number of hotels in Waikiki have their own rooftop hydroponic gardens, and at least one Maui resort harvests fresh tropical fruit and other produce from an organic garden that surrounds its parking lot.

A host of professional chefs were inspired by the daring dozen, and Hawaiian Regional Cuisine has become a palate-pleasing password even beyond island shores. Names such as Sam Choy and Roy Yamaguchi, both of whom own several restaurants, have published cookbooks, and hosted their own television cooking shows, have become synonymous with Hawaiian cooking. The current pantheon of greats includes George Mavrothalassitis, Peter Merriman and Daniel Thiebaut, each with their own signature restaurants. In 2012, "Top Chef" runner-up Sheldon Simeon, from Star Noodle in Lahaina, was added to that list.

Passion and pineapple

Local products have become as intrinsically linked to Hawaii's lifestyle as the ebbing and flowing of the tides. Residents and visitors alike have easy access to an abundance of fresh fruit, and we're not just talking pineapple and coconut. Equally common are the apple banana, the golden papaya, the pungent *liliko'i*, and the guava, a yellow, lemon-sized gem with a shockingly pink interior.

The lychee, prized for its juicy white flesh, can be spotted hanging in grape-like clumps on trees in Manoa Valley, while *poha* (cape gooseberry) thrives on bushes near Kilauea Volcano. The markets of Honolulu's Chinatown district are a good source of these and lesser-known fruits, like the tamarind, kumquat, starfruit, *rambuton* (sweet white fruit in a red, spiky shell), and *cherimoya* (with tart white flesh).

Visit Hawaii during the summer and you'll discover the joys of the mango. When mango trees start to blossom in May, it's as big a deal as seeing the first whales of winter. By July, the fruit is weighing down the branches, and neighbors distribute free bags of sweet, juicy mangos.

Each island also is known for certain naturally occurring "specialties." Think of a papaya and one thinks of the prolific trees of Puna on Hawaii Island. Onions conjure up images of cool upcountry Kula on Maui, where the sweetest variety is grown. Guava thrives in Kilauea on Kauai, and Molokai is known for its sweet potatoes, while fresh fish are pulled from the waters round all the islands.

Ocean harvests

What is harvested by land is matched by the bounty of the sea. The king and queen of Hawai-

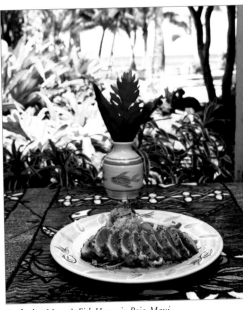

Seafood at Mama's Fish House in Paia, Maui.

ian fish are the *mahimahi* (dolphin fish) and *'opakapaka* (pink snapper), but *ulua* (jack crevalle), *ono* (wahoo), *ahi* (yellow-fin tuna), *onaga* (red snapper) and *tako* (octopus), which is served raw and marinated as *poke*, are equally memorable, whether blackened Cajun-style or baked in wafer-thin layers of crisp phyllo pastry. In the world of aquaculture, Hawaii Island, Kauai, and North Shore of Oahu are creating miniature ocean tanks and fishponds teeming with prawns, lobsters, abalone, and other delicacies.

Called *'opihi*, limpets are Hawaii's signature mollusk but are rarely found on restaurant menus. Locals have been known to scamper crab-like across shorelines, hanging on when the big waves roll in (not recommended; deaths are reported each year when waves overpower harvesters), in order to pick a bunch of quarter-sized shells off the lava rocks.

Perfection on a plate

Hawaii's homegrown extends to grain-fattened beef, grass-fed lamb, and free-range game. *Paniolos* (cowboys) on Maui and the Big Island saddle up in the pre-dawn mist to round up the beef that ends up on dinner plates. Ni'ihau is promoting its own special grade of lamb. Lanai axis deer has become a popular entrée laced with plum sauce, and

guava, and coconut, and one of US President Barack Obama's favorite treats. Those in the know order it with vanilla ice cream and sweet azuki beans on the bottom.

Additional snacks have a decidedly Asian flare. Try *manapua*, the tennis ball-sized steamed Chinese dumpling filled with pork or curried chicken. Enjoy a bowl of *saimin*, an Asian noodle soup topped with an encyclopedia of garnishes like sliced *char siu* (roast pork), fishcake, and green onions. Or pick up a bag of crack seed (preserved and flavored fruits), pickled plums, and *pipi kaula* (beef jerky).

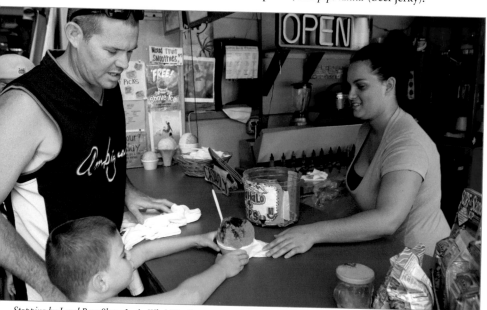

Stopping by Local Boys Shave Ice in Kihei, Maui.

Molokai venison makes for a tasty stew or toothsome sausage.

If all this choice sounds a little overwhelming, start with the basics. Try a "plate lunch" – the statewide institution defined by a few simple elements. You'll get a paper plate loaded with "two scoop rice," plus a mound of heavily mayonnaised macaroni salad. Order one with *teriyaki* beef, breaded pork or chicken (*katsu*), fried fish, or Spam, an unexpected passion among local people.

Other tasty goodies

There are other tasty treats to sample in Hawaii. On hot days, try a shave ice, a snowcone soaked in neon-colored tropical syrups like mango,

FOR THE LOVE OF SPAM

Spam has a special place in the Hawaiian diet; it is sometimes referred to as the "Hawaiian Steak." Residents of the islands consume more Spam per capita than any residents of any other place in the US. This popularity can be attributed in part to the military; in the years that followed World War II, the meat product was used as a substitute for fresh meat, and, gradually, surplus supply of it made its way into native diets. Today in the islands, the canned meat is most commonly eaten atop a rectangle of rice and bound with a piece of nori seaweed. The resulting sushi-like creation is called Spam musubi.

The Lu'au

The *lu'au* predates the modern dinner dance. And it's a great way to get a quick perspective on local culture.

Traditionally, the *lu'au* is a festival of food and dance, an amalgamation of Hawaiian culture unlike any other. These days, however, most of the *lu'aus* you'll discover will be the commercialized variety, complete with the comic hula and *Mai Tais*. While purists may find this a shallow version of the real thing, the *imu* ceremonies, hula, Hawaiian music, *kalua* pig and other culinary specialties, and good cheer are all rooted in Hawaiian tradition. If you can let go of prejudices about "authenticity," you're very likely to have a really good time.

Historic feasts

These modern *lu'aus* emerged from the *aha'aina*, or feasts of old, when women dined separately from men and were prohibited from eating some of the choicest of *lu'au* fare. Finally, after 1819, when Liholiho (King Kamehameha II) abolished the old *kapu* (taboo) system of restrictions, *lu'aus* became a lively tradition enjoyed by all. Today, an island wedding, baby's first birthday, or junior's graduation wouldn't be the same without a backyard bash for friends and family. The heart of any *lu'au*, commercial or private, continues to be the preparation and unearthing of the *imu*. Current *lu'au* food is reasonably authentic, except for such items as macaroni and potato salads or *teriyaki-beef*, which were added to suit all tastes.

Hawaiian specialties

You'll still find pig roasted to juicy tenderness in the *imu* (hole-in-the-ground oven filled with koa wood and heat-retaining rocks that continue to cook after the wood has burned off) accompanied by *poi*, sweet potatoes, marinated *lomilomi* salmon with chopped tomatoes and onions, and sometimes *'opihi*, a Hawaiian shellfish plucked from wave-washed rocky shorelines and eaten raw as a special delicacy. For uninitiated taste buds, it's best to sample *poi* with salty *kalua* pork or *lomilomi* salmon to enhance the flavors and textures.

Many *lu'aus* ladle out chicken long rice, a dish of chicken cooked with translucent noodles made of rice flour and garnished with green onions. Frequently you'll find *laulau*, little green bundles of taro leaf, which taste like spinach, steamed with pork and fish. For dessert, coconut cake is a new addition, but *haupia*, a coconut-milk pudding, has long been served as a sweet finale.

Island entertainment

The entertainment at one of these modern feasts is like taking a mini-tour through the island cultures of Hawaii, Tonga, Samoa, New Zealand, and Tahiti. Hawaii's contribution includes the haunting chants that perpetuate the genealogies and

Preparing the pig, the staple of lu'aus.

legends of the past, as well as the graceful hula. Some *lu'aus*, including the one at the Polynesian Cultural Center on Oahu, include pageantry with participants dressed like early Hawaiian royalty.

Whether visitors will get their money's worth from a commercial *lu'au*, which could range in price from $60 up to $125 per person, depends upon the individual, and the *lu'au*. If you are ready to throw yourself into the spirit of the night by donning your most colorful *aloha* shirt, taking off your shoes, and getting up on stage to learn a Tahitian *tamure* while your traveling companions cheer, and if you find unfamiliar foods intriguing, you'll have a good time. *Lu'aus* range from tacky to traditional, and you'll just have to look around for your style.

A still from the first season (2004) of the television series Lost which was filmed in Hawaii.

HAWAII ON SCREEN

With lush valleys, mind-bending waterfalls, and tropical paradise around every corner, Hawaii has become a darling of Hollywood.

You can't really blame Hollywood producers for falling in love with Hawaii. Between lush valleys, swaying palm trees, white sand beaches, and tropical vistas, the islands offer more authentic paradise than any studio set. Starting with a pair of one-reelers in 1913, more than 100 films have been shot in the islands since the 1950s, and countless other television shows have been filmed there, as well. Some islands, such as Kauai, are more famous than others. But all of the Hawaiian Islands wear the spotlight well; over the years Hawaii has become known as "Hollywood's Tropical Back Lot."

What makes Hawaii so appealing to producers and directors? Its versatility, for one. Hawaii has the ability to morph easily, making the audience believe it is anything from a South Pacific beach to a South African village to an exotic Peruvian rainforest.

The islands also are renowned for great weather and spectacular light – both of which are important considerations when filming for movies or TV. Another reason Hawaii is a big draw is that the islands beckon movie stars; if celebrities know a production is being shot in Hawaii they are that much more likely to sign up. Finally there's cost. You might think filming on location in a tropical paradise is expensive, but the truth is that tax breaks and other incentives make the endeavour almost as affordable as shooting in a studio back on the mainland. Add to this the only state-owned and -operated film studio in the country and a growing list of production facilities, an experienced pool of crew and talent, a comprehensive local inventory of state-of-the-art equipment, a well-established one-stop process for state film permits, and a film-friendly government and

Burt Lancaster and Deborah Kerr in the beach scene filmed on Oahu in From Here to Eternity (1953).

HAWAII THE CHAMELEON

Tropical jungle is tropical jungle, all over the world. For this reason, over the years Hollywood studios have not only depicted Hawaii as Hawaii in film; they also have used Hawaii to be other lush places, including the Amazon, Africa, and more. Perhaps the most famous example of this was the 1995 film, *Outbreak*. In this film, Kamokila Hawaiian Village, a throwback-type attraction along the Wailua River on the east side of Kauai, was turned into the African village where a deadly virus began. Visitors were able to tour the set until as recently as 2010, when site operators finally reclaimed the space.

community, and it's no wonder Hawaii has said "Aloha" to so much film production over the years.

The big splash

A number of small movies were filmed in Hawaii between 1913 and 1950, including *Bird of Paradise* in 1932 and *Waikiki Wedding*, with Bing Crosby, in 1937. Still, Hawaii's real Hollywood boom started following World War II. Perhaps the film that put the islands on the map was the original Hollywood adaptation of *From Here to Eternity*, starring Burt Lancaster,

television industries entered their respective heydays, more and more Hollywood studios saw Hawaii as a viable option for authentic, on-location tropical shoots. The islands' life in pictures had begun.

Kauai in the spotlight

Since then, if the Hawaiian Islands have had a "star" in Hollywood, it would have to be Kauai. Perhaps it's the remote location. Perhaps it's the green forests. Perhaps the island has captured more directorial imaginations than any other. Whatever the reason, Kauai has appeared on the

Jurassic Park used locations on Oahu and Kauai.

Frank Sinatra, Montgomery Clift, and Deborah Kerr. This movie dealt with a sensitive subject: the Japanese bombing of Pearl Harbor, on Oahu, in 1941. Still, thanks in part to a racy on-screen kiss between Lancaster and Kerr (and Oscars for Best Picture and Best Director), the movie became an instant classic, and remains one of the film industry's greatest accomplishments today.

Among directors, *From Here to Eternity* changed the landscape, opening up Hawaii as a destination for on-location spots. Over the next decade, dozens of films were filmed in Hawaii, including *Blue Hawaii* and *Girls! Girls! Girls!*, both starring Elvis Presley. In the second half of the 1960s, as the film and

silver screen (and the small screen) more than any other Hawaiian Island.

Fantasy Island; *Pirates of the Caribbean*; *Six Days, Seven Nights*; *Voodoo Island*; and *South Pacific* all are films that were at least partly on Kauai. Old buildings in the town of Hanapepe reportedly inspired backdrops for the Disney movie *Lilo & Stitch*. In recent years, the Garden Isle also has been a backdrop for the television show *Lost*; the George Clooney film, *The Descendants*; and *The Hunger Games: Catching Fire*. Clooney's film in particular has turned at least one destination into a veritable tourist goldmine; because the Tahiti Nui restaurant and bar in Hanalei has a cameo in the film, fans have lined up to dine and/or drink there ever since.

Other islands take center stage

Other Hawaiian Islands have had their proverbial 15 minutes of fame, as well. On Oahu, between 1968 and 1980, Honolulu and Waikiki Beach were the inspiration behind the Hawaii police show *Hawaii Five-O* (and a recent remake of the same show). Another popular television show filmed on Oahu: *Magnum P.I.*, with Tom Selleck.

Oahu also has seen its share of surfing movies (most notably *North Shore* and *Blue Crush*), and war movies including *Pearl Harbor*. Turtle Bay Resort, on the North Shore, was the setting for the 2008 romantic comedy *Forgetting Sarah Mar-*

Other islands in the Hawaiian archipelago have had less of a role in modern film and television. Hawaii Island has provided backdrops for *Waterworld* and *Planet of the Apes*, while Lanai appears in a modern version of Shakespeare's *The Tempest*, starring Helen Mirren. New Lanai owner Larry Ellison has said he will try to bring more film crews to that island in the coming years. There have been rumors of small-budget films happening someday on Molokai, as well.

Celebrating film on Hawaii

Hawaii is not only a popular destination for on-

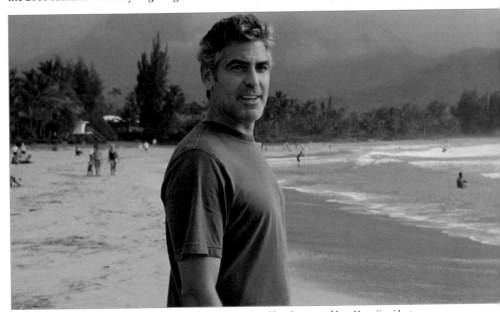

George Clooney in The Descendants, filmed on location in Hawaii and based on a novel by a Hawaii resident.

shall. And Kualoa Ranch has provided the backdrop for a number of films, including *Jurassic Park* and *50 First Dates*. The ranch now offers private bus tours on which visitors can get an inside look at filming sites; the experience actually has become quite popular among fans of *Lost*.

Maui has appeared in many films over the years, too. Lahaina took center stage in Clint Eastwood's *The Devil at 4 O'Clock*, and some of the island's beach locales were front and center as backdrops in movies such as *Just Go With It* and *Pirates of the Caribbean: At World's End*. *Baraka*, a 1991 documentary about life as humans (and, for the film geeks, shot in 70mm film), opened with an eerie shot from inside the crater atop Mount Haleakala.

location filming these days; it also has become a destination for festivals that celebrate films in general. With this in mind, a number of towns across the islands now sponsor annual film festivals through the year. Some of the largest of these parties include festivals on Maui and Hawaii Island and in Oahu. Many of these festivals screen independent movies; in 2013, for instance, the Maui Film Festival premiered *Nebraska* and *The Short Game*, a highly acclaimed documentary about young golfers.

The newest of the bunch, the Lanai Film Festival, started in 2013. Film buffs also might enjoy attending the Oiwi Film Festival, an annual event in Honolulu that celebrates films directed by indigenous Hawaiian filmmakers.

Surfers at Waipio Bay in Waipio Valley, Big Island.

Waikiki Beach with Diamond Head volcanic cone in the background in Honolulu, Oahu.

Hanakapi'ai Falls in the Hanakapi'ai Valley, Na Pali Coast State Wilderness Park, Kauai.

INTRODUCTION

They're part of the same archipelago,
but each of the Hawaiian Islands has
its own personality, history, and vibe.

Road sign on Kamehameha Highway near Hale'iwa town, Oahu.

Geologically speaking, the islands have all been cut from the same cloth; the volcanic vent that continues to make Kilauea erupt on Hawaii Island was responsible for the genesis of all Hawaii's islands. Since this creation, however, each one has developed differently. Here's a look at the islands from southeast (youngest) to northwest (oldest).

Hawaii Island, previously known as the Big Island, is, well, big – the biggest of all eight, actually. And it's getting bigger every day that Kilauea erupts. Against the backdrop of these explosions, the rest of the island operates quietly; more than half of the island is farmland.

The island chain encompasses 6,423 sq miles (16,635 sq km) of land area. Hawaii Island is twice the area of all the others combined.

Next up is Maui where the residents like to say, "Maui no ka oi," which translates into "Maui is the best." And the island certainly is awesome. Whether you're visiting the beaches of Ka'anapai, the jungles of Hana, or the slopes of Mount Haleakala, the spectacles are sure to impress.

Kaho'olawe, once a testing site for weapons, is now closed to visitors, but neighboring Lanai, once covered in pineapples, is being reborn as a rustic tourist destination – a great spot to have a luxury getaway and get away from the world.

Waimanalo Beach Park, Oahu.

The same can be said for Molokai, which is the most undeveloped of the islands and, as a result, is perhaps the most "authentic" of the bunch.

Then, of course, there's Oahu, the most populous island. The party rages nonstop on Waikiki Beach, and Honolulu is the seat of the state's government. Beyond this metropolis, however, the island boasts verdant mountain ranges, great surf spots, and cultural sites including Pearl Harbor.

On Kauai, the "Garden Isle," nature has shaped the land as she has wished; cutting into the island at Waimea Canyon and wearing it down into beautiful bluffs along the Na Pali Coast. In between is some of the most pristine paradise on Earth; no wonder Oscar Hammerstein immortalized the spot in "South Pacific." Finally, of course, is Ni'ihau, a lush island only open to native Hawaiians.

Eight islands, eight completely different personalities. Together, they comprise the Hawaii of today. This diversity only makes the local culture richer – and more fun to experience and explore.

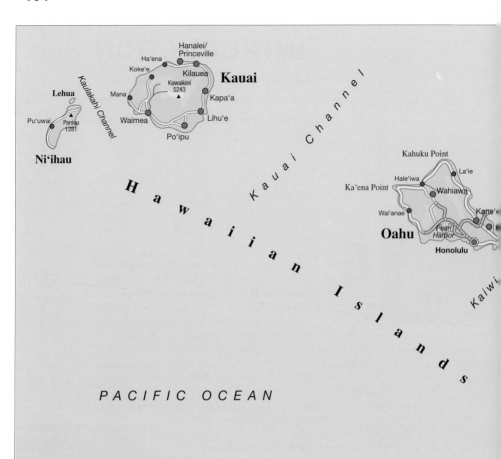

Hanalei/
Princeville

Ha'ena
Koke'e
Kilauea
Kauai
Kawaikini
5243
▲
Kapa'a

Lehua
Mana

Pu'uwai
Paniau
1281
▲
Waimea
Lihu'e

Ni'ihau
Po'ipu

Kaulakahi Channel

Kauai Channel

H **a** **w** **a** **i** **i** **a** **n** **I** **s** **l** **a** **n** **d** **s**

Kahuku Point

La'ie
Hale'iwa
Ka'ena Point
Wahiawa

Wai'anae
Kane'

Pearl
Harbor
Oahu
Honolulu

Kaiwi

PACIFIC OCEAN

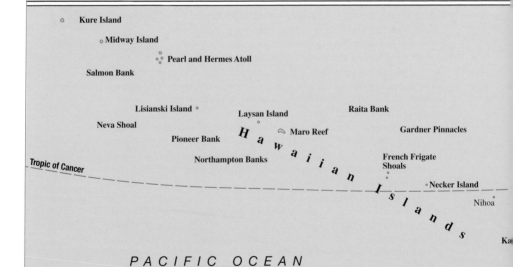

◌ **Kure Island**

◦ **Midway Island**

◦◦ **Pearl and Hermes Atoll**
◦

Salmon Bank

Lisianski Island ◦
Laysan Island **Raita Bank**
◦
Neva Shoal
⌒ **Maro Reef** **Gardner Pinnacles**
Pioneer Bank

H **a** **w** **a** **i** **i** **a** **n**
**French Frigate
Shoals**
Northampton Banks
◦
Tropic of Cancer
I **s** **l**
◦ **Necker Island**

Nihoa
◦

I **s** **l** **a** **n** **d** **s**

Ka

PACIFIC OCEAN

OAHU

The most populous of the Hawaiian Islands also is the most visited – with good reason: Honolulu is a happening place, and the North Shore's beaches are among the most picturesque in the world.

Waikiki Beach in Honolulu.

Scour the globe and you won't find another island quite like Oahu. Its varied attractions include dense rainforest in the center of the island, monstrous surfing waves on the North Shore, a multi-billion-dollar skyline at Waikiki, lively Honolulu, colorful history, epic hikes, volcanic craters, and a Disney resort. Every day, more than 75,000 visitors explore the island coast to coast, tip to tip, from Wai'anae in the west to Hale'iwa in the north, Pearl Harbor and Waikiki in the south, and Makapu'u in the east.

"O'ahu" is said to mean "the gathering place," and there is no doubt that Oahu plays that role today. Its 800,000-plus residents make up around 75 percent of the state's population. Honolulu is the seat of island and state government, and is the longest city in the world; because the city and county of Honolulu are one and the same, the metropolis extends 1,400 miles (2,250km) northwest up the Hawaiian chain to Kure Atoll, near Midway Island.

Honolulu proper lies on Oahu's southern coast, backed up against the Ko'olau Range. Its two best-known neighborhoods, downtown Honolulu, and Waikiki, 3 miles (5km) to the east, hold almost all its facilities and attractions for tourists. Waikiki is virtually a separate destination in itself, and many visitors to Hawaii never leave it except to reach the airport on the other side of Honolulu. The truth

Ko 'Olina Golf Club in Kapolei.

is that there is much more to Oahu than this famous beach. On the other side of the Ko'olau Mountains is the windward side, which is green and wet. Life slows down along the North Shore, whose waters are placid in summer but violent in winter with surfing's best waves. On the south coast to the west of Honolulu and Waikiki is Pearl Harbor, encircled by military bases and housing. Farther to the west are the Ko 'Olina resort area, the 'Ewa plains and the sunny Wai'anae coastal valleys, probably Oahu's most "local" area. You can experience five or six microclimates in a day, all without ever leaving Oahu.

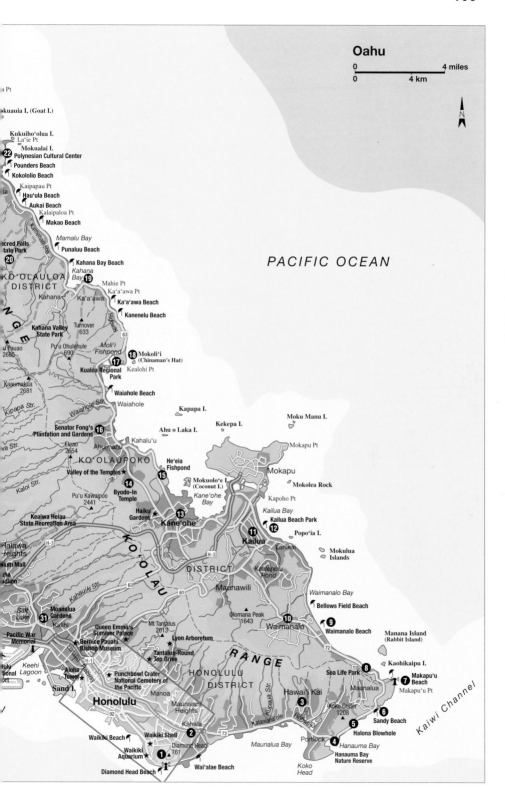

Oahu

0   4 miles
0   4 km

N

a Pt

kuauia I. (Goat I.)

Kukuiho'olua I.
La'ie Pt
Mokualai I.
22 Polynesian Cultural Center
Pounders Beach
Kokololio Beach
Kaipapau Pt
Hau'ula Beach
Aukai Beach
Kalaipaloa Pt
Makao Beach

Mamalu Bay
icred Falls
tate Park   Punaluu Beach
20
   Kahana Bay Beach
Kahana
KO'OLAULOA   *Bay* **19**
DISTRICT   Mahie Pt
Kahana   Ka'a'awa Pt
N   Ka'a'awa   Ka'a'awa Beach
G   Kanenelu Beach
E
Kahana Valley   Turnover
State Park   633   83
u Pauao   Pu'u Ohulehule *Moli'i*
2685   690   *Fishpond* **18** Mokoli'i
Kaaumakua   **17**   (Chinaman's Hat)
2681   Kualoa Regional   Kealohi Pt
Park
Kipapa Str.   Waiahole Beach
Waiahole Str.   Waiahole
va Str.   Kapapa I.
Moku Manu I.
Senator Fong's   Kekepa I.
Plantation and Gardens **16**   Ahu o Laka I.
va Str.   Kahalu'u   Mokapu Pt
Eleao   Ahuimanu
2654   He'eia
KO'OLAUPOKO   Fishpond   Mokapu
Valley of the Temples ★ **15**   Mokuolo'e I.
Kaloi Str.   (Coconut I.)   Mokolea Rock
Pu'u Kawaipoo **14**   *Kane'ohe*   Kapoho Pt
2441   Byodo-In   *Bay*
Temple   Haiku   *Kailua Bay*
Keaiwa Heiau   Gardens **13**   Kailua Beach Park
State Recreation Area   Kane'ohe **12**
aiawa   Popo'ia I.
eights   H-3   **11**
ium Mall   Kailua
dium   H-3   Lanikai   Mokulua
H-1   Islands
DISTRICT
Kahauiki Str.   *Kaelepulu*
63   *Pond*
Moanalua   61   Maunawili   *Waimanalo Bay*
Sak   Gardens
Lake   **31**   Kalihi   Olomana Peak   Bellows Field Beach
Pacific War   Queen Emma's   Mt Tantalus   1643   **10**   **9**
Memorial   Summer Palace   2013   Waimanalo   Waimanalo Beach
Bernice Pauahi   Lyon Arboretum   Manana Island
olu   Bishop Museum   72   (Rabbit Island)
Keehi   Tantalus-Round
tional   Top Drive   Kaohikaipu I.
ort   *Lagoon*   Aloha   HONOLULU   Sea Life Park **8**   Makapu'u
Tower ★   Punchbowl Crater   DISTRICT   **7** Beach
Sand I.   National Cemetery of   Maunalua   Makapu'u Pt
the Pacific   Manoa   Hawai'i Kai
Honolulu   **3**   Koko Crater
92   Maunalani   1208   **6**
Heights   Sandy Beach
Kahala   **5**
Waikiki Shell   72   Halona Blowhole
Waikiki Beach   Diamond Head   **2**   Portlock   **4**
Waikiki   761   *Maunalua Bay*   Hanauma Bay
Aquarium   **1**   Wai'alae Beach   Hanauma Bay
Diamond Head Beach   *Koko*   Nature Reserve
Head

PACIFIC OCEAN

Kealohi Pt

Kaelepulu
Pond

Kamehameha Hwy

Kahekili Hwy

Kaumualii St

Likelike Hwy

Pali Hwy

Kuneia Str

Kalaniana'ole Highway

KO'OLAU RANGE

HONOLULU DISTRICT

Kaiwi Channel

HONOLULU

A cosmopolitan metropolis in the middle of the Pacific Ocean. Sure, it seems strange. But that's what makes Honolulu worth a visit.

Honolulu – the name rolls off the tongue like a soft wave breaking off Waikiki. There's no mystery about its origin: *hono*, a bay, and *lulu*, protected. It explains why Honolulu has been the commercial, political, and cultural center of the Hawaiian Islands since the 1800s. Until Pearl Harbor was made navigable in the mid-19th century, Honolulu Harbor was the largest protected body of water within 2,000 miles (3,200km) of Hawaii.

Three miles (5km) west of the beaches of Waikiki, downtown Honolulu is a walker's delight. A stroll through Downtown with its grid of side streets, shops, oddball bars, and historic buildings can consume hours or days. The key to unlocking Honolulu is to treat it not like a city, but like the real gem that it is. You're on Hawaiian time now, so take it slow and easy.

Palace in paradise

Grand old 'Iolani Palace ❶ (364 S. King Street; tel: 522-0822; www.iolani palace.org; Mon–Sat 9am–4pm) is the only royal palace on US soil. It was built in a Victorian-era style called American Composite or American Florentine. Completed in 1882 during King Kalakaua's reign, it took three years and $350,000 to finish.

King Kalakaua and his successor-sister, Queen Lili'uokalani, lived in the palace, holding royal court from 1882 until 1893, when a group of American businessmen staged a coup d'état and abolished the monarchy. 'Iolani – Hawaiian for heavenly hawk – was renamed the Executive Building after the monarchy's overthrow, but the humiliation did not end there. In 1895, following a futile counter-revolution led by royalists, Lili'uokalani was convicted of misprision of high treason and was

Main Attractions
'Iolani Palace
Honolulu Museum of Art
Chinatown
Foster Botanical Gardens
Aloha Tower
Aina Moana State Recreation Area
Ala Moana Shopping Center

Gallery of 18th-century European art at the Honolulu Museum of Art.

TIP

In Honolulu, locals speak of a place as being *'Ewa* or *Diamond Head* of something else, not west or east. For example, Waikiki is *'Ewa* of Diamond Head. You'll catch on.

The grounds of 'Iolani Palace.

returned to 'Iolani Palace, where she spent most of the year living on the second floor under house arrest as a prisoner of the provisional government.

The palace was used as a capitol for the provisional, territorial, and state governments of Hawaii. In 1969, the state legislature and administration moved out of the palace and into the new capitol building and grounds just *mauka* (toward the mountains) of the palace. The state and a private non-profit-making group then began a $6-million effort to restore the palace to its former splendor. Original furnishings were tracked down and recovered and the palace proper now glows as it did when Kalakaua and Lili'uokalani hosted formal banquets and grand balls. This includes Corinthian columns, etched-glass door panels, chandeliers, the mirrored and gilded Throne Room, and the spectacular three-story *koa* (an indigenous hardwood) stairwell with carved balusters. Also back in operation are the first flush toilets known to have been installed in any palace

anywhere in the world, and Hawaii's first internal telephone and electric-light systems. A worthwhile museum of royal Hawaiiana is housed in the basement.

On the palace grounds are some other intriguing sites. The **Coronation Stand** was built in 1883 for King Kalakaua and Queen Kapi'olani's coronation. The stand's foundation was rebuilt in 1919, but the copper dome is the original and now plays host to free public concerts (every Friday at noon) by the Royal Hawaiian Band.

The **'Iolani Barracks** is a stone structure that served as headquarters and home to the Royal Household Guards from 1871 until the overthrow of the monarchy. The small building now includes a gift shop and the palace ticket office.

The **Royal Burial Ground and Tomb** is an inconspicuous, grass-covered mound surrounded by *ti* plants in the Diamond Head *makai* (towards Diamond Head and toward the ocean) corner. It was the site of the first Royal Mausoleum, built in 1825

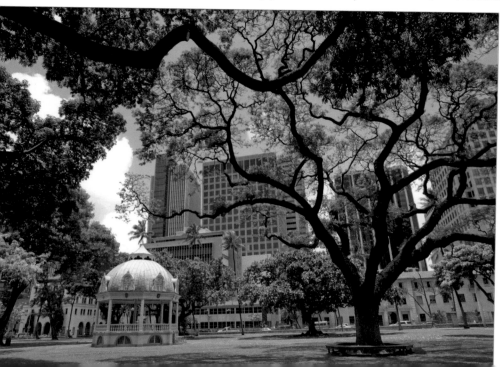

to house the remains of King Kamehameha II and Queen Kamamalu, who died of measles when they visited England in 1823. Later Hawaiian *ali'i* (royalty) were also buried there. But in 1865, with the tomb overcrowded with royal remains, all were moved to a new Royal Mausoleum in Nu'uanu Valley.

On the *makai* side of King Street, across from 'Iolani Palace, is the **King Kamehameha the Great Statue ❷**. Although this heroic bronze probably bears little resemblance to Kamehameha the Great, it's a Honolulu monument and a prime spot for camera-wielding tourists. The statue shows the king holding a barbed *polulu* (spear) in his left hand as a symbol of peace and his right arm outstretched in a welcoming gesture of *aloha*. Hanging from the king's shoulders is a large feather cloak and on his head is a *mahiole*, or feather helmet. Around his loins and chest he wears a feather *malo*, or loincloth, and a sash. When the Hawaiian kingdom's 1878 legislature commissioned this statue, King Kalakaua chose John Timoteo Baker, a local businessman, to serve as its primary model, as he was the most handsome man in court circles. Baker was mostly Anglo-Saxon, and only about one quarter Tahitian. Photos were taken wearing ancient clothing, and these plus copies of painted likenesses of Kamehameha were sent to Thomas B. Gould, an American sculptor in Florence. Unveiled during Kalakaua's 1883 coronation, the statue is a copy of the original, which is in Kapa'au, on Hawaii Island.

Behind the statue is the old **Judiciary Building** (tel: 539-4999; Mon–Fri 9am–4pm; free), originally designed by Australian architect Thomas Rowe to be King Kamehameha V's palace. The king's household plans changed, however, and after the building was completed in 1874, it was used instead as a courthouse and legislative building. The building – also known as Ali'iolani Hale (*hale* means house, and *ali'iolani* translates as "chief of heavenly repute") – is now home to the state's supreme court and the Judiciary History Center.

Every June, the Kamehameha Festival opens with a colorful lei-draping ceremony at the bronze statue of King Kamehameha I, with lei up to 18ft (5 meters) long.

Kawaiaha'o Church.

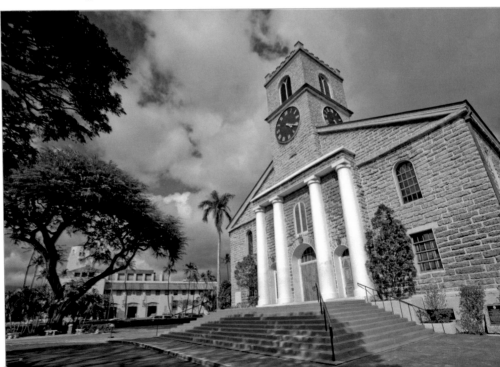

Kawaiaha'o Church

Towards Diamond Head up King Street from the Judiciary Building is Hawaii's most famous Christian structure, **Kawaiaha'o Church** ❸. On Sunday mornings, or when the church's Hawaiian choir is in rehearsal, the royal palms and hala trees in its grounds seem to sway with the lyrics of *"He A-kua he mo-le-le"* – "God is Holy," or *"E Ha-wai-i e ku'u o-ne ha-nau e,"* the opening words of "Hawai'i Aloha," which translates as, "Oh, Hawaii, my own birthplace, my own land."

For years this was the gathering place of missionaries and Christian Hawaiian *ali'i*. Even today, the church often serves as a meeting place where matters of serious Hawaiian interest are discussed. Designed by Reverend Hiram Bingham, who led the first Congregationalist mission to Hawaii in 1820, Kawaiaha'o Church was constructed in the late 1830s and early 1840s of some 14,000 large coral blocks cut from nearby reefs. Although the present Kawaiaha'o structure was dedicated in 1842,

it was preceded by four thatched churches also built under Bingham's direction, the first in 1821.

Kawaiaha'o, the "water used by Ha'o," was named after an ancient sacred spring that still flows in the church grounds. The grounds also hold a cemetery for early missionaries and faithful Hawaiian members of the congregation. It is estimated that as many as 2,000 Hawaiians were buried here in the 1800s, many the victims of diseases unwittingly introduced by the early sailors and settlers. Missionaries and their descendants were buried at the back of the church, while native Hawaiians and others were segregated in death on the harbor-side of the church.

One Hawaiian, who received special exemption from Kawaiaha'o's congregation: King William Lunalilo, the popular "Prince Bill," whose Gothic tomb stands just to the right of the churchyard's main entrance. Lunalilo, who died in 1874 after a one-year reign, requested on his deathbed that he be buried "among his people" at Kawaiaha'o, away from the "clannish" Kamehameha kings and queens who rested in vaults at the Royal Mausoleum in Nu'uanu.

It was at **Likeke Hale**, an adobe schoolhouse built on Kawaiaha'o's grounds around 1836, that early Congregationalist missionaries taught Hawaiian children the *palapala*, or Bible, and literature in general. Built of mud, limestone, and coral, the schoolhouse is the only survivor of the many adobe structures that were constructed during the early 1800s. It is still used today for Sunday-school classes and smaller church meetings.

Mission Houses Museum and around

Across from the schoolhouse is the yard where the missionaries lived, prayed, and printed the first of their many 19th-century publications. Now a museum complex, the **Mission Houses** ❹ (553 S. King Street; tel:

DISCOVERING HONOLULU HARBOR

European explorers didn't find Honolulu Harbor for more than 14 years after Captain Cook's arrival in 1778. But in late 1792 or early 1793, Captain William Brown, then busy in both the Pacific Northwest–China fur trade and a new Hawaiian gun trade, accidentally came across a nameless inlet. He described it in his logbook as "a small but commodious basin with regular soundings from 7 to 3 fathoms clear and good bottom, where a few vessels may ride with the greatest safety." Brown named it Fair Haven, which in an unusual reversal was translated into Hawaiian to become "Honolulu."

While Oahu's chiefs had always preferred Waikiki, with the arrival of sailing vessels and a new concept called money, other *akamai* (smart) Hawaiians, including Kamehameha, began moving to Honolulu's harbor. In Kamehameha's hands, Honolulu became the most important stopover point in the mid-Pacific ocean. Although Kamehameha eventually returned to Hawaii Island around 1812, he closely monitored commerce at Honolulu until his death in 1819, as did his sons. Later, during the whaling era, the Kamehamehas moved Hawaii's capital to the booming town of Lahaina, on Maui. Eventually the Hawaiian elite recognized that the future would play out in Honolulu, and in 1845, Kamehameha III moved back to Honolulu where he officially declared it the capital of the Hawaiian Kingdom in 1850.

447-3910; www.missionhouses.org; Tue–Sat 10am–4pm) rank among the oldest surviving Western-style structures in Hawaii.

The main white Frame House still stands as it was the day it was erected in 1821 of New England timbers, which were cut and fitted in Boston and shipped to Hawaii aboard the brig *Thaddeus*. It is the oldest wooden house in Hawaii, and was for many years home to several prominent missionaries. The Coral House, where the first printing in the north Pacific was made, was built in 1823. A third building, the Chamberlain House, used as a storehouse and home for the mission's purchasing agent, was built in 1831. All three structures belong to the Hawaiian Mission Children's Society, an exclusive *kama'aina* (long-time residents') club made up of missionaries' descendants. If you fail to coincide with a guided tour of the actual houses, you can settle instead for the museum in the separate visitor center.

From the front entrance of Kawaiaha'o Church, across King Street is **Honolulu Hale** ❺, the city's California-Spanish-style city hall built in 1927. Adjacent is a redbrick structure in a burst of Americana with white pillars, opposite the Mission Houses, which was dedicated in 1916 as the Mission Memorial Building to honor the original New England missionaries. Since 1947, it's been used as a city hall annex. 'Ewa (to the west) is the Greco-Roman **Hawaii State Library** ❻ (478 S. King Street; tel: 586-3500; Mon, Wed 10am–5pm; Tue, Fri, Sat 9am–5pm; Thu 9am–8pm; free), which has an extensive Hawaiian and Pacific Isles collection. Built in 1911–2, it was restored and modernized in the late 1980s.

State capitol and surroundings

Behind 'Iolani Palace is contemporary Hawaii's center of power – the **State Capitol Building** ❼, dedicated in 1969 and completely renovated in the mid-1990s. The structure's architectural lines were designed to suggest Hawaii's volcanic and oceanic

FACT

It was at Kawaiaha'o Church that Kamehameha III spoke what has become the State of Hawaii's motto – *Ua mau ke ea o ka'aina i ka pono*, or "The life of the land is perpetuated in righteousness." He spoke after the restoration of Hawaiian sovereignty following a brief 1843 British takeover of the islands.

Tomb of King Lunalilo at Kawaiaha'o Church.

The Frame House at the Mission Houses Museum.

origins. Its high and flaring support pillars represent royal palms. Paneling made of *koa* in offices and conference rooms gives the structure a distinctly Hawaiian touch. On the *makai* (ocean) side of the building stands a majestic, bronze **statue of Queen Lili'uokalani**, the last monarch of Hawaii (see page 46). An outstretched hand holds fresh flowers, placed there daily by admirers and supporters.

On the *mauka* (mountain) side of the capitol, along Beretania Street, fly the American and Hawaiian flags, and a blue, red, and starred governor's flag. Visitors to the islands are sometimes surprised to see the British flag in the upper left corner of Hawaii's red, white, and blue flag, designed in 1816 for Kamehameha the Great. It is thought that this flag includes the Union Jack out of consideration for the British sea captain George Vancouver, who presented Hawaii with its first flag when Kamehameha temporarily placed his islands under the protection of Great Britain. Other historians say

Kamehameha adopted the Jack-and-Stripes flag so that Hawaiian ships at sea would look both American and British, thereby discouraging pirates from pillaging his kingdom's vulnerable vessels.

On the same side, take a moment to study the bronze **sculpture of Father Damien (formerly Joseph De Veuster)**, the self-sacrificing priest who lived and died among sufferers of leprosy (now called Hansen's disease) at Kalaupapa, Molokai in the 1870s–80s. This blockish statue, created by Venezuelan sculptor Marisol Escobar, is a duplicate of one that stands in Statuary Hall at the US Capitol building in Washington, DC. Unveiled in 1969, the statue ignited controversy because the bold and tragic likeness was based on a photograph taken of the priest shortly before he died in 1888; a sufferer of the disease, his formerly handsome features were grossly disfigured. Controversy regarding the statue has subsided, but Escobar's Damien remains a powerful artistic statement, and a telling memorial.

The official residence of Hawaii's governor is a white Greek Revival mansion on Beretania Street, **Washington Place** ❽ (320 Beretania Street; tel: 536-8040; tours Mon–Fri by appointment only; free). It was built in 1846 for American sea captain John Dominis. His daughter-in-law, Lydia Kamakaeha, lived here between her marriage in 1862 and her accession to the throne as Queen Lili'uokalani in 1891, and returned just two years later following the overthrow of the Hawaiian monarchy. Washington Place remained a center of courtly social proceedings until Lili'uokalani's death in 1917, at the age of 79, and the deposed queen regularly sang her own compositions for visitors at the massive *koa* grand piano in her Music Room. The current governor, Neil Abercrombie, lives in a separate new building in the grounds.

Peek in next door at **St Andrew's Cathedral** ❾, a Gothic Revival structure built at a snail's pace between 1867 and 1958 of imported English sandstone. Another block 'Ewa (west) up Beretania Street is the **Cathedral of Our Lady of Peace** ❿, built by Roman Catholic missionaries from France. This coral building at the top of the Fort Street Mall was dedicated in 1843. Father Damien was ordained here in 1864.

The historic Richards Street YMCA building, immediately west of 'Iolani Palace across Richards Street, now houses the **Hawaii State Art Museum** ⓫ (250 Hotel Street; tel: 586-0300; Tue–Sat 10am–4pm). This highlights the state's impressive collection of art, purchased over a 25-year period as part of the Art in Public Places program. Exhibits are loosely divided between large-scale landscapes and natural-history displays in the eastern wing, and quirkier multi-media works in the western wing.

Honolulu Museum of Art

Down Beretania Street from Washington Place and the Capitol, towards Diamond Head, is the superb **Honolulu Museum of Art** ⓬ (900 Beretania Street; tel: 532-8700; www.honolulumuseum.org;

Statue of Queen Lili'uokalani, Hawaii's last monarch, near the State Capitol Building.

Washington Place.

In the central courtyard at the Honolulu Museum of Art.

Impressionist and Post-Impressionist gallery at the Honolulu Museum of Art.

Tue–Sat 10am–4.30pm, Sun 1–5pm). Housed in a magnificent Japanese-influenced former private home, built in 1927, the academy holds galleries of Asian and Western art, plus inner courtyards rich in flora and sculpture.

There are works by Modigliani, Picasso, Gauguin, Van Gogh, Monet, and Rodin, and some fascinating displays on how Hawaii has been depicted, and imagined, by the rest of the world. The true highlight, however, is one of the finest Oriental collections in America, including a wonderful range of artifacts from ancient China, statues and religious carvings from throughout southeast Asia, and the writer James Michener's collection of Japanese woodblock prints.

Big business and wealthy families

Anchoring Downtown is **Bishop Square** ⑬, a refreshing plaza with fountains at the intersection of Bishop and King streets. Named after Charles Reed Bishop, who established both the Bishop Estate and the Bishop Museum, **Bishop Street** contains the graciously porticoed suites of the "Big Five" *kama'aina* corporations – conglomerates built on sugar in the 19th century by business and missionary families.

Today, a bronze statue of the royalist Robert Wilcox shares their turf. Every Friday is Aloha Friday, when nearly every man on the street – Big Five type, banker, or otherwise – wears a crisp aloha shirt. A necktie on Friday is truly an odd sight, as is a sports coat or sweater.

Be sure to check a special events listing before heading downtown. You just might be able to catch a show at the historic **Hawaii Theatre** ⑭ (1130 Bethel Street; tel: 528-0506; www.hawaiitheatre.com), located at the corner of Bethel and Pauahi streets, two blocks 'Ewa (west) of Bishop Street. The 1,400-seat theater, which opened in 1922 and closed in 1984, was reopened in 1996, restored to its original glory: gold metallic leaf adorns the columns and grillwork moldings inside the theater; the lobby has new marble floors and counters. Lionel Walden's *Glorification of the Drama*, a stunning mural that presides over the proscenium arch, has been fully restored. Today, the theater showcases a wide range of musical and theatrical acts.

Chinatown and Hotel Street

Historic buildings vie with rising glass towers throughout Honolulu. Perhaps the most interesting of the historic structures outside of the capitol district are in an area near the harbor. This brick-built neighborhood is a pleasant four-block stroll from the Federal Post Office Building, down Merchant Street, Honolulu's old "Financial Boulevard." Many of the structures in this area escaped the demolition ball: some have been restored, while others add a somewhat seedy edge to parts of Chinatown.

Between Bethel Street and Nu'uanu Avenue, two immense stone lions flank **Hotel Street** to announce **Chinatown**, an area bounded by the harbor waterfront, Nu'uanu Avenue, and Beretania and River streets. In the late 1860s, Chinese plantation workers, after paying off their indentured labor contracts, gathered here and established new lives.

Chinatown comes into its own in a medley of Asian markets, noodle factories, shops, and art and antique galleries. Side streets cutting across Hotel Street and extending from King Street to Beretania Street tempt the curious. The **Maunakea Marketplace** ⑮ (1120 Maunakea Street; daily 5.30am–4pm) is a modern, open plaza nestled amid the old – look for the clock tower with Chinese numbers. Down on King Street, toward the waterfront, the **Oahu Market** ⑯ will rekindle a traveler's Asian memories with its early-morning hubbub of mongering and bargaining.

Hotel Street ends at River Street, which parallels the lower **Nu'uanu Stream** descending from the Ko'olau Mountains. On the *mauka* (mountain) side of Chinatown, on Vineyard Boulevard, is the **Kuan Yin Temple** ⑰, where Buddhist and Daoist images

Dim sum in Chinatown.

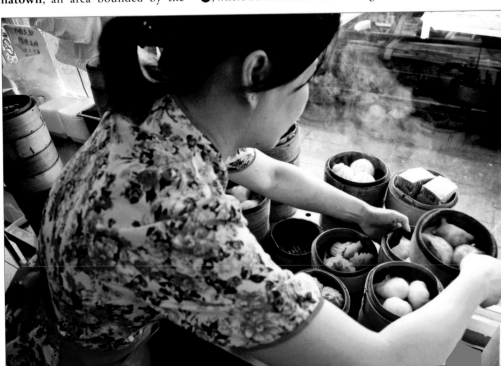

gleam and a 10ft (3-meter) statue of Kuan Yin, the Buddhist goddess of mercy, dominates.

A quiet respite can be found beneath hardy tropical trees in the spacious **Foster Botanical Gardens** (tel: 522-7065; daily 9am–4pm) on Vineyard Boulevard, just beyond the Kuan Yin Temple. Several plants, such as the fragrant and ever-blossoming cannonball tree, are the only specimen of their genus and species in Hawaii.

Along the harbor

Toward the waterfront, Fort Street Mall empties into **Ala Moana Boulevard**, an oceanside artery that starts as Nimitz Highway near the Honolulu International Airport and turns into Ala Moana (Ocean Street) when it reaches Downtown. Near here stood the old "fort" – Ke Ku Nohu, c.1816 to 1857 – that gave Fort Street its name. Cross Ala Moana and hop on the elevator to the top of the **Aloha Tower** ⑱ (observation deck daily 9am–5pm; free) for views that span Downtown, with Waikiki to the

Chinatown market.

east and the Wai'anae Mountains to the west. This pleasing 1925 structure is only 10 stories high – or 184ft (56 meters) – but it was once the tallest building in Hawaii. It is now dwarfed by the skyscrapers of downtown Honolulu.

Toward 'Ewa

From Aloha Tower, heading *'Ewa* (west) along the Nimitz Highway leads towards the airport and *'Ewa*, while traveling *Diamond Head* on Ala Moana Boulevard leads to Waikiki. Nimitz Highway is an unattractive gateway to Waikiki, a mess of traffic amid light industry and warehouses – an unfortunate introduction to Oahu's beauty, partly revealed on the crowded H-1 Freeway that also links the airport to Waikiki.

Toward Waikiki and Diamond Head

Along Ala Moana Boulevard, past the **Prince Kuhio Kalaniana'ole Federal Building**, the harbor and ocean disappear behind walls and buildings, including Restaurant Row, where a

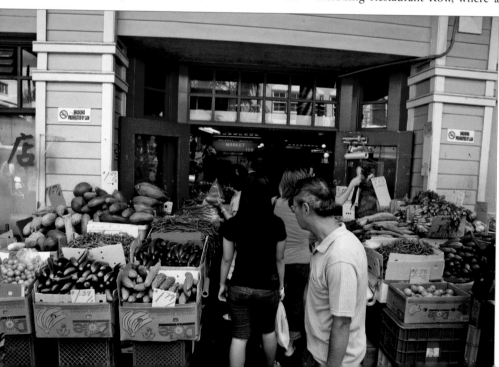

theater complex plays art films not offered elsewhere in Hawaii.

A mile or so farther on there's **Kewalo Basin** ⓳, where Honolulu's fishing fleet returns with the day's catch, and which serves as a departure point for coastal cruises and sport fishing. Opposite Kewalo Basin and on the other side of Ala Moana Boulevard, there are two popular shopping, restaurant, and movie theaters, malls, all part of the Ward Centers complex, **Ward Warehouse** and **Ward Center**.

On the *makai* (ocean) side, just past Kewalo Basin, begins the **Ala Moana Beach Park** ⓴ comprising 100 acres (40 hectares) of open space and beaches with good swimming and decent surfing to be found beyond the reef. The adjacent artificial peninsula, known locally as **Magic Island** ㉑, or **Aina Moana State Recreation Area**, is popular with joggers, cyclists, skaters, and walkers. Created by infilling a coral reef, this spot was originally intended as the site for a collection of new luxury hotels, but they were never built, and instead it holds a peaceful little sand-fringed lagoon.

Directly *mauka* (towards the mountains) from Ala Moana Beach Park you come to the **Ala Moana Shopping Center** ㉒, a huge development and Hawaii's largest shopping mall (as well as being the largest open-air mall in the world), which has more than 250 stores and eateries. Ongoing renovations and expansions mean that it now stands four stories tall, and holds a roster of top-name retailers that includes Neiman Marcus, Dior, Gucci, Prada, and Louis Vuitton.

On the extreme Diamond Head end of Ala Moana Beach Park, a bridge rises over the **Ala Wai Canal** and into Waikiki. The Ala Wai is a favorite training area for outrigger canoe paddlers.

On the west side of the canal rises the Modernist Hawaii Convention Centre; to the east looms the first of Waikiki's highrises. Oceanside, there are dozens of spindly sailing craft at the **Ala Wai Yacht Harbor** and yacht basin, towered over by the Hawaii Prince and Renaissance Ilikai hotels.

Aloha Tower.

"BOAT DAYS"

As recently as the 1950s, Aloha Tower smiled down upon Hawaii's famous "Boat Days," when luxury Matson liners would arrive and depart at piers 10 and 11 in a flurry of flowers and *hapahaole hula*. On and off the ships would go huge steamer trunks and travelers in white linen suits and ribboned hats. At pier side, local boys would dive for coins tossed into the water. Something of that spirit has returned as increasing numbers of cruise ships make Honolulu port-calls, with Boat Day arrivals reinstituted in the process. The half-hour long mix of hula, music, confetti launches and waterboat displays provides a festive atmosphere, with Aloha Tower as the centerpiece of an open-air shopping, restaurant, and entertainment complex. For the Boat Day schedule, call 528-5700.

Waikiki Beach with Diamond
Head in the background, Honolulu.

WAIKIKI

Crystal-clear water, fine white sand, and a host
of luxurious hotels nearby; to many, Waikiki
Beach might just be the best beach on Earth.

At 500 acres (200 hectares) in size, Waikiki covers less than 1 percent of Oahu's land area, yet it pumps more than $5 billion into Hawaii's economy annually, representing about 40 percent of the state's total tourism dollars. It provides about 40,000 jobs tending to Oahu's 388,000 monthly visitors, while somehow finding the room to house its 20,000 residents.

World-famous **Waikiki Beach**, actually a series of connecting beaches – Sans Souci, Queen's Surf, Kuhio, Waikiki, DeRussy, and Duke Kahanamoku – extends for more than a mile in a crescent of sand. The city has spent millions upgrading the Waikiki beachfront promenade, adding landscaped gardens, statues, historic story boards, and tourist facilities. Additional upgrades to Kapi'olani Park, Fort DeRussy, and along the Ala Wai Canal have greatly enhanced Waikiki's appeal, with extensive redevelopment in recent years to the heart of Waikiki, along Lewers Street, and Kalakaua and Kuhio avenues. The central showpieces of all this revitalization are the Beach Walk development on Lewers Street, which opened in 2007, and the Trump International Hotel Waikiki, which opened in 2009.

Early Hawaiians named this 1.5-mile (2.5km) -long coastal strip *Waikiki*, or spouting water, because its inland section was a wetland nurtured by mountain streams and springs. As early as the 1400s, Hawaiians capitalized on this water with a sophisticated irrigation system that fed aquaculture ponds and taro fields.

Until the 1920s, when completion of the Ala Wai Canal diverted water from the swamps and created dry land for future hotels, Waikiki's somewhat smelly interior was still a boggy place of fish ponds, taro patches, and rice paddies populated by quacking waterfowl and other damp creatures.

Main Attractions
Waikiki Beach
Royal Hawaiian Hotel
US Army Museum
Kapi'olani Park
Honolulu Zoo

Waikiki.

"If anyone desires such old-fashioned things as lovely scenery, quiet, pure air, clear sea water, good food, and heavenly sunsets hung out before his eyes...I recommend him cordially to the Sans Souci," wrote author Robert Louis Stevenson, pictured above in Honolulu.

Outrigger canoes mingle with beach parasols on Waikiki Beach.

The area's beaches, coconut groves, and fish-rich reefs, however, have long made this area a favorite spot among *ali'i*, or the Hawaiian royalty. All Hawaii's royals had homes here, as did the island's ruling chiefs before them.

Transport links and tourists

In the 1860s, a dirt road was built to link Waikiki's cool surf with hot and dusty Honolulu. Two decades later, a mule-drawn omnibus began making daily round trips to Waikiki; by 1888, a regular tram service was initiated, which was motorized in 1895. Most visitors stayed with friends or in one of downtown Honolulu's hostelries – notably the long-gone Hawaiian Hotel – until the 1880s and early 1890s, when a few Waikiki homes and cottages were converted into guest houses.

In 1884, Allen Herbert opened one such guest house near Diamond Head and named it **Sans Souci** (in French this means "without a care"), and later hosted the noted Scottish author Robert Louis Stevenson. To this day, the "heavenly sunsets" that

Stevenson loved take place off Sans Souci Beach, where the New Otani Kaimana Beach Hotel has replaced Stevenson's bungalow.

Reminders of the past

Once home to Oahu's chiefs, today's Waikiki offers intriguing hints of its past. Take, for example, the **Stones of Kapaemahu Ⓐ**, four imposing boulders at Kuhio Beach adjacent to the Honolulu Police substation. Approach the stones with respect, because, according to Hawaiian oral traditions, they possess the *mana*, or spiritual powers, of four *kahuna* – priests or wizards – who were renowned throughout Polynesia for their wisdom and healing abilities. These four wizards – Kapaemahu, Kahaloa, Kapuni, and Kinohi – came to Oahu from Tahiti in the 16th century, then left. A metal plaque notes that "before vanishing, the wizards transferred their powers to these stones."

Close by is the bronze **Statue of Duke Kahanamoku Ⓑ**. The statue includes a bronze surfboard representing Duke's classic 24ft (7.5-meter)

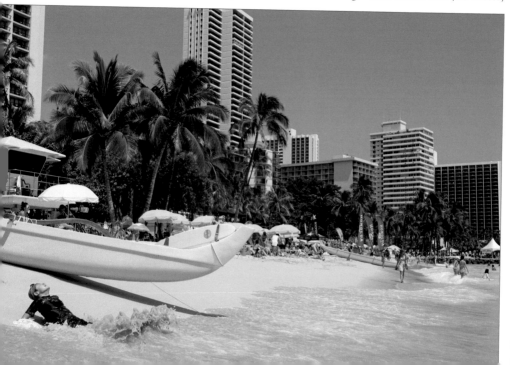

-long *koa* board. Short boards are the norm today, but some of the old long boards still in use can be found nearby in storage racks wedged between the Moana Hotel and the Honolulu Police substation. Duke Kahanamoku was a swimming world-record holder in three Olympics. He also brought surfing into the modern age, introducing Hawaii to the rest of the world. Beach boys here still paddle oversized surfboards out to surf spots like Queens, Populars, or Canoes.

A block beyond Duke is a statue of Prince Kuhio, royal champion of Hawaiian rights in the US Congress for 20 years after annexation. A statue of King Kalakaua graces Gateway Park, at the 'Ewa (west) end of Waikiki. A statue of his niece, Princess Kaiulani, is located on the street that bears her name, while statues of Mahatma Gandhi and Queen Kapi'olani are to be found in Kapi'olani Park.

The section of beach fronting the statue of Prince Kuhio is known as Kuhio Beach. Almost entirely enclosed by stone breakwaters, the inshore waters here offer Waikiki's safest swimming, and are therefore good for families. At dusk nightly at the beachside hula stand at Kuhio Beach, the lighting of torches begins an hour of music and dance. On select evenings, movies are shown beachside at the Kalakaua entrance to Kapi'olani Park.

The first luxury hotel

Since the mid-1950s, hotels in Waikiki have risen in escalating waves of concrete and steel, a Great Wall of Waikiki. At last count, there were more than 30,000 hotel rooms in Waikiki. However, for most of the 20th century, three Waikiki hotels anchored the beach, luxurious locales that are still regarded with respect by *kama'aina* (long-time residents) who knew them way back when.

The **Moana Surfrider Hotel** ⓒ, on the beach along Kalakaua Avenue near the Duke Kahanamoku statue, is the *tutu-kane*, or granddaddy, of them all. At its center is Hawaii's first luxury hotel, the **Moana**, which is what it is commonly called even today.

Opened in 1901 and geared to steamer-set tourists, it offered 75 rooms,

TIP

If you are renting a car, be aware that Honolulu's roads can be a little confusing. Entrances and exits for the H-1 freeway defy logic – they often don't come in pairs – and the routes into Waikiki are very convoluted and fussy.

Looking northwest along the beach at night.

NEVER-ENDING SANDPIT

It's no secret that Honolulu's Waikiki Beach is one of the most heralded beaches in the world. But with constant use and the consistent battering from seasonal storms, fighting erosion has proven to be a challenging task. In response to the situation, the state government in 2012 allocated $2.5 million to pump sand from offshore to fill in the beach. In just a year, the controversial project added a 37ft (11-meter) band of sand to a small stretch of beach from Kuhio Beach north to the Royal Hawaiian hotel. Experts seemed to think subsequent sand replacements would be approved every few years after this phase finishes in 2014. Some consider the sand replacement "mission critical." After all, without the beach itself, what would Waikiki really be?

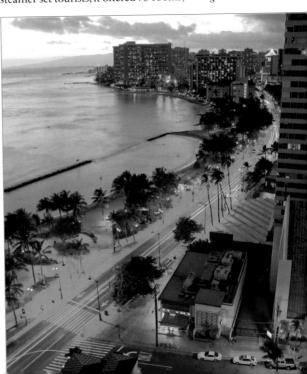

the beachside banyan tree. With one of Waikiki's superlative trademark sunsets as a backdrop, and no cover charge for a stage-front table, it's the perfect way to round off a day in paradise.

More stays in paradise

The newest luxury kid on the block along Waikiki is the **Trump International Hotel Waikiki** , a condo-hotel 'Ewa (west) along the beach from Halekulani and kitty-corner from the US Army Museum. The history of this property is relatively scant, since the place only opened in 2009. When the 462 units went on sale in 2006, they sold out in one day for a total of $700 million. Real estate experts say it was the fastest real estate sale in history.

At the far western end of the Waikiki Beach Waterfront, golden Kahanamoku Beach, once the home of the eponymous legendary surfer's family, is now dominated by the mighty towers of the **Hilton Hawaiian Village** . At the landscaped Ala Moana gateway you won't be able to miss the larger-than-life depictions of hula dancers. Take the time to wander through the Village's landscaped grounds, enjoying the collection of rare birds and the king's

The Royal Hawaiian Hotel.

ransom of giant *koi* (Japanese carp). Beachside, look up at the 30-story rainbow murals (the largest in the world) that make the Rainbow Tower a Waikiki landmark. On Friday nights there's an hour-long show of music and dance and a grand fireworks finale.

The Hilton Hawaiian Village is also a base of operations for **Atlantis Submarines** (tel: 973-9811), which offers fabulous underwater excursions to submerged shipwrecks a mile or so offshore.

US Army Museum

A short walk east of the Hilton, the oceanfront **US Army Museum** (Fort DeRussy on Kalia Road; tel: 438-2819; Tue–Sat 9am–5pm; free) displays warfare artifacts including weapons of ancient Hawaii, the American Revolution, Spanish–American War, World Wars I and II, and the Korean and Vietnam wars. Even for the pacifist, this is an interesting and underrated museum, located inside Battery Randolph, a massive bunker built in 1911 with walls on its seaward side made of 22ft (7-meter) -thick concrete. When the military tried to demolish the football-field-size bunker in the late 1960s, they couldn't do it – hence the museum. The battery had two disappearing 14in (35cm) shore guns, cut up in the late 1940s, capable of firing a 1,600lb (726kg) shell 14 miles (22km) out to sea. Today, the museum has an extensive archive that boasts information about every military unit that has served in Hawaii since 1898.

Kapi'olani Park

Kapi'olani Park , a complex of beaches, grassy picnic and play areas, amphitheaters, jogging courses, gardens, a zoo, and aquarium, at the eastern end of Waikiki, was dedicated on June 1, 1877, Kamehameha Day, as Hawaii's first public park. Opening day was celebrated with a slate of high-stakes horse races held on a new track laid out just below Diamond Head. (The park's Kamehameha Day races in the early years of the 20th century were outlawed by temperance and anti-gambling forces.) King Kalakaua named the park after his wife.

Today Kapi'olani Park remains one of Oahu's favorite recreational areas, and whether you're seeking tennis, soccer, kite-flying, surfing, or long tranquil walks under monkeypod and ironwood trees, you'll find it here.

Kapi'olani Park is also the finishing point for one of the running world's biggest and best-known marathons. The Honolulu Marathon takes place each December and draws competitors from around the world. The race, which was first run here in 1972, draws more than 30,000 runners annually, many of them from north Asia, and particularly Japan, where marathon-running has become extremely popular.

Across the street at **Queen's Surf Beach** – Lili'uokalani's beach house once stood here – beach boys gather for volleyball, and to listen to impromptu conga drum, guitar, and flute concerts held under a banyan tree, especially at sunset. The nearby **War Memorial Natatorium**, built to commemorate World War I veterans, was dedicated in 1927 as a world-class swimming facility.

Although the pool, long in a state of disrepair, was approved for an $11-million restoration program in the 1990s, that plan drew substantial opposition from the community and sparked legal challenges. To date, only the decorative arch and entry have been restored, while the pool remains off limits.

Also nearby is **Kaimana Beach**, a sandy beach that is popular among locals. The beach also was the endpoint of the first submarine communications cable between Hawaii and California. The first telegraphic message over that cable was sent on January 1, 1903, from Henry Ernest Cooper to President Theodore Roosevelt.

Zoo and aquarium

At the **Honolulu Zoo** ❶ in Kapi'olani Park (tel: 971-7171; www.honoluluzoo. org; daily 9am–4.30pm), you can enjoy the typical antics of assorted primates, lions, elephants, giraffes, and hippos. The zoo is the only place in Hawaii where you can see a live snake: there are no wild snakes in Hawaii and strict control is maintained on their import to keep it that way.

Except for sea birds, virtually all the birds you will see nowadays in

The Aquarium in Kapi'olani Park.

Learning to surf.

Duke Kahanamoku

One of Hawaii's great names,
the legendary Duke Kahanamoku
managed to literally swim his
way into the history books.

In his lifetime, he was an Olympic champion, a
Hollywood celebrity, a local sheriff, and one of
Hawaii's pre-eminent ambassadors of goodwill.
Duke Kahanamoku's most enduring legacy, how-
ever, lives on through thousands of surfers in
Hawaii and all around the world. Through it all,
Kahanamoku was first and foremost a beach boy.
He helped popularize surfing in places like
California, Australia, and New Zealand. Kings and
queens once governed Hawaii's lands, but it was
a Duke who ruled its ocean waves.

A full-blooded Hawaiian, Duke Paoa
Kahanamoku was born in Honolulu in August
1890. The Kahanamoku family moved to Waikiki
three years later, and the young Duke was never
far from the beach he would help make famous.
In 1911, in his first timed swims, he broke three
free-style world records at Honolulu Harbor.

Duke surfing at Waikiki Beach in 1929.

Kahanamoku, in fact, shattered the 100-meter
record by 4.6 seconds. When word was sent to
Amateur Athletic Union (AAU) officials in New
York, they replied sternly, "Unacceptable. No one
swims this fast!"

A year later, at the Summer Olympics in
Stockholm, Kahanamoku made believers the
world over by capturing the gold medal in the
100-meter free-style, and a silver medal as part
of the American 200-meter free-style relay team.
The handsome Olympic star became an international celebrity. In the 1920 and 1924 Olympics,
Kahanamoku again came home a medalist.

Life after gold

In the 1920s, Kahanamoku tried his hand at acting. In all, he appeared in nearly 30 movies, sharing the screen with Hollywood giants like Dorothy
Lamour, Ronald Coleman, and another Duke,
John Wayne.

Kahanamoku's most impressive performance,
however, came in 1925, when he used his longboard to rescue eight drowning men off Newport
Beach, in California. The local police chief called
his act of heroism "the most superhuman rescue
act and the finest display of surfboard riding that
has ever been seen in the world."

After returning to Oahu, he married Nadine
Alexander in 1940 (who died in 1997 at the age
of 92). Kahanamoku was elected Honolulu's
sheriff and was re-elected 12 times, finally giving
up his office in 1960 when the position was
abolished.

In January 1968, Kahanamoku suffered a
heart attack in the parking lot of the Waikiki Yacht
Club and died at the age of 77. An estimated
10,000 people attended his funeral at Waikiki
Beach. From outrigger canoes, family and friends
scattered his ashes in the waters off Waikiki
Beach. Reported the *Honolulu Star-Bulletin*:
"There is a strange sound in the booming surf in
Waikiki today, like the anguished cry of a mother
at the loss of her favorite son."

Waikiki Beach memorial

In 1990, on the centennial anniversary of his birth,
an imposing bronze statue of Kahanamoku,
sculpted by local artist Jan Fisher, was unveiled at
Waikiki Beach. Some beach boys lament the fact
that the statue is facing *mauka* (the mountains)
instead of the ocean. Perhaps only the Duke could
safely ignore the rule of the surf never to stand with
one's back to the ocean.

Hawaii are introduced species. Ironically, then, the zoo is probably the only place a visitor to Oahu – and most residents, as well – can see indigenous mountain birds, including the exquisite 'apapane (Hawaiian honeycreeper) at the Manyara Bird Sanctuary and the South American Aviary. It's also one of the few places that you are guaranteed to see a *nene*.

The Tropical Forest section here is filled with flowering plants, trees and gardens, and there is a Children's Zoo where youngsters can pet a llama or touch a monitor lizard. Over the past decade or so, the zoo has made significant improvements, including the opening of the expansive African Savanna exhibit.

Yet more exotic creatures can be found just a few minutes away at the small **Waikiki Aquarium** Ⓚ (2777 Kalakaua Avenue; tel: 923-9741; www. waquarium.org; daily 9am–4.30pm), established in 1904. Affiliated with the University of Hawaii since 1919, the Waikiki Aquarium is the third-oldest aquarium in the United States. Probably the rarest inhabitants here are

the monk seals; along with the hoary bat, these creatures are the only two mammals known to have been native to Hawaii when the first Polynesian settlers arrived. There are also some fascinating exhibits on the nautilus and the spawning of the *mahimahi*, perhaps the most popular fish for eating in the Hawaiian Islands.

If you are more interested in local art than flora and fauna, there is plenty around if you know where to look. Not far from here, at the Waikiki branch of First Hawaiian Bank (2189 Kalakaua Avenue) you will find the huge fresco mural *Early Contacts of Hawaii with Outer World*, by Jean Charlot.

If you're still feeling energetic after all this activity, it's possible to continue walking around the front of Diamond Head and into Kahala. There are spectacular views from Diamond Head Road overlooking the ocean, and the beach at Diamond Head Beach Park is a nice spot for a picnic. The loop from Kuhio Beach Park is about 4.5 miles (7km), so be sure to take plenty of water.

FACT

In 1927, world swimming records were set at the Waikiki Natatorium, a Beaux-Arts public pool that was a World War I memorial, west of Kapi'olani Park, by Buster Crabbe and Johnny Weissmuller, the future Hollywood Tarzan.

Moana Surfrider Hotel.

The WWII battleship USS Missouri.

GREATER HONOLULU

Outside Waikiki, away from the hustle and bustle of Downtown, Honolulu features mind-bending history, pristine valleys, and much more besides.

What can loosely be called Greater Honolulu stretches for around 15 miles (24km) along Oahu's southern shoreline. Its single most attractive feature has to be its physical setting, squeezed between the ocean and the soaring Ko'olau Mountains. Although the sharp, green-velvet ridge of the *pali* (cliffs) is often just three miles from the beach, the mountains are repeatedly indented by lush valleys. Several such valleys cradle characterful city neighborhoods, like Kalihi, Nu'uanu, and Manoa. Two major roads cross the mountains close to Downtown, the Likelike and Pali highways, while a meandering 8-mile (13km) route along Tantalus and Round Top drives enables visitors to enjoy some superb rainforest scenery.

Of course the biggest draw to this area is Pearl Harbor – named for the pearl oysters once found here – a cemetery and historic site that pays homage to those who lost their lives during the Japanese attack of Oahu on December 7, 1941. Few military memorials in the world offer the type of perspective that this one does.

Bernice Pauahi Bishop Museum

Greater Honolulu also is home to the world's greatest repository of Pacific and Polynesian artifacts: the **Bernice**

Pauahi Bishop Museum ㉓ (1525 Bernice Street; tel: 847-3511; www.bishopmuseum.org; Wed–Mon 9am–5pm). Anchoring the working-class neighborhood of Kalihi, 2 miles (3km) northwest of Downtown, the museum tells a colorful story of the history of the Hawaiian Islands, and how the region became a state. It is considered one of America's most important multi-disciplinary museums, a Smithsonian Institution in microcosm.

The museum was established in 1889 by Charles Reed Bishop as a

Main Attractions
Bishop Museum
Soto Zen Mission of Hawaii
Nu'uanu Pali Lookout
Lyon Arboretum
Pearl Harbor

Bernice Pauahi Bishop Museum.

FACT

The Bishop Museum also manages off-site attractions: a planetarium and astronomical observatory, the Falls of Clyde, and a four-masted sailing ship in Honolulu Harbor.

memorial to his wife Bernice, a princess and the last of the Kamehameha family. Today, with the help of grants and a steady endowment, the facility maintains natural history collections of nearly 20 million animal and plant specimens. Among the highlights of its central building, the cavernous and recently restored *koa*-paneled Hawaiian Hall (1903), are carved and feathered icons, capes, and many other remnants of pre-contact Hawaii; brilliant regalia from the time of Kamehameha the Great; the monarchical crowns, thrones, and court costumes used in 'Iolani Palace by King Kalakaua and his sister, Queen Lili'uokalani; and important pieces reflecting the experiences of Hawaii's many immigrant groups. Pacific Hall, which re-opened in 2013 after eight years of renovations, incorporates artifacts, photographs, and storytelling to take a broader look at island people from all over the Pacific.

Further galleries explore specific points in Hawaiian history, such as immigration, plantation-era island

life, and the push for statehood. Across the lawns, a modern building, the Richard T. Mamiya Science Adventure Center, explains vulcanology and Hawaiian natural history in an entertaining and kid-friendly way. Throughout the month, the museum hosts classes in a variety of aspects of Hawaiian culture, teaching visitors everything from hula to *lei*-making, basket-weaving, and more. It also has a small on-site café.

Oahu Cemetery

Nearby is the old **Oahu Cemetery**, where many names of rich or famous *haole* residents can be seen on tombstones. One in particular merits the attention of serious American sports fans: the layered, pink granite tomb with the inscription, "Alexander Joy Cartwright Jr. Born in New York City April 17, 1820. Died in Honolulu July 12, 1892." This austere monument, located at the center of the cemetery, marks the remains of the man who many believe to have invented modern baseball. After setting down the rules of the game – the first baseball

Interior of the Bernice Pauahi Bishop Museum.

contest played under Cartwright's rules took place in 1846 in Hoboken, New Jersey – Cartwright drifted west and eventually ended up in Hawaii. He founded Honolulu's first volunteer fire department and served as its fire chief from 1850 to 1859.

A few hundred yards/meters farther up Nuʻuanu Avenue is the **Royal Mausoleum** ㉔ (2261 Nuʻuanu Ave; Mon–Fri 8am–4pm; free), where the bodies of Kamehameha II, Kamehameha III, Kamehameha IV, Kamehameha V, Kalakaua, Queen Liliʻuokalani, and other members or favored friends of those royal Hawaiian families are buried. The only two Hawaiian monarchs not buried here are King Lunalilo, who at his own request was buried in the grounds of Kawaiahaʻo Church, and Kamehameha the Great, whose bones were hidden away in a secret burial place on Hawaii Island. The mausoleum, which lies on a 3-acre (1-hectare) site chosen by Kamehameha V, was prepared in 1865 to replace an overcrowded royal burial tomb on the grounds of ʻIolani Palace.

Queen Emma's Summer Palace

Half a mile (1 km) up the Pali Highway from its intersection with Nuʻuanu Avenue stands **Queen Emma's Summer Palace** ㉕ (2913 Pali Highway; tel: 595-3167; www.daughtersofhawaii.org; open daily 9am–4pm). This royal bower with a ginger- and *ti*-lined driveway was built in the late 1840s and later sold to John Young II, an uncle of Queen Emma and son of Kamehameha the Great's chief *haole* adviser, the Englishman John Young. Queen Emma and Kamehameha IV in turn bought it from Young and named it Hanaiakamalama, "the foster child of the moon," after a favorite Hawaiian demi-goddess.

Until Emma's death in 1885, the royal family used this home as a summer retreat, salon, and courtly social center. In 1890, the summer palace was bought by the Hawaiian government. The Daughters of Hawaii organization, a non-profit founded by women who were daughters of American Protestant missionaries, has maintained it as a museum since 1915.

The palace's rooms have been restored with many of the royal family's belongings. Among the items are a spectacular triple-tiered *koa* sideboard of Gothic design presented to Emma and Kamehameha IV by Britain's Prince Albert, the husband and consort of Queen Victoria; a heavy gold necklace strung with tiger claws and pearls given to Emma by a visiting maharajah; and various opulent wedding and baby gifts, which were given to the royal family by Queen Victoria, who was godmother to Emma's son, the Hawaiian Prince Albert. Among the most fascinating Hawaiian pieces is a stand of feather *kahili* (royal standards) in the queen's master bedroom. Behind and around the corner from the palace, off Puʻiwa Road, is a lovely little retreat, Nuʻuanu Valley Park, favored

Queen Emma's Summer Palace.

by lovers and daydreamers who like to lounge under its gigantic trees.

Nu'uanu

Just a half-mile or so inland from Chinatown (along Nu'uanu Avenue), and a mile east of the Bishop Museum, near the foot of the Pali Highway, **Nu'uanu** is perhaps Honolulu's prettiest valley. Even the name is beautiful – Nu'uanu, meaning the "cool height." There was no doubt among early *haole* settlers that Nu'uanu was the best place to live. Nu'uanu was the first suburb in which they built their Victorian mansions with broad *lanai*, and where they planted the monkeypods, banyans, Norfolk Island pines, bamboo, eucalyptus, African tulips, and golden trees that now tower over the valley's indigenous ferns, hibiscus, *koa*, and ginger. Many of these estates are still occupied by wealthy missionary descendants, but most have been sold or leased to institutions, churches, or Asian consulates.

Before exploring the valley's lush rainforest, listen for the "oms" vibrating out of the beautiful **Soto Zen Mission of Hawaii** (1708 Nu'uanu Avenue), a duplicate of a major Buddhist *stupa* at Bodhgaya, India, where Gautama Buddha gave his first sermon. This temple's towers would appear most at home on a Himalayan crag, but a few Japanese influences – gardens of tinkling water, sand, and bonsai – give its authenticity away. Built in 1952, the temple is somewhat similar to an even larger shrine, the nearby and hard-to-miss **Honpa Hongwanji Mission** (1727 Pali Highway), which was built in 1918 to commemorate the 700th anniversary of the creation of the Shin Buddhist sect.

Nu'uanu Pali Drive winds through the hanging vines, bamboo, wild ginger, jasmine, and cool air in two separate sections, east of the Pali Highway inland from Queen Emma's Palace. Along this wending path you'll spot stately mansions hidden away in the bushes, and, on rainy days, dozens of tiny waterfalls run wherever wrinkled Ko'olau ridges let them flow. **Waipuhia Valley Falls**, on the left side of Nu'uanu Valley just before you reach the Pali Lookout, is nicknamed

National Memorial Cemetery of the Pacific.

THE HAWAIIAN RAILWAY

In the heyday of the sugar cane industry, railroads were a popular way of transporting the product – and the people who harvested it – around each of the Hawaiian Islands. Today, however, the only railroad still operating on Oahu is the 'Ewa Train, which departs from the Hawaiian Railway Society's headquarters in 'Ewa, just outside of Honolulu, and runs to Nanakuli, about seven miles (11km) away. The train runs every Sunday with departures at 1pm and 3pm; each journey includes a historical narrative delivered by a volunteer. The Society also operates the only railroad museum in Hawaii; a small affair with artifacts and photographs from yesteryear. The on-site gift shop has a surprisingly large collection of Oahu Railway & Land Company branded merchandise.

"Upside Down Falls" because its waters are often blown straight back up a cliff and turn into mist before they can reach the precipice below. Waipuhia means "blown water."

The **Nu'uanu Pali Lookout** ㉖, just off the Pali Highway, is one of the most popular scenic attractions on Oahu, offering panoramic views of the *pali* (cliffs) and the Windward Coast. Gale-force winds rush up this Ko'olau palisade and literally stand one's hair on end. The view from the lookout is spectacular: sawtooth peaks rise like a great rampart, with lush flatlands facing a sea of all shades of blue.

Several spectacular trails start to the left of the lookout, including one atop an abandoned stretch of the old Pali Highway. From here, the Pali Highway continues down to the windward side and the bedroom communities of Kailua and Kane'ohe.

Punchbowl Crater and the National Memorial Cemetery

Another iconic Honolulu experience includes two areas above town between Nu'uanu and Manoa valleys, Punchbowl and Mount Tantalus. **Punchbowl Crater** ㉗, once a site of human sacrifices, was known to Hawaiians as Puowaina, or "the hill for placing [of sacrifices]." Like Diamond Head and Koko Head craters to the east, Punchbowl emerged during an eruption phase about 150,000 years ago. It was pushed upward by volcanic action through a vast coral plain that had built up around this side of the Ko'olau Mountains.

Today, Punchbowl is the site of the **National Memorial Cemetery of the Pacific**, where more than 40,000 war veterans and family members are buried. The small, flat, white headstones, set level with Punchbowl's expanse of grass, stretch across the crater's 112-acre (45-hectare) floor.

Perhaps the most famous person buried here was Ernest Taylor "Ernie" Pyle (1900–45), not a conventional war casualty but a journalist whose ability to write about the average foot-slogging GI during World War II made him one of the most widely read combat correspondents, and

View from Nu'uanu Pali Lookout.

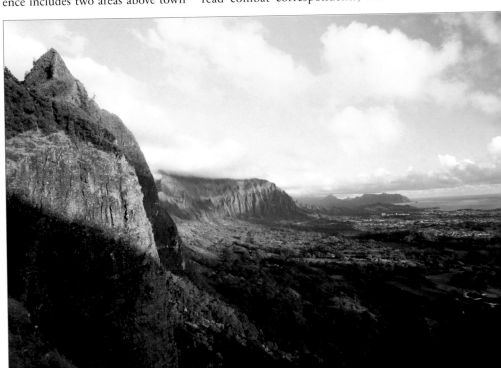

The University of Hawaii's Manoa campus, in the Manoa Valley.

earned him the Pulitzer Prize in 1944. The following year, he was killed by Japanese gunfire on a small Pacific islet. Pyle's burial here was allowed because he had served in the US Navy during World War I. More than 60 years after his death, cemetery officials have estimated that as many as 50,000 people a month visit his grave.

Tantalus

From Punchbowl's mountain-side entrance, Puowaina Drive crosses a bridge over Prospect Street and drifts along a steep valley through Papakolea, one of Oahu's few Hawaiian homestead communities. At the top of Puowaina Drive, turn right onto Tantalus Drive, a winding mountain road that twists and turns through some of Oahu's largest *kama'aina* estates. **Mount Tantalus** ㉘ has some of the coolest and most panoramic vantage points on this side of the island. You can hike one of the marked trails near the mountain's 2,013ft (610-meter) peak into groves of bamboo and fern. At the top,

Tantalus Drive connects with Round Top Drive, which descends down the ocean side to Makiki and Punahou.

There are at least a dozen knockout viewpoints on Tantalus, but locals agree that the best one, a panorama extending from Diamond Head to Pearl Harbor and the Wai'anae Mountains, is from **Pu'u 'Ualaka'a State Park** ㉙, on Tantalus's Diamond Head flank.

A few hairpin turns below this peak is a straight stretch of Round Top Drive beside a lava rock wall, with an unobstructed postcard view of Diamond Head, the University of Hawaii, and broad Manoa Valley. Down below in Makiki Heights is the **Spalding House** ㉚ (2411 Makiki Heights Drive; tel: 526-1322; www.tcmhi.org; Tue–Sat 10am–4pm, Sun noon–4pm), a beautifully maintained contemporary art museum hosting top-class, regularly changing temporary exhibitions, with a gift shop and an appealing café that is a good place for lunch. The facility existed for years as the Contemporary Museum, but changed its name and merged with the Honolulu Museum of Art in 2011. Admission to the Spalding House includes admission to the Honolulu Museum of Art on the same day.

Manoa

Manoa Valley ③, meaning "vast," has long been preferred by islanders as a residential refuge from the heat and hassle of Honolulu's coastal flatlands. Indeed, residents of both Manoa and Nu'uanu consider their valleys the closest one can get to Eden – both are verdantly green and consistently wet – and still manage to be near shopping centers and bus routes.

At the mouth of this easy-going valley is the center of higher education in Hawaii, the large **University of Hawaii** ③ Manoa campus, attended by some 18,000 full-time students. This institute has the academic and post-adolescent aura typical of any university in the world, except that its student body, like Hawaii itself, is generally more diverse and casual – loud T-shirts, shorts and sandals – and more ethnically mixed than the typical US university campus. The university's sports teams are nicknamed the Rainbow Warriors.

At the **East–West Center** – a federally funded institute on the university campus that promotes understanding in the Pacific Basin – are a Thai pavilion personally presented and dedicated by King Bhumibol Adulyadej of Thailand in 1967; a Center for Korean Studies building handpainted in the busy and intricate style of Seoul-area Yi dynasty palaces; and the center's main building, Jefferson Hall, which is fronted by large Chinese dog-faced lions and backed by a Japanese garden rich in sculptured grass, bonsai trees, and a lily pond full of nibbling koi carp.

Arboretum and falls

Half a mile or so beyond Punahou School and beyond the university is the junction of Manoa and East Manoa roads. Branching left, Manoa Road leads to the back of the valley and the University of Hawaii's **Lyon Arboretum** ③ (3860 Manoa Road; tel: 988-0456; Mon–Fri 8am–4pm, Sat 9am–3pm; free), established in 1907. Nearly 6,000 plants grow on the arboretum's 120 acres (48 hectares), on land rising from 300ft (90 meters) to 1,800ft (550 meters) above sea level. Tropical and native Hawaiian plants, conservation biology, and Hawaiian ethnobotany are the major themes here.

Nearby, cool **Manoa Falls**, accessed via a steep trail that climbs through spectacular rainforest for just under a mile, is fed by 160–200ins (4,065–5,080mm) of rain a year (and is a haven for insects; bring repellent and wear long sleeves).

Pearl Harbor

One of the major reasons why the US annexed Hawaii, at the end of the 19th century, was to acquire control of **Pearl Harbor** ③. This vast inlet, at the heart of Oahu's southern

The red cap cardinal is native to South America but was introduced to Hawaii in the 1930s.

Bamboo trail around Mount Tantalus.

Commissioned on December 7, 1942, the USS Bowfin was later mothballed in the Middle Loch of Pearl Harbor until it was brought out of retirement.

Inside the USS Arizona Memorial.

coast, is the finest harbor for 2,000 miles (3,200km) in any direction. As the base of the US Pacific Fleet, it became the target of the notorious Japanese surprise attack on the morning of December 7, 1941. Denounced by President Roosevelt as a "date which will live in infamy," it immediately precipitated US entry into World War II.

Japanese torpedoes and dive-bombers, launched from an armada 200 miles (320km) northwest, destroyed a total of 18 warships that day. Their most famous victim is now the focus of the **USS Arizona Memorial ㉟** (tel: 422-0561; www.nps.gov/usar; visitor center daily 7.30am–4.30pm; shuttle boats run 8am–3pm, weather permitting; to reserve tickets online (which is advised) visit www.recreation.gov.). US Navy boats ferry a constant stream of visitors to stand on the dazzling white platform that straddles the wreck of the USS Arizona, still visible, indeed still leaking oil, where it sank beneath the waters, carrying almost 1,200 of its crew to their deaths.

Designed by Honolulu architect Alfred Preis, the memorial was made possible in part by a benefit concert staged in 1961 by Elvis Presley, as his first public performance after leaving the US Army. It's the most popular free attraction on Oahu, with more than a million visitors annually – some 4,000 daily – so reserving online is advised to avoid at best a long wait or at worst the attraction being fully booked. The visitor center has a museum and bookshop to keep you occupied should you need to wait.

USS *Bowfin* and USS *Missouri*

A few minutes' walk from the USS *Arizona* Memorial visitor center, across the parking lot, brings you to the privately operated **USS Bowfin Submarine Museum & Park** (tel: 423-1341; www.bowfin.org; daily 7am–5pm). Would-be submariners and the curious can check out defused torpedoes, and descend into and walk through a completely refurbished World War II diesel-electric submarine, the USS *Bowfin*, which is credited with sinking 44 ships in nine patrols, many of them well inside Japanese waters.

Shuttle buses run from the *Bowfin* across a slender road bridge to reach Ford Island, which is otherwise barred to non-military personnel. Their destination is a decommissioned World War II battleship, moored a short way along from the USS *Arizona* Memorial – the **USS *Missouri*** (tel: 973-2494; www.ussmissouri.org; Sept–May 8am–4pm, June–Aug 8am–5pm). Known affectionately as the "Mighty Mo," this was the last battleship ever built by the US, in 1944 and was retired in 1992. You can visit the Missouri by yourself or take one of the guided tours – the 35-minute "Mighty Mo Tour" swings by the site of the surrender that ended World War II, while the 75-minute "Heart of the Missouri" tour ventures down the longest and widest passage on the ship. Whichever you choose to do, the highlight will be the precise spot on deck where Japan's surrender was signed in Tokyo Bay in September 1945.

USS Bowfin.

Another monument, considerably lower in profile and cost, can be found on Ford Island alongside the rusting hulk of the USS *Utah*. Civilians, however, can visit the site only if accompanied by a member or dependent of the United States military. At neighboring **Hickam Air Force Base**, a plaque marks the spot where the *Apollo 11* astronauts first touched earth after their walk on the moon in 1969.

The USS Arizona Memorial.

ORIGINS OF A MONUMENT

The USS *Arizona* Memorial grew out of a wartime desire to establish some sort of memorial at Pearl Harbor to honor those who died in the attack. Suggestions for such a memorial began in 1943, but it wasn't until 1949, when the Territory of Hawaii established the Pacific War Memorial Commission, that the first real steps were taken to make it a reality. Initial recognition came in 1950 when Admiral Arthur Radford, Commander in Chief, Pacific, ordered that a flagpole be erected over the sunken battleship USS *Arizona*. On the ninth anniversary of the attack, a commemorative plaque was placed at the base of the flagpole.

President Dwight D. Eisenhower, who helped achieve Allied victory in Europe during World War II, approved the creation of the Memorial in 1958. Its construction was completed in 1961 with public funds appropriated by Congress and private donations. The Memorial was dedicated in 1962. According to its architect, Alfred Preis, the design of the Memorial, "Wherein the structure sags in the center but stands strong and vigorous at the ends, expresses initial defeat and ultimate victory....The overall effect is one of serenity. Overtones of sadness have been omitted to permit the individual to contemplate his own personal responses...his innermost feelings."

SOUTHEAST OAHU

Beyond Diamond Head, Oahu becomes a mix of lush jungle, dense neighborhoods, and, of course, pristine beaches.

Main Attractions

Diamond Head
Koko Head Trail
Hanauma Bay
Makapu'u Point and
  lighthouse
Waimanolo Beach

On the trail to Diamond Head.

This is the part of Oahu where the city gives way to the country, where it appears humans have remembered that nature is in charge. The most noticeable landmark is mighty Diamond Head, which towers to the east of Waikiki and is the most conspicuous of the chain of ancient volcanic cinder cones that rise from the coastline. Rent a car and drive beyond Honolulu's most luxurious residential neighborhoods to some dramatic beaches and scenery, including the popular snorkeling site of Hanauma Bay,

the hiking trails of Makapu'u, and the soft sand of Waimanalo. As you go, take advantage of the many pull-outs – these are here for slower cars to allow faster traffic to pass, but they also are the perfect excuse to stop and enjoy the view.

Diamond Head

You can actually drive into the extinct volcanic tuff cone of **Diamond Head** ❶, and hike up the inner walls to its sea-side rim 761ft (231 meters) above the beach. It's well worth the short but steep hike. The view of

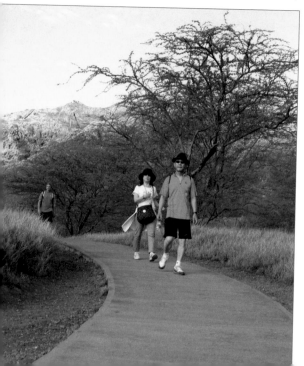

HIKE TO THE RIM

The hike to the rim of Diamond Head is, without question, the most popular (and most accessible) hike on the island of Oahu. Though the trail isn't long – most reliable GPS units clock it at less than 2 miles (3km) – the way to the top is almost entirely uphill, climbing 560ft (170 meters) from the trailhead. The hike begins on pavement, then switches to dirt and follows some switchbacks to a flight of stairs. From there, head through a tunnel and up more stairs before reaching old bunkers at the top. At this point, if you're not too winded, climb atop the bunkers for a 360-degree view of the island, the ocean, and Waikiki Beach. Another tip: bring sunscreen and lots of water, as there is almost no shade at all along the way.

Waikiki and Oahu's South Shore is one of the island's best, and atop one of the abandoned World War II gun emplacements there is a comfortable picnic spot. The crater's interior and exterior slopes are part of the 500-acre (200-hectare) Diamond Head State Monument. Inside the crater there's a visitor center, as well as civil defense and National Guard facilities, and an air traffic control facility of the Federal Aviation Administration.

Diamond Head is a nickname given the crater in 1825 by British sailors who mistook worthless calcite crystals found on its slopes for diamonds. Its original Hawaiian name was Lae'ahi, which means "brow" (*lae*) of the yellow-fin tuna (*'ahi*). Hawaiian legends say that the fire goddess Hi'iaka, Pele's younger sister, noticed the resemblance between Diamond Head's profile and that of the *'ahi* and named it Lae'ahi. In later years this was shortened by mapmakers to Leahi. Its steep slopes were favored for *holua* sliding, a tropical form of tobogganing over dry ground.

Long before this tuff cone became Hawaii's most famous landmark, Lae'ahi was the site of the Papa'ena'ena *heiau*, an important temple. According to historical accounts, some of the last human sacrifices ordered by Kamehameha the Great took place at this *heiau* following the decisive Battle of Nu'uanu Valley, in 1795. Early descriptions indicate that the *heiau* was located below Diamond Head's jutting brow. A lovely estate called La Petra, now the Hawaii School for Girls, is built on the site.

Kahala and Hawai'i Kai

Beyond Diamond Head, at the eastern end of the H-1 highway, stands the high-priced neighborhood of **Kahala** ❷. Following Hawaii's statehood in 1959, this part of the island became increasingly residential as Honolulu proper began running out of living space. Today, Kahala is one of Oahu's most desirable neighborhoods. At the end of ritzy Kahala Avenue is the Kahala Hotel & Resort. Built in 1959, the hotel has become the Hawaiian escape for those with money and status. A walk along Kahala Beach toward Diamond Head leads past immaculate

TIP

The drive between Hanauma Bay and Sandy Beach is stunning but challenging; the road is narrow and twisting, with many blind spots so keep your eyes on the road if you are driving.

View of Waikiki from the summit of Diamond Head.

Hawai'i Kai marina.

beachfront estates. In the other direction is the Wai'alae Country Club.

Further along Kalaniana'ole Highway, toward Oahu's southeastern tip, is the sprawling **Hawai'i Kai** , created by the late billionaire industrialist Henry J. Kaiser during the early 1960s. The development included converting Kuapa, once Hawaii's largest fishpond, into a marina for Kaiser's master-planned suburb, now home to more than 35,000 people. Check out the variety of water activities, from parasailing to snorkeling, offered by Hawaii Water Sports Center, located in Hawai'i Kai's Koko Marina complex (tel: 395-3773; www.hawaiiwatersportscenter.com); they will take you out into the neon-blue waters of Maunalua Bay. Once past Hawai'i Kai the Kalaniana'ole Highway cuts over a saddle ridge at **Koko Head**, yet another cinder cone, named either for the striking red earth common in the area or for the blood *(koko)* of a man bitten by a shark long ago. Koko Head also boasts one of the toughest summit trails anywhere in Hawaii; a hike that includes more than 1,000 wooden steps.

Coastline near Halona Blowhole.

Hanauma Bay and Sandy Beach

Even beach-loving tourists who otherwise never leave Waikiki during their entire trip emerge at least once to make the pilgrimage to gorgeous **Hanauma Bay** (tel: 396-4229; summer: Wed–Mon, 6am–7pm, winter 6am–6pm). Famed since Elvis Presley's 1961 movie *Blue Hawaii* as Oahu's premier snorkeling spot, Hanauma is also exceptionally pretty in its own right. Its name, meaning "curved bay," is an understatement. Cradled in what remains of an eroded extinct volcanic tuff cone, the bay is inhabited by enough protected but bold Hawaiian fish to seduce any snorkeler.

Daily visitor numbers are carefully regulated to minimize environmental harm – if you arrive any later than 9am you may not be allowed in – and the entire site remains closed every Tuesday. Snorkeling equipment is available for rent, and all visitors are obliged to watch an educational film. No food or water is sold at the beach, but if you bring your own supplies this is a great place to spend the whole day.

After Hanauma Bay, the feeling of a city evaporates. At the next cliffside turn, *makai* (the ocean side) of Koko Crater, tourists wait at a parking lot lookout to hear the **Halona Blowhole** , a lava formation that emits a geyser-like wheeze when incoming sea swells push up through its underwater entrance.

Appropriately, *halona* means "peering place." Just along the coast, before you round Makapu'u Point to Oahu's windward side, is **Sandy Beach** , a local favorite for bodysurfing, people-watching, and, in season, an occasional whale sighting. If you go, watch those waves – in winter, they're lethally dangerous to all but experts.

Makapu'u

Continue northward from Sandy Beach along winding Kalaniana'ole Highway and watch for **Makapu'u Beach Park** , which is bounded y rough open seas, sheer lava-rock liffs, and hill-sized dunes. Makapuʻu s prized for its bodysurfing waves. Lifeguards are stationed on the beach.

The rocky summit on the right s **Makapuʻu Point**, where a white ighthouse is perched on the craggy black-lava palisade. A paved road leading up to the lighthouse is closed to automobiles but is accessible by foot; the view of the coastline is well worth he easy hike.

On Makapuʻu's *mauka* (mountain) ide sits **Sea Life Park** ❽. Among the highlights is a 300,000-gallon (113,562-liter) Hawaiian reef tank, illed with sharks, rays, sea turtles, and teeming with fish of every color. The park also maintains a wildlife rehabilitation unit, and is called upon when marine animals are found in distress.

Waimanalo

f you are looking for a beach with plenty of empty space, an awesome mountain *pali* (high-cliff) backdrop, and warm waters to soak in, **Waimanalo Beach** ❾ has few eers, but it's one of those gems

that are often overlooked by visitors. **Waimanalo** ❿ is as local a town as anywhere in Hawaii, a place where the rural Hawaiian lifestyle is sustained. Perhaps the area's most notable resident was Gabby Pahinui (1921–80), a slack-key guitarist and one of Hawaii's finest musicians. Another famous son of Waimanalo is Chad Rowan, born here in 1969, a sumo star who fought in Japan under the name Akebono (Sunrise). In 1993, he became the first *gaijin* (foreigner) ever to ascend to the rank of *yokozuna*, or grand champion, in sumo.

Beyond Waimanalo and **Bellows Air Force Station** rises 1,643ft (499-meter) **Olomana**. Named for a giant who jumped from Kauai to Oahu, Olomana casts morning shadows over **Maunawili**, an emerald vale where two parting lovers inspired Queen Liliʻuokalani to write her timeless song *Aloha ʻOe*. Just minutes past Maunawili's pastures and farms are Oahu's second and third most populated towns – Kailua and Kaneʻohe (see page 149) – which unfurl in a hybrid of modern suburbia and natural setting.

Body boarding at Sandy Beach.

Snorkeling heaven at Hanauma Bay.

Touring the Hakipuʻu Valley in a 6x6 Swiss Pinzgauer from Kualoa Ranch.

WINDWARD OAHU

Lush, verdant mountains and valleys are the result of heavy winds and rain on the eastern coast of Oahu. Amid all this green, there's plenty to marvel at.

Map on page 108

In Hawaii, the "windward" side of each island is the side that is blitzed by wind and rain every winter. The result is forests like the ones on the television series *Lost*. On Oahu, this stretch begins near the beginning of the majestic **Ko'olau Mountains**. Like a massive curtain that parts now and then to expose lone spires, fluted columns, crystal falls, and deep green valleys, these sheer cliffs dwarf everything in their vicinity. Ko'olau wears, as the Hawaiians like to poetically say, *lei i ka noe*. (mist as a *lei*); on and on the mountains stretch, from Makapu'u in Southeast Oahu nearly to the North Shore, encircling enchanting towns such as Kailua in between.

Kailua

Take the Pali Highway up from Honolulu, and, dropping down the sheer flank of the Ko'olau Mountains beyond the Nu'uanu Pali Lookout, you will reach Oahu's second largest town, **Kailua ⓫**. This unremarkable suburb has become famous in recent years because it is where President Obama and his family celebrate Christmas, but the area also is known for the famous banyan tree on the corner of Oneawa Street and Ku'ulei Road. If you're entering **Kailua** around sunset, pass by the tree and

witness the wonderful sight of scores of mynah birds gathering to roost for the night, kicking up a squawking fuss. Of course the beaches in this area are top-notch, too. A fine beach stretches the length of **Kailua Bay**, and the most convenient access to this swathe of sand is at **Kailua Beach Park ⓬**. (Some locals might argue that beaches at Kalama and Lanikai are just as good.) The water just off these beaches often is the site of international windsurfing competitions. Beyond the surfsails, beyond

Main Attractions
Kailua
Kane'ohe Bay
Kualoa Regional Park
Kualoa Ranch
Polynesian Cultural Center

Outrigger at Lanikai Beach, Kailua.

the breaking waves, sit a number of small sanctuary islands named the Mokuluas and Popo'ia. All of them are swimmable from Kailua Beach Park.

Kane'ohe

North of Kailua, Kane'ohe is a bedroom community for Honolulu and the nearby marine base, with residential subdivisions that hug shimmering **Kane'ohe Bay** and the *pali* (steep cliffs). The large Kane'ohe Marine Corps Air Station dominates scenic Mokapu Peninsula. Just offshore, Mokuolo'e, better known as Coconut Island, is the site of the Hawaii Institute of Marine Biology, run by the University of Hawaii.

Stunning Kane'ohe Bay is a popular recreation area, protected by outlying reefs and good for most watersports. Several catamarans offer day trips to the bay's central sandbar. Kane'ohe means "bamboo husband." One interpretation says that a woman of ancient times compared the cruelty of her husband with a sharp bamboo knife; others suggest the name refers to one of his physical attributes.

Cultural attractions in the area include the serene **Byodo-In Temple** ⑭ (47-200 Kahekili Highway; tel: 239-8811; daily 9am–5pm), a termite-proof, cement replica of Kyoto's famous Byodo-In Temple of Equality. It is the major structure in the **Valley of the Temples Memorial Park**. A 7-ton bronze bell, a 2-acre (0.8-hectare) reflecting lake, peacocks, swans, ducks, meditation niches, and tinkling waterfalls enhance its imported architecture.

Of cultural and historical importance is a series of ancient fishponds that pepper windward shores north of Kane'ohe. The splendid **He'eia Fishpond** ⑮, on the Kane'ohe side of **Kealohi Point**, is Oahu's biggest. It has a wall 12ft (3.6 meters) wide and 5,000ft (1,500 meters) long, and once enclosed an area of 88 acres (35 hectares).

Visiting the site provides perspective on exactly how big fishpond operations were back in the heyday. A stop here also provides a good

Byodo-In Temple.

ROYAL GETAWAY

In past centuries, the beauty of the windward city of Kailua drew vacationing Hawaiian royalty. These days, at least some of that appeal is back: US President Barack Obama and his family have celebrated Christmas and New Year in the area every year since 2008. The American "royals" have spent most of those years in the same 5,000-sq-ft (465-sq-meter) beachfront home that rents for $3,500 per night. Because the house is white, locals have dubbed it the "Winter White House." Obama's draw to the place goes back decades; he spent time in Kailua as a child and apparently always had wanted to return with his family to enjoy what is now a chic beach town with a laid-back vibe and a beach that some claim to be Hawaii's best.

opportunity for personal reflection; something about the site today is almost sacred in nature.

Another worthwhile stop is **Senator Fong's Plantation and Gardens** 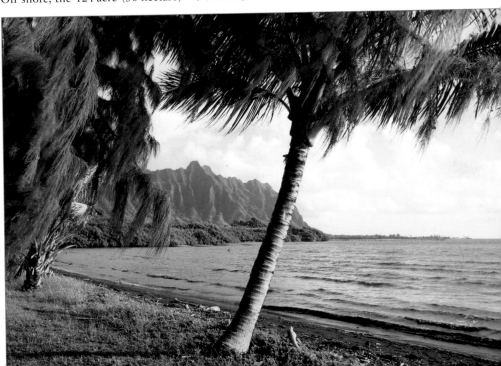 (47-285 Pulama Road; tel: 239-6775; www.fonggarden.com; daily 10am–2.30pm), a 725-acre (293-hectare) attraction owned by the former US Senator Hiram Fong, with gardens of exotic flowers, scenic views of windward Oahu, and guided tram tours.

Kualoa: park and ranch

At **Kualoa Regional Park**, heads usually crane seaward for lingering looks at a small, distinct island known to Hawaiians as **Mokoli'i** (which means the little *mo'o*, or lizard). Long ago, the conical island was nicknamed Chinaman's Hat. At low tide, one can easily wade out on the reef to this island (reef shoes are recommended), bask under palm trees, and photograph the graceful Hawaiian stilts *(ae'o)* and frigate birds *(iwa)* that soar overhead. On shore, the 124-acre (50-hectare)

Moli'i Fishpond, easy to spot with a 4,000ft (1,200-meter) -long retaining wall, has been in cultivation for 800 years. This is also a very good place to see endangered Hawaiian waterfowl. Kualoa has long been sacred to the ancient Hawaiians and was favored as a royal residence.

Inland is the **Kualoa Ranch** (tel: 237-7321; www.kualoa.com), the largest of the few working cattle ranches still left on Oahu. In recent years, the enterprising owners have developed it as a film location, notably for *Lost*, and as a popular tourist destination, offering activities like horseback riding, snorkeling, and jet-skiing at the beach park just across the street, plus helicopter tours that take in this spectacular stretch of coast and mountains.

Equally impressive is a sailing trip in a catamaran to Kane'ohe Bay's sweeping sandbar. Set in the middle of the bay's waters and backed by the towering *pali*, this is Hawaii at its most beautiful. For information call Captain Bob's Picnic Sail (tel: 942-5077).

FACT

Oahu once had nearly 100 fishponds used by Hawaiians to grow seafood. Now, only five are left intact. Four are on this Windward Coast: He'eia (north of Kane'ohe), Kahalu'u, Moli'i (off Kualoa Point), and Huilua (Kahana Bay). The fifth is at Oki'okiolepe, in Pearl Harbor.

On the beach looking towards Kualoa.

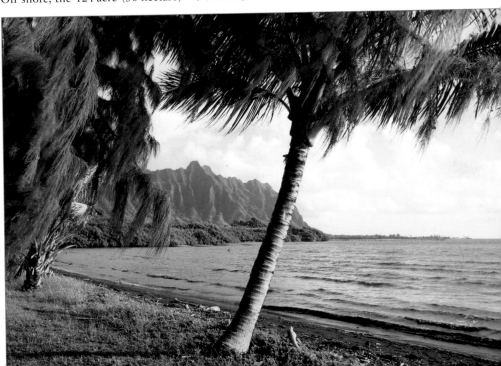

FACT

According to local legend, Kauhi, a demi-god from Tahiti, was imprisoned on a rock by the goddess Pele. But Kauhi fell in love with Pele's sister Hiʻaka and tried to escape to be with her. He was frozen into stone in a crouching position, which is why the rock is called the Crouching Lion.

Kahana and Hauʻula

Beyond Kaʻaʻawa is Mahie Point, which overlooks the *hala* (screwpine) groves, reedy lagoons, and whistling ironwood that rim the silent beauty of **Kahana Bay** ⓳. Off the point, there is a rock formation at the Point called **Kauhi**, better known as Crouching Lion.

Kahana Bay itself shelters a fine beach of grayish sand, while the valley behind, which is still farmed in the traditional manner by native Hawaiians, offers a couple of good hiking trails.

Straw baskets bulging with plump papayas, avocados, and Chinese bananas hanging inside weathered wooden stands compete with shell chandeliers for the traveler's dollar along this stretch to **Hauʻula**. Further hiking trails enable adventurous walkers to explore the hillsides behind the little residential community of Hauʻuh.

One place trails no longer go is **Sacred Falls State Park** ⓴, which is known as **Kaliuwaʻa Falls** in Hawaiian. Due to a landslide that claimed eight lives in 1999, the trail to Kaliuwaʻa has been closed indefinitely. Now, for those intent on getting back to see the area, the only option is a helicopter tour.

Polynesian Cultural Center and environs

Three miles (5km) north of Hauʻula is **Laʻie** ㉑, a predominantly Mormon community that's home to the Hawaii campus of Brigham Young University, as well as the chaste-looking **Mormon Temple**, built in 1919 by descendants of missionary Mormons living in this area since 1864. The temple is closed to non-Mormons; however, its visitor center is open to all.

Laʻie is very much on the tourist map, thanks to the **Polynesian Cultural Center** ㉒ (tel: 1-800-367-7060; www.polynesia.com; Mon–Sat noon–10pm), which manages to educate more than a million visitors each year about the history and culture of the Pacific islands, despite its decidedly theme-park presentation. Your hosts are native islanders

Horseback trekking through Kualoa Valley scenery.

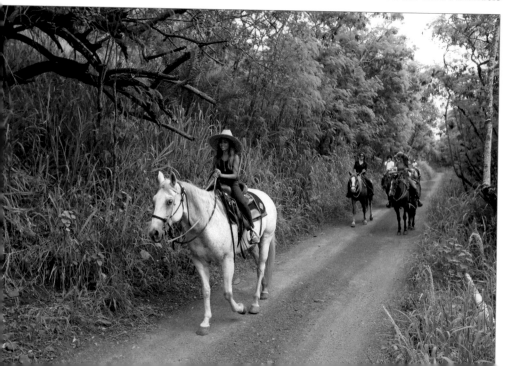

whose enthusiasm and warmth are infectious, and the activities range from the serious to the comical, with plenty to keep you occupied and entertained. There are boat rides, luaus, and even an IMAX theater that adds a high-tech element to the experience.

The center's main shows – performed nightly by young Mormon students from Fiji, Samoa, Tahiti, Tonga, the Marquesas, New Zealand, and Hawaii – are designed, according to brochures, to give visitors a "pure cultural view of Polynesia." Exactly how much you pay for the experience depends on which of the many possible packages, including meals and shows, you choose to buy, but it can easily run into hundreds of dollars. The center runs special buses from Waikiki if you'd rather not drive.

Just north of the cultural center is **La'ie Point**, at the end of Anemoku and Naupaka streets and where windward waters running hard from the north pound two little offshore isles – **Kukuiho'olua** and **Mokualai**

– with a frightening and beautiful force, especially in winter.

Kahuku ㉓ is an ex-plantation town where the only landmark is a former sugar mill (it closed in 1971). The site is now a rather run-down shopping mall, though sadly its towering chimney stack, deemed a health and safety hazard, had to be demolished in 2004. Here you will discover a place where workers' cafés, grocery stores, karate *dojo,* and tiny homes survive much as they did when residents awoke to the mill's morning steam whistle. A walk around this village, where ferns and orchids hang in bleach-bottle planters, is pleasant and usually highly rewarding.

Aquaculture is very big business in the Kahuku area. Shrimp, shellfish, and edible seaweed are all cultivated in large ponds that flank the James Campbell National Wildlife Refuge. Roadside stands offer the freshest and best catches of the day's harvest; if you drive past one, don't fret, as you likely will pass about six more before leaving the region.

Students from the University of Hawaii perform a traditional Samoan dance on a canoe at the Polynesian Cultural Center.

NORTH SHORE

Home to some of the best and most hallowed breaks in the world, Oahu's sleepy North Shore is where serious surfers go to catch some serious waves.

Main Attractions
Ted's Bakery
Waimea Bay
Hale'iwa
Pu'uomahuka Heiau
State Monument

The Banzai Pipeline reef break is off Ehukai Beach.

Both figuratively and literally, the North Shore is as far away from Waikiki as one can get without leaving Oahu. On the map, it's clear on the other side of the island. It's also got a totally different vibe; life here is just slower. And that's the appeal.

The first major landmark encountered on the North Shore, continuing from the windward side, is the **Turtle Bay Resort** , on a dramatic point extending into the ocean, with dramatic vistas of storms and waves. A few miles farther, the world's finest surfing waves crash onto offshore reefs and sandbars: Sunset, Rocky Point, Banzai Pipeline, Waimea Bay, Chun's Reef, Hale'iwa, and Avalanche. Each of these spots corresponds to a pocket beach off the main road. In summer, the beaches are ideal spots to witness Hawaiian Monk Seals or green sea turtles in the wild (just don't get too close). Year-round, **Ted's Bakery**, across the street from Sunset Beach, is a great place to grab a coffee and a slice of coconut cream pie.

Calm in summer and for much of the year, **Waimea Bay** ㉕ hosts monster waves when the North Shore feels the fury of winter storms in the Arctic that drive rough seas toward Hawaii. In December 1969, more than 30 homes between Kahuku Point and Hale'iwa were reduced to tinder as monstrous 50ft (15-meter) waves pounded the North Shore. The most jaded surfer will agree that a tubing, top-to-bottom wave off one of those reefs generates enough adrenaline to keep anybody going through at least a few nervous lifetimes, especially when Waimea Bay is breaking with waves so big that hundreds of people line the road like spectators at a gladiator show. The waves are so thunderous that the ground trembles underfoot. Only the best surfers paddle out toward the 20 to 30ft (7- to 10-meter) winter swells lifting like glossy black holes on the blue-gray horizon.

A good place to take in Waimea Bay, most of the North Shore, and the distant Wai'anae Mountains is from the

17th-century **Pu'uomahuka Heiau State Monument** ㉖, on a 250ft (75-meter) bluff above the **St Peter and Paul Church**. To get there, turn off from the main road onto Pupukea Road, at the fire station and supermarket.

At the very top of the bluff, on a marked side road, is an ancient *heiau*, or temple. It is one of Oahu's largest, and Hawaiians still leave offerings for the gods, usually lava stones wrapped in *ti* leaves, on its walls. It was known as Pu'uomahuka, the hill of escape, although historically not for some. In May 1792, two crew members (some accounts say three) of Captain George Vancouver's ship HMS *Daedalus* were offered in sacrifice at this *heiau* after being captured while filling water barrels at the mouth of the Waimea River. During that period, the Hawaiians had an insatiable desire to procure guns and ammunition.

When Vancouver was informed of what had happened, he pledged to track down and punish the culprits, and eventually he did. Three Hawaiians were executed with a pistol by their own chiefs in full view of islanders and crewmen. There is some debate as to whether the trio were the actual offenders. Some historians believe Oahu's wily ruler, Kahekili, rounded up three innocent people and "sacrificed" them to assuage the British captain. Whatever the truth may be, the *heiau* is a somber, foreboding place.

Where Waimea River enters Waimea Bay, on the *mauka* (mountain) side of the road, just east of the beach park, look for the entrance to **Waimea Valley** ㉗ (59-864 Kamehameha Highway; tel: 638-7766; www.waimeavalley.net; daily 9am–5pm). This 1,800-acre (728-hectare) botanical garden used to be run as a theme park, but now serves as a nature preserve. Trails leading well over a mile back into the valley, and culminating at a spectacular waterfall, enable visitors to enjoy more than 6,000 varieties of native and imported plants, many of which have magnificently colorful flowers.

Farther westward along the North Shore's surfing grounds, a small cement bridge funnels traffic over a little stream into **Hale'iwa** ㉘ (House of the Frigate Bird), an arty and funky

Lush vegetation in the nature preserve of Waimea Valley.

Waimea Falls.

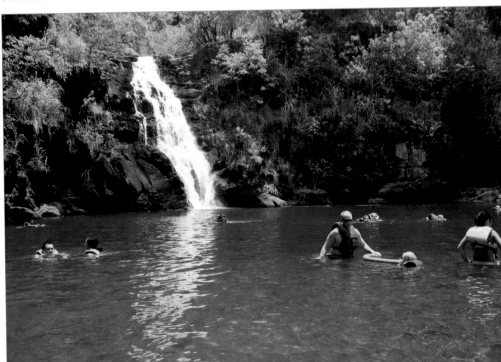

outpost – but the biggest town on this side of Oahu – where people of all ethnic backgrounds and lifestyles mingle. An eclectic mix of trendy cafés, art galleries, boutiques, and shops mix with remnants of the old plantation days. No visit to Hale'iwa would be complete without a stop at Matsumoto General Store (66–87 Kamehameha Highway; daily 9am–6pm), famous for shave ice, complete with azuki beans and ice cream at the bottom.

A mid-summer visit to Hale'iwa coincides with the height of the Japanese *Obon* season, when the **Hale'iwa Jodo Mission** has its annual lantern festival, *toronagashi*, with dozens of flickering lanterns – each a farewell light for an ancestor's spirit – floating on the dark sea to the east side of **Kaiaka Bay**. Hale'iwa also hosts the **Hale'iwa Festival** in July and the **Hale'iwa Taro Festival** in September, two celebrations that offer a hometown glimpse into Hawaiian culture.

Northwest Oahu

From Hale'iwa, continue south down the Kamehameha Highway through central Oahu and back to Honolulu, or head farther east past taro and banana patches to the old plantation town of Waialua. Beyond Waialua, on the *mauka* (mountain) side of Farrington Highway, is the **Mokule'ia Polo Farm**, where teams from around the world battle through chukkas of polo against local pony teams (most Sundays from March to July). Farther down the road is the **Dillingham Airfield** ㉙, where Honolulu Soaring (tel: 637-0207; www.honolulusoaring.com) take to the skies alongside the 2,000ft (610-meter) -high Wai'anae *pali*. The more courageous can skydive with Skydive Hawaii (tel: 637-9700; www.hawaiiskydiving.com), which also departs from Dillingham. At the end of the road beyond Mokule'ia, a foot trail continues to **Ka'ena Point** ㉚, the westernmost tip of Oahu where the Hawaiians believed the souls of the dead departed to the afterlife. The surrounding area is now a wildlife conservation district. Beyond, on foot, is the Wai'anae Coast. Waves as high as 50ft (15 meters) have been witnessed off Ka'ena Point.

Hale'iwa.

Surfing

Surfing is said to have started in Hawaii, and it makes sense that the sport has established itself as the unofficial pastime of the island chain.

Surfing is as much a part of Hawaiian culture as hula, *lu'aus* and *'ukulele* music. Some historians believe that a primitive form of surfing originated somewhere in the Pacific around 2000 BC. It is likely that when the first Polynesians migrated to the Hawaiian Islands around AD 400, they were already well versed in the sport.

Early Hawaiians called surfing *he'e nalu*, which literally translates as "wave sliding." Hawaiian chants dating from the 15th century recount surfing exploits, indicating that *he'e nalu* had become so developed that competitions were held among famous surfers, usually royalty, or *ali'i*. These were widely heralded affairs, sometimes pitting chiefs against each other; crowds of supporters would indulge in high-stakes gambling by placing property bets on a favored wave rider.

One Hawaiian legend tells the story of Kawelo, whose wife was taken by his brother, the ruling chief 'Aikanaka. Full of anguish, Kawelo was plotting his revenge when he suddenly noticed a crowd on the beach, enjoying *he'e nalu*. Overcome with desire, Kawelo at once forgot completely about his wife and 'Aikanaka and headed for the beach to engage in his favorite pastime. No wonder one long-time surfer says, "Perfect waves are miracles. When they come, everything else stops, including romance."

Waves of change

Gone are the days when *ali'i* rode on large *koa* boards weighing 150lbs (70kg). Also gone are early 20th-century Waikiki-style boards made of California redwood. And just as extinct are the balsa "pig boards" that were popular in the early 1950s. Thanks to modern technology, today's surfboards are made of foam and fiberglass, and can weigh less than 5lbs (2kg). The serious surfer today maintains not just one surfboard, but an all-purpose "quiver" of boards, ranging in function and size. Short-boards are slightly more than 6ft (2 meters) in length, while long-boards (more buoyant and stable, they permit the surfer to perform more creative maneuvers) are about 9ft (3 meters) in length. – one that cannot begin without the proper training. Visitors to Hawaii usually sign up for some sort of lessons; there are a handful of surfing instruction schools on Oahu. If you are especially confident and have plenty of time to kill, you can usually get informal lessons from willing beach boys in Waikiki.

Know the lingo

Of course, you can't become a true surfing aficionado without first knowing the language. Useful surf terms to be mastered include breaks (waves), and gonzo (highly enthusiastic or raring to go). To hang ten refers to a maneuver usually performed on long boards, which entails placing all 10 toes over the nose or front of the board. Finally, to wipe out means to crash and splash, and it should be only on a big, big wave.

For those who just want to watch, the best time to be a spectator of big-wave surfing is in November and December, when the **Triple Crown of Surfing** is held on Oahu's North Shore. The Triple Crown consists of three separate competitions featuring professional surfers from around the world. Binoculars are a critical tool to help watch the events unfold.

Surfing at Waipi'o Valley on the Big Island.

Taro, a Hawaiian staple crop, grows at Hawaii Plantation Village in Waipahu.

CENTRAL OAHU AND THE WAI'ANAE COAST

Wedged between the mountains of the old Wai'anae and Ko'olau volcanoes, central Oahu is an eclectic mix of resort living, farmland, ancient sites, and untamed wilderness.

There's something for everyone in central Oahu: resorts, golf courses, farmland, ancient sites, stellar beaches, and miles upon miles of open space. Hotels in the Ko 'Olina resort area – especially Disney's Aulani – have become some of the most popular on the entire island, and many travelers like stopping at the Dole Plantation for some pineapples on the drive to the North Shore. The US military also has quite a presence. In short, the area might be the most eclectic portion of the entire island. Which is precisely why so many visitors like it so much.

Ancient Moanalua

Just off the H-1 freeway is **Moanalua Gardens** ❸❶, a tranquil retreat graced with huge, umbrella-like monkeypod trees. A popular picnic spot and site of July's Prince Lot Hula Festival, the gardens are privately owned but are open to the public. A country home built by Kamahameha V in Victorian style with Chinese accents graces the setting. Behind is **Moanalua Valley**, an even more spectacular wilderness area where there are tall white hibiscus trees shading a stream, and Hawaiian petroglyphs and an ancient medicinal pool surrounded by colorful morning glories, gardenias, ferns, and fragrant vines. The valley is now owned by the

state, which has pledged to ensure continued access for hikers.

Aloha stadium

Also off the H-1 as you approach Pearl Harbor, you'll easily spot the 50,000-seat **Aloha Stadium** ❸❷, Oahu's prime but plagued-by-rust outdoor venue for major sports and special events like the annual State Fair. Home of the annual Pro Bowl football game, which features National Football League all-stars, the stadium was built in 1975 and can be realigned into baseball or

Map on page 108

Main Attractions
Aloha Stadium Swap Meet
Dole Plantation
Aulani
Makua Beach
Ka'ena Point

On the Farrington Highway heading for Ka'ena Point State Park in Wai'anae.

football configurations. Concession workers here sell Chinese crack seed and *saimin* noodles along with the usual hot dogs and burgers.

Aloha Stadium's parking lot doubles as the site for one of Oahu's biggest attractions, when some 30,000 residents and visitors flock to the **Aloha Stadium Swap Meet** (tel: 486-6704; Wed & Sat, 8am–3pm, Sun 6.30am–3pm). Here are row upon row of vendors hawking everything from *aloha* shirts to zucchini.

Just *mauka* (toward the mountains) of the stadium is **Stadium Mall**, a retail complex, unremarkable except that it is home to **The Ice Palace** (tel: 487-9921), a popular ice-skating venue that occasionally hosts hockey competitions.

Beyond the stadium lie the east, middle, and west lochs of Pearl Harbor (see page 141) and the towns of **'Aiea**, **Pearl City**, and **Waipahu**, largely bedroom communities for Honolulu.

Central plateau

Dole Plantation's pineapple maze.

On the drive north and inland on the H-2 freeway, Oahu's central plateau rises gradually until it reaches the **Schofield Barracks** ❸ army post and **Wahiawa**, the highest residential community on Oahu. Wahiawa ("Place of Noise") can be bypassed altogether by staying on Highway 90, which separates the town from Schofield Barracks. But military enthusiasts will enjoy a stop at Schofield's **Tropic Lightning Museum** (tel: 655-0438; www.garrison.hawaii.army.mil/tlm/index.html; Tue–Sat 10am–4pm; free), which houses artifacts, photographs, and archival materials documenting the history of Schofield Barracks and the famed "Tropic Lightning" 25th Light Infantry Division.

Others, more interested in a place of quiet than a place of noise, might care to stop in Wahiawa to take a look at the visually unspectacular **Healing Stones**. The stones sit on a simple altar inside a concrete shelter on California Street. Until the late 1920s, pilgrims regularly visited these stones, which, according to legend, were two sisters from the island of Kauai who were petrified by greater powers. Other myths attribute alternative origins to the stones but, whatever the explanation, they are still thought to emanate healing powers. Offerings are regularly left here. Also in Wahiawa is the **Wahiawa Botanical Garden** (1396 California Avenue; tel: 621-7321; daily 9am–4pm; free).

Birth stones

On the north side of Wahiawa, to the left of Kamehameha Highway and just beyond Whitmore Avenue, are sacred stones of a different sort. These are the **birth stones of Kukaniloko** ❸❹. This eucalyptus-fringed clearing in a pineapple field has been venerated by Hawaiians as far back as the 12th century. The wives of high-ranking chiefs bore their children on the gently curved surfaces of these stones. Attendant chiefs, high priests, and physicians would gather around the newborn infant and, during an impressive ceremony marked by great drum rolls, chants, and offerings, the royal child would be named and the umbilical cord cut and ritually hidden away.

From this open-air site, to the west in the direction of the Wai'anae Range, you can look up the side of Leilehua Plain to the broad **Kolekole Pass**, which was used by low-flying Japanese bombers as a convenient cover and western approach for their sneak attacks on Schofield Barracks and adjacent **Wheeler Army Air Field**. In 1969, when the joint American-Japanese movie *Tora! Tora! Tora!* was being filmed, the sight of Japanese Zeros, Kates and Vals roaring through Kolekole and raining simulated bombs and machine-gun fire on Schofield Barracks and Wheeler Air Force Base produced a chilling sense of *déjà vu* for anyone who had been here during World War II.

Pineapple world

Although the Dole company no longer grows pineapples on Oahu on a significant commercial scale, its former headquarters, just north of Wahiawa, have been converted into a flourishing tourist attraction known as the **Dole Plantation** ❸❺ (Kamehameha Highway; tel: 621-8408; www.dole-plantation.com; daily 9am–5.30pm; free but entrance fee to specific attractions). The central building is a large store that sells all kinds of pineapple-related products, along with coffee, Hawaiian plants, and T-shirts

TIP

Throughout the islands you will encounter *lei*- or *ti*-covered objects at sacred sites. These are religious offerings of Native Hawaiians and should be left undisturbed. They are not tourist souvenirs.

Sampling the goods at Dole Plantation.

PINEAPPLES

Europeans first came across pineapples in South America and the West Indies. Quickly adopted as a crop, they were transplanted throughout the world, and were reportedly grown in Hawaii as early as 1813. However, the commercial selling of pineapple in Hawaii did not begin until 1899, when an Oahu entrepreneur, James D. Dole, planted 60 acres (24 hectares) of Wahiawa land with the fruit. Two years later, Dole organized the Hawaiian Pineapple Company, and by 1906 he had begun building a cannery at Iwilei, near Honolulu Harbor. Dole's father was a cousin to Sanford Dole, president of the Hawaiian Republic from 1893 to 1900 and one of the group of businessmen and landowners responsible for overthrowing the monarchy.

Plantation-era living room at Hawaii Plantation Village.

displaying the company logo. There's a little yellow train, the Pineapple Express, which makes regular 20-minute tours of the fields, accompanied by a helpful narrative. There is also what's claimed to be the world's largest maze (it was featured in the 2001 edition of the *Guinness Book of World Records*), an intricate tangle of hedgerows with six distinct "centers," and more than 10,000 colorful plants, including varieties of hibiscus, the state flower.

Wai'anae Coast

The Wai'anae Coast is perhaps the most misunderstood and maligned area of Oahu. It is true that this 20-mile (32km) coastline is hotter, dustier, and drier than the rest of the island. And with the exception of the Ko 'Olina Resort at the southern end, and Makaha's golf club, it lacks the usual tourist attractions. But dig deep, and you'll find that West Oahu has considerable natural and cultural beauty to offer a respectful and adventurous traveler.

Question any long-time resident of Nanakuli, Ma'ili, Wai'anae, or Makaha about the West Side, and they may

Hawaii Plantation Village.

just spend hours explaining why it's paradise: "It's the closest thing to an unspoiled Hawaiian place on this island," says a truck driver from Lualualei. A Nanakuli elder states flatly that "You've never been to a real *lu'au* until you've been to a big one on this side." Indeed, wedding or first-birthday *lu'aus* (see page 91) on this side of the island are legendary, remembered by participants by the number of *kalua* pigs and kegs of beer consumed.

Just over 35,000 people live along Wai'anae's jagged shorelines and dry mountain slopes. Before the arrival of Captain Cook, the west coast of Oahu was a major center of Hawaiian civilization, probably because of the rich fishing grounds in the clear offshore waters between Nanakuli and Ka'ena Point. It was here, according to oral traditions, that the demigod Maui lived and first learned to make fire after he arrived in Hawaii. Also along this coast, several myths refer to the infamous man-pig Kamapua'a, renowned throughout Hawaii as a god who both charmed and harassed mortal worshipers with his capricious antics.

Just past Pearl City and a quick dash off the H-1 Freeway, lies the town of **Waipahu** ㊱, which is over a century old. Until the mid-1970s, it was devoted to growing sugar cane, but today employment is provided by other industries, such as tourism and leisure.

The past is still celebrated at **Hawaii Plantation Village** (tel: 677-0110; www.hawaiiplantationvillage.com; Mon–Sat 10am–2pm). Plantation-era houses reveal the diverse cultures of eight ethnic groups in Hawaii that were a part of the sugar industry's century-long flowering. Guided tours of the 3-acre (1.2-hectare) site are offered.

The southwest corner

The **Ko 'Olina Resort** ㊲ has the requisite golf course plus a spa and a series of beach-lined lagoons. Anchoring the resort is **Aulani**, the biggest and most popular: a Disney resort that blends the familiar faces of Mickey

Mouse, Minnie Mouse, Donald Duck, and the gang with a Hawaiian motif. The resort, which opened in 2009 and underwent expansion in 2013, is popular among Disney devotees, especially since the characters are omnipresent. The resort also has one of the best spas outside of Waikiki. Also worth exploring is the **JW Marriott Ihilani Ko 'Olina Resort and Spa**, perched on one of the lagoons and white-sand beaches. Film buffs will recognize the hotel from *Blue Crush*, a 2002 surfing movie starring a young Kate Bosworth. Several large *lu'aus* (feasts) are held adjacent to the resort (there's a bus link to Waikiki). Each Wai'anae coast beach has its own character and devotees. 'Ewa Beach Park, for example, is famed for its abundance of *limu* (also called *ogo* in Japanese), or edible seaweed.

Just outside Ko 'Olina is **Hawaiian Waters Adventure Park** ❸ (400 Farrington Way; tel: 674-9283; www.hawaiianwaters.com; opening times vary), with 25 acres (10 hectares) of waterslides and wave pools. Favored by surfers, **Kahe Point** ❹ is a beach past Ko 'Olina, opposite an electric power plant on the main road, which parallels the western coastline. This spot is called the Kahe Point Beach Park, but locals call it Tracks because remnants of the old narrow-gauge train tracks still run parallel to the highway traveling northward.

Ku'ilioloa Heiau ❹, on the extreme fingertip of Kane'ilio Point on the south side of Poka'i Bay, is surrounded by water on three sides. This *heiau*, or temple, of coral and lava rock was built in the 15th or 16th century in honor of Ku'ilioloa, a giant dog that often protected travelers in the area.

Protection by giant dogs was appreciated here. This area is said to have been populated in ancient times by cannibals preying on passers-by. According to J. Gilbert McAllister, who wrote a 1933 Bishop Museum survey entitled *Archaeology of Oahu*, these highwaymen apparently hid behind high ridges and ambushed unwary victims who came their way. The largest town on this coast, Makaha, meaning fierce or savage, takes its name from these marauders.

"For many years these people preyed upon the traveler," McAllister wrote, "until at one time men from Kauai, hairless men *(olohe)* came to this beach. They were attacked by these cannibals but defeated them, killing the entire colony. Since then, the region has been safe for traveling."

Makaha: coast and valley

Several reefs and points of land along this coast have long been favored as surfing spots, but perhaps the most famous is Kepuhi Point in **Makaha** ❹, where the annual Makaha International Surfing Championships were once held. In recent years, an oldie-but-goodie surfing event at Makaha has caught the fancy of wave-riding old-timers: the annual Buffalo's Longboard Contest, which began in 1978. Makaha Beach commander Buffalo Keaulana and other *kama'aina* (long-time residents) organized it to renew interest in the style of surfing that was in vogue during the 1950s and 1960s.

TIP

The Wai'anae Coast has developed a reputation for not embracing tourists. Break-ins of parked rental cars underline this impression. Still, if you behave respectfully you may find yourself liking this part of the island and its residents best of all.

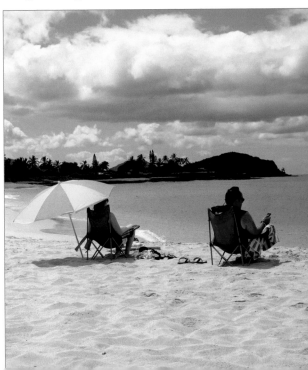

Makaha Beach.

Wander into the back reaches of **Makaha Valley** to the impressive **Kane'aki Heiau** 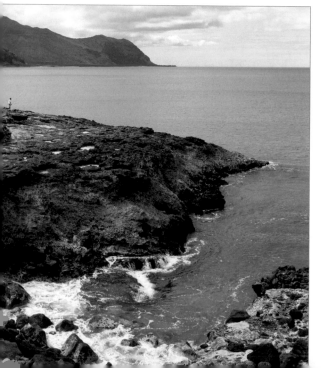 (Tue–Sun 10am–2pm; free), which has been restored by the National Park Service, Bishop Museum, and the Makaha Historical Society. This 17th-century *heiau*, one of the best-preserved on Oahu and tucked away in a spectacular setting alongside Makaha Stream, was rebuilt entirely by hand, using indigenous *pili* grass, *'ohi'a* timber and lava stones much as they were utilized by ancient craftsmen. To get there, head up into Makaha Valley toward the Sheraton Makaha Golf Club and continue through the golf course to the gate for Mauna 'Olu Estates. The guard will direct you to the *heiau*.

Kaneana and Keawa'ula Bay

Another famous site you can walk into is about 3 miles (5km) north of Makaha: **Kaneana** ⊕, the Cave of Kane. Although this cave is 100ft (30 meters) high in places and about 450ft (135 meters) deep, it is not a lava tube. Rather, it was carved out by the sea 150,000 years ago when its entrance was at or below sea level. According to a local story, this cave was occupied by a fierce character, Kamohoali'i, who was able to alternate at will between being a human and a shark. Kamohoali'i had a fondness for human flesh, so in his guise as a mortal, he would periodically jump on people and drag them into this cave for dinner. Eventually, this human disguise was discovered and Kamohoali'i had to flee into the sea, but he was captured and destroyed later by vengeful Makua residents.

Makua Beach ⊕ is the photogenic area where much of the epic motion picture *Hawaii*, based on James Michener's novel of the same name, was filmed in 1965. Film producers recreated an entire set on this beach representing the old Maui whaling town of Lahaina. That set has long since been carted away, but the same spectacular backdrop remains.

Moments later, Farrington Highway ends and briefly becomes a modest road that terminates at **Keawa'ula Bay** ⊕, a favorite board- and bodyboarding spot known to residents as **Yokohama Bay**. This sandy playground received the Japanese name at the turn of the 20th century when the Oahu Railway train between 'Ewa and Hale'iwa would stop here to let off Japanese fishermen, who favored the fishing at Keawa'ula.

Beyond Yokohama Bay, the landscape loses its sandy character and turns into a jangle of black lava, thorny scrub brush, and sand dunes at **Ka'ena Point**. Like an arrow, Ka'ena points slightly to the northwest and the island of Kauai. It can be traversed on foot or bicycle – but not by car. Continuing farther on and around Ka'ena Point would lead you to the North Shore. Ka'ena Point is now a state wildlife preserve, home to nesting albatross, the occasional Hawaiian Monk Seal, and rare flora.

Ka'ena is said to be named for the brother or cousin of Pele, the fire and volcano goddess, and ancient Hawaiians were reluctant to cross it, for it was a place from which souls departed the earth – the good to the right, and the not-so-good to the left.

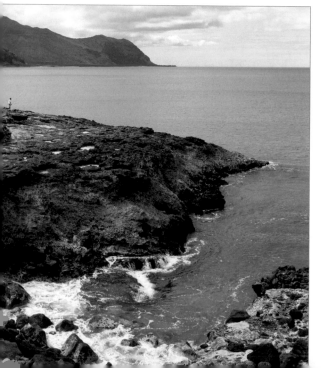

View towards Yokohama Bay from Ka'ena Point State Park.

The Leeward Islands

Oahu County continues west from Honolulu, encompassing thousands of miles and dozens of islands where nature reigns supreme.

For most travelers, Honolulu ends at the sharp, beaky tip of Ka'ena Point on northwest Oahu. Unknown to many, however, including most Honolulu residents, is that Honolulu is the most far-flung city in the world. The city's jurisdiction not only includes Oahu, but also dozens of smaller points of land that stretch some 1,400 nautical miles (2,200km) to the northwest.

These shoals, atolls, and desert isles have names like Nihoa, Necker, French Frigate Shoals, Gardiner Pinnacles, Maro Reef, Laysan, Lisianski, Pearl and Hermes Reef, and Kure Island. The better-known Midway Islands are also within Honolulu's sprawling city limits, but they were placed under military jurisdiction at the start of the 20th century.

Some 2,000 US Navy personnel and dependants – as well as hundreds of thousands of goony birds – live at Midway, but the other islets are uninhabited, except for Tern Island at French Frigate Shoals, which supports an airstrip and Loran navigation station maintained by the US Coast Guard. Midway, partially converted to eco-tourism in the 1990s, is no longer open to visitors, pending a new management contract.

Collectively, these islands are often referred to as the Leeward Islands, although, officially, they are the Northwestern **Hawaiian Islands Marine National Monument**. Eight of these islands and reefs have been combined to form the Hawaiian Islands National Wildlife Refuge.

Wildlife haven

Largely because of their remoteness, these isles are a favorite breeding ground of the Hawaiian Monk Seal, an endangered species. This sea mammal prefers solitude over congregating in groups, hence the name "monk" seal, and can grow to over 7ft (2 meters) in length and weigh nearly 500lbs (230kg).

Each spring, adult green sea turtles – Hawaiians called them *honu* – migrate to the wildlife refuge, where the females lumber ashore to lay eggs. The turtles can grow up to 4ft (1.2

meters) in length and weigh up to 400lbs (180kg). They are known to bask on the beach on these uninhabited Hawaiian islets, an activity rare among sea turtles. The monk seals and green sea turtles are federally protected and should not be disturbed.

Ornithologist's delight

Among the interesting birds that populate these islands and excite ornithologists are Hawaiian noddy terns, sooty terns, red-footed and blue-faced boobies, Laysan albatrosses, shearwaters, frigate birds, wandering tattlers, Pacific golden plovers, Laysan honey eaters, bristle-thighed curlews, and Laysan teals (said to be the rarest ducks in the world). Nihoa, also known as Bird Island, has several endemic species including the Nihoa Millerbird and the Nihoa Finch.

For biologists, the region also has become a special spot for observing rare bivalves, mollusks, and other forms of simple sea life. Today it is considered the foremost place for spotting nudibranchs, a hard-to-find cousin of the snail. Many of these animals were photographed for the 2005 book *Archipelago* (National Geographic Society).

A Laysan albatross nests on Sand Island, part of Midway Atoll National Wildlife Refuge on Midway Atoll.

Waterfalls near the Hana Highway.

MAUI

With resorts aplenty, remarkable beaches, and one of the largest volcanoes on Earth, Maui is a mix of natural beauty and manmade elegance.

I f the Hawaiian Islands had a prom, Maui would be crowned queen for all it has to offer. The island's economy is growing more quickly than the economies on other islands, and it has weathered the recession better than anywhere else in Hawaii. Resorts are swanky and full. Humpback whales visit every winter like clockwork. And the beaches one is more spectacular than the next. Together with Lanai and Molokai, the other islands that comprise Maui County (also known as Greater Maui), the center of the Hawaiian archipelago is by far the most exciting part these days.

In ancient times, Maui was a strong and stable island kingdom. Then, in the late 1800s, the Maui town of Lahaina was capital of the newly united Hawaiian kingdom. Nowadays, Maui sustains itself with three basic industries: tourism, sugar cane production and information technology. The island also has spawned a variety of cutting-edge businesses, including floriculture (the growing of flowers) and wind energy.

For a relatively small island – if it were square, it would only be 27 miles (43km) on each side – Maui possesses an amazing natural diversity. The island is composed of two entirely different volcanic masses. The island of Maui is dominated by a single landmark – mighty Haleakala that makes up Eastern Maui. This massive dormant, three-sided shield volcano – capped with a Manhattan-sized *caldera*, a national park, and a space-age research facility – offers the adventure of lofty, sometimes snowbound, heights. It's also a great place from which to watch the sun rise.

Surfers at Ho'okipa Beach Park, Paia town.

West Maui is anchored by the island's older and second volcano: Komohana (or, depending on whom you ask, Kahalawai). Adding to this diversity are two other neighboring islands that comprise the County of Maui – Molokai and Lanai. Together with uninhabited Kaho'olawe, this row of sheltering islands forms one side of the 'Au'Au Channel, which protects Maui's dry shores from the open ocean and creates a haven for humpback whales.

People visit Maui for all of these reasons: the beaches, the watersports, the glamour, whale-spotting, and the scenery. Of course they also come for the golf and resorts – some of which rank among the best in the world. As the island grows, though, locals are increasingly concerned about water, traffic, and overcrowding. So far, thankfully, none of these problems has arisen.

Kanounou Pt.

Poelua
Bay

Honolua Bay

Blowhole

Kapalua ⑩
Napili Bay

Honolua

Honokohau ⑪

Pohaku Kani
(Bellstone)
Kahakuloa ⑫

Kahakuloa Head

Mokeehia I.

Napili

Kahana

LAHAINA

Honokohau Str.

340

Honokowai
Beach
Honokowai

West Maui
Airport

West Maui

Kahakuloa
Section

Hulu I.

Waihe'e River

Waihe'e Beach

Ho'okipa

Black Rock
Ka'anapali ⑨
Whaler's Village

W
E
S
T

Eke Crater
4480

Honokowai
Section

Waihe'e

Waiehu Beach

Maui Jinsha
Shinto Shrine

H.P. Baldwin Beach

Kuau

Pa'ia ⑱

Kau
Buc
Mis

Hanakaoo Beach

Hahakea

Natural Area

Kahului
Bay

Kanaha
Pond

Kahului
Airport

Holy Ros
Chu

Lahaina ⑧
Lahaina Harbor
Courthouse, Banyan Tree

M
A
U
I

Pu'u Kukui
5788 ⑤
Panaewa
Section

'Iao Needle
2250 'Iao Valley

Wailuku ③
'Iao Valley State Park

Kahului ②
①

Kanaha Pond
State Wildlife Sanctuary

Alexander & Baldwin
Sugar Museum

Unio

Maluulu O Lele Beach

M
O
U
N
T
A
I
N
S

Reserve
DISTRICT

④
Kepaniwai
Heritage Gardens

Ka'ahumanu
Church (1837)

Hale
Ho'ike'ike
Museum

WAILUKU

Haleakala Highw

Puamana Beach

Lihau
Section

Hanaula
4616

Wailuku Heights

Hawaii
Tropical
Plantation

Waikapu

DISTRICT

350

Pu'unene ⑥

Ditch

Lowr
e Ditch

Puk

Olowalu Str.

30

380

Haliu

Mokulele Highway

Puehu

Road

Sugar Mill Ruins

Olowalu

Mopua

Hekili Pt.

30

Honoapiilani Highway

Kealia Pond Nat.
Wildlife Refuge

MAKAWA

Ukumehame Beach

Ma'alaea
⑦

Maui
Ocean
Center

Papawai Pt.

Ma'alaea Bay

Kapoli Beach

Capt. Vancouver
Monument

David Malo's
Kilolani Church

Mai Poina Oleau Beach

Kihei ⑬

31

Waipuilani

Kaa

'
A
u
'
a
u

C
h
a
n
n
e
l

Kalama Beach

Kamaole

Kamaole
Beach

Keawakapu

Keok

Wailea ⑭

Kula High

37

Kaho'olawe

0   2 miles
0   2 km

Molokini
Island ⑯

Makena

Keawala'i Church
(1832) ⑮

'Ulupalakua
Ranch ㉒

'Ulupalakua

Tedeschi Wi ㉓

Cape Kukui

Oneloa Beach

Last Lava Flows
on Maui (1790)

Kanaio

Kuhe'eia Bay

Kanahena
Ahihi Bay

Ahihi-Kina'u
Natural Area Reserve

Kanaio
Area

Ahupu Bay

Ahupu Gulch

Lua Makika
452

Kanapou
Bay

Cape Kina'u

Honokoa Bay

MAKAWAO DISTRICT

La Pérouse Bay ⑰

Lae Paki Pt.

Kanaloa

Cape Hanamanoia

Kamanamana Pt.

Pohakuea
Pt.

Kealaikaihiki Pt.

Wai

Honu

Waikahalulu
Bay

Kamohio
Bay

Kuakaiwa Pt.

Kaka Pt.

Maui

0   5 miles

0   5 km

N

PACIFIC
OCEAN

Pauwela
Pt.

Papanui o Kane I.

Uaoa Bay

Pauwela

Kuiaha

Waipio Bay

28

Kaulanapueo
★ Church (1853)

Ha'iku

Utumalu

Huelo

29

Hoalua Bay
Kahalau I.

Kailua

Ka Puka a Maui Pt.

Kaupakulua

Keopuka Islet

Honomanu Bay

Kokomo

400

Kaumahina
State Wayside

30

360

Ke'anae
Pt.

31

aile

Makawao

20

Puohokamoa ★
Falls

Ke'anae

St Gabriel's Church

Moku Mana I.

Ke'anae
Arbretum

Wailua
Lookout

32

Waialua Bay

Wailua

Waiohue Bay

Moku Huki I.

Nahiku

33

Kapukaulua Pt.

377

Waiale

Pua'a Ka'a
State Park

Kalahu Pt.

Puleku

DISTRICT

Ke'anae Valley

Hanawi Str.

Kuhiwa Valley

Upper
Nahiku

National Tropical
Botanical
Garden

★

34

Hana Airport

Pukaulua Pt.

Wai'anapanapa
State Park

35

Church of the
Holy Ghost (1897)

Vaiakoa

Ko'olau Gap

Park
Headquarters

Hanakauhi
8907

Kalapawili Ridge

HANA

Kawaipapa

Hotel Hana-Maui

Birthplace of Ka'ahumanu (1768)★

360

Hana Bay
Hana Beach

Kula Botanical
Gardens

Kalahaku Overlook

25

Holua Cabin

Wananalua Church (1838)

36

Hana

uli

Haleakala
Visitor Center

Pu'u 'Ula'ula (Red Hill)
10023

Haleakala

24

Pohakupalaha
8105

Silversword
Garden

Haleakala Basin

Laie
Cave

Science City

Kapalaoa ★
Cabin

Haupaakea Peak
9159

Kaupo Gap

Haleakala
8201

27

Paliku Cabin

National

Kaumakani
4576

Hana
Ranch

Waihoi Valley

Kipahulu Valley

Hamoa

Koki Beach

Alau I.

37

Hamoa Beach

Kahalulu

DISTRICT

Waihiumalu
Falls

Puuiki
Haou

Koali

ol Springs State
eation Area

Manawainui

Pi'ilani Highway

31

Natural Arch

Huakini
Bay

Mamalu
Bay

Kailio
Pt.

Palapala Ho'omau Church (1857),
Sugar Mill (1890-1922)★

Huialoha Church
(1859)

Kaupo

26

St Joseph's
Church (1861)

Mokulau
Islets

Lelekea
Bay

Ahole Rock

Wailua
Falls

38

Catholic Monument

39

Ohe'o Gulch

40

Kipahulu

31

Puhilele
Pt.

Aloe Rock

oa Pt.

Wekea Pt.

Alenuihaha Channel

West Maui mountains in 'Iao
Valley State Park, near Wailuku.

CENTRAL MAUI

The urban center of Kahului anchors the isthmus connecting the island's two volcanoes. But it is the sun and surf of the west coast – and Lahaina's whaling history – that seduce visitors.

Think of Maui like a suspension bridge; the volcanoes rise like supports on either end, and sloping farmland stretches in between. This farmland – technically it's an isthmus – is the island's prime agricultural region, and was created when the Haleakala volcano filled in the gap between it and the much older West Maui volcano. This farmland isn't the brazen moneymaker that it used to be, but the production of both pineapples and sugar cane remains important here today.

Kahului

Kahului ❶, Maui's deep-water port on the north side and the site of the island's primary airport is the island's commercial hub, with shopping malls, a community college, and the **Maui Arts and Cultural Center** (Kahului Beach Road; tel: 242-2787; www.mauiarts.org). Created by an heroic grass-roots fund-raising campaign, the center includes the elegant, 1,200-seat Castle Theater, several smaller performance spaces, an amphitheater, and an art gallery, and public installations by local artists.

Kahului is important for another reason; just off the highway between the airport and downtown Kahului is **Kanaha Pond State Wildlife Sanctuary ❷**, the state's most

important waterfowl sanctuary and the home of several species of native birds. Three indigenous species in particular make the pond particularly worthwhile given their relative rarity on other islands: the Hawaiian Coot, the Hawaiian Duck, and the Hawaiian Stilt.

Wailuku

Wailuku ❸ is perched in the western foothills above Kahului like an older and wiser sibling. Once centered around a now-defunct sugar

Main Attractions
Maui Arts & Cultural Center
Hawaii Nature Center
'Iao Needle
Home Maid Bakery
Maui Ocean Center

A charter boat docks at Ma'alaea harbor in Wailuku.

mill, Wailuku is the seat of the Maui County government, administering not only Maui, but the islands of Molokai, Lanai, and the contentious but uninhabited Kaho'olawe.

In Wailuku's historic district in the heart of town stands **Ka'ahumanu Congregational Church**, built in 1876 of white-painted wood and plastered stone to honor Queen Ka'ahumanu, who played an important role in establishing Christianity in the islands.

The church is often closed except when services are being held, but if you attend one of the services you will hear hymns sung in the Hawaiian language.

An early example of Western architecture touched with Hawaiian influences is the stone- and timber-built **Bailey House** (tel: 244-3326; www.mauimuseum.org; Mon–Sat 10am–4pm), a small museum operated by the Maui Historical Society. The structure was built in 1841 for Edward Bailey, headmaster of the former Wailuku Female Seminary. The museum conveys the spirit of

missionary life and exhibits paintings of old Maui by Bailey himself.

West Maui Mountains

Beyond Wailuku at the end of the road are the wet, lush remnants of the West Maui crater and **'Iao Valley** ❹ (pronounced *ee-ow*, meaning "cloud supreme"). At the valley's mouth is **Kepaniwai Heritage Gardens**, a country park with gardens and pavilions representing the many ethnic groups that have settled in Maui. It was established in counterpoint to an historic and vicious Hawaiian battle waged in the area; during the battle of 'Iao Valley, Kamehameha's forces pushed Maui warriors back into the valley and slaughtered them, choking the river with their lifeless bodies. Kepaniwai means "water dam."

Next to Kepaniwai is the **Hawaii Nature Center** (tel: 244-6500; www.hawaiinaturecenter.org; daily 10am–4pm), an environmental education project with particular emphasis on programs for children. The Interactive Science Arcade offers

Making malasadas (fried, powdered pastries) in Wailuku.

30 hands-on natural history exhibits and daily guided nature hikes in the afternoons.

Farther up, the scenic road ends in 'Iao Valley State Park, a lush mountain terrain dominated by 'Iao Needle, the exposed core of an old cinder cone that rises 1,200ft (365 meters) above the stream at its base. There is a parking lot at the end of the road, and a path leads down to the stream and up to various sheltered spots for a view of the valley.

Surrounding this compact, spectacular valley are the 5,788ft (1,764-meter) walls of Pu'u Kukui ❺, the summit of the eroded remains of the West Maui volcano and one of the wettest places in the islands, with more than 400ins (10,000mm) of rain annually. The summit is a natural wonderland, as it has one of the greatest selections of native species in Maui, but unfortunately it is totally inaccessible to visitors.

On the isthmus

Just to the east of Kahului is the plantation town of Pu'unene ❻

and a sugar mill that is still in operation. The former plantation manager's house next to the mill is now the Alexander & Baldwin Sugar Museum (tel: 871-8058; www.sugar museum.com; daily 9.30am–4.30pm), with working exhibits and an informative look at the lives of early migrant laborers on Hawaii's sugar plantations.

On the south side of the central isthmus is Ma'alaea ❼, a small coastal village and harbor, and also a departure point for fishing and whale-watching charters; it also has one of the best surf breaks on the island. Ma'alaea's star attraction is undoubtedly the Maui Ocean Center (tel: 270-7000; www.maui oceancenter.com; daily 9am–5pm), a brilliantly designed aquarium dedicated to the Hawaiian marine environment. Exhibits include live coral, a gigantic walk-through open-ocean tank, a turtle pool, plenty of kids' activities, and a touch pool. The center also allows qualified scuba divers to dive with the sharks in the tank (reserve in advance).

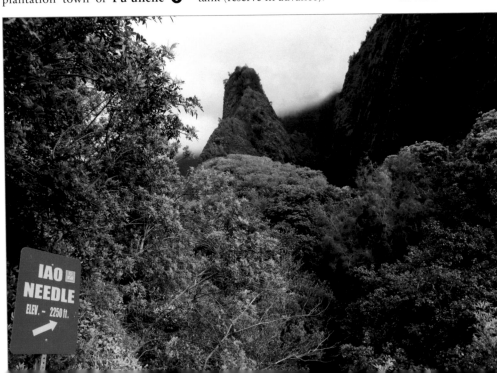

'Iao Needle.

IAO
NEEDLE
ELEV. - 2250 ft.

WEST AND SOUTH MAUI

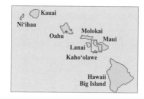

Most of Maui's resorts are clustered in the south and the west, making these parts of the island prime spots for golf, beaches, and good eats.

Main Attractions

Lahaina
Whale-watching (Lahaina
  and Wailea)
Ka'anapali
Whaler's Village Museum
Kapalua Beach

Front Street, Lahaina.

Maui's most protected beaches are on its south and western shores. Naturally, then, these are the places where, in the 1960s and 1970s, resort development happened first. Since then, resort communities have sprouted in places such as Wailea, Ka'anapali and Kapalua. Along the way, the historic whaling village of Lahaina has evolved to become perhaps the island's most sophisticated and visitor-friendly tourist town. It's worth noting that humans aren't the only visitors who enjoy these parts of this great island; humpback whales do, too. Every winter, these marine mammals migrate to Hawaii from Alaska to mate, birth, and rear their young. Watching the leviathans is quite an experience – and, at least between the months of December and April, something you simply cannot avoid.

Lahaina

After Honolulu, **Lahaina ❽**, on the western coastline of West Maui, is Hawaii's best-known town, partly for the nearby beaches of Ka'anapali, partly for its history, and nowadays for its party atmosphere.

The city has quite a history. In the early 1820s, King Kamehameha III made Lahaina the capital of his kingdom, and it remained so until 1845. By then, New England whaling ships had begun visiting. Missionaries followed in 1823, sponsored by Queen Keopuolani, mother of Kamehameha II and Kamehameha III. She helped the missionaries establish a grass church called Waine'e, the site of today's Waiola Church. Keopuolani is buried at the site, on Waine'e Street in Lahaina.

By the 1840s, Hawaii had become the principal forward station of the American whaling fleet. All the actual hunting of whales took place in the northern Pacific; humpback whales were never the prey. Lahaina was a favorite port-of-call because of its protected offshore waters in **'Au'au Channel** that are sheltered y nearby Molokai and Lanai. The whaling ships have long disappeared from Lahaina, but this waterfront town, once a magnet for whalers and seamen on shore leave, continues to preserve the lively spirit and look of the salty 1800s – although sometimes with a decidedly commercial or Hollywood veneer. It's a superb walking town, nonetheless, compact and manageable for any traveler.

The heart of Lahaina lies along **Front Street**, between Shaw and Papalaua streets, parallel to the waterfront. The narrow streets that Mark Twain and Herman Melville walked are now lined with cafés and restaurants (some perched over the water in weathered buildings), art galleries, T-shirt boutiques, and fashionable shops. In 1962, the town was designated a National Historic District, and since then, the Maui County Historic Commission and the non-profit Lahaina Restoration Foundation have worked to encourage the preservation of older buildings and the construction of harmonious new ones. The result is a blend of seaport nostalgia and contemporary living (peppered nonetheless with some gaudy schlock), found nowhere else in Hawaii.

Exploring the town

The **Pioneer Inn** Ⓐ, built on the harbor in 1901 and wedged between Wharf and Front streets, is nothing if not nostalgic. On its walls are fading photographs of early ships and sailors, whaling equipment, and other memorabilia, including the original house rules: "Women is not allow in you (sic) room; if you burn you bed you going out; only on Sunday you can sleep all day." Downstairs is a veranda restaurant and a popular and noisy bar.

Kamehameha's Brick Palace once stood nearby; it is thought to have been Hawaii's first Western-style building. Built around 1798 of locally produced brick, it was commissioned by Kamehameha the Great, using the labor of two ex-convicts from a British penal colony in Australia. Unfortunately, all traces of the ruins have now disappeared.

In a plaza next to the Pioneer Inn is the expansive **Banyan Tree**, planted in

FACT

Herman Melville, author of Moby Dick, unsuccessfully looked for work in Lahaina. He finally found a job in Honolulu as a store clerk and then as a pin-setter in a bowling alley. He later went home to Boston, never to return to the Pacific.

Wo Hing Society Temple, Lahaina.

Humpback Whales

Humans aren't the only mammals to visit Maui with regularity; every winter, thousands of humpback whales descend on the island, too.

The humpback whales that visit Hawaii each winter spend their summers in Alaska, where the rich waters fatten the whales with krill, a type of shrimp. Around November, the whales start heading for Hawaii's warmer waters, where they mate and give birth. By the end of May, they have disappeared again.

Scientists believe that at least 10,000 humpback whales make the journey to Maui; they have no idea how many of these animals pass through the 'Au'au Channel in any given season. What they do know is that the number of whales that winter in Hawaii is steadily increasing each year; great news for a population once feared to be headed to extinction (and one that, technically, still sits on the endangered species list).

Of the behaviour displayed by the humpbacks, breaches (where the whale jumps out of the

Breaching humpback whale.

water), are the most spectacular to watch; between January and March, you can do so from most of the waterfront cafés in Lahaina and on Ka'anapali. Whales also can be seen from charter boats – many of which are available for hire out of Lahaina and Ma'alaea harbors. Most of these boats are inflatable speedboats; some have fiberglass hulls. If you opt for this method of whale-watching, don't expect to get too close; federal and state laws require whale-watchers in Hawaii to keep a distance of 300ft (90 meters), and the law is strictly enforced. (That said, there is no law prohibiting whales from checking out boats of their own accord.)

Other types of behavior one can witness off Maui are flipper-slapping, spyhopping (poking a head above the surface), and lobtailing (slapping the tail flukes on the surface of the water). Each fluke is unique, a whale "fingerprint." Researchers photograph the flukes to track the mammals.

Song of the humpbacks

Female humpbacks spend most of their time in Hawaii being mothers or being pursued by males. Scientists believe that when in Hawaiian waters, males attract females to areas called arenas by singing. (Not all whale species, however, have songs; and not all humpback songs are about attracting females – males also sing in other social situations.) It is not known whether the information contained in the songs is simple or complex. What is known is that during the winter season, males repeat the song in a precise sequence and that, over time, the whale song changes and evolves.

The songs are composed of thematic sets sung repeatedly in a specific order. The average song session lasts maybe a quarter of an hour, although they have been known to last as long as 22 hours. Whale songs sound like creaks and groans of different lengths in many pitches. Because sound travels well underwater, it's easy to hear these enchanting tunes if the whales are singing nearby.

When the humpbacks leave Hawaiian waters in spring, the singing stops, to resume again the following winter in almost exactly the same spot in the song as where they broke off months earlier. Humpbacks in Hawaii sing the same evolving song as humpbacks in Mexico; some scientists believe this indicates communication between regional whale "cultures."

873 by the town sheriff. It is the largest known banyan tree in the islands: more than 60ft (18 meters) high and covering 0.6 acres (0.25 hectares) with its canopy. Next to it is the old courthouse building, now an art gallery and information center. Opposite the Pioneer Inn on Front Street is the **Baldwin Home ⓑ** (tel: 661-3262; daily 10am–4pm). Formerly the home of Dwight Baldwin, a Protestant medical missionary, it was a focus of Lahaina missionary life in the mid-19th century. The home has been fully restored and is now a museum.

Hale Pa'ahao ⓒ ("Stuck-in-Irons House"; Mon–Fri 8am–3pm; free) is the old prison, located a few blocks up – where else? – Prison Street. It's a worthwhile stop just for its cool, quiet courtyard. Step inside one of the whitewashed cells and imagine a confined life in paradise. The prison had inmates convicted of the usual perfidy, including some convicted of "furious riding" – 89 in 1855 but just 48 in 1857. In that same year, one person was imprisoned for "neglect of parent to send children to school."

A few blocks to the east is **Malu'uluolele Park**, once a pond with an island where Maui chiefs lived. Kamehameha III enjoyed showing visitors the ornate coffins and burial chamber embellished with mirrors, royal feather standards, and velvet drapes. A well-known *mo'o*, or lizard god, inhabited the pond. Today, the place is a ball park.

Farther north along Front Street, the **Wo Hing Society Temple ⓓ** (tel: 661-3262; daily Sat–Thu 10am–4pm, Fri 1–8pm) is a fascinating museum of early Chinese life in the islands. The early 1900s-era building was a cultural and social home for Chinese immigrants, mostly male and single. In the former cook house next door, old Thomas Edison movies are projected amongst the pots and pans. At the north end of Front Street is the seaside **Jodo Mission Buddhist Cultural Park**, with the largest Buddha outside of Asia.

Lahainaluna High School ⓔ is located up Lahainaluna Road and behind the now defunct Pioneer Sugar Mill. It opened as a general

Inside the Wo Hing Society Temple on Front Street.

Ka'anapali Beach.

academic school in 1831 under the name "Lahainaluna Seminary." This is the oldest American high school west of the Rockies. Californians once sent their children here rather than to the East Coast schools, which ran the risk of Indian attack. The original printer's shop, **Hale Pa'i** (tel: 661-3262; visits by appointment only; donation suggested), is where the first Bible in the Hawaiian language was published.

Ka'anapali

When the **Ka'anapali Resort** ❾ began to be developed during the early 1960s, less than 5 miles (8km) north of Lahaina, Maui entered the global tourist industry, starting the expansion that has since doubled the island's population. This complex of hotels, shopping centers, golf courses, and condominiums also lays claim to what some people consider to be Hawaii's finest beaches: two 1-mile (1.6km) -long stretches of sand separated by a promontory made of lava rock. Hotels line both stretches, though the less-urbanized North Beach is slightly less built up.

The **Whaler's Village** shopping center includes the **Whaler's Village Museum** (tel: 661-5992; daily 9am–10pm; free), a small but sophisticated museum with wonderful exhibits, including one of the country's best collections of baleen and scrimshaw.

A rebuilt 1890s-vintage sugar cane train, the **Lahaina Ka'anapali Railroad** (tel: 667-6851; www.sugarcanetrain.com), regularly puffs over a 6-mile (10km) route between Lahaina and Ka'anapali, transporting tourists through the cane fields. Narrow-gage tracks follow the haul-line road that was used by the Pioneer Mill until the early 1950s.

The first of Ka'anapali's hotels, the Sheraton Maui, opened in 1963, sits at the northern end of Ka'anapali Beach at a rocky point called **Black Rock**, or **Pu'u Keka'a** ("The Rumble"). This *'uhane lele*, or sacred place, was where the souls of the dead departed for ancestral spirit worlds. Whether you are staying at one of the Ka'anapali deluxe resorts lining the beach – which include the Hyatt Regency Maui, Westin Maui,

Whaler's Village shopping center.

and Maui Marriott – or not, enjoy a walk along Ka'anapali Beach, timed to coincide with the sunset, if possible, for the spectacular, torch-lighting, cliff-diving ceremonial that ends the Ka'anapali day.

Northward

From Ka'anapali, Honoapi'ilani Highway passes through **Honokowai**, **Kahana**, and **Napili**, a clustering of condos and apartment hotels. Just beyond Napili Bay is **Kapalua Resort** ❿, renowned for its golf courses (the best in Hawaii) and beautiful setting at the base of the West Maui Mountains offering the islands best views and trails, along with its luxury accommodations The Ritz-Carlton, Kapalua.

Beyond Kapalua, the road arcs eastward over the northern end of the West Maui Mountains, passing the beach at the **Honolua/Mokule'ia Marine Preserve**, a hugely popular surfing destination that is also great for snorkeling (visited by catamaran). Park roadside (the long line of cars makes the site obvious) and it is then only a short hike down to the beach.

Situated nearby is the small bay of **Honokohau** ⓫. Beyond the Marine Preserve, the landscape becomes wilder, with beautiful panoramic coastal and mountain views. Although the road has some rough stretches (not suitable for large rental cars), it is possible to travel all the way to **Wailuku**. Make sure you stop in the rustic town of **Kahakuloa** ⓬, a scenic rural enclave where taro is still grown and the lifestyle is quintessentially Hawaiian.

South Maui

In the past 25 years, the area known as South Maui has come to rival West Maui as the island's main resort destination. The name is somewhat misleading; South Maui is not along the island's southern coast, but at the foot of the west-facing slopes of Haleakala. This region is nothing like as green as West Maui, in fact it used to be a virtual desert, but what it lacks in scenic beauty it makes up for in reliable sunshine, and, crucially, sheltered sandy beaches. Roughly half of Maui's guest rooms are now

One of Kapalua Resort's golf courses.

located in the neighboring communities of Kihei and Wailea, which are not so much towns as simply elongated strips of low-rise hotels, condos, and restaurants.

Kihei

Stretching for seven miles (11km) along the shoreline of Ma'alaea Bay, **Kihei** ⑬ consists largely of endlessly repeated condominium rentals and shopping centers with little aesthetic appeal. They are at least here for a good reason: the adjacent beaches are actually quite decent, and offer spectacular sunset views and whale-watching during winter months. Some of the best deals in accommodations can be had here. Broadly speaking, the more northerly beaches, where the swimming is poor, are mainly used by windsurfers heading out into the sheltered waters of the bay, while the further south you go, the better the beaches become for bathing.

Wailea and Makena

Immediately south of Kihei lies the far more upscale resort of **Wailea** ⑭, home to a succession of glorious crescent beaches – Wailea and Polo beaches are the best of all – a fancy, luxury-oriented shopping mall, and several extravagant oceanfront hotels (including the Grand Wailea, the Four Seasons, Maui and the Fairmont Kea Lani.) As elsewhere throughout Hawaii, you don't have to be a hotel guest here to visit any beach you like. Higher up the landscaped slopes of Haleakala, there are five 18-hole golf courses.

South again from Wailea, little **Makena** ⑮ has just one hotel, the Maui Prince. Makena did at least exist before the tourist boom, so it retains one or two vestiges of the past, in the shape of the pretty Keawala'i Church, and the remains of its former harbor. There's yet another lovely beach in front of the Maui Prince, but the finest of all South Maui's beaches lies another mile (0.5km) farther south. Known to everyone as "Big Beach," but officially named both Oneloa Beach and Makena State Park, this magnificent 1-mile (0.5km) -long expanse of broad golden sand is a wonderful place for walking and taking pictures, but unless you're

Molokini island.

THE MAUI FOOD SCENE

When Sheldon Simeon nearly won "Top Chef" Season 10 in 2012, the national spotlight shone brightly on Lahaina, where Simeon works as chef at Star Noodle, an Asian restaurant. The attention was long overdue; for years, South and West Maui have boasted some of the most celebrated chefs in the islands – chefs whose expertise, flair, and culinary creations are so great, diners often travel great distances to enjoy them. Like Chef Miguel Cedeno's sushi at Sansei in Kapalua. Or the treats from chef Tylun Pang at Ko, in Wailea. There are so many delicious food options in this part of Hawaii that one could make an entire trip out of eating. The only downside is fitting into that bathing suit when it's time to hit the beach.

an expert boogie-boarder the waves are too dangerous for swimming.

Molokini and Kaho'olawe

Looking out seaward from the resorts of South Maui, it's easy to spot the small crescent island of **Molokini** ⑯, an eroded tuff cone whose submerged crater offers spectacular snorkeling. Daily diving and snorkeling boats to Molokini depart from several points along the shore, especially from Ma'alaea.

Beyond Molokini, looming low and red on the horizon, lies uninhabited **Kaho'olawe**, the smallest of Hawaii's eight major islands. The ancient Hawaiians used Kaho'olawe as a center of religious practices and a navigational school. Sites on the island have been placed on the National Register of Historic Places.

During World War II the US Navy appropriated the island for use as a gunnery range, where the military practiced firing and detonating weapons. Native Hawaiian Rights activism from the 1970s onward resulted in the eventual return of the island to the state in 1994. A major rehabilitation program, involving the removal of debris and unexploded ordinance, has been underway for several years, and is not likely to be completed in the foreseeable future. Each year, there is a lottery to select volunteers to assist as part of the clean-up efforts, but priority is given to Native Hawaiians.

La Pérouse Bay

You can drive another 3 miles (5km) beyond Big Beach (and past multi-million-dollar mansions) on a road that finally ends at **La Pérouse Bay** ⑰, another popular snorkeling and kayaking spot. The first Westerner to land on Maui, the French explorer Jean-François de La Pérouse (Captain Cook had earlier sailed past without stopping), wrote in 1786 that "during our excursion we observed four small villages of about 10 or 12 houses each, built and covered with straw." Shortly after his departure, around 1790, the whole area was covered by lava from Haleakala's last volcanic eruption. Much of the landscape here remains a lava desert to this day.

Makena State Park, also known as Big Beach.

Windsurfing at Ho'okipa Beach.

HALEAKALA AND UPCOUNTRY

Up on the slopes of Maui's volcano,
life is a mix of cowboy culture and
geologic wonder.

Of the sunrise from atop Maui's Haleakala, Mark Twain wrote: "It was the sublimest spectacle I ever witnessed, and I think the memory of it will remain with me always." Travelers continue to be awed by dawn at the 10,023ft (3,055-meter) summit of **Haleakala**, which means "House of the Sun." But from a distance, this gently sloping shield volcano, which is dormant, not extinct, lacks pretension. The first European to sight Haleakala, Captain James Cook, who did not land on Maui, described it as simply "an elevated hill... whose summit rose above the clouds."

Indeed, as with Hawaii Island's Mauna Kea and Mauna Loa (also shield volcanoes,) the Haleakala that is visible is only part of the story. It towers 2 miles (3km) above sea level, but below, it extends another 3.5 miles (6km). The exact dimensions of the part above ground weren't fully known until 1841, when an American expedition surveyed the summit basin and found it to be 3,000ft (915 meters) deep and 19 sq miles (49 sq km) in area, with a circumference of 21 miles (34km).

The island's namesake, the demigod Maui, was a magician and mythical figure in Polynesia long before the Hawaiian Islands were inhabited. According to legend, the sun was fond of sleeping late and then racing across the sky to make up time. With the short days, Hina, Maui's mother, had trouble drying *kapa* cloth that she pounded from the bark of the mulberry. Noticing that the sun appeared each morning over Haleakala, Maui wove a rope of coconut fiber and climbed up to the summit basin's edge one night to await dawn. When the sun awoke, Maui lassoed its rays and threatened to kill it. The sun begged for mercy and promised to behave more

Above the clouds at Leleiwi Lookout, Haleakala National Park.

TIP

It can be quite cool in Upcountry – many homes have fireplaces – and it's increasingly colder as one ascends the slopes of Haleakala. In the morning and late afternoon, the winds atop Haleakala are often cold if not frigid.

responsibly. For most contemporary travelers watching the sun rise or set from the summit of Haleakala, it still moves too fast. To witness the sunrise or sunset from atop Haleakala, one must first ascend the lower slopes of the volcano, an area commonly called **Upcountry**.

Upcountry

Say that you're heading Upcountry and envious listeners will know that shortly you'll be smelling eucalyptus suspended in cool air and following rolling grassy contours reminiscent of Ireland. Upcountry is the lower-slope area of Haleakala that over-looks the isthmus connecting the volcano with West Maui. Far below one can see the white ribbons of beaches, but in Upcountry, there are farms, flowers, and fireplaces. There are two routes in to Upcountry: from Kahului on the Haleakala Highway or, preferably, through Pa'ia and Makawao.

Once a sugar town, **Pa'ia** ⓲ has been changed in large part by the winds and waves at **Ho'okipa Beach** ⓳, one of the world's finest windsurfing places. Pa'ia now reflects a demographic shift from plantation worker to windsurfer, arti-san, and hipster. The town has become a haven for celebrities visiting Maui, and its main drag, Baldwin Avenue, is lined with just as many chi-chi bou-tiques as restaurants and tourist stores.

Just outside of Pa'ia is the **Man-tokuji Mission**, a Japanese Buddhist temple with an oceanfront cemetery of more than 600 burial markers, most of them traditional Japanese. Higher up, **Pukalani** (Heavenly Gate) and **Makawao** ⓴ (Forest Beginning) lie at the geographical entrance to Upcountry. Makawao and surround-ing villages were once home for both sugar plantation laborers and cattle cowboys. In recent years, Makawao has been rejuvenated by a diverse col-lection of newcomers ranging from upscale professionals to counter-cul-ture refugees. Even with the influx of cafés and boutiques, Makawao has retained a rough-hewn rustic feel from its days as a ranch town. On the Fourth of July, a wide variety of peo-ple turn out for the annual Makawao

Small surf-town life in Pa'ia.

parade and rodeo, one of the biggest local events on Maui.

North of Makawao, on the flanks of Haleakala, stop for a picnic at **Ali'i Kula Lavender Farm**, the biggest such farm in the islands. Beyond Makawao and Pukalani, the **Kula** area is blessed with a mild climate and rich, deep soil. As a result, its agriculture is probably the most diversified in Hawaii. During the California Gold Rush of the mid 1800s, Kula farmers grew potatoes, corn, and wheat for export to California. Nowadays, farmers harvest lettuce, cabbage, turnips, carrots, and peas. Most delectable, claim the gourmets, are the extra-sweet Kula onions, which are said to be unparalleled. Flowers of all colors and purposes are yet another Upcountry product, including many of the exquisite tropicals like heliconia, bird-of-paradise, and protea.

Highway 37 is the road that stretches from Makawao to Kula, and continuing south on this road brings visitors through the back portion of Upcountry. The road passes through **Waiakoa** and the **Church of the Holy Ghost**

㉑. This octagonal church, dating from the late 1890s, was built by Portuguese families who had settled on Maui two decades earlier.

Beyond Kula and **Keokea** (a good place to stop for coffee) on a narrow two-lane road, the 18,000-acre (7,300-hectare) **'Ulupalakua Ranch** ㉒ marks a terrain shift from green and cool to brown and hot. Started as a sugar plantation in the 1850s, 'Ulupalakua is today a working cattle ranch of about 5,000 head, with additional sheep and elk. The ranch's general store offers *paniolo* gear and a deli. 'Ulupalakua Ranch is also home to Hawaii's only commercial vineyard, **Tedeschi Winery** ㉓ (tel: 878-6058; www.mauiwine.com; daily 10am–5.30pm), which produces a rather diverse assortment, from pineapple wine to "champagne." The vineyard offers free tastings, tours, and a small museum.

From the winery at 'Ulupalakua Ranch, the view downslope south to the coast and **La Pérouse Bay** (see page 183) is as unobstructed as one could hope for.

Horses graze in Makawao.

UPCOUNTRY COWBOYS

Cowboys in Hawaii? It is perhaps an unexpected combination, but in 1838, King Kamehameha III invited Spanish-Mexican vaqueros from California to teach Hawaiians how to manage wild herds. Today, cowboy culture is alive and well in Makawao, home of the *paniolo*, the Hawaiian word for cowboy. Short of attending the annual Makawao Rodeo, the best place to live like a cowboy is Pi'iholo Ranch, where resident wranglers host a variety of horseback riding excursions across protected land on the slopes of Haleakala. Some of these tours include a picnic lunch; all of them make a stop at a local rehabilitation area for the Hawaiian Goose. For true thrill-seekers, Pi'iholo also operates a zipline park where riders "zip" across tree canopies, mountain valleys, and more.

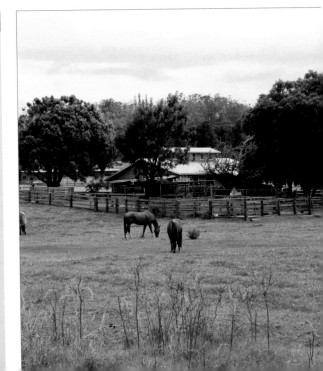

FACT

Although the vast depression atop Haleakala is usually called a crater, it is actually a basin or caldera created by the collapse and erosion of the summit rim.

Atop Haleakala

Another road from Kula and Maka-wao climbs to the summit of Halea-kala in more than 30 switchbacks, delivering exquisite views at every turn. More than half a million people visit **Haleakala National Park** annually, many venturing into the basin either by foot or on guided horseback trips along a 30-mile (50km) system of trails.

As far as visitors are concerned, the park consists of two distinct and mutually inaccessible sections, the main section at the top of the volcano, and another one extending down Haleaka-la's southeast flank to the Hana Coast and the 'Ohe 'o Gulch (Seven Pools). The National Park Service maintains two campgrounds in the basin for visitors, and another coastal campsite adjacent to 'Ohe 'o, which is approximately 10 miles (17km) past Hana.

Park Headquarters (tel: 572-4400; www.nps.gov/hale; daily 8am–3.45pm) offers information and a telephone, but no gas or food, and the Visitor Center (daily sunrise–3pm) at the summit has displays, restrooms, and

shelter from the high-altitude cold winds. There are good overlooks of the summit basin itself at several spots along the way to the summit. At the **Kalahaku Overlook** ㉕, one may be lucky enough to see the striking Haleakala silversword, a native member of the sunflower family that flowers once a year, then dies.

Pu'u 'Ula'ula (Red Hill), the summit of Haleakala, now has a space-age tenant. Here at **Science City**, scientists track satellites across the sky and bombard the heavens with laser beams, while University of Hawaii researchers operate lunar and solar observatories. Both facilities are closed to the public.

Crater hikes

To drive yourself to the summit of Haleakala in time to see the dawn, you'll need to start early and leave almost any hotel in the island by around 3am. Commercial tours pick up passengers even earlier than that and some tour operators offer the option of rolling back down the mountain on a bicycle.

Street scene in Makawao.

If you have the time and energy, it's well worth venturing down into the caldera itself, an extraordinarily desolate yet compelling wilderness of cinder cones and ash. After even the shortest of hikes, you'll have to walk steeply uphill in order to exit the crater, at an altitude of 10,000ft (3,000 meters), so prepare for a serious physical challenge. The most obvious route is to take the Sliding Sands Trail, which drops down from close to the visitor center. Distances are very deceptive once you're in the caldera, but you need to allow three or four hours for the round-trip if you want to descend at all far. A full day's hike will take you right into the heart of the caldera, and out again via the other major route, the Halemau'u Trail.

The back side of Haleakala

There's another way to see Haleakala: from the back. Beyond 'Ulupalakua Ranch, Highway 37 becomes Highway 31, the Pi'ilani Highway, and begins a slow descent, rounding the southwest slopes of Haleakala and cutting across dry, open range where cattle roam. Pastures along this route are scarred by lava flows and abandoned stonework. Now parched and uninhabited, this vast leeward side of Haleakala once supported dryland forests and a population of Hawaiians.

In **Kaupo** ㉖, 5 miles (8km) of the road are unpaved, and most rental car contracts prohibit driving the unpaved sections due to risk of rockfalls. Check locally before you set off. Kaupo is about 1.5 miles (2.5km) past pavement's end (coming from Upcountry) just beyond **St Joseph's Church**, built in 1861. A well-defined trail winds up the southern slope and through the 8,200ft (2,500-meter) **Kaupo Gap** ㉗ into the basin atop Haleakala. Assuming it's clear, the road beyond Kaupo continues to Kipahulu and the Hana Coast, and eventually back to Pa'ia. Even if you were planning to turn around here, consider going a little farther to the eternally windswept setting of **Huialoha Church**, which was built in 1859 and is still in use.

Cinder cones seen from the Leleiwi Lookout in Haleakala National Park.

Paragliding over Kula.

Beach near the Ke'anae Peninsula.

THE HANA COAST

On the rainy side of Haleakala, at the end of the windiest drive in Hawaii, Hana sits like an oasis, a spot almost too beautiful to be real.

Both geography and climate have conspired to keep the Hana district, the east-facing bulge of Haleakala, a separate world. Between Hana and the rest of Maui stretches the windward face of the mountain, and in Hawaii that means the rainy side of the island. Hana is so separate from Maui proper that ruling chiefs from the Big Island often claimed it as their own and defended it successfully against the challenges of Maui chiefs. Lovely, rounded Hana Bay, backed by lush grasslands and a mountainous wilderness of rain forest and waterfalls, was the site of some fierce fighting in the old days.

The road to Hana – also known as the Hana Highway – twists through jungle, over bridges, past waterfalls, and along cliff-edges for 35 miles (56km), finally straightening out in the town itself. It slices through a landscape scoured by water, cut with deep gulches, and choked with the enthusiastic flora of the rainforest. Despite infrastructure improvements over the years, the trek remains a stomach-churning drive of twists and turns, lasting a minimum of two hours, more if you divert to picnic or explore.

From the town of Hana, it's another 30 minutes along the Pi'ilani Highway to Haleakala National Park at Ohe'o Gulch, promoted, erroneously, as the "Seven Sacred Pools." At that point, one can turn back, or else, assuming the

highway is currently clear, continue on through Kaupo to completely encircle Haleakala. Either way, start early and plan to put in a long day. Remember that local people drive the road every day. They know every twist and turn, and they usually have a good reason to keep moving. It's polite to use the passing places and let *kama'aina*, or residents, go by.

The road to Hana

Properly speaking, the **Hana Highway** begins at the one-mile marker (look for

Main Attractions

Hana Highway
Wai'anapanapa State Park
Pi'ilani Highway
Pools at Ohe'o Gulch
Laulima Farmstand

Surfing in Hana Bay.

TIP

Souvenir T-shirts
promote the drive to
Hana as if it were a
transcontinental
expedition. It's not; it's
just a slow, winding
road. It is narrow, with
several one-lane bridges.
If cars pile up behind
you, pull over and let
them past.

Hana Bay.

the green rectangular signs on the road-side) at the bottom of Kaupakalua Road in **Haʻiku** ㉘. The gateway to the Hana Coast and the winding road is the quiet community of **Huelo** ㉙, with its small Congregational church, **Kaulanapueo** ("Owl Perch"), built in 1853. Maui's mood and *ʻaina* – land – begin to shift here, slipping away in the tropical wet-ness. From this point on, you'll be driv-ing pretty slowly for most of the way, as pasture and open forest give way to ever-thickening jungle. Many of the bridges offer easy turnouts and places to swim. The best of these is the pool at mile 11, with the added bonus of a waterfall and covered pavilion.

Another good resting spot is at **Kaumahina State Wayside** ㉚. The park's carefully tended grounds, with restrooms and picnic tables, include labeled examples of plants common to this coast. You can retrace your steps a few hundred yards/meters for a refresh-ing swim at **Puohokamoa Falls**. Or from the Kaumahina parking lot, hike to the upper left side of the park and experience a spectacular view of the **Keʻanae Peninsula**. The view here is

due east, which may explain the name Kaumahina, or Rising Moon.

The road next drops into spectacular **Honomanu** (Bird Bay), with a rocky, black beach and canyon walls choked with flowering trees. Just after Hon-omanu, at about mile 16, is **Keʻanae** ㉛, a community of taro farmers who still maintain *loʻi*, or irrigated fields, that were first established over 500 years ago.

A narrow road leaves the highway and curves 0.5 miles (800 meters) down to a scattering of houses, a tiny cemetery, and a Congregational church built in 1860. Decades ago, when only a horse trail connected Keʻanae and Hana, there were two country grocery stores here, and the field behind the church was a baseball diamond. The school building used to face in the opposite direction, but a lethal tidal wave in 1946 spun it around on its foundations. The shoreline down here consists of jagged black lava rocks, lashed endlessly by crashing white surf.

Near the turn off to Keʻanae is the **Keʻanae Arboretum**, which offers a look at taro cultivation and pleasant walks among tropical and Hawaiian native plants.

Cultural landscape area

Three miles (5km) farther is **Wailua** **32**, another traditional taro-growing region. The state has designated this entire area as a Cultural Landscape, and life here follows patterns established long before Hawaii was discovered by Cook. Wailua's tiny **St Gabriel's Church** was one of the first to be built on this coast. The lookout on the Hana Highway above Wailua has picnic benches and a captivating view.

Continuing toward Hana, the highway offers another popular roadside stop, **Pua'a Ka'a** (Rolling Pig) **State Park**, between mile markers 22 and 23. Located here, where one least expects it, are a pay telephone, restrooms, and picnic tables, along with a natural waterfall and pool. You are approaching **Nahiku** **33**, the wettest stretch of this coast. At the end of the 19th century, it was the home of America's first rubber plantation, with thousands of acres of rubber trees. The vigorous community was serviced by a small railroad and barges.

The most impressive accomplishment along this coast, however, is still active and clearly visible along the roadside as flumes, tunnels, engineered ditches, and watergates. In the late 19th century, the East Maui Irrigation Company built a water-delivery system that is arguably the boldest engineering accomplishment in post-discovery Hawaii, especially considering the awesome logistics of transporting all construction materials by horse, mule, and human power. The waterworks transformed Maui's arid central plain into verdant and extremely productive sugar cane fields.

The road begins to become easier at about mile 30. The **Hana Airport** **34**, which has a limited commuter service to Honolulu and Kahului, is just beyond. One mile farther, **Wai'anapanapa State Park** **35** offers a lava coastline ornately sculpted by nature, one of Maui's best campsites, hiking trails, and cabins set along a jet-black sand beach. Inland are a couple of caves with anchialine pools (linked to the ocean) that are great for swimming. Unfortunately, this is some of the only swimming available here; perhaps the only downside of Wai'anapanapa is that the ocean is often too rough to enjoy.

Flags fly in the breeze at Hana Bay.

Spectacular ocean views on the road to Hana.

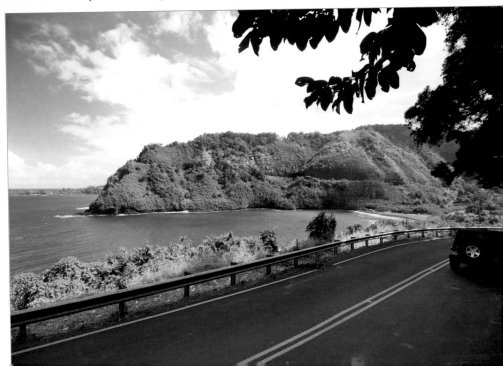

TIP

If you like quiet, and you want a special place mostly for yourself, spend the night in Hana. The place is bewitching in the morning and evening hours, when the day-trip visitors are absent.

Nearby, visit the large **Pi'ilanihale Heiau** (temple). The rock platform of the *heiau* overlooks the coast and is part of an escorted or self-guided tour of **Kahanu Gardens** (tel: 248-8912; Mon–Sat 9am–2pm). Plant collections from Pacific islands is the focus here, including the world's largest collection of breadfruit cultivars.

Hana and beyond

Finally, the tortuous road unravels into the rolling hills and ranch pastures of **Hana ㊱**. Hawaiians say that "the sky comes close to Hana," and, indeed, moody clouds often hang low off the hills here. A local legend tells of a deity who once stood atop **Ka'uiki Hill**, the prominent cinder cone that forms the right flank of Hana Bay, and who was able to throw his spear right through the sky. Ka'uiki ("The Glimmer") served as a fortress during the wars with Kamehameha the Great. A cave, now marked with a plaque, was the 1768 birthplace of Queen Ka'ahumanu, the favorite of Kamehameha's many wives.

Directly above the bay and to the right, the **Hana Cultural Center &**

Museum (tel: 248-8622; daily 10am–4pm; donations accepted) offers a brief, but thought-provoking glimpse into the area's history. Next to the museum is the small former courthouse dating to 1871, and a reconstructed *kauhale* – a compound of authentic thatch buildings constructed in the ancient style of the region. Several historic 19th-century churches add to Hana's appeal.

For a magnificent view of the Hana area, hike through the pasture above the town to the large stone cross on the hill; the cross is a memorial to Paul Fagan, founder of the 3,000-acre (1,200-hectare) **Hana Ranch**, which owns much of the land in these parts. Pedestrian access to the memorial is from the parking lot across from the **Travaasa Hana**, a low-profile luxury retreat. A trail from the hotel's oceanfront cottages leads to the isolated red sands of Kahailulu. In addition to the hotel, camping and bed-and-breakfast accommodations are options for an overnight stay in Hana.

There are two markets in Hana. One of them is the well-known Hasegawa General Store. Rural Hawaii grew

One of the pools at Ohe'o Gulch.

up on family-owned stores like this, established a generation or two ago by descendants of Japanese immigrants. Hasegawa Store is a general store in the fullest sense of the word, covering all the bases but with a totally eclectic inventory; prices are, given the scarcity of retail opportunities in town, usually on the high side.

The road beyond Hana, known as the **Pi'ilani Highway**, passes through several miles of grassy ranchland. Watch for the next big cinder cone, Ka'uiki's twin, **Kaiwio Pele** ("Pele's Bone"), site of a legendary battle to the death between Pele, the volcano goddess, and the earth deity Kamapua'a, a pig-man. Tiny **'Alau Island**, just offshore, marks the spot where Maui, the demi-god, fished the Hawaiian Islands out of the sea with a magic hook. The spur road that curves down to the sea here passes two of Hana's most accessible beaches. **Koki Beach**, at the foot of the cinder cone, is shallow and sandy for a long way, and great for bodysurfing, but watch for rip tides. As the road bends back to the main highway, it passes **Hamoa Beach** ③⑦, a favorite of James Michener. The

Travaasa Hana maintains facilities for its guests here, but the beach is open to the public.

From here to the Kipahulu district, the road encounters deep glades, sheer cliffs, and cascading waterfalls. **Wailua Falls** ③⑧ is the most accessible. Then, 13 miles (21km) out of Hana, the road enters the lower portion of **Haleakala National Park** and crosses an arched, stone bridge that overlooks **Ohe'o Gulch** ③⑨, a common turn-around spot for drivers heading back the way they came.

Just past the bridge, a 0.6-mile (1km) trail leads down to the lower pools, which are wonderful swimming holes. Be aware that 250ins (6,350mm) of rain falls annually in the forests above, and the stream and pools can quickly become raging torrents. Near the bottom-most pools and along the cliffs fronting the ocean are the stone foundations of an ancient fishing village. Just south of this area is a campground, with tent sites along the dramatic basalt cliffs. Campers may stay for up to three days at a time. Fires are forbidden, but barbecue pits are provided,

Waves pound the rocky shore at the Travaasa Hana resort.

Wailua Falls.

as well as restrooms. Bring your own water, however.

One of the most rewarding hikes on the island begins directly across the road from the parking lot: a 2-mile (3.2km) climb inland to **Waimoku Falls**. Rangers have built two mildly spectacular bridges, and also a boardwalk to keep the ground virginal while passing through the heart of an enormous bamboo forest. Still, the trek is not easy. Waimoku Falls is high (400ft/120 meters), sheer, and powerful enough to keep observers at a distance. Afternoon showers in the hills can mean flash flooding.

Kipahulu and Kaupo

Beyond Ohe'o Gulch is the drier, grassy Kipahulu district and the village of **Kipahulu** ⓭. About a mile past the pools lie the ruins of the **Kipahulu Sugar Mill**, a relic of the early 20th century. Below the ruins, a narrow, paved road leads toward the ocean and to tiny **Palapala Ho'omau Church**, erected in 1857. This is the burial place of aviation pioneer Charles Lindbergh, the first person to fly solo from Paris to New York. The church is open to visitors.

The road beyond is paved except for about 5 miles (8km) of rugged, jaw-rattling dirt toward Kaupo; driving on the unpaved sections of the road is prohibited by most car rental companies. It is always liable to be blocked by rock falls; check locally before you set off. The road breezes past the soft pastures of Kipahulu, touches a cove, then climbs a spine-tingling, cliff-side grade into the sterner landscape of Kaupo. Cattle guards mark the entrance to **Kaupo Ranch**, a large cattle operation since the late 19th century. A windswept and surf-pounded peninsula juts out below the road, where **Huialoha**, a restored old Congregational circuit church is sited. Huialoha was built in 1859, when Kaupo was almost totally isolated, accessible only by sea and a primitive trail. The crumbling walls behind the church were once a school. Offshore is an ancient surfing area once known as **Mokulau** ("Many Islets"), named for the lava islets sprinkled just offshore. The winds here seem to never stop.

The small store in **Kaupo** was once the only local source of food and supplies on this part of the island, but it now caters mostly to travelers in rental cars and minivans. From here, the road continues to Upcountry.

Toward the mountain, the slopes of Haleakala rise to a deep slash at the top called the **Kaupo Gap**, 8,200ft (2,500 meters) above sea level, which opens into Haleakala basin. In ancient times, the gap was the primary route taken by Hawaiians traversing Maui on foot. It was easier to climb the mountain than to bushwhack through the coastal jungle. Horseback trips are available; hikers also make the climb, though it's nearly all up hill and can be jarring on joints.

Kipahulu Valley, on the Hana side of the gap, is a protected natural science reserve that is closed to the public. The reserve shelters vast expanses of native trees like *koa* and *'ohi'a*, and endangered birds like the Maui parrotbill and Maui *nukupu'u*.

A more gentle beach near Travaasa Hana.

Swimming in the tiered pools of Oheʻo Gulch.

DISAPPEARING FLORA AND FAUNA

No doubt both the Polynesians and Europeans had good intentions, but both groups introduced plants and animals that have decimated Hawaii's own flora and fauna.

The Hawaiian Monk Seal is shy, keeping to itself in the uninhabited islands and atolls of northwestern Hawaii. You may encounter one on the less frequented beaches of the major islands; if you do, it is illegal to approach or touch it. It is one of only two indigenous mammals in Hawaii; the other is the hoary bat. The Polynesian rat, introduced by ancient Polynesians, is considered by some to have evolved enough to count as a Hawaiian species.

Avian decline

Many species of Hawaii's native birds, evolving through the centuries with few natural predators, have all but disappeared. The mongoose, introduced to combat rats, prefers eggs and has decimated native birds. Other introduced species threaten Hawaii's birds everywhere except Kauai. The mynah, introduced by Europeans, is a pushy creature, and it has forced many other bird species from their habitat. Another serious threat to both indigenous and introduced bird species is the brown snake from Guam, a potential arrival as a stowaway on commercial and military aircraft.

Flora

Prior to the arrival of people, the level of endemic plant species was higher in Hawaii than anywhere else on the planet. Today, the flora we associate with Hawaii – plumeria, hibiscus, pineapples, bananas, guavas – are all introduced species. Hawaii's indigenous plants are fighting for survival, and many are already extinct.

The nene is Hawaii's state bird. Males and females look identical.

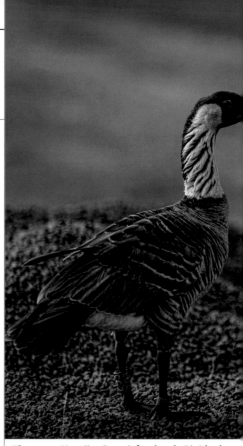

The nene, or Hawaiian Goose, is found on the Big Island, Maui and Kauai, usually at higher elevations. Unlike other goose species, the nene lacks webbed feet; it has claws that are more useful on the volcanic slopes.

Pigs, introduced by Polynesians, and goats and cattle, introduced by Europeans, have destroyed Hawaii's native plant species.

Silversword plants in Haleakala National Park, Maui. The silversword is adapted to high-altitude life, but walking to close to it will crush its roots.

HAWAII'S BENIGN EVOLUTION

Statistically speaking – at least before the first humans arrived 1,500 years ago – a new species had become established on Hawaii every 15,000 years. Hawaii's extreme remoteness gave those animal and plant species that arrived a unique environment in which to grow, independent of outside influence. By the time we humans showed up, nearly 9,000 kinds of flora and fauna unique to the islands had evolved, including the silversword.

In the absence of mammals and other interlopers, plants did not develop defenses such as thorns and toxins, nor did birds develop types of behavior that protected them from predators. When people introduced numerous animal species – from birds to grazing cattle – Hawaii's indigenous species in populated areas were poorly equipped for survival.

The good news is those native plants and birds that were not in populated areas survived. Many of these specimens are found largely in inaccessible places such as the cliffs of Molokai's north shore, the boggy highlands of Kauai, and the restricted and fenced-in Kipahulu Valley of eastern Maui. Biologically, they keep the old days alive.

...other introduced mammal, the mongoose, has decimated ...ny of Hawaii's indigenous birds. Brought by Europeans to ...trol rats, it preferred birds – it is a day mammal and rats ...efer the night.

...e reclusiveness of the Hawaiian Monk Seal (hence, the ...onk") has probably assured its species' survival. Rare is the ...hting of a grown Monk Seal (seen here on Poipu Beach Park ... Kauai), much less a seal pup. Wisely, they prefer ...inhabited islands.

The black-necked stilt is one of Hawaii's native birds, but lacks the necessary defensive behavior against introduced predators. Found only in a few inland wildlife sanctuaries, such as on Maui's central isthmus, the stilt is a delightful sighting for a birdwatcher.

Plumeria trees in bloom in Kaunakakai.

*Okala Island and cliffs viewed
from Kalawao.*

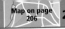

MOLOKAI

Quiet and underdeveloped, Molokai retains a colorful history, and a distinctive "Hawaiian" ambiance.

There's not much happening on Molokai, and that's precisely its appeal. Tourist resorts are few. Tiki bars are practically non-existent. And those big bus tours that you might spot on more populous islands such as Oahu and Maui? They are nowhere in sight.

No, life on Molokai is wonderfully slow, affording visitors the opportunity to sit down and talk with locals and learn about the island's history the old-fashioned way: through stories. Some of these stories undoubtedly will spotlight the cliffs in the north, the world's tallest ocean cliffs. Other stories will focus on the historic colony of those suffering from Hansen's Disease (formerly known as leprosy). Still others will spotlight the fish ponds, the vistas, and the untrammeled beaches. By the end of your visit, after four or five days on Molokai, you'll "get" what the place is all about.

The island is a haven for adventure-seeking travelers who want to immerse themselves in authentic Hawaii – the Hawaii they won't get anywhere else. It's for travelers who will be comfortable in hotels that are clean but not luxurious. It's also pretty much exclusively for adults; because activities are minimal, Molokai is a place where young kids would get bored and older kids might get a little stir crazy after a while.

Riding mules in Kalaupapa.

For those who give it a chance, however, who stick around and open their minds to the island's brilliance, the experience can be rewarding, even life-changing. Molokai is just about as Hawaiian as the Hawaiian Islands get.

Volcanic origins

On a map, Molokai appears to be shaped like a slender slipper, 38 miles (60km) long and 10 miles (16km) wide. The island has three geological anchors, each created by volcanic activity millions of years ago. **Mauna**

Main Attractions
Kaunakakai
Pepe'opae Trail
Pala'au State Park
Kalaupapa National
    Historical Park
Halawa Valley

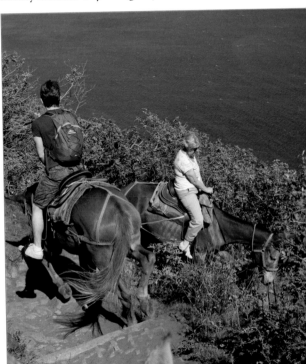

Loa, a 1,380ft (420-meter) tableland at the western end of the island (not to be confused with the active volcano of the same name on Hawaii Island), was noted in ancient times for an adze quarry, *holua* slides (snowless sledding), and as a source of wood for sorcery images.

Later, the east Molokai volcano erupted, and **Mauna Kamakou** was pushed up to 4,970ft (1,515 meters) to become the island's highest point. Kalaupapa Peninsula, properly called Makanalua, was born even more recently, when 400ft (120-meter) **Kauhako**, a small shield volcano, poured forth its lava to shape a flat tongue of land in the center of the northern coast. It is separated from the rest of the island by a fortress-like barrier of *pali*, or high cliffs, perfect for isolating a colony of exiles.

Agricultural Molokai

Molokai's land is primarily agricultural, and development has been limited. And, perhaps best of all for the adventurous traveler, tourists are few. Only a few paved roads transit

Molokai, and some of its more spectacular sights and places of archeological interest require a 4x4 vehicle, boat or helicopter to view.

Ho'olehua Airport ❶ is situated 7 miles (11km) away from the town of **Kaunakakai ❷**, which is on the southern coast. More than half of the island's 7,500 people live near Kaunakakai. Ala Malama, the main street contains old buildings that have probably changed very little since the "Cockeyed Mayor of Kaunakakai," who was made famous in a *hapa-haole* (semi-Caucasian) song popular during the 1930s, strolled along its streets.

A wharf – the longest in the entire State of Hawaii – extends several hundred yards/meters out to sea at Kaunakakai; barges were loaded with pineapples here until the plantations closed down in the 1970s and 1980s. The focus is now on crops such as corn, watermelon, coffee, and onions. Before becoming king in 1863, Kamehameha V spent his summers on Molokai. The nearby **Kapuaiwa Coconut Grove** (Kapuaiwa means "Mysterious Taboo"), which originally contained 1,000 coconut trees on 10 acres (4 hectares) of land, was planted for him in the 1860s.

The rainforest

Shrouded as often as not by clouds, the summit of Molokai's eastern mountain, Mauna Kamakou, holds a remarkable unspoiled expanse of Hawaiian rainforest. The only route to the top is up a gravel road that branches east just south of the junction of Maunaloa Highway and the highway to Kaunakakai, and soon degenerates into muddy ruts that are only passable in a high-clearance 4x4 vehicle. Most of this area is accessible only on monthly guided tours from The Nature Conservancy, and the tours fill up months in advance. To get on the list, call the **Nature Conservancy Office** (tel: 553-5236; www.nature.org).

Nine miles (14km) up from the highway, the curious **Sandalwood**

Riding mules on the beach in Kalaupapa.

boat ❸ is actually a hole in the ground roughly the size and shape of a 19th-century sailing ship's hold. Hawaiian laborers would fill this pit with the amount of sandalwood that such ships could carry, before selling it to Western traders. Sandalwood was once common throughout the Hawaiian Islands, but demand from China, where it was appreciated for its fragrance, encouraged the Hawaiian king to harvest it until there was no more left.

Waikolu Lookout and the Pepe'opae Trail

A mile further on, the **Waikolu Lookout** offers a first glimpse of the beautiful and rugged cliffs of Molokai's northern shore, the highest sea cliffs anywhere in the world. It also marks the start of the Kamakou Preserve, which protects unique Hawaiian plants and birds. A little over 2 miles (4km) farther on, you reach the **Pepe'opae Trail**, one of Hawaii's greatest hikes, an hour-long stretch of springy boardwalk that leads through extraordinary high-altitude mountain boglands and stunted forest to reach

further verdant views. The two deep valleys along this shore, Wailau and Pelekunu, cannot be reached on foot. The expensive and spectacular way to see them is by helicopter. Trips depart from Maui, or in summer you can also take a boat trip from Kaunakakai.

Central Molokai

Branching north off Maunaloas Highway, onto Kala'e Highway, just beyond the rainforest turn off, brings you to **Kualapu'u**, an old Del Monte company town; there are several unusual attractions en route, between Kaunakakai and the end of the road lookouts. A bit farther down the road is the **Molokai Museum and Cultural Center**. Adjacent to the historic **R.W. Meyer Sugar Mill** (tel: 567-6436; Mon–Sat 10am–2pm), the center provides a Molokai perspective on the Hawaiian past.

Pala'au State Park

Still heading north, you come to **Pala'au State Park** ❹, where the park road passes through an attractive forested area of *koa*, paperbark,

Boats in Kaunakakai Wharf.

Storefronts in Kaunakakai.

FATHER DAMIEN

Father Damien (formerly Joseph De Veuster) arrived in the islands in 1862 from Belgium. He came to Molokai in 1873 and remained until his death 16 years later. During that time, Damien organized the colony at Kalaupapa into a true community, establishing a church and small clinic. Land was cleared, crops were grown, and a modern water system installed. By 1883 Damien had contracted Hansen's Disease and six years later he died, just 49 years old. He was buried in Kalaupapa, but his body was returned to Belgium in 1936. In 1907, the writer Jack London traced the priest's footsteps around Kalaupapa, writing a number of short stories about Hansen's Disease after his visit, including a chapter in *The Cruise of the Snark* about the Kalaupapa residents.

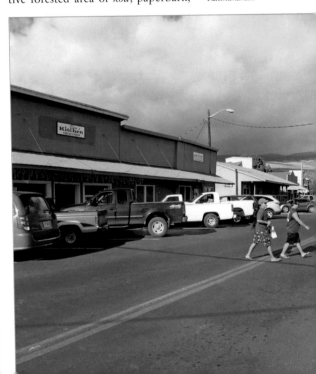

ironwood, and cypress trees. A small arboretum with more than 40 species of trees and a picnic area await at the end of the road. From the parking lot, it's a short walk and a slight climb to **Ka Ule o Nanahoa** ("Penis of Nanahoa"), a phallic rock 6ft (1.8 meters) high and once visited by those who believed it was a cure for infertility. The **Kalaupapa Overlook** ❺ offers a spectacular view from atop the 1,600ft (485-meter) -high cliffs above the former leprosy colony.

Kalaupapa

In his novel *Hawaii*, published in 1959, James Michener described the **Makanalua Peninsula** ❻ (often referred to as the **Kalaupapa Peninsula**, after the settlement) as "a majestic spot, a poem of nature… In the previous history of the world no such hellish spot had ever stood in such heavenly surroundings."

This area has had a colorful history to say the least. In 1866, the year of Mark Twain's visit to Molokai, the Hawaiian government began transporting victims of Hansen's Disease,

or leprosy, to Molokai. The exiles wer literally pushed from the boat into th peninsula's rough coastal waters, wit little care whether or not they woul survive. Over the years, more tha 8,000 people were exiled to Kalau papa. In later years, when Father Dam ien was dispatched to Molokai to loo after these patients, more than 1,00(exiles lived here. Now there are fewe than 10 residents in Kalaupapa. The all live there voluntarily.

Kalaupapa National Historical Park

Today, Kalaupapa is protected by th **Kalaupapa National Historica Park**, which was established in 198(and is jointly administered by th National Park Service and the Stat of Hawaii. Permission to visit the his torical park is easily obtained throug Makani Kai airlines, through an outfi ter or by contacting the Hawaii Stat Department of Health in Honolulu o Molokai. Children under the age of 1(are not permitted to visit Kalaupapa.

There are two ways to arrive: by ai which takes you to a small airpor on the peninsula, or from the top of the cliffs down a steep trail. The most colorful way to manage the trail, which drops 1,800ft (550 meters) to the peninsula, is on the back of a nimble-footed mule, which you can organize with the **Kalaupapa Rare Adventure** (tel: 567-6088; www. muleride.com; Mon–Sat departs 8.30am, returns 3.30pm). Only 100 permits are allowed for people to enter Kalaupapa each year; visitors must go through Damien Tours (tel: 567-6171), and can either charter a plane, ride the mules, or hike. Tours book up in advance so call ahead. State law prohibits photographing residents without their permission. Although some residents still suffer from Hansen's Disease, they are no longer confined to the island; as previously mentioned, they live here by choice. The disease can now be cured, and, despite the fears that surrounded it for so many years, is contagious but not easily contracted.

East across the Kalaupapa Peninsula is the abandoned settlement of **Kalawao** ❼, site of the original colony. **Siloama Church**, the Church of the Healing Spring, was built here by Protestants in 1871. The Catholic church nearby, **St Philomena's**, has a monument to Father Damien, marking his original burial spot. The plan is to preserve Kalaupapa as a living community until the last resident has died or departed, then to preserve it as a historic park.

Eastern Molokai

East from Kaunakakai, the Kamehameha V Highway runs for 28 miles (61km) along the southern coast to Halawa. There is much to see along this road, the second half of which is a narrow lane twisting along the coast. It is a long drive, and a slow one. Just a few miles past Kaunakakai is **Oneali'i Park** (Royal Sands), a beach with campsites. For a small daily fee, campers may stay here for two weeks but must renew their permit every three days.

If you have the time, hiking Halawa Valley is perhaps the best way to get to know the real Molokai. The hike crosses private lands and therefore requires permission from the landowner, **Anakala Pilipo Solatorio** (tel:

A phallic stone thought to enhance fertility in Pala'au State Park.

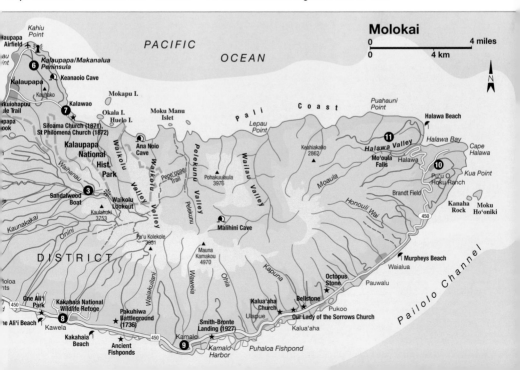

Western Molokai

Back through Kaunakakai and up past Hoʻolehua Airport, the Maunaloa Highway runs through a dry landscape for about 10 miles (16km). **Maunaloa** , itself a former plantation town, lies at the end of the road.

Much of this dry leeward side of the island is composed of grazing land owned by the 40,000-acre (16,000-hectare) **Molokai Ranch** ⑬, the largest local landowner. When the Dole Company closed down its pineapple operations here in 1976, the firm returned almost 10,000 acres (4,000 hectares) to the ranch, much of which has been planted with hay, grown for commercial purposes. Cattle rearing continues to be the mainstay of the ranch's operation, which currently runs as many as 600 head across its pasture lands.

Not far away, but hidden away from the gaze of casual visitors, is one of the most sacred spots in Hawaii. Dedicated to Laka, the goddess of hula, a difficult-to-find *heiau* (temple) is said to be the birthplace of this ancient dance form. *Halau hula* (hula school) students and their *kupuna* (elders)

Kalaupapa coastline.

gather here before sunrise to make offerings before performing at the annual Molokai Ka Hula Piko festival in May. Parts of this festival are open to the public, but if you plan to attend it's best to go with a local guide who can explain what is happening.

Kepuhi Bay

A number of spurs branch off the main highway and wind down to the coastline. Condominiums on the west side, at **Kepuhi Bay** ⑭ near the northwestern tip, have closed in recent years, basically eliminating overnight accommodations in this area. That said, neighboring Papohaku Beach, a vast expanse of golden sand, is worth a visit, and on clear nights the lights of Oahu and Diamond Head are visible across the 26-mile (42km) -wide Kaiwi Channel. Only the strongest swimmers should venture into the ocean along the beach. The treacherous current and pounding waves nicknamed the Oahu Express, can sweep the unwary out to sea. Camping is allowed by permit at **Papohaku Beach Camp** ⑮.

LANAI

Privately owned but open to visitors, Lanai has changed its focus from pineapples to luxury resorts, and is primed for the big time.

Main Attractions
Lanai City
Sweetheart Rock
Munro Trail
Shipwreck Beach
Garden of the Gods

Lanai, Hawaii's sixth-largest island, is lots of things at once: from quintessential Hawaiian palm trees to barren red-rock landscape and whole days without sunshine up in the hills. The island's beaches are among the best in the state. With high-tech billionaire Larry Ellison now owning 98 percent of the island, Lanai is primed for significant development, as infrastructure is refreshed and new condos for a higher calibre of tourists are built. In short, the place is on the cusp of something big.

The visitor experience

Lanai offers a number of microclimates in a relatively small amount of surface area – 18 miles (29km) long and 13 miles (21km) wide, to be exact. Beaches are breathtaking; the beach fronting the Four Seasons Resort Lanai at Manele Bay is great for sunbathing and swimming, and other beaches such as Hulopo'e offer epic snorkeling, too. Up in the mountains, in the tiny town of Lanai City or at the Four Seasons Resort Lanai, The Lodge at Ko'ele, the vibe is completely different, with pine trees, putt-putt golf, and much more manic weather than down at the beach.

Outside of these tourist-centric areas, Lanai is full of adventure. Visitors rent 4x4 vehicles and go off-roading in the Martian landscape of an area known as the Garden of the Gods. On the windward side of the island, people putter from cove to cove, trying desperately to stay out of the gusts. You can drive on a dirt road to Polihua Beach in the north; you also can hike to the Kaunolu Village site and brush up on local history or go tidepooling in the surf. Perhaps the best part of these activities: you've got most of them all to yourself.

Historical overview

The ancient Hawaiians felt Lanai was inhabited by spirits and, according to legend, people stayed away from the island until one day a hero named Kaulula'au, the son of a chief from Lahaina, crossed the channel and rid the place of danger.

The first Western residents were Mormons, who in the mid 1850s arranged generous lease terms with chief Ha'alelea of Oahu. James Dole, a persevering businessman from Boston, purchased Lanai in 1922 for $1.1 million, and planted the island with pineapple almost immediately, Dole then created a deep-water harbor at Kaumalapau and laid out a nearby town for the Japanese and Filipino immigrants who came to work on his Lanai plantation.

Dole's Hawaiian Pineapple Company prospered and was later purchased by one of Hawaii's original "Big Five" *kama'aina* (resident) corporations, Castle & Cooke, which kept Dole's name and operated the plantation as the Dole Pineapple Company. In 1987, California investor David Murdock bought controlling interest of Castle & Cooke. Like Dole, Murdock moved quickly, building two world-class hotels, two golf courses, new homes for the island's residents,

and a recreational complex in the middle of Lanai City. Stunning the locals but acting pragmatically given the competition of cheaper Asian pineapples, he plowed up more than 13,000 acres (5,260 hectares) of what was once the world's largest pineapple plantation. Fewer than 500 acres (200 hectares) of pineapple land remain on Lanai – token fields to provide pineapples for the island's three hotels. Other fields are being replaced by experimental crops such as citrus, onions, papayas, macadamia, coffee, and grains used for cattle and other livestock feed.

Lanai hit the big time when Microsoft CEO Bill Gates got married there in 1994. Since then, celebrities and athletes have frequented the island with abandon. Finally, in 2012, Lanai became the private property of someone else: Larry Ellison, CEO of Oracle Corp. Ellison was reported to pay about $600 million for the island, and has vowed to spend a reported $500 million more on infrastructure improvements. Those improvements could pave the way for considerable

FACT

Lanai's trademark tree, the tall and dark Cook Island pine, creates water for the thirsty island. Mists collect in the trees' tight branches and drip like rain. One tree can produce as much as 40 gallons (150 liters) a day.

Garden of the Gods.

*Sweetheart Rock (Pu'u
Pehe) in Hulopo'e Bay.*

*En route to the
Garden of the Gods.*

luxury condominium developments
on the island over the next few years.

Seeing the sights

The heart of the island is a lone volcanic crater, **Palawai**, long extinct and
weathered into a subtle depression
surrounded by a great saucer of fertile
but dry farmland. The **Palawai Basin**
❶ once sustained the largest pineapple plantation in the world; today,
its grassy fields glimmer in the soft,
muted light.

Lanai City ❷, built by Dole in the
early 1920s, is home to virtually all
2,600 residents of the island. Located
inland at the base of the Lana'ihale
ridge, it's a classic plantation town –
quiet, modest, and orderly, designed
around rectangular Dole Park edged
with stores, the headquarters of the
Lanai Company, and the vintage
10-room **Hotel Lanai**. Nearby is The
Lodge at Ko'ele, one of the two award-
winning Four Seasons resorts that now
sustain the island's economy. Three
paved roads connect Lanai City with
the coast. One, heading southwest,
leads to the airport and **Kaumalapau**

Harbor ❸. When the pineapple was
king on Lanai, more than a million
pineapples a day were loaded onto
barges here for shipment to the Honolulu cannery 60 miles (100km) away.
Now, infrequent incoming barges are
filled with supplies for the island, and
a ferry from Maui deposits passengers
three times daily.

A very rough road off the highway
leads down to **Kaunolu Bay**, but you
must hike more than 3 miles (5km) on
rocky trails; it is off-limits for rental
vehicles – 4x4 or otherwise. At the
hike's end are the hard-to-locate ruins
of **Kaunolu** ❹, an ancient fishing
village, and Kamehameha's summer
home. Kaonolu is rich with the *mana*,
or spiritual power, of old Hawaii.
Nearby is Kahekili's Leap, a scenic
lookout named after the Maui chief
renowned for diving into the waters
below. The coastal views from here are
breathtaking.

Hulopo'e marine life

It's a much easier 20-minute drive
on a paved road from Lanai City to
Hulopo'e Bay ❺. The bay, a nature

A REAL "SWEETHEART"

Lanai's most photographed spot, Sweetheart Rock, is a triangular-shaped rock
just offshore in Hulopo'e Bay. Pu'u Pehe
is the centerpiece of a tragic love story in
Hawaiian legend that revolves around
two lovers: Pehe and her warrior boy-
friend, Makakehau. Taken at face value,
the tale bears eerie similarities to
Shakespeare's "Romeo and Juliet." The
climax of the story occurs during a ter-
rible storm; when Pehe drowns in the
storm surge, Makakehau takes her body
out to the rock and buries her near the
80ft (24-meter) summit. Stricken with
grief and out of his mind, he jumps to his
death in the churning sea below.
Hawaiians believe the rock has stood as
a memorial to their love ever since.
Today the rock is only accessible (by
kayak or stand-up paddleboard) on days
when the water is flat-calm.

conservation district that's off-limits to nearly all boats, is home to spinner dolphins, turtles, and an abundance of other marine life. Hulopo'e is the best place on the island to swim and snorkel. You can also hike along the eastern coast to reach the panoramic lookout that takes in Sweetheart Rock, with Maui rising majestically above the horizon. Conveniently, the Manele Bay resort stands in a commanding position directly over Hulopo'e Bay; a trail leads down from the hotel to the beach. Frequent shuttles carry people from The Lodge at Ko'ele, a 20-minute drive away. The state even allows camping at six sites on the grass above the beach. Permits are available from Lanai Company for a maximum stay of seven days. Just around an easterly point from Hulopo'e Bay is **Manele Boat Harbor ❻**.

Off-road excursions

Lanai's most unusual touring route is surely the **Munro Trail**. This is a 4x4 dirt track that climbs along the island's eastern ridge, cresting at **Lana'ihale ❼**, the high point at 3,370ft (1,030 meters). On a clear day, all the major Hawaiian islands except Kauai and Ni'ihau can be seen on the horizon. The Munro Trail continues down past **Ho'okio Gulch**, scene of a 1778 battle involving Kamehameha the Great, to Ko'ele and back to Lanai City. Start from Manele Road end, because descending is easier than ascending on the mushy, slippery Ko'ele side. The trail is impassable during rainy weather.

Another popular excursion heads out to the island's convex northeast coast. It can be reached by following Keomuku Road until it forks near the shoreline. To the left is a track to **Shipwreck Beach ❽**, so named because of the rusting hulk of the *Helena Pt. Townsend*, a tanker that has sat impaled on a reef in 12ft (4 meters) of water for over 50 years. To the right is a better road to the abandoned village of

Keomuku ❾. The trip to Keomuku takes about 45 minutes; the village was abandoned after the 1901 collapse of the Maunalei Sugar Company. A short distance down the road is an oblong stone marker, a sad memorial to the Japanese immigrant workers who died of a plague during Keomuku's plantation days.

The **Garden of the Gods ❿** can be reached by driving northwest along the Polihua Road, which turns into a dirt track that passes through grasslands. This is a strange playground of strewn boulders and disfigured lava formations that look spectacular at sunset, when they glow an unearthly orange. The route to the Garden of the Gods also passes one of the largest examples of a dry-land forest in Hawaii at **Kanepu'u**. Protected by high fences, it has been donated to the Nature Conservancy to preserve its vegetation. Beyond the Garden of the Gods, magnificent Polihua Beach stretches along the north coast. With its fearsome currents, it's no place for swimmers, but the views across to Molokai are stunning.

TIP

There's excellent snorkeling just outside the breakwater at Manele Boat Harbor, or you can take a snorkel cruise to the clear waters off the south coast with **Adventure Lanai Ecocenter** (tel: 565-7373; www.adventure lanai.com).

The rusty hulk of a ship run aground at Shipwreck Beach.

Canada-France-Hawaii Telescope and Gemini North Telescope at the summit of Mauna Kea.

Flora along the beach of
Waipi'o Valley.

HAWAII: THE BIG ISLAND

The most rugged of the major Hawaiian
islands and the largest, Hawaii promises real
adventure, perfect beaches, and much more.

*Ki'i (wooden images)
surrounding the Hale o
Keawe temple in Pu'uhonua
'O Honaunau National
Historical Park.*

The island of Hawaii, until recently was called the Big
Island for a reason: it's huge. So huge, in fact, that it's
almost too big to explore adequately from a single base.
Instead, it's best to split a visit into two parts. And if you
time your trip right, you might even get to see snow atop
Mauna Kea.

Geologically the youngest of the Hawaiian islands and
twice the size of all the others combined, the Big Island is
a geological exhibit of considerable proportions. In Hawaii
Volcanoes National Park, since 1983 the volcano goddess
Pele has brought Kilauea to life, pouring ribbons of crimson
lava from rifts and vents on the southeastern coast.

On the dry western side, upscale resorts stretch from
Kohala in the north to Kona in the south. Save for the lush-
ness of North Kohala, where Kamehameha the Great was
born, most of the land on the western side is dry and expansive, and peppered with petroglyphs, ancient fish ponds, and
other archeological treasures. It was here that Kamehameha
the Great planned his conquests in the 18th century.

To the south in Kona District, Kailua is the Big Island's
center of tourism and play. Once the playground of Hawaiian royalty, the sun-washed town today is crowded with
boutiques, hotels, condominiums, and tourists. Down by the
waterfront, delve into history at Hulihe'e Palace, 'Ahu'ena
Heiau, and Moku'aikaua Church – built of black stone from
an abandoned *heiau* (temple) and cemented with white coral.

*Solidified lava along the Chain
of Craters Road in Hawaii
Volcanoes National Park.*

Continuing south, the highway rounds the island at South Point, or Ka
Lae, the southernmost point in both Hawaii and the United States.

On the wetter eastern coast, a half-hour's drive to the northeast of
Kilauea, is rustic Hilo, the island's seat of government. Hilo is a tranquil
town, with much of its charm originating in its quiet, unassuming residents. North of Hilo is the lush Hamakua Coast, where sugar plantations
once reigned. One can continue beyond Hamakua and cross over through
the highland town of Waimea to Kohala and the western coast. Overall,
the island is perhaps best known for the volcano and coffee plantations
outside of Kailua-Kona. A number of outfitters offer helicopter and boat
tours of the volcano; visitors can drive to a handful of coffee plantations
and tour the facilities on foot.

Hawaii (Big Island)

Alenuihaha Channel

PACIFIC OCEAN

0 ——— 10 miles
0 ——— 10 km

N

Limukoko Pt.
'Upolu Pt.
King Kamehameha I
Birthplace
Mo'okini Heiau
State Monument
Kauhola Pt.
Hawi
Kapa'au
Keokea Beach
Halawa Valley
Kohala
Mahukona Beach
Lapakahi State Historical
Park
Pololu Valley Lookout
Paokalani I.
Moku Puku I.
Puakea I.
NORTH
KOHALA
DISTRICT
Nunilii
Kehena
Pololu Valley
KOHALA MOUNTAINS
Kahua
Ranch
Pu'ukohola Heiau National Historic Site
Kawaihae Bay
Mauna Kea Beach Hotel
Hapuna Beach State Park
Puako Petroglyph Field
Mauna Lani Resort
Waikoloa Resort
'Anaeho'omalu
Bay
Kawaihae
Kawaihae Coast
Kaniku
Ranch
Puako
Waikoloa
Waimea
Waipi'o Valley
Overlook
Waimanu
Valley
Waipi'o Bay
Waipi'o Valley
Kukuihaele
Kawaihae-Kohala
Airport
Parker Ranch Museum
and Visitor Center
Honoka'a
Kamakoa
Kemole
Auwaiakeua
Keamoku
Ke'amoku
Waiki
Kukuihaele
Kapohakimauela
Kohakohau Road
Umikoa
Kaohaluu
SOUTH
KOHALA
DISTRICT
Haina
Pa'auilo
Pa'auhau
Honoka'a
Kahana
Honokaa
HAMAKUA DISTRICT
Hamakua
Mud Lane
Niu Village
Milo Village
Scenic
Valley
Laupaho'eho'e
Laupaho'eho'e
Train Museum
Laupaho'eho'e Beach Park
Papa'aloa
Ninole
Scenic
Valley
Laupaho'eho
Natural Area Reserve
Weloka
Hakalau Nat.
Wildlife Refuge
Hakalau Nat.
Wildlife Refuge
Nauhi Str.
Hakalau Str.
Kolekole Str.
Kagoe Str.
Honolii Str.
Wailuku
NORTH
HILO
DISTRICT
Kolekole Beach
Honomu
Pepe'ekeo Pt.
Pepe'ekeo
'Akaka Falls
Wailea
Onomea Bay
Papa'ikou
Kaiwiki
Hilo
Bay
Hawaii Tropical Botanical Garden
Honolii Beach
Lili'uokalani
Gardens
Hilo
Hilo
International
Airport
Mahika I.
Keaukaha
Papai
Macadamia Nut
'Imiloa Astronomy
Center of Hawai'i
Boiling Pots
Pu'u Huluhulu
6758
Nukupahu
Aweki Str.
SOUTH
200
Pohakua Military
Training Area
Humu'ula Saddle
6670
Pu'u Ah
Saddle
200
Pu'u Huluhulu
Puaar
Pu'u O'o
Mauna Kea Ice Age
National Area Reserve
Keck Observatory Complex
(University of Hawaii)
Mauna Kea 13796
Keanakakoi
Crater
Onizuka
Astronomy
Complex
HAMAKUA DISTRICT
NORTH
KONA
DISTRICT
Pu'u Wa'awa'a
Ranch
Hualalai
8271
Huehue
Pu'u Wa'awa'a
3967
Mahaiula
Bay
Kaloko-Honokohau
Nat. Historic Park
Kona Int'l Airport
Ellison S. Onizuka
Space Center
Kalaoa
Honokohau
(Palani Junction)
Kailua-
Kona Village Resort
Hualalai Resort
Kiholo Bay
Kekaha Kai
State Park
Ahuena Heiau
Ka'upulehu
Saddle
270
190
190
19
19
19
11
200
200
200
240

① ② ③ ⑩ ⑪ ⑫ ⑬ ⑭ ⑮ ⑯ ⑰ ⑱ ⑲ ⑳ ㉑ ㉒ ㉓ ㉔ ㉕ ㉖ ㉗ ㉘ ㉙ ㉚ ㉛ ㉜ ㉝ ㉞ ㉟ ㊱ ㊲ ㊳

Carved wooden images at Hale o Keawe temple, Pu'uhonua 'O Honaunau National Historical Park.

KONA AND KOHALA

Hopping towns, lush farmland, posh resorts, and ancient sites are all on offer on the western coast of Hawaii Island.

The leeward side of Hawaii Island is its dry side, meaning that the volcanoes that tower over this western coast catch the moisture-rich trade winds from the northwest and release their rain on the island's windward side. This makes the districts of Kohala and Kona prime destinations with some of the world's finest resort hotels, with beaches on this coast some of the best in Hawaii (the state) for swimming and sunbathing.

The northern part of this side of Hawaii Island is called Kohala (after the island's northernmost volcano), while the southern part is known as Kona (after the city of the same name). In the past, the only way to drive from Kohala to Kona was along a narrow road far uphill from the ocean. Today, however, a highway named for Kamehameha's wife, Ka'ahumanu, connects Kawaihae in Kohala with Kailua and Kona. The highway passes through some of the driest land in Hawaii, where beaches and archeological sites are strung along the coast. Expansive views range inland and along the coast, the landscape scarred by lava that flowed as recently as the 19th century.

The main town on this side of the island is known to locals as **Kailua**; with the district being called **Kona** ❶, it is known to the post office as **Kailua-Kona**. Generally, they're interchangeable, but Kona is commonly

used for the town, the district, and the coast. Dominating North Kona is 8,271ft (2,521-meter) **Hualalai** ❷, an awesome volcano that last erupted in 1801. The **Kona International Airport** ❸ lies on one of its lava flows at Keahole. Legend has it that an 1801 eruption of Hualalai was initiated by Pele, the fire goddess, because she was jealous of the successful Kamehameha the Great. When Kamehameha followed the advice of a *kaula*, a seer, and made offerings to Pele, the eruption ceased. Today, Hualalai is home to

Main Attractions
Kailua town
Captain Cook
The Fairmont Orchid
Pu'ukohola Heiau National Historic Site
Parker Ranch Museum and Visitor Center

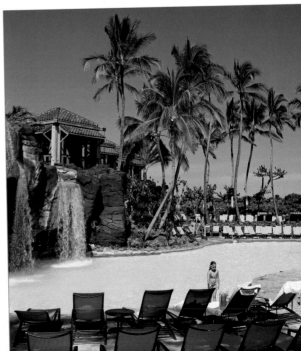

One of the pools at the Hilton Waikoloa Village.

Moku'aikaua Church on Ali'i Drive.

game birds, and sheep, goats, and pigs wander over its dormant heights foraging on dry shrubs and grasses.

Pu'u Wa'awa'a, a pumice cone around 100,000 years old, rises sharply 4,000ft (1,200 meters) on the flanks of Hualalai. The typical lava flow in Hawaii is 15ft (5 meters) thick, but flows from Pu'u Wa'awa'a reached 900ft (270 meters) in thickness. Glassy black obsidian, formed by rapidly cooled lava and historically used for making sharp tools and weapons, is found here. The only other place in the Hawaiian Islands where obsidian is found is on the island of Kaho'olawe. On Hualalai's southwest flank, at about 1,500ft (460 meters), is **Holualoa ❹**, home to those seeking refuge from the hectic pace of Kailua-Kona below. It sits on the high road surrounded by coffee plants and wonderful views. A growing number of visitors are discovering the town's small galleries.

Kailua

Sea spray crashes against Ali'i Drive's seawall by Kailua Bay.

The town of Kailua is one of those places noted for sun and nightlife – with the sun outshining the nightlife

by far. **Kailua Bay**, a harbor skirted by Ali'i Drive and a seawall, is the downtown focus. At the north end, on the grounds of King Kamehameha's Kona Beach Hotel, is an ancient temple or *heiau*, **Ahu'ena**, that was once used for human sacrifices. It was later restored by Kamehameha the Great and used as his personal *heiau*, when he settled here at the royal compound called **Kamakahonu**, or "turtle eye." This is where Kamehameha the Great retired and later died in 1819. Loyal attendants hid his bones, to prevent them being defiled by his enemies or the *mana* (spiritual essence) abused. Occasionally, someone claims to have found the burial site – caves were traditional burial locations – but it remains undiscovered. Possibly it was sealed by a lava flow, or it may even be under water, as the island's west coast has sunk an average of 9ins (23cm) every 100 years for the past eight centuries. The Ahu'ena Heiau site, which was partially demolished to build the Kona Pier, was later restored. The site provides a unique perspective for those on the nearby beach.

Ali'i Drive leads south along the harbor past the Royal Kona Resort, which is hard to miss as it juts out on a promontory through a jungle of condominiums and apartments into the ocean. The harbor area along Ali'i Drive, situated between the King Kamehameha and Royal Kona hotels, is a walking district for both shoppers and those interested in the history of the stretch.

The charming **Hulihe'e Palace**, built in 1838 by the brother of Queen Ka'ahumanu, sits right on the ocean just down from Ahu'ena Heiau. Its grounds were once part of Kamakahonu. Restored in 1927, it is a wonderful museum evoking the old days when it served as a royal getaway. Opposite the palace on Ali'i Drive, **Moku'aikaua Church** was built in 1837. The original church, with a *pandanus* roof and foundations of old *heiau* stones, was dedicated in 1823 but destroyed in 1835.

Sheltered from the prevailing trade winds, the waters off the Kona Coast are home to game fish considered among the best in the world. Each summer, the Hawaiian International Billfish Tournament is staged here. Blue marlin weighing 1,000lbs (450kg) have been caught within an hour's run from the pier. *Ahi* (tuna), *ono* (bonefish), *ulua* (jack crevalle), *mahi mahi* (dolphin fish), and swordfish are regularly caught.

South Kona

Up above Kailua, on the slopes of Hualalai and Mauna Loa, the climate is cooler. Moist air, bright sunshine, and porous volcanic soil produce one of the world's finest gourmet coffees: Kona coffee. Schools in this area used to close during coffee-bean harvest season so that children could help their families fill burlap sacks of the bright-red beans for delivery to the local mill. The coffee industry expanded substantially in the 1990s, riding the wave of growth in coffee drinking in the US. There are numerous boutique mills throughout the Kona region that welcome visitors. All along the upcountry stretch of highway south of Kailua to the town of **Captain Cook ❺** are tasting rooms where various types of Kona coffee are sold; be sure to stop and sample a cup.

Konane, a game similar to draughts, was played by Hawaiians before Captain Cook's arrival in Hawaii.

KONA NIGHTINGALES

No, Kona Nightingales are not birds: they are feral donkeys. And they are as much a part of the history of the western coast of Hawaii Island as volcanoes, coffee, and more recently the Ironman contest. Members of this breed of free-roaming animals get their names from the sound they make; their bray is more like a bird call than a whinny. It is said that this dates back to when lone donkeys on local farms called out to donkeys on other farms in the night. A population of hundreds of former worker donkeys once roamed the area, but numbers have dwindled to next to nothing in recent years. Efforts have been made to protect the remaining herd by enclosing an area away from a nearby highway to protect both the animals and passing motorists.

FACT

Over the last two decades, Kailua (and the surrounding Kona region) also has become famous for another contest: the Ironman World Championship, held every October.

The entire South Kona region has diversified, both in spirit and in economics, since the 1960s, when the area was a haven for self-exiled counterculture types, then later for artisans and craftspeople. Other newcomers settled here to become farmers by leasing land from large estates and buying up farmlands. Much of that new farmland went not into coffee production, but into vegetables, citrus fruits, and cocoa, with beans that, when processed, compare with the finest European chocolate.

Higher up Mauna Loa's slopes are forests of native trees. Around their trunks, wild *maile* wraps itself. *Maile* is prized for making *lei*, but with an increasing population, *maile* has become scarce. Sandalwood once covered many of these slopes; today, few trees remain. Whole forests of the creamy, aromatic wood were cut and sold by Kamehameha the Great and his heirs for profitable shipment to China.

The site of Cook's demise

Far below today's coffee farms, Captain Cook met his death at **Kealakekua Bay** 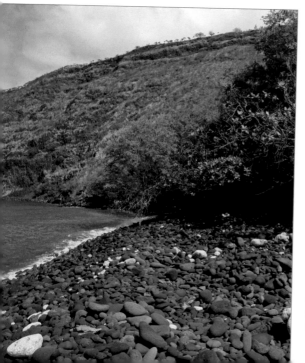, now a state marine

Kealakekua Bay State Historical Park.

conservation district. Visitors arrive on day-cruises from Kailua, or drive here on a paved road descending through relatively recent lava fields. A white obelisk, on a parcel of land that is officially British territory, marks the spot where Cook and some of his crew died. It is accessible only by water, or on foot via a strenuous trail. Archeological surveys between Kealakekua Bay and Kailua have mapped at least 40 *heiaus* (temples) in the area, with one of the best preserved at Napo'opo'o overlooking a rocky beach.

Travelers sailing south from Kealakekua Bay would be startled on reaching **Honaunau Bay** by the sight of fierce, hand-carved, wooden *ki'i* (sacred sculptures), and an immense stone platform with thick walls topped by thatched roofs. In this ancient *pu'uhonua*, or place of refuge, now known as the **Pu'uhonua 'O Honaunau National Historical Park** ⑦, (tel: 328-2326; www.nps.gov/puho; daily 7am–sunset), Hawaiians pardoned violators of *kapu* (taboos) and war criminals who reached sanctuary here, but only if they vowed to do penance. Over the centuries, this *pu'uhonua* gained importance and accumulated *mana* (spiritual power), as more and more chiefs were buried here. Its *heiau* and Great Wall (1,000ft (300 meters) long, 10ft (3 meters) high and 17ft (5 meters) wide), have been meticulously restored.

Near the main road and up from the historical park, **St Benedict's Painted Church** ⑧ is one of Hawaii's special little places. The interior was painted with biblical scenes and motifs by a Belgian priest sometime around the year 1900. Outside stands a bust of Father Damien, the priest who worked in the Molokai leper colony (see page 205).

South along this jagged Kona shore, the people of **Miloli'i** ⑨ still fish for a living. In few places on Hawaii is there a feeling of neighborliness so strong as in this little village of hand-built stone walls topped with night-blooming cereus and no electricity or mains water supplies. Farther south along the highway, lava flows from the 1920s lift the road higher onto Mauna Loa's slopes and toward **Ka Lae**, or **South Point**, the southernmost tip of the Big Island and the United States. Too dry for farming, but with rich harvests from the sea, this was an early site of Polynesian settlement. Past South Point, the road turns northeast and ascends to Hawaii Volcanoes National Park and eventually to Hilo.

North Kona

About two miles (3km) north of town is the first of three access roads that are part of the **Kaloko-Honokohau National Historical Park**. This mile-long coast park has a visitor center (daily 8.30am–4pm; tel: 326-9057), which offers a self-guided tour made interesting by display boards. It's hot and dry (like the rest of this side of the island), so bring bottled water. A *heiau* (temple) platform, fishpond walls, and an ancient *holua* (sled run) provide great insight into Hawaii's past.

Just north of Kaloko and south of the airport is the **Hawaii Ocean Science and Technology (HOST) Park** (tel: 327-9585; weekday tours at 10am, reservations necessary) where aquaculture and energy programs have been underway for more than 20 years.

North of the Kona International Airport is a controversial yet historic spot: the **Kona Village Resort ⑩**. The property was built in the 1960s as a string of luxury bungalows without TVs, phones, or anything else that disrupts the serenity of the setting. It was designed to look like the ancient village of Kalpulehu, and was hailed for years for being a different, more traditional lodging option. Then, during a tsunami in March 2011, the property sustained significant damage and has been closed ever since. Creditors and owners have feuded over renovation, rehabilitation, and just about everything else. Locals hope the property ultimately returns to its former glory. Until then, for the kitsch factor alone, it's worth a peek.

Other parts of the area have recovered much better from that big wave. The elegant **Hualalai Resort ⑪**, for instance, with its Four Seasons Hotel, 18-hole golf course and condominiums, is just as lovely as ever, providing

Keone'ele Cove in Pu'uhonua 'O Honaunau Park.

Carved image at the ancient place of refuge, Puʻuhonua ʻO Honaunau.

visitors with plenty of options to dine and relax. There's also an impressive cultural center.

A great collection of ancient petroglyphs can be found at the Waikoloa Resort at **ʻAnaehoʻomalu** **⑫**, where they have been joined by both a golf course and relatively modern petroglyphs from the late 1800s that include English words, and figures bearing rifles. Also well preserved here are ancient fishponds on the ocean side of the Outrigger Waikoloa Resort.

The grand-scale Hilton Waikoloa Village has 1,200 rooms. The hotel's three towers are connected by mechanically guided boats in a canal, a sleek electric train and a mile-long walkway lined with Asian and Pacific Island art. As the oceanfront here is very rocky, the hotel is laid out around an artificial lagoon with sand to create a pretty good approximation of a beach. This is the setting for the resort's popular Dolphin Quest "swim with a dolphin" program (tel: 248-3316), under which guests can pay to share a few minutes' water time with a brace of sleek dolphins.

Windswept trees at Parker Ranch, Waimea.

South Kohala

A few minutes further north is **Mauna Lani Resort** **⑬**, with two elegant hotels, The Fairmont Orchid and Mauna Lani Bay Hotel and Bungalows. In earlier days, Mauna Lani was known as Kalahuipuaʻa, a site of aquaculture ponds that the Mauna Lani Hotel has preserved. A walking trail leads from the hotel toward Keawanui Bay and the palm-lined ponds. Of six major ponds, the largest is 5 acres (2 hectares) in size and 18ft (6 meters) deep. A trail heads inland to a lava field, where caves have yielded an ancient canoe paddle and large fishhooks, probably for catching sharks.

Kamehameha the Great maintained a canoe landing here, marked by a replica of an old canoe shed; inside is a full-sized replica of an outrigger canoe. Beyond is the Eva Parker Woods Cottage Museum, built in the 1920s and later moved to its current seaside location. Ancient Hawaiian artifacts are displayed inside.

A 5-minute walk up the coast, in **Pauoa Bay** fronting the Fairmont Orchid, is a submarine freshwater spring. Ancient Hawaiians would dive to the spring's opening and fill gourds with fresh drinking water.

The shoreline trail to the south follows an ancient footpath that connected fishing villages in pre-contact Hawaii. Along the path are ancient fishing platforms, a house site, and some anchialine pools – low-sited caves that were once flooded with seawater. Brackish water now fills these natural depressions in the lava.

Just north of the Mauna Lani Resort is one of Polynesia's best collections of petroglyphs, the **Puako petroglyph field** **⑭**. Years ago, access was through the village of Puako. Now a well-marked road at the Mauna Lani Resort ends in a parking lot, where a self-guided trail leads to a field of several thousand petroglyphs etched into the lava. The age of these petroglyphs has not been determined. Many are of uncertain meaning; others, like the circles with a dot inside, called *piko* (navel) holes, are thought to have been receptacles for the umbilical cords of newborns. Most Hawaiian petroglyphs were chiseled into smooth *paho'eho'e* lava along major trails. Long sections of this rock-lined trail are still to be found along the coast, at Koloko and at each of the Kona and Kohala resorts.

The low roads in both North and South Kohala are lined with *kiawe* trees and prickly-pear cacti. The *kiawe* tree is burned into first-rate charcoal, and the cactus blooms develop into a tasty fruit. On land found too dry for cattle, Laurance Rockefeller commissioned a luxury resort in the 1960s, the **Mauna Kea Beach Hotel** ⓯, piping in water for its grounds and golf course all the way from Waimea. For 40 years, Mauna Kea was the standard by which other Hawaii resorts were measured. Other resorts have caught up in recent years, but the Mauna Kea still is one of the island's finest.

Half a mile south lies **Hapuna Beach State Park** ⓰, with the island's largest natural white-sand beach. The Hapuna Beach Prince Hotel opened in 1994 at the northern end of Hapuna Beach, and local people continue to use the popular public beach side-by-side with visitors. In summer, its warm turquoise waters offer truly superb swimming, but look for warning signs if you're here in winter, when the waves are so fierce that they scoop away enough sand to cut the beach into two separate halves.

Pu'ukohola Heiau National Historic Site

Continuing northward, hot, dusty, and dry South Kohala looks like parts of the western United States – rock-strewn grasslands but with a seacoast, and with fewer than 9ins (230mm) of rain a year. Where Highways 270 and 19 from North Kohala and Waimea meet and continue south stands the largest restored *heiau* (temple) in Hawaii: **Pu'ukohola Heiau National Historic Site** ⓱ (tel: 882-7218; www.nps.gov/puhe; daily 8.15am–4.45pm; free), built in 1791 by Kamehameha the Great for his war god, Kuka'ilimoku, a prelude to his military conquests. When it was finished, he invited his main Big Island rival and cousin, the high chief

Paddling an outrigger canoe at the Fairmont Orchid resort.

The lava flows of Kona and Kohala are rich with petroglyphs. Although carved in rock, they are fragile.

Trees and dry scrubland along the Kohala Coast.

Keoua, to a ceremony at the *heiau*. As Keoua's canoe landed he was killed by Kahamanu's father, Ke'eaumoku. The temple was dedicated with Keoua's body on the altar. In 1991, at a re-dedication of the site, descendants of the once-warring clans were reconciled in an impressive *'awa* ceremony, complete with costumed pageantry.

Today the site comprises a number of different parts: the old temple, which visitors can only walk around; the remnants of a coastal village, which visitors can walk through; a shoreline path with interpretive signs about how the site was used; and a visitor center. Time your visit right and you might see archeological excavations in progress. Because the site has no shade, it gets very hot during summer; be sure to bring plenty of water.

Waimea

Waimea ⑱, sometimes called **Kamuela**, is a cool and often misty town at nearly 3,000ft (910 meters) above sea level. That mellow upland climate has made it hugely in demand as a residential community for rich local people,

who, amazing as it may sound to most of us, weary of the endless sunshine on the coastal plain below. As such, this sleepy farming community is home to some of the most expensive real estate in the state.

The history of Waimea as a town dovetails with the history of a local farm, Parker Ranch. Captain George Vancouver and other early Europeans introduced goats, sheep, and cattle to the newly united island kingdom of Kamehameha the Great. The traditional low stone walls of the Hawaiians were unable to contain these domesticated stock animals, and in less than a decade, feral herds were ravaging cultivated farmlands and gnawing down young indigenous trees and plants.

In 1815, a New England farmer named John Palmer Parker offered to round up the animals in exchange for homestead land. Kamehameha gave him 2 acres (1 hectare) in the Kohala. These 2 acres grew to become what was at one time the largest privately owned ranch in America. Today, the cowboys of **Parker Ranch** run some 50,000 head of cattle over 210,000 acres (85,000

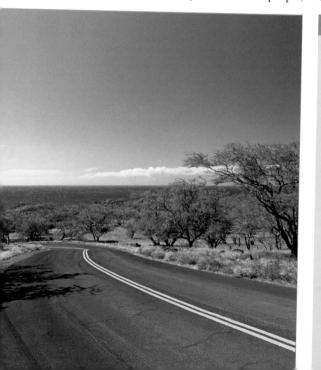

CHINESE SOCIETY

Chinese laborers founded the **Kohala Tong Wo Society** ("Together in Harmony") in 1886, the last of Hawaii Island's many Chinese societies. The society had emerged in 16th-century China to overthrow the Manchus, and flourished wherever Chinese settled. Sun Yatsen came to Hawaii in the 1880s and in the early 1900s, seeking help from the societies to overthrow the Qing dynasty. The **Kohala Tong Wo Society building** in Kapa'au was a social center. At night, the men gambled or climbed a rope ladder for opium breaks in the loft. As a man neared death from old age, he moved to the "death house," where he would await death and be buried on the society grounds. The main building was restored and re-dedicated in 1971. Plaques engraved with proverbs and phrases surround the doors and windows.

hectares) of pasture. In the 1960s, Parker's descendant, Richard Smart, sold large, unproductive coastal tracts in South Kohala to resort developers.

Although the ranch is now administered by a trust, the Parker name still crops up all over Kohala. At **Parker Ranch Museum and Visitor Center** ⑲ (tel: 885-7655; daily 9am–5pm) in Waimea, visits can be arranged to the century-old family home, Mana, and a second, more modern, home, Pu'uopelu, which has an extensive art collection.

Like the 19th-century sugar barons, Parker had to import workers for his ranch, primarily Spanish-speaking cowboys from Mexico who were called *paniolos* (derived from the Spanish word, *español*) by Native Hawaiians. Today, all cowboys in Hawaii are called *paniolos*, and ranchlands are known as *paniolo*-country. In later years, Portuguese joined them, and local men were trained as ranch hands, too, as were Asian immigrants. Today, *paniolos* have no racial or ethnic identity.

For years, Parker Ranch supplied most of the locally produced beef in Hawaii, butchering it at a company-owned slaughterhouse in Honolulu. Until a port was built, cattle were herded to the surf at **Kawaihae** ⑳ and forced to swim through the ocean to waiting ships, which hauled them aboard in slings. Nowadays, they are driven through gates onto enclosed barges.

North Kohala

In 1968, archeologists excavated a 600-year-old Hawaiian fishing village, Lapakahi, near Highway 270 that skirts North Kohala's coastline. The area is protected as **Lapakahi State Historical Park** ㉑ (daily 8am–4pm; free). The park, which offers self-guided tours, preserves the restored foundations and stone enclosures of this commoners' fishing village. It is also the entry point to the part of the island known as North Kohala. Essentially, the region encompasses the entire northern tip

of Hawaii Island, and is one of those windswept, wide-open places enveloped in mysticism.

Literally at the end of the road is the Big Island's northernmost point, **'Upolu Point** ㉒ (named for an island in Samoa). Past a small airfield along the coast, is the well-preserved and partially restored **Mo'okini Heiau** ㉓, built around AD 800, it's said, by a *kahuna* (priest) from Tahiti. Today, a *kahuna* from the Mo'okini family of North Kohala still maintains the *heiau*. Within sight of the *heiau* is the **birthplace of Kamehameha the Great**, *c.* 1752. Signs mark both Mo'okini Heiau and Kamehameha's birthplace, and the *heiau* in particular is well worth the short side trip on an unpaved road that's frequently rendered impassable by rain.

The backbone of North Kohala

Defining North Kohala are the **Kohala Mountains**, the remains of an extinct 700,000-year-old volcano. In addition to the coastal road on the west side, Highway 250 ascends from Waimea to the ridge line and then through ranchland

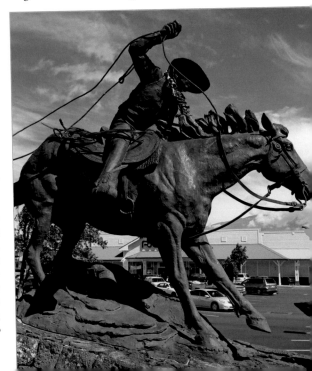

Statue of the famous Hawaiian cowboy Ikua Purdy by Fred Fellows, at Parker Ranch.

and groves of trees planted decades ago as windbreaks. The winds, called 'apa'apa'a, that whip across the Kohala ridge are powerful and persistent.

At the north end of the peninsula is **Hawi** ㉔, an old sugar town that has sprouted a surprising amount of character and many good restaurants in the last few years. In adjacent **Kapa'au** ㉕, in front of the town's historic civic center, is the original **Kamehameha the Great statue**. It was lost at sea off the Falkland Islands and later recovered and taken to the Big Island town of Kapa'au. Its replacement stands opposite 'Iolani Palace in Honolulu.

In the 1880s, Kohala led the island in sugar production. Chinese laborers were hired by a businessman to construct a narrow-gauge railway from **Niuli'i**, beyond Kapa'au, to the port of Mahukona, on North Kohala's western coast. Formally opened by King Kalakaua, the railroad was abandoned half a century later when trucks replaced trains.

From Kapa'au, the road continues until the **Pololu Valley Lookout** ㉖ with its expansive coastal views, alternating seacliffs and valleys leading to the **Hamakua Coast**. A steep, quadriceps-burning trail leads down to Polulu Valley's rocky beach, which is partially visible from the lookout. You can hike the trail independently, or join Hawaii Forest and Trail (tel: 800-464-1993; www.hawaii-forest.com) on a memorable horseback and hiking excursion to waterfalls deep into the valley. Note that the trail can be slippery after a rainstorm.

Dense forests cover the round, eroded highlands of Kohala, scarred by deep-cleft valleys and ravines. Along their eastern ocean faces, water seeps out of cracks in the cliffs and plunges 1,000ft (300 meters) to the sea. At the turn of the 20th century, a technique for tapping this mountain water was established. Christened in 1906, the **Kohala Ditch** was a watercourse 18 miles (29km) long that funneled the headwaters of Waimanu Valley to Honokane, terminating in an 850ft (260-meter) artificial waterfall. Immigrant Japanese laborers bored and blasted 44 tunnels. At least six men died and countless others suffered from exposure and chills while working in the icy darkness of the flooded tunnels.

Ensconced in a hammock in Hawi.

'Akaka Falls, near Honomu.

HILO AND THE WINDWARD SIDE

While the windward side of Hawaii Island is one of the wettest regions in the US, don't let the weather put you off from discovering all it has to offer.

Wet, warm, and sensuous in its appeal, the windward side of Hawaii Island is a tropical paradise unlike any other. Terrain is lush and verdant. Rivers and streams are almost permanently swollen. Waves and sea conditions are nightly news. And the seafood is second to none. Beaches and waterfalls grab most of the attention, but the big mountain of Mauna Kea towers over everything, serving as the only place in the islands you can build a snowman with natural snow. It is a place where Mother Nature rarely lets humans forget who is in charge.

Hilo

Hilo ㉗ is undeniably a tropical city. Unpretentious and subtle, it can yield its charm quickly or take forever, depending upon a traveler's receptiveness. Named for the first night of a new moon, or possibly for an ancient Polynesian navigator, Hilo has been a center of trade since ancient Hawaiian times. At the **Wailuku River**, which spills into **Hilo Bay** at the northwest end of today's Hilo, ancient Hawaiians shouted their bargains across the rapids and gingerly made their exchanges. Later, foreign ships found deep anchorage between the coral heads of its wide bay, and eventually a channel was dredged so that larger steamships could anchor. Blacksmiths,

missionaries, farmers, jewelers, tailors, teachers, and dentists dropped anchor in Hilo, opening shops, churches, offices, and schools.

Nearby, visitors marvel at plant life inside the Hawaii Tropical Botanical Garden, wonder at the volume of water while watching 'Akaka Falls, and embrace authentic local culture at places such as Honoka'a and in the Waipi'o Valley below. While a drive up Mauna Kea is great for perspective (especially on clear days), the region's big volcano pales in comparison to the

Main Attractions
Pacific Tsunami Museum, Hilo
'Imiloa Astronomy Center
Wailuku River State Park
Akaka Falls
Waipi'o Valley
Keck Observatory

Outrigger canoe on the beach of Waipi'o Valley.

lava light show available daily down near Kilauea in the national park. The best place to see the active volcano is in Puna, a city that is still very much part of the windward vibe.

Hilo's history

The Japanese especially embody Hilo's growth. The first generation that came as sugar cane laborers raised English-speaking children, the *nisei*, or second generation, who flocked not to the plantations for work but to government service and free enterprise. Respectful of their parents, the *nisei* and later *sansei* – third generation – descendants have run the island with particular sensitivity to the needs of older people.

Hilo's importance once revolved around its sheltered harbor. While cruise ships, freighters, and kayaks still ply its waters, the heart of town has moved inland, along Kanoelehua Avenue. Hilo's downtown buildings are dilapidated, although several have been artfully restored, with wooden awnings overhanging the sidewalks. Along **Waianuenue Avenue**, iron

rings to which horses were once tethered are still embedded in the curb.

Downtown Hilo once stretched along the black-sand harbor, so the town was nicknamed the Crescent City. But in 1946, a *tsunami* swept half the town inland, then dragged the debris seaward. Hilo was rebuilt, and a stone breakwater was constructed across the bay to shield the harbor. Then in 1960 another *tsunami* broke through and blasted the shore. This time there was no rebuilding. Lowland waters were drained and a hill of 26ft (8 meters) was raised above sea level, where city planners built a new government and commercial center, calling it **Kaiko'o**, or the strong seas. The old buildings that survived form a historical downtown district with a time-worn veneer that makes Hilo unique; the so-called Renaissance-Revival style was obviously popular for buildings from the early 1900s.

Downtown Hilo has undergone a partial restoration, and a fine walk that mixes old plantation ambiance with trendy hipness takes in the central area, bordered by Kino'ole Street,

Stallholder at Hilo Farmers' Market.

Furneaux Lane, Kamehameha Avenue, and Waianuenue Avenue.

The **Pacific Tsunami Museum** 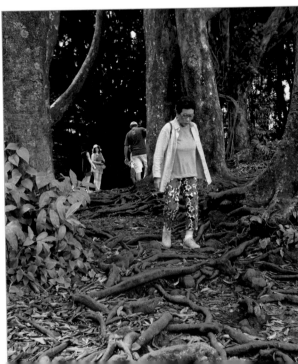 (tel: 935-0926; www.tsunami.org; Mon–Sat 9am–4pm) in the heart of old Hilo tells the dramatic story of the *tsunamis* that have hit the islands.

A few blocks inland is the **Lyman Mission House and Museum** Ⓑ (276 Haili Street; tel: 935-5021; www.lyman museum.org; Mon–Sat 10am–4.30pm), a reminder of the island's early missionary days. Built in 1839, the restored house is the oldest frame building in Hilo. Next door, a newer museum complex features Hawaiian and other ethnic history exhibits; upstairs is a world-class shell and mineral collection. Contemporary arts are on view at the East Hawaii Cultural Center Gallery (tel: 961-5711) on Kalakaua Street.

A couple of miles farther inland stands the innovative '**Imiloa Astronomy Center** Ⓒ (600 'Imiloa Place; tel: 969-9703; www.imiloahawaii.org; Tue–Sun 9am–5pm). This sets out to explain the work and discoveries of the various observatories atop the Big Island's highest mountain, Mauna Kea, and also to acknowledge Hawaiian religious beliefs about the entire cosmos, as well as the sacred mountain.

At the other end of the harbor to the east is the venerable **Banyan Drive** Ⓓ, a crescent road lined with voluptuous banyan trees shading most of Hilo's finer hotels. Japanese-style **Lili'uokalani Gardens** Ⓔ, nearby and off Banyan Drive, have stone bridges, lanterns, and a tea ceremony pavilion.

From the Naniloa Volcanoes Resort, one of several Hilo hotels with superb harbor views, 13,800ft (4,200-meter) **Mauna Kea** dominates the western horizon. Dark forests circle the mountain above bright-green sugar cane, thinning out as the altitude rises, and finally vanishing – along with shrubs, grasses, and bird life – at the alpine heights where snow in winter gives the mountain its Hawaiian name, White Mountain. A long and broad saddle separates Mauna Kea,

the island's older main volcano, from Mauna Loa, or Long Mountain. The road that traverses this saddle –appropriately it's named Saddle Road – provides the only access to the mountain.

Perhaps once in a generation Mauna Loa erupts. In 1975, lava flowed to within a short distance of Hilo. It wasn't the first time lava had put Hilo at risk. In the late 1880s, a perilous flow from Mauna Loa headed toward Hilo, stopped only, it is said, when the volcano goddess, Pele, heeded pleas from a high princess. In 1942, American military aircraft dropped water and explosives on the leading edge of a similar flow to halt the lava. The danger remains very real; volcanic activity in 2007 was assessed as posing a potential threat to Hilo.

Like the town itself, nearby scenic sites are quiet and contemplative places. **Rainbow Falls** in the **Wailuku River State Park** Ⓕ sport a prismatic halo in early mornings and late afternoons, when the sun is oblique to its cascade. Further upstream are the odd **Boiling Pots** Ⓖ, a section of bubbling water at the base of Pe'epe'e Falls.

TIP

A note of caution if you are traveling to Hawaii Island in April, around Easter. Hilo is the site of the state's most popular hula competition and performance, the annual Merrie Monarch Festival. Hotel rooms for this week are reserved a year in advance. Book as far ahead as you can (see page 83).

Rainbow Falls.

FACT

Honoli'i is said to be where the demigod Maui came to his end while chasing a young maiden up a tree. He had turned himself into an eel during the pursuit, but a passing *kahuna* (priest) killed him.

North of Hilo

When sugar was king along the **Hamakua Coast** north of Hilo, a railway carried cane, freight, and commuters between the sugar mills of Hamakua and Hilo. A simple, winding road between the workers' camps carried cars and horse-drawn carts, with palm trees for fence posts along the sea cliffs. After the 1946 *tsunami* undercut most of the railway bridges, the tracks were torn up. Trucks took over, clogging the old road until a new highway was built.

You can return to plantation times and enjoy a glimpse of an old-fashioned part of Hawaii by driving along the deserted road, using the main highway to bridge its gaps. A turn-off leads to **Honoli'i**, a river estuary and beach park with the only reliable, year-round surfing waves in the Hilo vicinity.

After picking up the highway, a right turn past **Papa'ikou** marked "Scenic Drive" follows a beautiful 4-mile (6km) stretch along the coast past **Onomea Bay**, once a major sugar port. **Hawaii Tropical Botanical Garden** (tel: 964-5233; www. htbg.com; daily 9am–5pm) is a 17-acre

(7-hectare) privately owned preserve with 2,000 species of plants and flowers, including palms, bromeliads, ginger, heliconia, and orchids. Take a self-guided walk through the property along a trail that turns from raised boardwalk to packed dirt and back to boardwalk again, and meanders through fern and palm groves.

The old road rumbles over single-lane wooden bridges covered with bright-red African tulip flowers in spring and squashed guavas in autumn. Plantation workers have, by and large, left the camps to buy homes on company land. Near **Pepe'ekeo**, their fine gardens and flower beds are turning old cane fields into lush, warm neighborhoods. At the town of **Honomu**, a spur road leads to the 400ft (120-meter) **'Akaka Falls** , and their neighbor, **Kahuna Falls**, both of which can be seen on an undulating mile-long hiking trail that appears seemingly out of nowhere. Somewhere in the area is a special rock, a stone of the fire goddess Pele, which causes the sky to cloud over and rain whenever struck by a branch of the *lehua 'apane*.

The Hamakua Coast

Change comes so slowly to Hamakua that few people notice it. A new house, a new car, a new storefront appear, but never anything startling. Places like **Papaʻaloa**, **Laupahoʻehoʻe**, **Paʻauilo**, and **Paʻauhau** look and feel much as they have for generations. On weekends, families secretly wager on the cockfights brought from their home islands in the Philippines. Fathers and sons take their dogs into the muddy forests on pig-hunting expeditions. Children and old men play softball in the parks. The paternal mills and the fraternal labor unions made Hamakua's plantation workers the highest-paid agricultural workers in the world. But as elsewhere in Hawaii, sugar died here. The largest mill and employer closed in 1996, and the fields of untended cane have rapidly vanished. What will replace the fields and the jobs still remains to be seen. Some agri-businessmen have hedged their bets by planting macadamia trees, which take a long time to mature but then bear nuts for decades. It is a lucrative market, but the competition from foreign producers is fierce. Another alternative to sugar cane is a fast-growing eucalyptus tree, which is harvested for paper, pulp, and as a source of fuel.

Slicing through the Hamakua coast are three great gulches: Maulua, Laupahoʻehoʻe, and Kaʻawaliʻi. The streams that cut through these volcanic channels have their sources far uphill where few people venture. With permission from neighboring ranchers to unlock their gates, the occasional hunter or forester rides up into the high terrain of the **Laupahoʻehoʻe Natural Area Reserve** 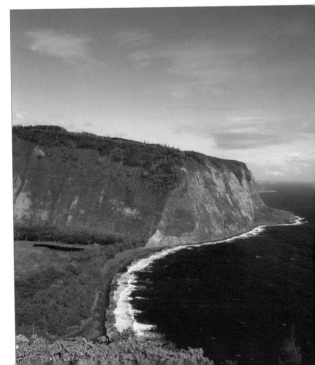, which protects the watershed of the island's windward side, a landscape misty in summer and frosty in winter. Here, the tall indigenous *koa* and *ʻohiʻa* trees stand. Hidden in the reserve are some cold-weather trees that were planted in the 1920s by foresters: spruce, cypress, maple, Dutch elm, and redwood.

The **Laupahoʻehoʻe Train Museum** (tel: 962-6300; Thu–Sat 10am–5pm)

is worth a stop, containing historic images of what impressive early 20th-century engineering.

Waipiʻo Valley

Nine miles (14km) beyond **Honokaʻa**, a rustic former sugar town, lies the broad and deep **Waipiʻo Valley**, the first of several windward valleys along North Kohala's wilderness coastline. Waipiʻo was a population center before European contact, home to thousands, including fishermen and farmers who built irrigated terraces to grow taro in the rich earth, which was said to have become red when Kanaloa, one of the four primary gods, beat Maui against the rocks.

Waipiʻo's **Hiʻilawe Falls** fed a river stocked with fish that skilled men and women would catch with their bare hands. The black-sand beach knew the keels of dozens of canoes that crossed treacherous currents to trade with neighboring valleys, but by the early 20th century, young people had moved away to work on the plantations or to live in more accessible towns. In the valleys, rice replaced taro grown by

View over Waipiʻo Valley from Waipiʻo Lookout.

TIP

You can get a tour to Waipi'o valley with Waipi'o Na'alapa Trail Rides (tel: 775-0419; www.naalapastables.com) or Valley Wagon Tours (tel: 775-9518; www.waipio valleywagontours.com).

Japanese and Chinese settlers. After World War II, two *tsunamis* flooded the valley floor and it was largely abandoned. Today, a few families call Waipi'o home. Most visitors take in Waipi'o from the clifftop lookout. The valley is accessed via a steep dirt road, technically off-limits by rental car companies (though 4x4s manage the road in good conditions) but open to hikers or on organized tours.

In the 1960s, the Peace Corps, newly initiated by President Kennedy, trained volunteers here to prepare them for life in rural Asia. Today, the Peace Corps village is gone, but visitors may pitch a tent a short hike away from a natural swimming hole below 300ft (90-meter) Hi'ilawe Falls. Dedicated hikers can cross the beach and scale the trail on the far side toward **Waimanu Valley** ㉝, 7 miles (11km) north over mostly irregular terrain.

The highest point in Hawaii

The Hilo and Kona sides of Hawaii have never been directly linked. The only overland road through the center of the Big Island, winding between Mauna Kea and Mauna Loa, is **Saddle Road** ㉞, which connects Hilo with Waimea.

Most rental car companies prohibit travel on the Saddle Road, but if you're brave enough to disobey, head skyward to the summit of **Mauna Kea** ㉟, which towers over the Pacific at 13,796ft (4,185 meters). It is the highest point in Hawaii and the Pacific Basin. Measured from its base below the ocean's surface, it is the tallest mountain on earth at more than 30,000ft (9,100 meters). Now dormant, Mauna Kea last erupted 3,500 years ago. More than 15,000 years ago, a glacier chilled the slopes of Mauna Kea. Today, a continual layer of permafrost sustains **Lake Wai'au**, close to the summit. Poli'ahu, the snow goddess and enemy of the fire goddess Pele, is said to live atop the volcano. It is said that when the gods disapproved of someone's presence on the mountain, they would turn him or her into stone; there are a lot of stones on the mountain.

Supplies of a dense and steel-hard basalt for use in adzes attracted ancient Hawaiians to the area. The Mauna Kea adze quarry, 11,000ft (3,350 meters) above sea level, is a National Historic Landmark. It covers nearly 8 sq miles (21 sq km). The site contains 40 *heiaus* (temples) and other shrines, and a trail leads to Lake Wai'au.

No site in the Northern Hemisphere is so high, so clear, so free from light and heat, and so easily accessible as Mauna Kea's summit. To take advantage of this unobstructed view of the heavens, the University of Hawaii and the governments of the US, Canada, Japan, and the UK have built 13 giant telescopes on summit cinder cones. The **Keck Observatory** ㊱ (tel: 935-6268 (for information on weather and road conditions); www.keckobservatory. org; Visitors' Gallery Mon–Fri 10am–4pm) is the most powerful optical telescope in the world, with mirrored segments aligned by computer to create a light-gathering surface of 33ft (10 meters). The observatory at the summit of Mauna Kea provides a visitors'

Hiking in Waipi'o Valley.

gallery with exhibits describing the site's research and operations. You need a 4x4 vehicle for the trek up a road that angles off Highway 20 toward the peak of Mauna Kea (off-limits to rental cars). Hawaiian Forest & Trail offers summit tours (tel: 331-8505; www.hawaii-forest. com). For details, call Mauna Kea Support Services (tel: 961-2180) at the Mauna Kea Visitor Information Station. Plans for additional observatories have been staunchly opposed by environmentalists, and those who consider the summit a sacred site. At a lower elevation is the **Onizuka Astronomy Complex** ㊲ (variable hours; tel: 961-2180), with evening star-gazing and displays in honor of Hawaii's first astronaut, who was killed in the 1986 *Challenger* space shuttle disaster.

Saddle Road history

A direct Kona–Hilo road has long been in the pipeline. In 1849, Kamehameha III approved a plan to survey and build a road over Crown lands from Kona, the seat of government, to Hilo, the only deep-water port. Convict laborers began at the edge of the forest and followed a nearly straight line. After 10 years they had reached halfway to Hilo when Mauna Loa erupted. A broad river of lava poured down the mountain and covered part of the road; the project was not completed until the 1940s, when the US military built an access road that was poorly maintained for decades.

In the last decade, however, county, state, and federal governments have teamed together to resurface portions of the old road and build new sections, as well. The last of the new sections opened in September 2013; it has breathtaking views of the coastline and the Hualalai and Kohala volcanoes. In the future, plans are to complete a section of Saddle Road to intersect with State Route 19.

A scant 400 yards/meters from the edge of the 1859 flow, high up in what is called the **Saddle**, stand the stone remains of a monument to a 16th-century king, 'Umi, the first known king of the Big Island. He completed his military unification of Hawaii here on a desolate plateau inland behind dormant Hualalai, which, at 8,271ft (2,521

Steep gradient warning on Mauna Kea; holes in the sign prevent it being blown down by the wind.

WONDER WAIP'O

You don't have to descend from the end of Route 240 into the Waipi'o Valley to experience the valley's beauty. That said, getting from the road to the bottom of the valley will enable you to fully appreciate some of what makes the valley so unique. For starters, consider the one-mile road itself: one of the steepest roads in the world with an average 25 percent grade for the entirety of its 900ft (270-meter) descent. Then at the bottom, there's the black-sand beach and, in addition to about 50 full-time human residents, the valley is home to nearly a dozen wild horses, and countless wild boar. Finally, of course, is the history: the valley once was a choice gathering spot for island royalty, and was home to Kamaehameha I when he was a child.

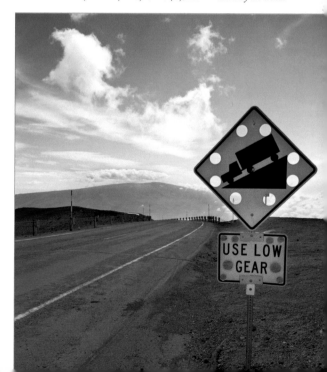

*Subaru and Keck
telescopes on the
summit of Mauna Kea
at sunset.*

meters), is the island's third-largest
volcano. At this location, Mauna Kea,
Mauna Loa, and Hualalai appear
nearly the same size. 'Umi, according to some stories, ordered a census.
Stones were used to represent people,
animals, and units of land. These heaps
of stones were fashioned into a place of
worship, Ahua 'Umi Heiau, and probably decorated with offerings.

It has been 500 years since armies
bivouacked on the plain in this geographical center of the island, but
only a few miles away in the Saddle
at **Pohakuloa**, the American military
practices war games. Near the Saddle's
high point is the **Kipuka 'Ainahou
Nene Sanctuary** ❸, one of the preserves of Hawaii's indigenous goose,
or *nene*. The bird can also be found in
Haleakala National Park on Maui and
Koke'e on Kauai.

Mauna Loa

Unlike Mauna Kea, Hawaii's southern
volcano, **Mauna Loa** ❸, is not yet
dormant. Indeed, the Big Island districts of Kona, Ka'u, Hilo, and Puna
remain vulnerable to a possible major
eruption. Mauna Loa's last eruption
was a 1984 fountain inside the summit caldera of **Moku'aweoweo**, a
name that refers to the *'aweoweo* fish
whose red color has obvious volcanic
parallels. Mauna Loa has erupted 36
times since European contact. Several
times, it has threatened Hilo, situated
on its northeast flank; in 1984, flows
stopped just 5 miles (8km) away.

Mauna Loa is a shield volcano, growing through the accumulative stack-
ing of thin lava flows 10–15ft (3–4.5
meters) thick. This process gives the
shield volcano its gentle convex shape,
in contrast to dramatically explosive
volcanoes such as Mt Fuji and Mt St
Helens. Lower than Mauna Kea, at
13,679ft (4,169 meters), Mauna Loa
("Long Mountain") has more mass
than any other mountain on the planet,
with more volume (almost 10,000 cubic
miles/40,000 cubic km) than the entire
Sierra Nevada range in California. For
most hikers, the trail to the summit is
a two-day climb, with a cabin at Red
Hill providing overnight shelter. With
fog and sudden storms a possibility, the
summit hike can be risky.

From the summit caldera, two prominent rift zones, which are fractured areas of weakness, extend deep into the ocean. The first rift zone passes through South Point at the bottom of the island, and the second, the northeast rift zone, extends toward Hilo.

South of Hilo

Travelers often bypass the **Puna** area south of Hilo off Highway 130. The road that once linked Puna to Hawaii Volcanoes National Park (see page 247) was closed in 1984 after lava covered it in several places. Scores of homes, the village of Kalapana, and several historic sites have been destroyed by the slow flows of Kilauea, whose most recent period of activity began in 1983. All of this history confirms that Puna is the best place outside the Hawaii Volcanoes National Park to see the active volcano of Kilauea today.

The gateway to the Puna area is the town of **Pahoa** ⓵, once a major supplier of *'ohi'a* wood to the railroads, which used the wood for ties. Its small downtown area is interesting, with raised wooden sidewalks and old buildings along its main street. The historic Star of the Sea painted church was moved here after lava covered its original site near the coast. The area surrounding Puna is known for producing tropical flowers, papaya, and illegal *pakalolo* (marijuana).

In 1790, lava flows flooded then drained a rainforest, leaving shells of solidified lava around now-vaporized trees. The lava-tree mold forests of **Lava Tree State Monument** ⓵ are eerie, especially in early mornings before the mists have lifted.

Costal Route 137 leads to volcanically heated thermal springs at Ahalanui Beach Park, and naturist sunbathing at Kehena. To the North lies the island's westernmost point, **Cape Kumukahi** ⓶, which grew dramatically after eruptions in 1955 and 1960. The Cape's namesake may have been one of two men: a chief who mocked Pele or a migratory traveler from Tahiti. Either way, Kumukahi means "first beginning." Partially covered by the recent flows is a cemetery for Japanese immigrants. The coastline of Puna is volcanic and rough, with few satisfactory beaches.

Lava flow from Kilauea.

HAWAII VOLCANOES NATIONAL PARK AND KA'U

There's more to Hawaii Volcanoes National
Park than watching an active volcano do
its thing; there also are great hikes and a
crash-course in Earth Science.

The best sights to see on the Big Island are nature at its most awesome, a spectacle that unfolds daily inside **Hawaii Volcanoes National Park** ⑱ (tel: 967-7311; www.nps.gov/havo; daily). The main attraction is Kilauea, an active volcano that has erupted consistently since 1983. Getting to the part of the park where you can see molton lava takes time; most visitors spend a full day. Other parts of the park to explore are canopied, misty rainforests filled with giant tree ferns; dried lava flows from yesteryear; the windswept deserts of Ka'u; and interpretive exhibits at park visitor centers. There also are great hikes up to the top of **Mauna Loa**. The park is so big, you could visit every day for a week and still miss more than half the park.

An active volcano

On Mauna Loa's slopes is a rift zone, where lava that sometimes feeds the summit crater oozes from cracks lower on the mountain. This is the Big Island's biggest draw, along with the beaches of Kohala and Kona. All of the current activity is from **Kilauea** ⑭, the youngest of Hawaii's volcanic mountains, which has erupted steadily since 1983, the longest continuously erupting volcano in the world. Like all Hawaiian volcanoes, Kilauea is a dome-like shield volcano with deceptively gentle slopes. It rises southeast of Mauna Loa, more than 20,000ft (6,000 meters) above its base on the ocean floor.

At the **Kilauea Visitor Center** ⓐ (daily 7.45am–5pm), the latest information about eruptions, road closures, and flow activity is displayed on maps, information boards and on film. Geologists and other experts also are on hand to provide lectures and answer questions about what's happening in the right outside, and down where the lava hits the sea.

A tenacious plant takes root in solidified lava.

Heed the warning signs in the Volcanoes National Park.

From the visitor center, the 11-mile (17km) **Crater Rim Drive** passes over some of the Pacific's most bizarre scenery as it skirts past wheezing steam vents at **Steaming Bluff (Sulfur Banks) Ⓑ**, where seeping ground water hits hot rock; there are several breathtaking views of the caldera. Lava flows in the caldera just below the first stretch of road and the Volcano House hotel date from 1919.

The **Hawaiian Volcano Observatory Ⓒ** (closed to the public), operated by the US Geological Survey, is one of the world's premier volcanology and geophysical research centers. Next door, the **Thomas A. Jaggar Museum Ⓓ** (tel: 967-7643; daily 8.30am–5pm) has informative exhibits and presentations. It also displays equipment used by scientists in the past to study the volcano (including working seismographs), as well as an exhibit of clothing and gear from scientists who got a bit too close to lava.

The primary vent of Kilauea

The road slips into the Southwest Rift zone, crossing lava flows from 1971, 1974, and 1921 to an overlook of **Halemaʻumaʻu Crater Ⓔ**, the collapsed depression within Kilauea Caldera. From the parking lot near the crater, whiffs of sulfuric gases escaping the earth along the short trail are reminders that there is still plenty going on down below. Halemaʻumaʻu is the primary vent of Kilauea. The crater of Kilauea is 2.5 miles (4km) by 2 miles (3km) in size, its walls a set of step-like fault blocks that form cliffs as high as 400ft (120 meters). From the early 1820s until 1924, Halemaʻumaʻu was a lake of active lava, then it went into a period characterized more by steam. In 2008, lava eruptions returned to the crater and have been going off pretty much daily ever since. Halemaʻumaʻu is said to be the fire goddess Pele's current home. At the crater's rim, offerings of *lei*, *ti*-wrapped stones, and money are left for Pele's appeasement.

Compared to explosive volcanoes in the Mediterranean or around the Pacific Rim, Hawaii's volcanoes are relatively benign, allowing visitors "drive-through" access to eruptions

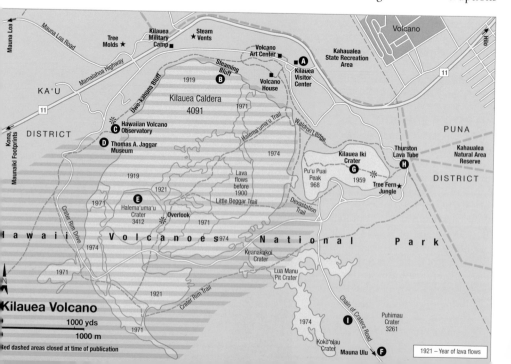

Kilauea Volcano

1000 yds
1000 m

Red dashed areas closed at time of publication

1921 – Year of lava flows

and lava flows. Only twice in recorded history have dangerously explosive eruptions occurred in Hawaii. The most recent was in 1924, when steam pressure expelled Kilauea volcano's plug and enlarged Halema'uma'u's diameter from 1,200ft (360 meters) to 3,000ft (900 meters), and left a hole 1,300ft (400 meters) deep. An eight-ton block of basalt was tossed 3,000ft (900 meters) from Halema'uma'u's center. Dust clouds rose to 20,000ft (6,000 meters).

Historic hot spots

In recent decades, Kilauea's eruptions have been primarily along the Southwest Rift and the East Rift zones, areas of structural weaknesses in the shield volcano. The Southwest Rift extends through Ka'u, and the East Rift to Puna. The most accessible of these sites since 2008 has been in the heart of the Halema'uma'u crater. During daylight, the robust plume of volcanic gas is a constant and dramatic reminder of the molten rock churning in a lava lake beneath the crater floor. After sunset, the crater continues to thrill with a vivid glow that illuminates the clouds and the plume as it billows into the night sky.

Earlier this millennium, a vent on the East Rift, **Mauna Ulu** *F*, was the biggest attraction. Over the years that vent has buried almost 13 miles (19km) of park road, some of it under 300ft (100 meters) of lava, and added more than 600 acres (243 hectares) of land to Hawaii Island.

Kilauea Iki Crater *G* was where a 2,000ft (600-meter) volcanic geyser erupted in 1959, possibly the highest volcanic fountain ever recorded. Another popular stop is the **Thurston Lava Tube** *H*, where a short trail weaves through primal groves of fern to a short lava tube.

It is very likely that by the time of publication, another eruption zone will have appeared inside Hawaii Volcanoes National Park. For all of the latest updates on eruptions, where to see them and when are the best times to go, visit the park website or – on the island itself – ask a hotel concierge. Just about all of the modern-day eruption sites are accessible

Horses graze along South Point Road in the Ka'u district.

ALL ABOUT LAVA TUBES

Lava tubes are naturally occurring conduits that are formed by flowing lava that hardens on the outer edges as this outside layer starts to cool. Tubes can be actively draining lava from a volcano during an eruption, or can be extinct, meaning the lava flow has ceased and the rock has cooled and left a long, cave-like channel. Inside Hawai'i Volcanoes National Park, there are a number of these tubes, many of which are big enough to walk through. Perhaps the most famous of these tubes is Kazumura Cave, which has been surveyed at almost 41 miles (66km) long and 3,614ft (1.1km) deep, making it one of the longest and deepest lava tubes in the world. A number of private outfitters lead tours of this cave.

via the **Chain of Craters Road** , which cuts off the Rim Road and descends along the East Rift, passing prehistoric pit craters and heading toward the ocean toward a fault scarp covered with lava flows that look like black molasses. Because lava flows change all the time, the National Park Service maintains facilities at roadblocks on this road. From those roadblocks, there are usually marked walks to safe viewpoints. Caution is required when hiking off the marked trail, as the lava cover can be unstable, and deaths have occurred here. It was once possible to continue along this road to Hilo. In the 1980s and 1990s, lava flows obliterated scores of homes, the village of **Kalapana** ⑤, archeological sites, the road itself, and the national park's Waha'ula Visitor Center. In 1997, the **Waha'ula luakini heiau**, once used for human sacrifices, was finally swallowed up, too. Waha'ula was first established by a Tahitian priest in the 13th century, and later used by Kamehameha the Great. According to legend, when a young chief passed through smoke

coming from the *heiau* – a taboo, as the smoke was considered a shadow of the *heiau's* god – he was killed and his bones were thrown in a pit.

About 25 miles (40km) out at sea, 3,000ft (900 meters) below sea level, a new island-to-be, **Lo'ihi**, is developing on the East Rift. Thousands of years from now, it will surface as either a new island or an extension of the Big Island itself.

Volcano

Just outside of the national park boundary, on the road to Hilo and not far from the Kilauea Visitor Center, **Volcano** ⑯ is a small town set amid forests and mists situated 3,700ft (1,100 meters) above sea level. There are several bed-and-breakfast guesthouses in the town for those wanting to stay up here, rather than returning the same day to Hilo or Kona. The well-appointed Kilauea Lodge (tel: 967-7366; www.kilauealodge.com), with its popular restaurant, is well worth an overnight stay, as are the many village bed-and-breakfasts. Green Goose Lodge (tel: 808-985-7172; www.greengooselodge.com), Volcano Rainforest Retreat (tel: 800-550-8696; www.volcanoretreat.com), and the 1920s-vintage Hale Ohia (tel: 967-7986; www.haleohia.com) are all reliable choices, provided you don't require luxurious accommodations. Volcano Places (tel: 877-967-7990; www.volcanoplaces.com) coordinates the rental of a number of vacation homes, as well.

The Volcano area attracts artisans, writers, and craftspeople. Many of their works are offered for sale at the **Volcano Art Center** (tel: 967-7511; www.volcanoartcenter.org; daily 9am–5pm) next to the Hawaii National Park headquarters and housed in the *c.*1877 **Volcano House** (tel: 967-7321; www.volcanohousehotel.com), once perched on the caldera's edge, but moved back in subsequent years to avoid lava flows. The original Volcano House holds the distinction of being

Halema'uma'u Crater, the primary vent on Kilauea.

the oldest hotel on Hawaii Island. The current incarnation, a 33-room hotel that overlooks Halema'uma'u is comfortable but rustic. Volcano House is the only hotel inside the national park and is a short walk from the visitor and art centers. During the day, it's crowded with visitors, but in the evenings it's quiet and pleasant.

From the main highway and still inside the national park, a side road leads to **Kipuka Pua'ulu** ❼ (Bird Park), an idyllic hideaway with a nature trail through meadows and one of the thickest concentrations of native plants in Hawaii.

A *kipuka* is an isolated ecosystem created when a lava flow shunts around an "island" of older growth or a habitat, isolating it. These *kipuka* are important biological research areas where native species continue to flourish independent of outside influences. Biologists often create artificial *kipuka* for research. In 1968, the National Park Service isolated an area near the coast with fences, protecting it from the wild pigs and goats that roam the Big Island. Something grew within the fenced *kipuka* that had never been seen before by modern scientists: a large bean plant with purple flowers. Until the fence was put up, island goats had eaten the bean plants before they could mature.

Ka'u

To the southwest of Kilauea and Volcano is **Ka'u Desert**, downwind from the summit and where noxious gases and dehydrated breezes inhibit vegetation. In 1790, an eruption of gas and dust suffocated a phalanx of warriors headed to battle Kamehameha the Great. Their footprints pressed into the hardening cinder, as they unsuccessfully sought to escape, can still be seen at **Maunaiki** ❽, preserved under glass at the end of a mile-long trail, and accessed from the main highway coming from South Point.

From the national park, the road descends along the Southwest Rift of Kilauea. **Punalu'u Beach** ❾ is a black-sand beach near the small Sea Mountain Resort, and it's worth a stop. If the tiny black sand crystals made of eroded lava rock don't impress, the wildlife will: the beach is frequented by endangered hawksbill and green turtles, which can often be seen basking on the black sand. There also are at least three *heiaus* here.

Beyond Punalu'u is Na'alehu, a traditional Hawaiian town billed as the southernmost in the USA, with a bakery renowned for its sweet bread. Turning off the main highway, a dead-end road traverses 12 miles (19km) of cattle range southward to **Ka Lae** ❿ (The Point), or **South Point**. Along the way, the road passes immense wind turbines, spinning in the unceasing winds that whip this cape; privately owned **Kamoa Wind Farm** ⓻ feeds electricity into the island's main power grid.

Somewhere along South Point, some of the first Polynesians landed in Hawaii, calling it Ka Lae.

Old lava flows surround the Chain of Craters road in Hawaii Volcanoes National Park.

Modern-day visitors sense somehow that this is a special place. Clear, blue waters smash against the 50ft (15-meter) -high basalt cliffs. Small fishing boats are often tied up below. The ocean is tempestuous, the wind forceful, and the isolation nearly complete.

The ancient Hawaiians built the **Kalalea Heiau**, a temple dedicated to fishing, right on the cliff's edge. Today, this is the southernmost place in the United States. Due south from here lies Tahiti.

A 3-mile (5km) hike east from South Point through a grassy plain leads to the unique **Papakolea Green Sand Beach ❷**. Here, an entire cinder cone of olivine has collapsed into a little bay and been reduced into polished sand by the surf. The beach is one of only four green-sand beaches in the World (the others being Talofofo Beach in Guam; Punta Cormorant in the Galápagos Islands; and Hornindalsvatnet, in Norway).

Signs at the trailhead indicate it is possible to drive a vehicle down to the beach, but don't be fooled; the road is rough and you might not make the distance. If you'd rather not hike, some locals have been known to drive out tourists for $10 apiece. Be sure to negotiate a price first.

Moving north through **Ka'u District**, you will notice an increase in gray and black lava – a consequence of the Mauna Loa flows of 1907, 1919, 1926, and 1950. Where the local microclimate has permitted, lichens, grass and *'ohi'a* – usually the first tree to appear in lava flows – sprout from the new earth. This is one of the least-populated places in Hawaii.

During the 1950s and 1960s, however, unscrupulous real estate salesmen trafficked in these barren lava acres, hawking them sight-unseen to unsuspecting Americans as properties in paradise. Nevertheless, some of those living here came knowing full well how barren the land was going to be and they've come to love it, even if swaying palm trees and white-sand beaches are distinctly lacking.

Entering a lava tube.

A STATE OF FIRE IN THE PACIFIC OCEAN

Hawaii Island is one of the few places in the world to witness a volcanic eruption in relative safety, due to the type of volcanic craters that characterize the Hawaiian archipelago.

The islands of Hawaii sit almost in the middle of the Pacific Plate, a piece in the giant jigsaw puzzle that is the Earth's crust. This Pacific Plate is moving slowly to the northwest. Each of the islands in the Hawaiian chain, from the smallest atoll in the northeast to Hawaii Island, was formed as the plate moved over a "hot spot" 50 miles (80km) deep in the Earth's mantle.

The oldest Hawaiian Islands are in the northeast near Midway Islands. The process of island growth continues. Kilauea Volcano, on Hawaii Island, offers the world's most active continuing eruption, since 1983.

Volcano creation

Hawaii's volcanoes are called shield or dome volcanoes. Shield volcanoes form in massive but gently rising oval shapes because they are fed by lava flowing repeatedly through a conduit, slowly and benignly.

Two Hawaii volcanoes, Mauna Loa and Kilauea, have summit calderas, created when lava drains from an underground magma chamber, causing the volcano summit to sink. In contrast, Maui's Haleakala has neither crater nor caldera, but rather a summit basin created by erosion.

Mauna Kea is the world's tallest volcano, measured from its base 18,000ft (5,500 meters) below sea level. Mauna Loa, also on the Big Island, is the planet's most massive mountain, at 10,000 cubic miles (16,000 cubic km) in volume.

A ranger from Hawaii Volcanoes National Park about to measure the levels of hazardous gases being emitted from the opening of a lava tube near Kalapana, on the Big Island.

Established in 1916, Hawaii Volcanoes National Park on the Big Island displays the results of hundreds of thousands of years of volcanic activity, migration, and evolution – processes that thrust a bare land from the sea and clothed it with complex and unique ecosystems.

Pu'u 'O'o vent, Kilauea Volcano: the rare and spectacular sight of a rift opening and lava spurting into the air in a fountain.

An offering to Pele, the goddess of fire, left on the rim of the Kilauea caldera.

PELE: GODDESS OF HAWAII'S FIRE

Stay in Hawaii long enough and you'll encounter the name of Hawaii's goddess of fire, Pele.

Traditional beliefs attribute the current eruptions of Kilauea to Pele. Nomadic by disposition, she arrived in Hawaii from Tahiti in a canoe provided by the god of sharks. After arriving in Ni'ihau, a small island to the east of Kauai, she traveled along the islands looking for a volcano to call home.

The only suitable location was Hawaii Island. Arriving there, she went after the reigning fire god, Aila'au, hoping to move in with him. Her reputation had preceded her, especially the stories about her awesome power and rather tempestuous personality. By the time Pele reached Kilauea, Aila'au had already fled.

A visit to Hawaii Volcanoes National Park will reveal the reverence that many contemporary Hawaiians have for Pele. Offerings pepper the caldera rim of Halema'uma'u. Even outsiders learn of her power. Tourists who've taken lava souvenirs home often later return them to national park authorities, hoping to rid themselves of the bad luck that suddenly befalls them.

Kilauea's usually passive flows can take on explosive force when reaching the cooler ocean or during the more spectacular fountaining.

...ecently constructed house sits atop a lava flow that engulfed ...lapana in September 2013.

...shly cooled lava on Kilauea Volcano. The ropy, smooth ...racter of paho'eho'e lava, seen along the Chain of Craters ...ad near Kilauea, is easily distinguished from the jagged and ...gh texture of 'a'a lava. Lava flows create new land but also ...troy nearly everything in their path.

Crossing the Hanakapi'ai Stream on the Hanakapi'ai Falls Trail, Hanakapi'ai Valley.

Kilauea Lighthouse.

KAUAI

Long the most reclusive and independent of Hawaii's islands, Kauai attracts hikers, kayakers, and others with its laidback lifestyle and dramatic landscape.

Waves break upon the black rocks at Po'ipu Beach Park, Koloa.

The historian Edward Josting called Kauai a "separate kingdom" when he detailed the history of this idyllic island, for it remained stubbornly independent after all the other Hawaiian islands had succumbed to Kamehameha the Great's conquest in the 1790s.

That moniker still is true today. Kauai moves at its own pace, has its own style of beach living, and harbors miles upon miles of challenging but breathtaking hiking trails. There's also lots of forest – they don't call it the "Garden Isle" for nothing.

Anchoring this nearly circular island, reportedly the wettest place on earth, is the summit of Wai'ale'ale. Down by the coast, the island is ringed by perfect, white-sand beaches that stretch from Ha'ena Point on its northern coast to the Po'ipu Resort on its southern shore. The beaches continue to broad and beautiful Polihale Beach in the west.

On the southeastern coast is Lihu'e, Kauai's largest urban center and main airport. Northward from Lihu'e, the road passes through the green and wet Windward Coast to the spectacular North Shore, Hanalei Bay and Lumahai Beach. The road stops here. Beyond is the 14-mile (22km) long Na Pali coast, accessible only by foot or boat. Westward from Lihu'e is the dry side of the island, along with some of Kauai's most important historical sites. At Waimea, Captain Cook first set foot in the Hawaiian Islands. Nearby, an ascending road leads inland along spectacular Waimea Canyon to Koke'e, where mists compete with the sun, providing stunning views from 4,000ft (122-meter) lookouts.

Hanakapi'ai Falls, Na Pali Coast State Wilderness Park.

More than half of this 550-sq mile (1,430-sq km) island is reserved for conservation and preservation. Alaka'i Swamp, a boggy dwarf forest high in the verdant interior, provides safe harbor for a number of endangered plants and birds. Elsewhere are many nature preserves and botanical gardens. Retreat to the seemingly silent places of Kauai, and sometimes you'll hear the song or catch a flash of the red or yellow feathers of a rarely seen 'apapane or 'akialoa, two types of Hawaiian honeycreepers.

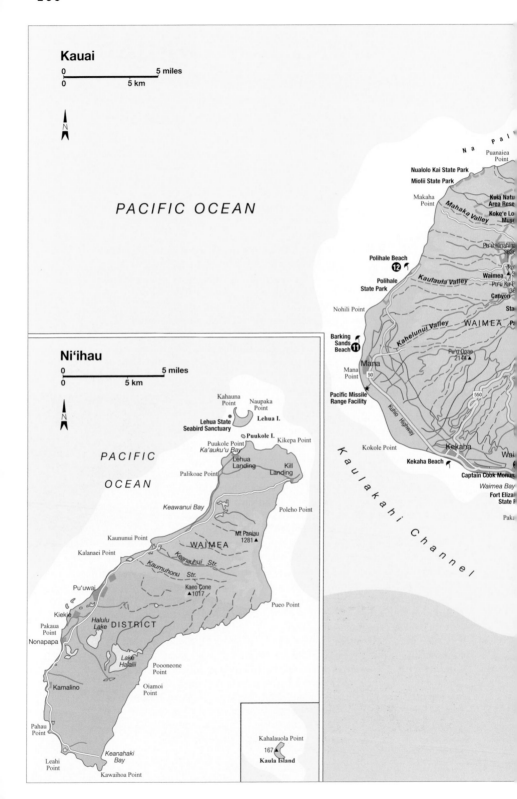

Kauai

0   5 miles
0   5 km

N

PACIFIC OCEAN

N a   P a l

Puanaiea Point

Nualolo Kai State Park

Miolii State Park

Makaha Point

Mahaka Valley

Kula Natu Area Rese

Koke'e Lo Muse

Pu'u Hinahin 383

Pu

Polihale Beach

⓬

Waimea

Pu'u Ka'

Polihale State Park

Kaulaula Valley

Canyon

Nohili Point

Kahelunui Valley

WAIMEA

Sta

P

Barking Sands Beach ⓫

Pu'u Opae 2144 ▲

Mana

Mana Point

50

Pacific Missile Range Facility

Kuhio Highway

550

Kokole Point

Kekaha

Kekaha Beach

Wai

Captain Cook Monur

K a u l a k a h i   C h a n n e l

Waimea Bay

Fort Eliza State F

Paka

Ni'ihau

0   5 miles
0   5 km

N

PACIFIC

OCEAN

Kahauna Point

Naupaka Point

Lehua I.

Lehua State Seabird Sanctuary

Puukole I.

Kikepa Point

Puukole Point

Ka'auku'u Bay

Lehua Landing

Kill Landing

Palikoae Point

Keawanui Bay

Poleho Point

Kaununui Point

Mt Paniau 1281 ▲

WAIMEA

Kalanaei Point

Keanauhui Str.

Kaumuhonu Str.

Pu'uwai

Kaeo Cone ▲ 1017

Pueo Point

Kiekie

Halulu Lake

DISTRICT

Pakaua Point

Nonapapa

Lake Halalii

Poooneone Point

Kamalino

Oiamoi Point

Pahau Point

Kahalauola Point

167 ▲

Kaula Island

Leahi Point

Keanahaki Bay

Kawaihoa Point

NORTH AND WEST KAUAI

Kauai is considered the "Garden Isle," and the lush landscape of the north and west of the island are a big part of how it earned this moniker.

Tropical paradise is different for every one of us, but in the original show, *South Pacific*, the notion takes the form of a place called Bali Hai. When the show was made into a movie, this mystical and magical spot was filmed in a mystical and magical part of Hawaii where a lush ridge of green traces a line high on the horizon, then drops all the way to meet the sea. Not surprisingly, it was filmed in Hanalei Bay, on the windward North Shore of Kauai.

All of the "Garden Isle" is green, but perhaps nowhere is the island greener than it is here. Taro fields; palm trees; you name the tropical flora, and it more than likely grows here. The north is home to the Na Pali Coast, some of the most stunning coastline anywhere in the world; the Kalalau Trail, one of the most iconic hikes on American soil; Tunnels, one of the most fabled surfing spots; and the Princeville, one of the most luxurious resorts in the world. The forests surrounding these spots have proven to be an uncrowded refuge for endemic plants and native birds; of all the Hawaiian Islands, Kauai has lost the fewest of its native feathered friends.

This eco-conscious vibe continues in the western quadrant of the island, where nature's beauty takes a very different form in Waimea Canyon. Known as the "Grand Canyon of the

Pacific," this site – and the area that surrounds it – is remarkable for what it represents; just as geologic forces built Kauai, so too are geologic forces (in the form of erosion) slicing it in two. Put simply, in a state with a multitude of incredible natural features, there simply is nothing like this.

Kilauea and Hanalei Bay

Technically speaking, north Kauai begins at the small town of **Kilauea**. A tiny downtown stretch is notable for its coffee shops, but the

Main Attractions
Hanalei Bay
Na Pali Coast
Kalalau Trail
Waimea Canyon
Koke'e

Hanalei.

Admiring the view towards Hanalei Bay.

main attraction here is the **Kilauea Point National Wildlife Refuge** (tel: 828-0383; daily 10am–4pm), where visitors can follow trails and look for sea birds that roost here year-round. If you have the time, follow the trails to the Kilauea Point Lighthouse on the point and take a tour. The structure was built in 1913, is a National Historic Landmark, and was renovated to commemorate its 100th anniversary.

A few miles beyond Kilauea Point is **Princeville** ❷, a 2,000-acre (800-hectare) resort area containing several golf courses and a large clubhouse, airport, shopping center, private houses, several luxurious condominium projects, and the elegant Princeville Hotel. Princeville offers striking views of Hanalei Bay and the sheer mountains at Hanalei, which is one of the wettest and greenest parts of the island. When rain mists the mountains, countless waterfalls hang like strands of silk thread from the dark green cliffs. It was in these lush mountains that films such as *Jurassic Park* and *Raiders of the Lost Ark* were

Limahuli Garden and Preserve.

filmed. In the distance, near where the sun sets, is the stretch that served as *South Pacific's* Bali Hai; a small peak that rises where the mountains enter the ocean. Beginning at Princeville and continuing to the end of the road at Ha'ena are several valleys, each fronted by a curved, white, and sandy beach.

Hanalei Bay ❸, the largest bay on Kauai, is a favorite spot for yachts in summer. In winter, when big surf from the north makes anchorage riskier, the bay's outer reef provides a challenge for the island's surfers. Sheltered from the open sea, Hanalei is spared the largest surf that crashes against Kauai's North Shore. Waves generated by storms in the north Pacific can reach 30ft (9 meters), although surf of 10–20ft (3–6 meters) is more common. From fall to spring, the huge waves create clouds of floating sea mist known as *'ehukai* all along the North Shore. In late afternoon, the descending sun gives the mist a golden cast. At **Tunnels Beach**, just outside of Hanalei Bay, these waves can be epic – both for humans and sharks alike.

MARKET OF MARKETS

On an island like Kauai, where plants and fruits and vegetables reign supreme, pretty much every farmers' market is a good one.

One market, however, rises above the rest: the weekly event on Saturdays on the main park in downtown Hanalei. To say the produce is spectacular would be an understatement; in addition to selling traditional Hawaiian items such as taro and poi, vendors peddle beautiful tomatoes, lettuce, and other fruits and veggies they have grown organically.

The market also always features flowers – everything from orchids to bird of paradise flowers. The market also has a slew of craft vendors. Perhaps the only downside is demand; produce tends to sell out quickly so get there early.

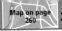
Lumaha'i and Limahuli

Beyond Hanalei is an 8-mile (13km) stretch of scenic coast, a glorious mix of mountains, beaches, and sea, known as the North Shore. Highlights include the photogenic series of beaches called **Lumaha'i ❹**, where brilliant white sands are interspersed with black lava-rock promontories. The blue of the sea shimmers beyond the sand, and the green of *hala* trees (also known as *pandanus*) glows behind it. Access to the beach is down a short dirt trail overhung with exotic *hala* trees. This is the beach where Mitzi Gaynor sang to the world in the movie *South Pacific* that she'd "wash that man right out of my hair." And there's the long stretch of reef-sheltered beach up against that other stand-in for *South Pacific*: the beach at Princeville in Hanalei Bay, which boasts good snorkeling as an additional reward.

Past these beaches, **at least b**otanically speaking, the North Shore becomes Kauai at its most tropical, with waving palms, hibiscus, plumeria, ginger, and a host of other flowers. The **Limahuli** section of the National Tropical Botanical Garden (tel: 826-1053; www.ntbg.org; open Tue–Fri, Sun 9.30am–4pm), 5 miles (8km) on from Lumaha'i Beach, is dedicated almost entirely to native plants such as these and includes a 900-acre (360-hectare) natural preserve that encompasses much of this striking valley. Walking the grounds and experiencing some of the terraced hillsides is an education in island farming techniques that have survived for centuries.

Wai'oli Hui'ia Church, Hanalei.

The Na Pali Coast

The volcano goddess, Pele, was associated with Kauai long before she established her current home at Kilauea on the Big Island. One story about Pele places her at beautiful **Ha'ena ❺**, beyond Hanalei Bay and at the end of the road before Na Pali, during a big hula festival. In order to join the dancing, Pele took the form of a beautiful young woman, then fell in love with a handsome Kauai chief, Lohi'au. The remnants of the hula platform can still be found on the hillside, to the west of **Ke'e Beach ❻**, where the road ends. This is a

Hanalei.

NA PALI'S PAST

There remains some evidence of the large numbers of people who once inhabited Na Pali's valleys. Extensive stonework that formed the taro paddies of Nu'alolo-aina (*'aina* means sea), a hanging valley, and the remains of a fishing village at Nu'alolo-kai (*kai* means fertile land) survive. The people of Nu'alolo-aina had access to the sea, while the people of Nu'alolo-kai had little land or fresh water, so they formed a trading relationship, a single community built, of necessity, in two valleys.

In centuries past, the people who lived here maintained the trails, but they are impassable today. A tree trunk that spanned a section of cliff between Honopu and Awa'awapuhi has rotted away, and a ladder that once connected the two sections of the Nu'alolo-aina and Nu'alolo-kai trail is long gone.

popular spot that marks the start of the **Na Pali Coast State Wilderness Park ❼**, perhaps one of the world's most exquisite places. Though inaccessible to vehicles, this coastline can be enjoyed in a number of ways: by helicopter, kayak, paddleboard, or boat. Most people go by boat, preferring to experience the 4,000ft (1,220-meter) cliffs that drop into the ocean from the comfort of a floating vessel with a full bar. Charter tours are available in rigid-hulled inflatable boats or in catamarans. Almost all of these trips leave from Hanalei Bay.

Geologically speaking, the Na Pali Coast is a wonder. After the island was created hundreds of thousands of years ago, two forms of erosion have been working to create the natural rock spires we see today. From the bottom, wind and surf have chipped away at the rock to create caves and sea stacks. From the top, rain in the form of waterfalls has worn away saddles that, eventually, have become chasms. Over time, the cliffs have developed their unique appearance.

A traditional grass hut in Limahuli Garden and Preserve.

The Kalalau Trail

There is another way to traverse the Na Pali Coast: by foot. From Ha'ena, a short oceanside trail leads to an ancient *hula heiau* (temple) plus spectacular scenic views. A far longer, 11-mile (18km) trail has become established as one of the most iconic hikes in all of America: the Kalalau Trail. The trail begins gradually, rising on a ridge and dropping into lush **Hanakapi'ai ❽**. This area boasts a valley with a lovely pool and waterfall toward the cliffs, and a crescent of white sand on the ocean side. The ocean here becomes extremely dangerous in winter, and numerous unwary visitors have drowned. Hiking to and from Hanakapi'ai usually takes at least three hours.

From Hanakapi'ai, the Kalalau gets serious, zigzagging a heart-thumping course upward, scurrying in and out of valleys and across a sheer cliff face to **Hanakoa ❾**, a hanging valley. Like several others here, Hanakoa sweeps from the heights in a flourish of vegetation and ends abruptly, hanging over the ocean, its stream turning into a misty waterfall that falls on the rocks and sea below. After passing a rough trail shelter, more jungle and an infinite number of shallow valleys and cliffs, the trail drops and then ends in **Kalalau Valley ⑩**, the largest of Na Pali's valleys. The section of the trail from Hanakoa valley can only be tackled by those who have a permit to camp overnight at Kalalau or at Hanakoa. Permits are available from the state parks office in Lihu'e but are limited and often sell out up to a year in advance especially in summer. (See www.hawaiistateparks.org/parks/kauai/napali.cfm for more information). Conditions at these campsites are rustic at best.

The wonderful west

Kauai provides its residents with many avenues to the sea, as the island is ringed with sandy beaches. The largest is the stretch of nearly unbroken sand along the western coast, from Waimea stretching northward more than 15 miles (24km) along Highway 50 through sugar plantations and shorefront property. Along the beach north of Waimea is the Pacific Missile Range Facility at **Barking Sands ⑪**, which remains the site of controversial military testing. At the end of the highway – and the end of this long stretch of sand and former cane fields – is **Polihale ⑫**. A state park, this beach is Hawaii's longest at over 15 miles (24km); it is usually empty due in part to the rough access road, and often dramatically draped with mist. Polihale offers campsites and showers; permits are available from the park's office in the state office building in downtown Lihu'e. Hidden in the cliffs at the Na Pali coast end are a couple of *heiaus*, or temples. Unless you know exactly what you're looking for, however, you'll not find them. There is no public access trail from here to the looming cliffs of the Na Pali coast.

All along this western coast, the modest rise of **Ni'ihau** breaks the horizon less than 20 miles (32km) offshore.

Waimea Canyon

Perhaps the region's most notable feature is a giant gash in the landscape on the back side of the Na Pali Coast: a naturally occurring geologic phenomenon known as **Waimea Canyon ⑬**. The chasm often is referred to as "The Grand Canyon of the Pacific," and the nickname is apt. Over the course of tens of thousands of years, the Waimea River has helped cut this canyon into the hillside. Today, the waters that continue to do the cutting start high in the bogs of the Alaka'i Swamp. After every major storm, waterfalls tumble from the swamp, through the canyon and into deep valleys carpeted in green. As the plum- and guava-dotted valleys converge into gorges, a change in flora occurs. The wetness of the swamp is left behind as the vegetation becomes sparse.

Downstream, the *ohi'a* gives way to *kukui*, the candlenut tree. The gorges meet with the main canyon, and the *kukui* gives way to dry country trees: the native *wiliwili* and introduced *kiawe* (mesquite) and *lantana*. The weather lower down is hot and dry, and

Hiking the Hanakapi'ai Falls Trail, Na Pali Coast State Wilderness Park.

the streambed holds the only moisture. Red dust blows from barren hillsides; by the time the **Waimea River** meets the sea at Waimea town, its currents carry a heavy suspension of red earth.

The scenery is still elegant and primal, but visitors should arrive early before the mists have cleared, before the rainbows have had time to form, and before the caravans of other tourists in rental cars and tour buses gather. For the more experienced hiker, there is the **Kukui Trail**, which drops in a steep, zigzagging course down the side of the remarkable Waimea Canyon. If you hike here, be on the lookout for others who might be sharing the path – a herd of mountain goats, for example.

Koke'e

Just after the second canyon lookout, **Koke'e** is the only inhabited place in Kauai's higher elevations. There are a dozen state-owned cabins here that anyone can rent as long as reservations are made well in advance. The cabins, which are basic and rustic, are managed from **Koke'e Lodge**, which offers facilities including a restaurant, bar, store,

and information center. Educational activities are also run from here.

Next to the lodge is the **Koke'e Museum** (tel: 335-9975; daily 9am–4.30pm; donation requested) with displays on the natural history of Kauai and the other islands. Prints and living examples of important plants are exhibited. Maps and guidebooks are also sold here. Located in the state park, the lodge and museum are fronted by a spreading lawn where protected *moa*, or wild Hawaiian chickens, strut.

Activities in the Koke'e area include a casual stroll around the **Iliau Nature Loop**, or a drive to **Kalalau Valley Lookout** at the end of the road reveals one of the world's finest views on a clear day: the panorama of Kalalau Valley, the largest valley along the Na Pali Coast.

The view from that 4,000ft (1,200-meter) -high lookout will reward the twisting drive to Koke'e. Low clouds sometimes obscure the view of the valley, but the lookout offers a fine opportunity to see some native birds, such as the red-and-black *'apapane* and vermilion-colored *'i'iwi*.

Hanakapi'ai Falls.

Waimea Canyon State Park.

Rock pooling at Po'ipu Beach Park, Koloa.

SOUTH AND EAST KAUAI

There are beaches, and then there are the beaches of Po'ipu and Kapa'a – some of the most intimate strips of sand in all of Hawaii. No wonder so many visitors flock to south and east Kauai.

Main Attractions
Kalapaki Beach
Kauai Museum
Po'ipu
Koloa Rum Company
National Tropical Botanical Garden
Hanapepe

Not much happens on Kauai, but when it does, it happens in the south and east. Here, on white-sand beaches such as Po'ipu, Kalapaki, Hanama'ulu, Waipouli, and Kapa'a, visitors come in droves to kick back, sip Mai Tais and escape the madness of other-island resorts. The eastern part of the island always has had a bit of a buzz about it; as recently as a few decades ago, this was sugar cane country and the site of Kauai's first processing plants and first railroad. Today, these historic sites provide an informative overview as to how the most remote major island managed to survive. In the south, the name of the game is innovation. Hanapepe Town comes to life every Friday night when visitors descend for an up-close look at the local art scene. Waimea Town, technically the first place Captain Cook made landfall in the Hawaii (before he moved along to Hawaii Island), has become a hub for technological innovation. Along with its lush jungles and glorious beaches, Kauai certainly has its share of secrets to discover.

Lihu'e

On the island's southeast coast, Lihu'e ⑯ is the seat of county government, the island's major business district and shopping area, and the site of Kauai's airport. Nearby, **Nawiliwili Harbor**, the island's major port, plays host to a growing number of cruise ships on inter-island and trans-Pacific itineraries. It's also home port to a number of deep-sea fishing charters. Also nearby: **Kalapaki Beach**, a quiet, locals-only, white-sand beach that fronts the beautiful Haupu mountains and looks out onto Nawiliwili Harbor.

Since the 1850s Kauai has been a sugar-producing island, and the

Cycling on a trail beside the Kuhio Highway, outside Kapa'a.

Kauai has ten different golf courses at seven venues; some are part of resorts, others are independent.

Kayaking on the Wailua River.

history of sugar's heyday can be studied at two highly recommended museums in Lihu'e. In the center of town, on Rice Street, **Kauai Museum** (tel: 245-6931; Mon–Sat 10am–5pm) is, without question, the best museum on the island. In addition to collections that tell the story of life on Kauai in the past, the museum frequently displays the work of local artists. It also occasionally offers courses in such activities as *lau hala* weaving and *lei*-making. Located off Nawiliwili Road (Highway 58), also in Lihu'e, is the **Grove Farm Homestead & Sugar Plantation Museum** (tel: 245-3202; Mon, Wed, Thu: tours 10am and 1pm, reservations required). For close to a century this was a plantation-owner's home; today it provides insights into the era of plantation agriculture in Hawaii.

Both museums offer a good introduction to the contributions made by Kauai's elite *kama'aina* (long-time resident) families, with names that become more familiar during one's stay on the island: Rice, Wilcox, Sinclair, Gay, and Robinson. Many had

missionary roots but later made their fortunes in sugar and ranching. Some of these *kama'aina*, such as William Harrison Rice and his son, William Hyde Rice, had a strong affinity for Native Hawaiian people and their culture, and did a great deal to keep the language and legends alive. Kauai Museum was founded by Rice's progeny, while Grove Farm Homestead was established by George N. Wilcox, whose parents were among the earliest American Protestant missionaries to Hawaii; they left a legacy of land and sugar.

The Wilcox holdings comprise some of the largest privately owned land on Kauai, including one of the few remaining plantations in the islands. With the decline of the sugar industry, Grove Farm has branched into land development, including Kukui Grove, Kauai's largest shopping mall. The Wilcox family also retains extensive holdings on the North Shore and developed a shopping center in Hanalei. The Sinclair-Robinson-Gay clan, which purchased the tiny island of Ni'ihau in 1864, continues to be active in cattle ranching and sugar cultivation. The Robinsons, who manage Ni'ihau, are perhaps the most secretive of the *kama'aina* families.

Waipouli and Kapa'a

The stretch of coastline east from Lihu'e is sometimes called the Coconut Coast because of its preponderance of palm trees, bays, and beautiful beaches. This stretch runs from **Waipouli** to Kapa'a, and since 1990 this area has become one of the island's biggest resort areas, complete with condominiums, supermarkets, gas stations, and all of the other amenities to serve visitors. (It's also one of the best places on the island to buy shave ice.)

Up Kuamo'o Road toward the mountains and the spectacular beach at Opaeka'a Falls, just outside **Wailua** is a large gathering of rocks that includes a birthstone and a *piko* (navel) stone. Modern-day attractions in the area include the Wailua Golf Course, a municipal 18-hole facility; Wailua Beach; the Wailua River,

which carries tour boats to the **Fern Grotto**, a natural though commercialized wedding site; and the modern Coconut Plantation Marketplace.

Heading inland on Route 53, there's a turnoff for **Kamakilo Village**, where you can visit a reconstructed *hale*, a type of a traditional Hawaiian village house (tel: 823-0559; 9am–5pm). Farther along, off Kaholalele Road, look out for the spires of **Kauai's Hindu Monastery**, a religious retreat built on acres of lush, rainforested valley. The San Marga Iraivan Temple has existed here for years, while the Kadavul Temple is a more recent addition. Five different tours are offered daily by warm and welcoming devotee-guides (tel: 822-3012).

Po'ipu and beyond

On Kauai's southernmost point, **Po'ipu** is the sunniest of the island's districts. It has several large hotels, plus many smaller hotels and condominiums, and has evolved as an enclave around this stretch of overnight accommodations. Most

Koloa Rum Company's tasting room and store on the Kilohana Plantation.

Outside the Kauai Museum, Lihu'e.

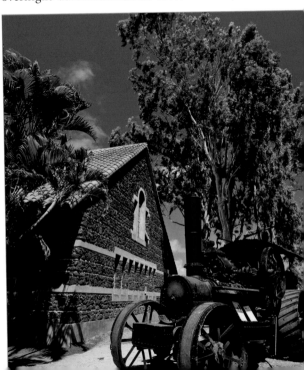

OPAEKA'A FALLS

It's not as tall as some of the waterfalls outside Hanalei, but this 151ft (46-meter) cascade, along the Wailua River on the east side of Kauai, has become one of the island's most popular waterfalls. The popularity stems from accessibility; the attraction is 2 miles (3km) up Kuamo'o Road from Highway 56, and there's a roadside lookout. The name of the waterfall tells a bit of history; opaeka'a means "rolling shrimp," and when freshwater shrimp were abundant in the stream, they would roll in the water from the force of the falls. On the opposite side of the road near the falls is the relatively well-preserved ancient temple of Poli'ahu Heiau. It is named after the snow goddess, Poli'ahu, sister of Pele.

Salt Pond Beach Park, in Hanapepe, has the only natural salt pond in Hawaii that is still used to make salt during the summer.

Opaeka'a Falls, Wailua River State Park.

of the hotels face the ocean; on the other side of the main road through the area, you'll find restaurants, supermarkets, and shopping centers designed to serve the tourists who come and stay a while. In addition to the white-sand beaches (with water that generally is calm), there are several scenic spots in the area, such as **Spouting Horn**, a natural water spout in the shoreline rocks of an old lava flow, and **Brennecke's Beach**, renowned for its great body-surfing waves. This portion of the island suffered most from the wrath of 1992's Hurricane 'Iniki. Although many homes, especially those along the coastline leading to Spouting Horn, were destroyed, they have all been rebuilt.

The coast westward from Lihu'e, the dry leeward side, might as well be a different island from the opposite side. Little rain falls past Kalaheo a town in the heart of the Anahola Mountains in the center of the island.

Kauai's "Hawaiianness" is obvious, but since 1835, when Hawaii's first commercial sugar plantation was started at **Koloa** ⑳, the island's ethnic character has gone through radical changes. As in other parts of Hawaii, sugar attracted a diverse set of people willing to work in its dusty, itchy fields and pungent mills. First came the Chinese, then the Japanese, Portuguese, Puerto Ricans, and lastly the Filipinos. Thus many of Kauai's communities developed as plantation towns, with the different races separated into camps. Koloa is one of these towns, welcoming visitors with rustic charm and a cluster of shops and restaurants. One of its newest attractions, the **Koloa Rum Company** (3-2087 Kaumuali'i Highway; tel; 246-8900; www.koloarum.com; daily 9.30am–5pm), offers tours of the on-site spirits production facility and tastings in a bar. The town also has a monument to its plantation past, a Buddhist temple, and several historic churches to add flavor to a visit.

Today, many of the sugar firms that started the towns are gone or have merged with other companies, but the communities themselves persist. Waimea, Numila (the Hawaiian

THE LITTLE PEOPLE

It's difficult to visit Kauai without hearing at least a handful of references to the *menehune*, little people who are reputed to have inhabited the island in the distant past. As the legend goes, these pint-sized humans were believed to farm remote valleys on the island's North Shore, and were reportedly responsible for several stone constructions across the island. Menehune were seldom seen, working only after dark, and it was said that they accepted as payment only a single shrimp per worker. Among the construction projects associated with them are the Menehune Ditch near Waimea on the leeward coast, which exhibits a knowledge of stonework not seen elsewhere in Hawaii, and the 'Alekoko Fishpond, also called the Menehune Fishpond, near Lihu'e's Nawiliwili Harbor.

pronunciation of New Mill), Puhi, Kealia, and Kilauea are a few of the towns that have lost the plantations that helped build them. In 2009, Gay & Robinson, Kauai's last big sugar company, closed its mill at Makaweli and got out of the business all together.

National Tropical Botanical Garden

The prestigious **National Tropical Botanical Garden ㉑** (tel: 742-2623; www.ntbg.org; Mon–Sat 8.30am–5pm; reservations essential) in Lawa'i Valley is a facility that saves endangered tropical plants, and locates and grows flora of medicinal and economic importance. In recent years, the garden has begun collecting and propagating Hawaii's unique endemic plants. The gardens also include **Lawa'i Kai**, the verdant estate of John Gregg Allerton, who willed his estate to the nation upon his death. Lawa'i Kai is a wonderland of vegetation and statuary at the base of Lawa'i, where it meets the sea in a clean, white-sand beach. The estate's lovely gardens and buildings, including Queen Emma's summer home are open to the public (tours at 9am, 10am, 1pm, 2pm; for details of the gardens' Limahuli site on the North Shore, see page 265).

Hanapepe and Waimea

West of Koloa on the south shore sits **Hanapepe ㉒**, known lovingly as "The Biggest Little Town" on Kauai. This is a place built on salt; a group of pre-contact salt ponds that have been worked by local Hawaiian salt gatherers for generations lie just beyond the main drag. In recent years, the town's historic buildings have become chock-full of art galleries and tiny cafés. Hanapepe Town celebrates its artists every Friday, from 6–9pm, as painters, sculptors, and craftsmen open the doors of their galleries and studios to introduce newcomers to their respective work. For an island that never has too much happening, Friday nights in Hanapepe are about as hopping as things get.

Waimea ㉓, a historic seaport, is not far from where British discoverer

FACT

John Gregg and his adoptive father, Robert, spent many years traveling all over the world, collecting art and botanical species. Robert died in 1964 and John Gregg in 1986.

Wailua River in Kapa'a.

Trees create a tunnel over the road linking the east side of Kauai to Koloa and Po'ipu.

Po'ipu Beach Park, Koloa.

different Hawaiian history would be if the *ali'i* had been home.

Today, Waimea is an off-the-radar spot that is worth exploring. On the south bank of the Waimea River is the old Russian **Fort Elizabeth** , now protected as a state park. In 1816, an agent of the Imperial Russian government came to Kauai to recover the cargo of a ship that had broken up on the island's shore. The agent, Dr Anton Sheffer, convinced Kauai's King Kaumuali'i that together they could conquer the rest of the islands. Sheffer's Machiavellian bid for Hawaiian power failed miserably, but ruins of the fort, named after Czar Alexander I's queen, remain as a testimonial to Sheffer's adventurism and folly.

Captain James Cook first landed in Hawaii in 1778. When Cook arrived, the local chiefs had moved their courts from the warmth of the island's leeward side to cooler Wailua on the east side of the island, and were nowhere to be found. Cook left Waimea before these chiefs could return to greet him. He eventually found his welcome, and end, on Hawaii Island, but it's hard to visit Waimea and not contemplate how

For a more modern monument, check out the **West Kauai Technology & Visitor Center** (9565 Kaumuali'i Highway tel: 338-1332), a great place to learn more about Kauai's past. The center features exhibits, programs and weekly activities that reflect the diversity of Kauai's agricultural community.

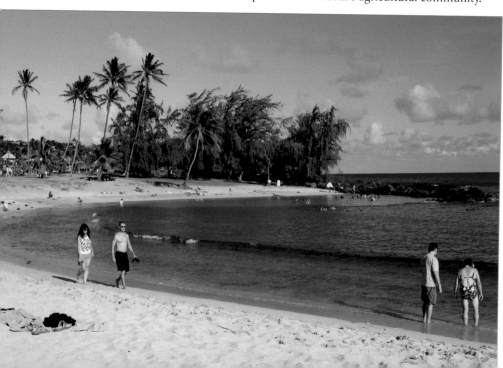

Ni'ihau

Across the Kaulakahi Channel from Kauai's west side, Ni'ihau rises dimly through sea mists like some slumbering prehistoric creature 17 miles (27km) away.

It sees little rain because it falls in the lee of Kauai, whose mountains collect most of the moisture. The mystique of this windswept, privately owned island, whose estimated 120 residents are seemingly caught in a 19th-century time warp, has been perpetuated by the owner's patriarchal restriction on visitors.

Owned by the Robinson family since 1864, Ni'ihau has been cloaked in myth from the time the first Polynesian explorers came upon the 6- by 18-mile (10 by 29km) sliver of arid land. Early chants relay that Ni'ihau and its tiny islet neighbors, **Lehua** and **Ka'ula**, were triplet siblings born to the ancestral gods Papa and Wakea.

Another chant postulates that Pele chose Ni'ihau as her first home. Interestingly, many volcanologists now theorize that Ni'ihau was the first of the current Hawaiian islands to break the surface of the ocean. Seventh largest in the chain, its highest point is 1,281ft (390 meters) above sea level. Ni'ihau was Captain James Cook's second stop (following Kauai) in the islands during his voyage of exploration in 1778.

Elizabeth Sinclair

In 1864, King Kamehameha V sold it to Elizabeth (McHutcheson) Sinclair, widow of a Navy officer who had perished, along with their eldest son, in a shipwreck. Mrs Sinclair saw Ni'ihau lush after two years of abundant rainfall and believed it would make a good ranch home for her remaining five children. For her $10,000, she acquired not only an island, but also the 300 Hawaiians living on it.

Modern island life

Today, family heirs Keith and Bruce Robinson manage the ranch and island. They continue to guard the privacy of Ni'ihau's Hawaiian populace to the extent that the island is one of the last true enclaves of a lifestyle that has long since disappeared elsewhere. Life on the island, however, is quite unembellished and without frills.

Ni'ihau is the only island in Hawaii where Hawaiian is the primary language. Today, children attend a grammar school with three classrooms in **Pu'uwai**, the island's only village. Though many homes do not have electricity and most do not have indoor plumbing or telephones, the school has solar-powered computers. Other schools for Ni'ihau's children are on Kauai, where kids go to live with relatives. They must go to Kauai or Oahu to attend high school.

State education officials and tax officers visit the island, and a couple of doctors make infrequent checks on the populace. Otherwise, access is limited to visitors who pay for an expensive helicopter tour (tel: 335-3500) or less costly daylong snorkeling tours to remote ends of the island, which do not allow passengers to set foot on the soil (tel: 335-0815). There are virtually no county services, no county roads, and no sewers. Few people use cars; horses and bicycles are more common.

Nearly all residents still work for the Robinsons, rearing cattle and sheep, making charcoal from *kiawe* trees and gathering honey. Twice a week a barge arrives at Ka'auku'u Bay to carry goods across the sea to market and to deliver mail and other necessities.

Making a Ni'ihau shell necklace.

INSIGHT GUIDES TRAVEL TIPS
HAWAII

Transportation

Getting there........................ 280
  By air.................................. 280
  By sea................................ 281
Getting around..................... 281
  By air.................................. 281
  By bicycle.......................... 281
  On foot............................... 282
  By bus................................ 282
  By car................................. 282
  By sea................................ 283
  By taxi............................... 283

Accommodations

Choosing a hotel................... 284
  Hotel companies................ 284
  Accommodation agents..... 284
  Camping............................. 285
  National parks................... 285
  State parks........................ 285
  County parks..................... 285
Oahu..................................... 286
Maui...................................... 288
Molokai................................. 290
Lanai..................................... 290
Hawaii (Big Island)................ 291
Kauai..................................... 293

Eating Out

Choosing a restaurant........... 294
  Where to eat...................... 294
  Drinking notes................... 294
Oahu..................................... 295
Maui...................................... 296
Molokai................................. 297
Lanai..................................... 297
Hawaii (Big Island)................ 298
Kauai..................................... 299

Activities

The Arts................................ 300
  Art galleries...................... 300
  Performance art................ 301
  Movies............................... 301
Children's activities.............. 301
  Children's museums.......... 301
  Steam trains...................... 301
  Theater............................... 302
  Water-themed attractions. 302
  Zoos.................................. 302
Festivals............................... 302
  January............................. 302
  February............................ 302
  March................................ 302
  April.................................. 302
  May................................... 302
  June.................................. 303
  July................................... 303
  August............................... 303
  September......................... 303
  October............................. 304
  November.......................... 304
  December.......................... 304
Nightlife............................... 304
  Bars.................................. 304
  Dinner cruises and lu'aus.. 305
  Live music......................... 305
Shopping.............................. 305
  What not to buy................. 305
  What to buy....................... 305
  Where to shop................... 306
Sightseeing tours.................. 308
Sports................................... 308
  Participant sports.............. 308
  Spectator sports................ 308
  Outdoor activities.............. 308

A – Z

Admission charges................ 310
Animals................................. 310
Budgeting for your trip........... 310
Children................................. 310
Climate and weather.............. 311
Crime and safety................... 311
Customs regulations.............. 311
Disabled travelers................. 311
Emergencies......................... 312
Embassies and consulates.... 312
Electricity.............................. 312
Gay and lesbian travelers...... 312
Health and medical care........ 312
Internet................................ 312
Maps.................................... 312
Media................................... 312
Money.................................. 313
Opening hours....................... 313
Postal services..................... 313
Public holidays...................... 313
Tax....................................... 313
Telephones............................ 313
Time zone.............................. 314
Tipping.................................. 314
Tourist information................ 314
Tour operators...................... 314
Visas and passports.............. 314
Weights and measures.......... 314
What to bring........................ 314
What to wear......................... 314

Language

Background............................ 315
  A language of the Pacific ... 315
  Pronunciation guidelines... 316

Further Reading

Non-fiction............................ 317
Fiction.................................. 317

TRANSPORTATION

GETTING THERE AND GETTING AROUND

GETTING THERE

Because Hawaii is an archipelago, and because those islands sit right in the middle of the Pacific Ocean, getting to them often presents visitors with one of the biggest challenges of their respective trips. In reality, there are only two options – you either fly in or come by sea.

By air

Hawaii is regularly serviced from the US mainland, Canada, Europe, the South Pacific, and Asia. Flying time is about 10 hours from New York, eight hours from Chicago, and five hours from Los Angeles. The Hawaiian Islands also are a major stopover point for flights traveling between US mainland and Asia, Australia, and New Zealand.

Oahu

It might be Hawaii's most populous island but Oahu only has one commercial airport, **Honolulu International Airport** (tel: 808-836-6411; www.hawaii.gov/hnl). However, over the years this has become one of the busiest airports in the entire US: in 2012, the airport recorded 21 million passengers. Most planes touch down on a series of reef runways, completed in 1977 on a shallow reef-lagoon between Honolulu Harbor and Pearl Harbor. The interior of the airport's main terminal is adorned with Hawaiian arts and crafts created by top local artists. (In 1967, a Hawaii legislative act designated one percent of all appropriated public works funds for the purchase of artwork for state buildings, including the airport.)

Japanese, Hawaiian, and Chinese gardens also enhance the terminal's promenade areas.

In addition to the main terminal building, the airport operates two other terminals: the inter-island terminal and the commuter-airline terminal. The airport operates a free shuttle system between these buildings from 6am to 10pm.

Maui

Maui has three airports. The main one, **Kahului Airport** (tel: 808-872-3830, www.hawaii.gov/ogg), handles a growing number of direct flights from the US mainland and many inter-island hops. The airport boasts a Visitor Information Center, major rental car counters, and taxi and shuttle stands.

The two other airports, the **Kapalua-West Maui Airport** (tel: 808-665-6108; www.hawaii.gov/jhm) and **Hana Airport** (tel: 808-248-4861; www.hawaii.gov/hnm), are significantly smaller; both are served by inter-island airlines (see page 281). Flying to Hana from one of the other Maui airports is a fast and efficient option if you don't want to drive the Hana Highway. Be warned: these flights can be expensive.

Hawaii Island

Hawaii Island has two main airports, **Kona International Airport** at Keahole (tel: 808-327-9520; www.hawaii.gov/koa) on the popular west side, and **Hilo International Airport** (tel: 808-961-9300; www.hawaii.gov/ito) on the outskirts of Hilo. A third airport, dubbed Waimea-Kohala Airport (tel: 808-887-8126; www.hawaii.gov/mue) is used for inter-island commutes. It is called Kamuela Airport by locals.

Kauai

On Kauai, **Lihu'e Airport** (tel: 808-246-1448) has direct flights daily from San Francisco and Los Angeles on the US mainland, as well as numerous inter-island flights from Honolulu and other neighboring island airports. It is the smallest of all the airports on the four major Hawaiian Islands.

Molokai and Lanai

Molokai's Ho'olehua Airport (tel: 808-567-9660; www.hawaii.gov/mkk) in south-central Molokai, handles inter-island flights only. The same is true at **Lanai Airport** (tel: 808-565-

Distances from Honolulu

Anchorage 2,781 miles/4,475km
Auckland 4,393 miles/7,068km
Equator 1,470 miles/2,352km
Hilo, Hawaii Island 214 miles/344km
Hong Kong 5,541 miles/8,915km
Kailua-Kona, Hawaii Island 168 miles/270km
Kahului, Maui 98 miles/158km
Kure Atoll 1,367 miles/2,200km
Lanai 72 miles/116 km
Lihu'e, Kauai 103 miles/166km
London 7,226 miles/11,627km
Los Angeles 2,557 miles/4,114km
Manila 5,293 miles/8,516km
Midway Is. 1,309 miles/2,106km
Molokai 54 miles/87km
New York 4,959 miles/7,979km
North Pole 4,740 miles/7,631km
Papeete, Tahiti 2,741 miles/4,410km
San Francisco 2,397 miles/3,857km
Tokyo 3,847 miles/6,190km
Vancouver 2,709 miles/4,359km

ACCOMMODATIONS

EATING OUT

ACTIVITIES

A – Z

LANGUAGE

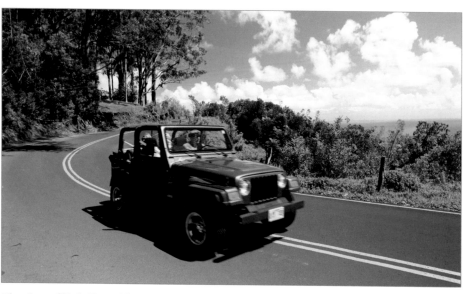

Hire a Jeep and hit the Hana Highway on Maui.

7942; www.hawaii.gov/lmn), 10 miles from Lanai City. For more information about aircraft that serve these destinations, visit www.hawaii.gov/dot/airports.

Trans-Pacific Airlines

Alaska Airlines
Tel: 800-252-7522
www.alaskaair.com
American Airlines
Tel: 800-433-7300
www.aa.com
Delta Airlines
Tel: 800-221-1212
www.delta.com
Hawaiian Airlines
Tel: 800-367-5320
www.hawaiianairlines.com
United Airlines
Tel: 800-864-8331
www.united.com

By sea

Numerous cruise ships including **Crystal Cruises** (www.crystalcruises.com), **Princess Cruises** (www.princess.com), and **Royal Caribbean** (www.royalcaribbean.com) now make Hawaii a port-of-call, stopping in Honolulu as well as the neighbor islands as part of their itinerary. A few lucky souls, of course, arrive by private yacht.

GETTING AROUND

Once you're in Hawaii, getting around can be easy or difficult,

depending on where you're headed and how much you're willing to spend to get there. If you're staying on one island, the best option is to rent a car; it's cheaper than taking taxis everywhere and more reliable (and efficient) than public transportation. If you're island hopping, you'll either have to fly or take a ferry, though ferries only run between Maui, Lanai, and Molokai.

By air

Flights between islands are frequent, every half hour or hour. There is one primary carrier, **Hawaiian Airlines**, which use jets between all major airports.

A newer arrival, **Go!**, offers discounted fares on the same routes. In addition, **Island Air**, a subsidiary of Aloha Airlines, uses small propeller craft to smaller airports such as the one near Princeville, on Kauai. There are also fixed-wing and helicopter flights for inter-island travel. **Mokulele Airlines** and **Pacific Wings** are smaller airlines that offer small-plane flights from many of the major airports to smaller airports (such as Hana and Lanai).

With the exception of morning and late afternoon commuter times, when local workers and business-people are returning to their home islands, you can usually get a seat on one of these inter-island flights at short notice. If one flight is full, there is another flight in about 30 minutes

to an hour. However, weekends and holidays are busy times; reserve ahead if possible. Inter-island flights are short, from 20 to 45 minutes, depending on the route.

Hawaiian Airlines often offers hotel and rental car deals with its flights, again often on very short notice. The first couple of early-morning flights and the last couple of flights at night are sometimes also discounted.

Inter-island flights

Go! Airlines
Tel: 888-435-9462
www.iflygo.com
Hawaiian Airlines
Tel: 800-367-5320
www.hawaiianairlines.com
Island Air
Tel: 800-652-6541
www.islandair.com
Mokulele Airlines
Tel: 888-435-9462
www.mokuleleairlines.com
Pacific Wings
Tel: 888-575-4546
www.pacificwings.com

By bicycle

Cycling aficionados love riding around Hawaii – many say the Aloha State offers some of the most challenging and rewarding road system in the US. The same rules of the road apply to bicycles and cars; bicyclists are expected to ride with traffic and obey all traffic signals. If you're cycling, be aware that some drivers may have trouble spotting you. It's also a good idea to bring raingear; though the weather on the islands is usually sunny especially in winter it can rain at any time.

On foot

When all else fails, when you have no other method of getting around the Hawaiian Islands, you always can walk. Pedestrians are permitted on all local roadways, provided they are in the shoulder. Hitchhiking also is quite common, especially in surfing areas. If you are walking at night, use caution and wear reflective clothing so drivers can see you. And if you do choose to hitch, be careful which vehicles you enter; if you feel the slightest bit unsafe, keep walking or dial 911.

By bus

All four of the major Hawaiian Islands have some form of mass transport. Depending on where you want to get to and how long you're willing to wait to get there, utilizing these systems may make sense during your visit.

Oahu

Without question, the bus system on Oahu, dubbed **TheBus, is the best in the state. This bus** system covers the entire island, and the fare is the same regardless of whether you travel six blocks or all the way around. TheBus is especially

efficient in downtown Honolulu, with buses stopping every 15 minutes around Waikiki and the Ala Moana Shopping Center.

As of late 2013, fares for TheBus were $2.50 per ride. Each ride includes one transfer, but you must ask the driver if you want a transfer ticket. Exact change is required and dollar bills are accepted. A four-day pass of unlimited rides costs $25 and is available at ABC convenience stores in downtown Honolulu. Important route numbers for Waikiki are 2, 4, 8, 19, 20, 58, and the City Express Route A. Route booklets listing other routes are available all over town.

The open-air **Waikiki Trolley (tel: 591-2561,** www.waikikitrolley.com) is another reliable option for getting around town. This system has four lines and makes dozens of stops. The Honolulu City Line (Red Line) travels between Waikiki and the Bishop Museum. The Ocean Coast Line (Blue Line), hugs Honolulu's southeastern coastline, including Diamond Head and Hanauma Bay. The Ala Moana Shuttle Line (Pink Line) stretches from the DFS Galleria Waikiki or Hilton Hawaiian Village to the Ala Moana Shopping Center. Finally, the Local Shopping & Dining Line (Yellow Line) starts at Ala Moana Center and stops at popular shopping destinations, including Ward Warehouse. A one-day, four-line ticket costs $30; four-day tickets (also good for all four lines) cost $52. There are discounts when ordering online.

Maui

There has been talk of implementing an island-wide public transportation system on Maui for years. Until it happens, the best option for this island is **Maui Bus** (tel: 871-4838; www.mauicounty.gov/bus). Operated by Roberts Hawaii, this system offers 10 routes between various communities. Two routes – the Upcountry and Haiku Islander routes – include a stop at Kahului Airport. Buses cover all of the island's major destinations, and fares are $2 per person.

Hawaii Island

The best bus option on Hawaii Island is the **Hele-On Bus** (tel: 961-8744; www.heleonbus.org), which covers all major towns and runs the four-hour trip from Kona to Hilo three times each day. Fares for this system are $1 per ride.

Kauai

On the Garden Isle, The Kauai Bus (tel: 246-8110, www.kauai.gov/transportation) runs hourly from Hanalei to Kakaha every day except Sunday. It also provides a midday shuttle around Lihu'e. Fares are $2 per ride.

By car

Most visitors to Hawaii prefer to rent cars. This option provides travelers with the flexibility to go where they want, when they want. (On Molokai, renting a car is the only way to explore without the help of a tour

Watch out for donkeys crossing in Waimea, Big Island.

outfitter.) It also is more affordable than taking taxis (see page 283); most rates start at $25–35 per day for economy cars, and child car seats are an additional charge of $5–8 per day.

All major car rental companies operate in Hawaii and many have 24-hour counters at most airports. Book in advance – or through online travel agents – for the best deals. Drivers generally are required to be 25 years or older, have a valid driver's license (non-US license holders should check if their car rental company requires an international license), and a major credit card. It's also a good idea to fork over the extra cash for the loss/damage waiver; rental agencies in Hawaii are notoriously nitpicky about dings and scratches on their cars, and this surcharge covers you against any faults they may find. Car rental agencies in Hawaii include:

Alamo tel: 800-462-5266; www.alamo.com
Avis tel: 800-230-4898; www.avis.com
Budget tel: 800-527-0700; www.budget.com
Dollar tel: 800-800-3665; www.dollar.com
Enterprise Rent-a-Car tel: 800-261-7331; www.enterprise.com
Hertz tel: 800-654-3131; www.hertz.com
National tel: 800-CAR-RENT; www.nationalcar.com
Thrifty tel: 800-847-4389; www.thrifty.com

Orientation

Local folks share a common vernacular for directions, which has nothing to do with cardinal directions or where the sun rises and sets. Rather, it deals with *local* geographical features.

The two most common directional terms are *mauka* ("upland" or "toward the mountain") and *makai* ("toward the sea"). In Honolulu, directions are also given in relation to '*Ewa*, a plantation town just west of Pearl Harbor, and to *Diamond Head*, the famous landmark to the east side of Waikiki. Those four orientations – *mauka, makai, 'Ewa* and *Diamond Head* – are regularly used among residents. Say north, south, east, or west and you'll receive looks of bewilderment.

A tram in Honolulu, Oahu.

Driving

It is worth noting that driving in Hawaii is much like driving on the US mainland. Traffic advances on the right side of the road, and it is legal to make right turns on red lights unless posted otherwise. All passengers must wear seatbelts and infants and young children must be strapped into car seats or booster seats as appropriate. Pedestrians, whether in a crosswalk or not, always have the right of way. Most roads are paved; highways are well maintained; signs are in English and/or international symbols; speed limits and distance are indicated almost exclusively in miles and miles-per-hour.

All car rental companies offer emergency roadside assistance; don't hesitate to dial the numbers on your contract for any reason during your trip (including flat tires). Another option in the event of a breakdown is to contact **AAA Help** (tel: 800-222-4357). If you or one of your passengers appears injured, dial 911.

Though the islands are not nearly as populated as urban centers on the mainland, some of the busiest roadways still experience traffic during rush hour (7–9am and again from 4–6pm). Traffic is the worst on Oahu in and around Honolulu, where drivers have been known to inch forward on freeways for miles. In recent years, Maui has started to see rush hour traffic, as well – especially between Lahaina and the Kahalui area. Thankfully, traffic on Hawaii Island and Kauai generally only is a result of construction or unexpected lane closures on major roads.

Gasoline prices are higher on the islands than they are on the mainland, but usually can be obtained for $4–5 per gallon. For the latest information about gas prices across the state, visit www.hawaiigasprices.com.

By sea

For seafaring types, **Norwegian Cruise Line** (tel: 866-234-0392; www.ncl.com) offers weekly seven-day cruises that depart Honolulu for Kauai, Maui, and the Big Island. Tours, in-port activities and rental cars are all optional.

There is daily ferry service between Lahaina, Maui and Manele Bay, Lanai, with **Expeditions Lanai Ferry** (tel: 214-1467, www.go-lanai.com). The 9-mile (14km) crossing takes 45 minutes, depending on ocean conditions (which, especially in the afternoon, when the winds pick up, can almost guarantee seasickness). The **Molokai Ferry** (tel: 866-307-6524; www.molokaiferry.com) offers twice-daily ferry service between Lahaina and Kaunakakai, Molokai. Travel time on that route is about 90 minutes. Reservations are recommended for both ferries.

By taxi

Taxi service is available on all islands, including Lanai and Molokai. Rates vary from island to island; all taxis are metered, and most are available for sightseeing at a fixed rate. Honolulu, of course, has the most taxis, but don't expect to flag one down on the street. If a taxi is required, go to a nearby hotel. On other islands, it may be necessary to call a taxicab company and pre-arrange a ride.

There are dozens of cab companies on every island. On Oahu, try The CAB (tel: 422-2222, www.thecabhawaii.com). On Maui, use CB Taxi (tel: 243-8294, www.cbtaximaui.com). On Hawaii Island, book with Laura's Taxi (tel: 326-5466, www.laurastaxi.com). And on Lanai, try Pono Taxi (tel: 634-4744, www.ponotaxi.com). For additional listings, look to the Hawaii Tourism Authority (www.gohawaii.com) or check the yellow pages under the heading "Taxicabs."

ACCOMMODATIONS EATING OUT ACTIVITIES A – Z LANGUAGE

ACCOMMODATIONS

HOTELS, YOUTH HOSTELS, BED & BREAKFAST

CHOOSING A HOTEL

Considering that Hawaii attracts travelers of every kind, the islands abound in accommodations of every persuasion. Resorts, hotels, inns, rental condominiums, bed-and-breakfasts, hostels, and campsites – the islands have them all.

Because there are so many different classifications of accommodations in Hawaii, the quality of these accommodations varies widely. Many of the international luxury hotel chains have built brands around a certain standard of excellence; if you can afford these properties (often at upward of $500 per night), you probably know what you're looking for. On the flipside, the quality of rooms at properties on the lower end of the scale can vary widely. Definitely do your research (both here and online, at property websites) before you book.

Prices fluctuate considerably in Hawaii; they are most commonly dictated by season and location. During rainy season, for instance, especially in resort areas such as Wailea on Maui, some of the highest-end rooms might be $200–$300 less than they are during high season (which is summer). Location also determines price; the closer you are to a "beachfront" location, the more expensive your nightly rate likely will be. When you are ready to book, note that most accommodations offer booking online (at their respective websites). All of them also take reservations by phone. Some even can be booked through local companies in Hawaii that handle reservations for certain types of lodging. Finally, it may pay to book your rooms through an online travel agent such as Expedia,

where bundling a room with airfare and rental car could save you big bucks.

One last note. If you are particular about the exact location of your accommodation, you should either confirm the location with the property or call the reservations company. Because towns in Hawaii are so spread-out, mailing addresses sometimes don't reflect the true location of a hotel or condominium. Lahaina, for example, is often the mailing post office for places across West Maui. The same is true on Molokai and Lanai, where one postal code covers each of the islands, respectively.

Hotel companies

A number of reputable hotel chains have established a presence in Hawaii. In many cases, contacting the chains directly could score you seasonal specials or other freebies such as free continental breakfast for stays longer than five nights.

Aqua Resorts
Hotels and condominium rentals on Oahu, Maui, Lanai, Molokai, Kauai, and Hawaii Island
Toll free: 866-940-2782
www.aquaresorts.com/

Aston Hotels & Resorts
Hotels and condominium rentals on Oahu, Maui, Kauai, and Hawaii Island
Tel: 924-2924
Toll free: 877-997-6667
www.astonhotels.com

Castle Resorts & Hotels
Hotels on Oahu, Maui, Kauai, Molokai, and Hawaii Island
Tel: 545-3510
Toll free: 800-367-1912
www.castleresorts.com

Fairmont Hotels & Resorts
Hotels on Maui and Hawaii Island
Toll free: 800-257-7544

www.fairmont.com
Four Seasons Resorts
Hotels on Oahu, Maui, Lanai, and Hawaii Island
Toll free: 800-819-5053
www.fourseasons.com
Hilton
Hotels and condominium rentals on Oahu, Maui, Kauai, and Hawaii Island
Tel: 800-445-8667
www.hilton.com
Marriott
Hotels and condominium rentals on Oahu, Maui, Kauai, and Hawaii Island
Tel: 888-236-2427
www.marriott.com
Outrigger Hotels & Resorts
Hotels and condominium rentals on Oahu, Maui, Kauai, and Hawaii Island
Tel: 303-369-7777
Outrigger toll free: 866-956-4262
www.outrigger.com
Starwood Hotels & Resorts
Hotels and condominium rentals on Oahu, Maui, Kauai, and Hawaii Island
Tel: 877-946-8357
www.starwoodhotels.com

Accommodation agents

Hawaii is home to a number of booking agents who can help travelers reserve specific types of accommodations for the duration of their stays. The following listings are not comprehensive and they do not carry endorsements. For travelers wanting a more inclusive and comprehensive listing, telephone the **Hawaii Visitors Bureau** on 923-1811 for a current *Accommodations and Car Rentals* guide or visit www.gohawaii.com.

Bed and breakfasts

Bed-and-breakfast accommodations offer a more intimate overnight experience: smaller rooms, fresh breakfasts every morning, and communal sitting areas. Standards of these places vary widely (as they are regulated less than hotels), but most places that have survived the test of time offer a modicum of cleanliness and comfort. The reservation companies listed below book for most of the islands.

BedandBreakfast.com
Tel: 800-462-2632
www.bedandbreakfast.com
Bed & Breakfast Inns Online
Toll free: 800-215 7365
www.bbonline.com
Better Bed and Breakfasts
www.betterbedandbreakfasts.com
BnBFinder.com
Toll free: 888-547-8226
www.bnbfinder.com
Hawaii's Best Bed & Breakfasts
Tel: 263-3100
Toll free: 800-262-9912
www.bestbnb.com

Rental condominiums

Vacation rentals offer yet another option: apartment-style living for longer-term stays. Family travelers appreciate this option because most rental condos come with kitchenettes or full kitchens, enabling the guests to prepare their own meals. Other types of travelers swear by this option because it usually affords more space. Some condos offer daily maid service; others offer housekeeping once or twice a week for a fee. The reservation companies listed below book for most of the islands.

CyberRentals
Tel: 512-684-1098
www.cyberrentals.com
Vacation Rentals by Owner
www.vrbo.com
One Fine Stay
www.onefinestay.com
FlipKey
www.flipkey.com

The unmistakeable pink facade of The Royal Hawaiian, Honolulu.

AirBnB
www.airbnb.com

Alternate lodging

For truly budget-minded travelers, Hawaii offers still other options for lodging – namely home exchanges and farm stays.

HomeExchange.com
Toll free: 800-877-8723
www.homeexchange.com
HomeLink International
Toll free: 800-638-3841
www.homelink.org
Intervac
Toll free: 800-756-4663
www.interfac-homeexchange.com
WWOOF (World Wide Opportunities on Organic Farms) Hawaii
www.wwoofhawaii.org

Camping

Because many visitors who visit Hawaii go to commune with the natural environment, camping has become a popular option for overnighting under the palms and stars. The vast majority of campsites on the islands are run by the National Park Service, the State of Hawaii, and county governments. Plan outings ahead of time, as campsites are usually very popular.

National parks

The two largest national parks – Haleakala and Hawaii Volcanoes – each have a number of campsites available for overnight camping.
Haleakala National Park
www.nps.gov/hale
The park boasts one drive-in campground near the summit (Hosmer Grove), and another in Kipahulu, at the 'Ohe'o Pools. At Hosmer Grove, sites are first-come, first-served and permits are issued upon arrival

at the park. In the Haleakala basin itself, there are three hike-in cabins available, as well. These are assigned by lottery reservations. Book three months in advance.
Hawaii Volcanoes National Park
www.nps.gov/havo
This park has two campgrounds. Permits are not required, as sites run on a first-come, first-served basis. The park also offers rustic camper cabins (bedding included) at the Namakani Paio campground; payment can be made at the Volcano House hotel in the park.

State parks

There are more than 60 state parks throughout Hawaii, run by the state's Department of Land and Natural Resources. Some of the camping facilities at these parks are well developed, others are primitive. Many are true gems. Permits for overnight camping are required. For general information about camping permits, call 587-0300. For information about fishing licenses, call 587-0109. For information online, visit www.hawaii. gov/dlnr.

Regional offices
Oahu
1151 Punchbowl, Honolulu
Tel: 587-0300
Maui (includes Molokai)
54 High Street, Wailuku
Tel: 984-8109
Big Island
PO Box 936, Hilo
Tel: 974-6200
Kauai
3060 Eiwa Street, Suite 306, Lihu'e
Tel: 274-3444

County parks

County governments run parks in Hawaii, as well, and many of these have campsites available for overnight use. Permits are required at most of these parks; many of them are free. In all cases, the campsites are run by the counties' respective departments of parks and recreation.
Honolulu/Oahu
650 S. King Street, Honolulu
Tel: 523-4525
Maui (including Molokai)
1580 Ka'ahumanu Avenue, Wailuku
Tel: 270-7389
Hawaii (Big Island)
25 Aupuni Street, Hilo
Tel: 961-8311
Kauai
4444 Rice, Suite 150, Lihu'e
Tel: 241-6660.

OAHU

East Oahu

The Kahala Hotel & Resort
5000 Kahala Avenue
Wai'alae-Kahala
Tel: 739-8888
www.kahalaresort.com
Formerly the Kahala Mandarin, this resort is a 10-minute drive east of Waikiki, and is especially valued for its secluded oceanfront location. The dolphin lagoon is home to Atlantic bottlenose dolphins and tropical fish. 370 rooms. **$$$**

Honolulu

Ala Moana Hotel
410 Atkinson Drive
Honolulu
Tel: 955-4811
www.alamoanahotelhonolulu.com
Conveniently located next to Ala Moana Center, this hotel is great value considering it's also a 10-minute walk to Waikiki. Rooms are like small apartments, with mini refrigerators and microwave ovens. Rumours nightclub is in the lobby. 1,134 rooms. **$$$**

Best Western Plaza Airport Hotel
3253 N. Nimitz Highway
Honolulu
Tel: 836-3636
www.bestwesternhawaii.com/hotels/best-western-the-plaza-hotel
Efficiency is the name of the game at this airport hotel, which is primarily used by business travelers and visitors with late-night or early-morning flights. Considering its customer base, the hotel offers a 24-hour airport shuttle. 274 rooms. **$$**

Manoa Valley Inn
2001 Vancouver Drive
Honolulu
Tel: 947-6019
www.manoavalleyinn.com
Built in 1912 and listed in the National Register of Historic Places, this country-style inn is located in a residential neighborhood close to the University of Hawaii at Manoa. Rooms are designed with a country flair; breakfast is included with each stay. There's also a small pool out back. 8 rooms. **$$**

Pagoda Hotel & Terrace
1525 Rycroft Street
Honolulu
Tel: 941-6611
www.pagodahotel.com
Set amidst high-rise apartment buildings and strip malls in downtown Honolulu, this hotel is a short walk to the Ala Moana Center. Rooms are dated but clean; the Pagoda restaurant downstairs serves pan-Asian fare. 359 rooms. **$$**

North Shore

Turtle Bay Resort
57-091 Kamehameha Highway
Kahuku, North Shore
Tel: 293-6000
www.turtlebayresort.com
Perched on the edge of Kuilima Point, this resort represents the North Shore's best. Guest rooms average 500 sq ft (51 sq meters), and families love the 80-ft (23-meter) water slide. The resort's best claim to fame? It has appeared in countless television shows and films, most famously *Lost* and *Forgetting Sarah Marshall*. 437 rooms. **$$$**

Waikiki

Aqua Waikiki Joy Hotel
320 Lewers Street
Waikiki
Tel: 923-2300
www.aquawaikikijoy.com
The most eccentric amenity at this boutique hotel on a Waikiki sidestreet is the karaoke studio, which is open to the public. Upstairs, rooms have a tropical theme; most of them boast lanais. Guests also receive free continental breakfast every morning. 93 rooms. **$$**

Halekulani
2199 Kalia Road
Waikiki
Tel: 923-2311
www.halekulani.com
White is the theme at this elegant and chic resort, as all of the rooms are robed in what the place calls its "Seven Shades of White." Private registration in your guest room adds to an exclusive feel. 453 rooms. **$$$$**

Hawaii Prince Hotel & Golf Club
Waikiki
100 Holomoana Street
Waikiki
Tel: 956-1111
www.hawaiiprincehotel.com
This hotel, which fronts Ala Wai Yacht Harbor, is the only resort in Waikiki with a golf course; the 27-hole course is a 45-minute ride from the hotel. Floor-to-ceiling windows make up for the lack of balconies in the rooms. 578 rooms. **$$$$**

Hilton Hawaiian Village Beach Resort and Spa
2005 Kalia Road
Waikiki
Tel: 949-4321
www.hiltonhawaiianvillage.com
Five towers comprise what has become the largest hotel in Hawaii. The resort spans 22 acres in all, including landscaped gardens, ponds, and a pool complex that is great for kids. The resort even has its own pier (where the Atlantis submarine docks). All rooms have lanais. 3,860 rooms, 639 condos. **$$$**

Holiday Inn Waikiki Beachcomber Resort
2300 Kalakaua Avenue
Waikiki
Tel: 922-4646
www.waikikibeachcomberresort.com
Centrally located in the heart of Waikiki. Once home of the legendary Don Ho show, the property now hosts a new stage show, dubbed the "Magic of Polynesia." All rooms have balconies; free Wifi available on site. 501 rooms. **$$$**

Hyatt Regency Waikiki Resort and Spa
2424 Kalakaua Avenue
Waikiki
Tel: 923-1234
www.hyattregencywaikiki.com
Centrally located just across the street from Kuhio Beach, this hotel has an unobstructed view of the Pacific. One highlight: the 10,000-sq ft (900-sq meter) Na Hoola spa, which boasts treatments including massages for soothing sore feet. 1,248 rooms. **$$$**

Lotus Honolulu at Diamond Head
2885 Kalakaua Avenue
Waikiki
Tel: 922-1700
www.lotushonoluluhotel.com
This boutique-style hotel is situated on the oceanside border of Kapiolani Park, a short walk from central Waikiki. Formerly the W Honolulu, the property has incorporated whites to soften some of its former sleek and upscale vibe. 50 rooms. **$$$$**

Moana Surfrider, a Westin Resort & Spa
2365 Kalakaua Avenue
Waikiki
Tel: 922-3111
www.moana-surfrider.com
Built in 1901; this Honolulu icon mixes nostalgic, early 20th-century ambiance and comfort from modern times. Enjoy tea-time on the veranda surrounding a huge banyan tree. The *lu'au* here also is considered the best on Waikiki. 796 rooms. **$$$$**

The Modern Honolulu
1775 Ala Moana Boulevard
Waikiki
Tel: 943-5800
www.themodernhonolulu.com

Turtle Bay Resort, Kahuku, Oahu.

Arguably the trendiest hotel in town, the Modern is edgy and slick without being overbearingly so. Don't miss the pool complex, which includes an adults-only version of a wading pool, surrounded by 100 tons of sand. 383 rooms. **$$$$**

New Otani Kaimana Beach Hotel
2863 Kalakaua Avenue
Waikiki
Tel: 923-1555
www.kaimana.com
Situated on the "quiet end of Waikiki" (technically it's on Sans Souci Beach), this resort is one of the closest to Diamond Head and the Waikiki Aquarium. Oceanfront on Sans Souci Beach, at the foot of Diamond Head in Waikiki. Rooms are spacious but dated. 125 rooms. **$$$**

Outrigger Waikiki On The Beach
2335 Kalakaua Avenue
Waikiki
Tel: 923-0711
www.outrigger.com
Located on the beach at Waikiki, this hotel is the best known of the Outriggers on Oahu. The property underwent a massive renovation in 2012. Check out the good food and contemporary Hawaiian music at Duke's Canoe Club. 554 rooms. **$$$**

Pacific Beach Hotel
2490 Kalakaua Avenue
Waikiki
Tel: 923-4511
Toll free: 800-367-6060
www.pacificbeachhotel.com
Located in Waikiki, across from the beach, this hotel comprises two towers; every room has a lanai. The centerpiece of the property is a spectacular 3-story, 280,000-gallon indoor oceanarium tank, visible from the hotel's three restaurants. 839 rooms. **$$$**

Park Shore Waikiki
2586 Kalakaua Avenue
Waikiki
Tel: 923-0411
www.parkshorewaikiki.com
Across Kapahulu Avenue from Kapi'olani Park and a half-block from the beach; this quiet hotel is great value. Rooms are small but modern; most have lanais and partial ocean views. On-site Starbucks is one of the closest to the beach. 226 rooms. **$$**

Queen Kapi'olani Hotel
150 Kapahulu Avenue
Waikiki
Tel: 922-1941
www.queenkapiolani.com
Located at the Diamond Head end of Waikiki, this boutique hotel is comfortable and quiet. Rooms are spacious; they all come standard with refrigerators. The open-air, rooftop pool deck boasts a spectacular view of Diamond Head. 315 rooms. **$$$**

The Royal Hawaiian, a Luxury Collection Resort
2259 Kalakaua Avenue
Waikiki
Tel: 923-7311
www.royal-hawaiian.com
With its coral-pink stucco and Moorish-Spanish design, the "Pink Palace of the Pacific" is a landmark on Waikiki Beach. The hotel, which received an $85 million renovation in 2009, sits smack in the middle of Waikiki's shopping area. **$$$$**

Sheraton Waikiki
2255 Kalakaua Avenue
Waikiki
Tel: 922-4422
www.sheraton-waikiki.com
Few hotels in Waikiki have a view of Diamond Head as spectacular as this one. Rooms were renovated in 2011, so accommodations here are among the most modern on the beach. Hotel is mere steps from shopping, restaurants. 1,636 rooms **$$$$**

Trump International Hotel Waikiki Beach Walk
223 Saratoga Road
Waikiki
Tel: 683-7777
www.trumphotelcollection.com/waikiki
Chic, modern, and sophisticated, this property opened in 2009 and is one of Waikiki's newest hotels. Rooms boast apartment-style living, complete with mini-kitchens and luxurious bathrooms. A beach concierge sets up guests with bags and umbrellas for the beach across the street. 432 rooms. **$$$$**

Waikiki Beach Marriott Resort & Spa
2552 Kalakaua Avenue
Waikiki
Tel: 922-6611
www.marriottwaikiki.com
On the eastern edge of Waikiki, this flagship Mariott sits across from Kuhio Beach. The Spa Olakino, owned by Honolulu celebrity stylist Paul Brown, is one of the largest on Waikiki. Resort also has a 24-hour fitness center. 1,510 rooms. **$$$**

Waikiki Parc Hotel
2233 Helumoa Road
Waikiki
Tel: 921-7272
www.waikikiparc.com
This modern hotel is the boutique version of its sister property, the Halekulani. Rooms are minimalist but still retain tropical décor. Eighth-floor pool is private and quiet. Enjoy a complimentary wine mixer in the lobby every Friday night. 297 rooms.

West Oahu

Aulani, a Disney Resort & Spa
92-1185 Aliinui Drive
Ko 'Olina, Kapolei
Tel: 674-6200
Resorts.disney.go.com/aulani-hawaii-resort
Representing Disney's first hotel and timeshare development not connected to a theme park, this hotel mixes "The Mouse" with tropical paradise to create a kid-friendly atmosphere complete with roaming Disney characters in Hawaiian garb. An extensive pool complex includes a lazy river, a dive tank, and two water slides. In 2013, the resort also opened an adults-only infinity pool. 375 rooms, 481 timeshare units. **$$$**

PRICE CATEGORIES

$ = below $100
$$ = $101–200
$$$ = $201–300
$$$$ = above $301

TRANSPORTATION

ACCOMMODATIONS

EATING OUT

ACTIVITIES

A – Z

LANGUAGE

J.W. Marriott 'Ihilani Resort & Spa
92-1001 Olani Street
Kapolei
Tel: 679-0079
www.ihilani.com
Located in West Oahu, about a
30-minute drive from Honolulu
International Airport, 'Ihilani sits on
one of the Ko 'Olina Resort's seven
lagoons. Standard rooms are among
the largest on the island and boast
high-tech control systems for lighting
and climate. 387 rooms. $$$$

Condominiums

Aston Waikiki Beach Tower
2470 Kalakaua Avenue
Waikiki

Tel: 926-6400
www.astonwaikikibeachtower.com
One- and two-bedroom suites are
available at this luxurious tower
set back from Waikiki Beach. All
units receive daily housekeeping
and nightly turndown service. The
recreation deck boasts a pool and a
paddle-tennis court. 140 suites. $$$

Aston at the Waikiki Banyan
201 'Ohua Avenue
Waikiki
Tel: 922-0555
www.astonwaikikibanyan.com
Located on Diamond Head side of
Waikiki, this property is the largest
condominium in Honolulu. Rooms are
all one-bedroom suites, with kitchens

and washer/dryer units. Elsewhere on
property guests will find a children's
playground, tennis courts, and
barbecue area. 876 suites. $$$
Castle Waikiki Shore
2161 Kalia Road
Waikiki
Tel: 952-4500
http://www.castleresorts.com/Home/
accommodations/waikiki-shore
The only condominium resort located
on Waikiki Beach offers roomy studio,
one- and two-bedroom units. All
suites include kitchens (some include
full kitchens), washer/dryer units,
free high-speed internet access and
daily housekeeping service. 168
suites. $$

MAUI

Hana

Travaasa Hana
5031 Hana Highway
Hana
Tel: 888-820-1043
www.travaasa.com/hana
Casual elegance is perfected at this
intimate and upscale resort in Maui's
most remote town. The property
comprises two adjacent sites; one
where families are welcome, and
another for adults only. All guests
have access to a multitude of
activities each day. Both the spa
and on-site restaurant are stellar. 96
rooms. $$$$

Ka'anapali

**Hyatt Regency Maui Resort and
Spa**
200 Nohea Kai Drive
Ka'anapali
Tel: 661-1234
www.maui.hyatt.com
Water features, museum-quality art,
and penguins welcome guests to this
bustling resort at the southern end
of Ka'anapali Beach. The property
has become known for its spa, Spa
Moana, and its lu'au, the spectacular
"Drums of the Pacific" show that
draws visitors from all over the island.
806 rooms. $$$$
Ka'anapali Beach Hotel
2525 Ka'anapali Parkway
Ka'anapali
Tel: 661-0011
www.kbhmaui.com
The least upscale of Ka'anapali's
hotels is also it's most storied; KBH
has been welcoming guests for
almost 50 years. The staff are well-
versed in local knowledge they can
share with guests one-on-one or
during classes throughout the week.

Rooms are decorated in Hawaiiana
style – kitschy but fun. 432 rooms.
$$$
Outrigger Maui Eldorado
Ka'anapali
2661 Keka'a Drive
Ka'anapali
Tel: 661-0021
www.mauieldorado.com
Technically, this is a condo complex,
but it's run like a hotel. Décor of
the rooms varies, but the rooms
themselves come in three flavors:
studio, one-, and two-bedroom.
Perhaps the biggest draw is access
to a beach cabana on a semi-private
beach; there's nothing else like it in
the area. 204 units. $$$
Royal Lahaina Resort
2780 Keka'a Drive
Ka'anapali
Tel: 661-3611
www.royallahaina.com
Dating back to 1962, when it debuted
as Ka'anapali's first hotel, this
property remains the Grand Dame
of the resort stretch. Rooms are
decorated with dark teak furnishings,
part of a 2009 renovation. For a
taste of yesteryear, hit the Don the
Beachcomber bar, which is reputed
to be the home of the Mai Tai. 511
rooms. $$$$
Sheraton Maui Resort & Spa
2605 Ka'anapali Parkway
Ka'anapali
Tel: 661-0031
www.sheraton-maui.com
This white resort sits next to and
on top of the 80ft (23-meter) -high
Puu Kekaa, from which divers leap
in a nightly torch-lighting and cliff-
diving ritual. Rooms are spacious
with modern touches such as
stereo systems. There's also great

snorkeling right off the beach. 508
rooms. $$$$
The Westin Maui Resort & Spa
2365 Ka'anapali Parkway
Ka'anapali
Tel: 667-2525
www.westinmaui.com
Waterfalls and lagoons connect the
two towers of this resort, which is
great for families. All rooms boast
Westin's signature Heavenly Bed,
and also contain a sofa bed. The
Wailele Polynesian Lu'au includes
Maui's only fireknife dance. There's
also a free shuttle to Lahaina, where
parking can be difficult. 758 rooms.
$$$$

Lahaina

Best Western Pioneer Inn
658 Wharf Street
Lahaina
Tel: 661-3636
www.pioneerinnmaui.com
Built in 1901, this historic hotel
looks out on the bustling harbor
and sits next to the city's famous
banyan tree. Rooms sport décor to
match the building's century-old
roots. If you need quiet, ask for
a room facing the courtyard. 34
rooms. $$
Lahaina Inn
127 Lahainaluna Road
Lahaina
Tel: 661-0577
www.lahainainn.com
This restored 1860s boutique hotel
is located off Front Street in Lahaina,
putting it right in the center of all of
the town's action. Rooms feature
antique furnishings and all guests
receive breakfast every day. No
children under 15 years. 12 rooms.
$$$

Paia/Kuau

The Inn at Mama's Fish House
799 Poho Place
Kuau
Tel: 579-9764
www.mamasfishhouse.com
Mama's isn't only a restaurant; a handful of one- and two-bedroom cottages are tucked into the gardens just behind the famous eatery. Units are eccentric; many have one-of-a-kind art- and tile-work built into the walls. Each comes with a private patio. 12 units. **$$$**

Paia Inn
93 Hana Highway
Paia
Tel: 579-6000
www.paiainn.com
Originally built as a boarding house in 1927, this property in 2008 was converted into a modest inn. Rooms are surprisingly modern and come with an iPod clock/radio and a fully stocked minibar. One word of warning: there is no elevator. 15 rooms. **$$**

Wailea, Kihei, and Makena

Aston Maui Lu
575 S. Kihei Road
Kihei
Tel: 879-5881
www.astonmauiluhotel.com
Located on 28 acres (11 hectares) of historic coconut grove, this hotel is one of the only beachfront options in Kihei. Rooms have wood-paneled ceilings and arts and crafts from around the islands. As of 2013, guests also had the option of reserving Playstation2 consoles. 120 rooms. **$$**

Fairmont Kea Lani Maui
4100 Wailea Alanui Drive
Wailea
Tel: 875-4100
www.fairmont.com/kealani
With white spires and tiled archways, this resort looks like something out of Morocco. All rooms are suites; 37 of them are two-story villas. A host of family-friendly programs are available year-round. Ko, the on-site restaurant, serves authentic Hawaiian cuisine. 450 suites. **$$$$**

Four Seasons Resort Maui at Wailea
3900 Wailea Alanui Drive
Wailea
Tel: 874-8000
www.fourseasons.com/maui
Elegant furnishings, fresh flowers, and sumptuous bed linens characterize rooms at this iconic Four Seaons on Wailea Beach. On-site restaurants include Wolfgang Puck's Spago and DUO Steak & Seafood.

Pool services include Evian spritzers and hand-passed freshly cut fruit. 380 rooms. **$$$$**

Grand Wailea Resort Hotel & Spa
3850 Wailea Alanui Drive
Wailea
Tel: 875-1234
www.grandwailea.com
You've never seen a pool like the one at this 40-acre (16-hectare) resort; it features a "canyon riverpool," slides, caves, a Tarzan swing, and a water elevator. The water theme continues inside Spa Grande, which offers one of the most comprehensive hydrotherapy programs on the island. 780 rooms. **$$$$**

Makena Beach & Golf Resort
5400 Makena Alanui
Makena
Tel: 874-1111
www.makenaresortmaui.com
Located near Makena Beach, south of Wailea, this resort (formerly known as the Maui Prince) offers scenic views of neighboring islands and access to Maui's most popular public beach. The hotel also offers on-site tennis courts, as well as activities such as diving and snorkeling. 310 rooms. **$$$**

Hotel Wailea
555 Kaukahi Street
Wailea
Tel: 874-0500
www.hotelwailea.com
Set back from the beaches of Wailea, this resort trades in true luxury. All of the rooms are suites that include comfortable furniture, private lanais, and deep soaking tubs. The on-site spa specializes in facials. 72 suites. **$$$$**

Wailea Beach Marriott Resort & Spa
37000 Wailea Alanui Drive
Wailea
Tel: 879-1922
www.waileamarriott.com
Sometimes there are benefits to old age: because this property was built before current zoning laws, rooms sit closer to the beach than they do at other resorts. Rooms have a modern and residential feel; each has its own lanai. 554 rooms. **$$$**

Wailea Beach Villas Resort
3800 Wailea Alanui Drive
Wailea
Tel: 891-4500
www.waileabeachvillasresort.com
Understated luxury is in full effect at this resort adjacent to the shops at Wailea. Accommodations come in the form of two-, three- and four-bedroom villas, each with a marble kitchen, spacious bathrooms, comfortable furniture, and the latest in high-tech

gizmos. On-site pools are private; one is exclusively for families. 98 suites. **$$$**

Wailuku

Old Wailuku Inn at Ulupono
2199 Kaho'okele Street
Wailuku
Tel: 244-5897
www.mauiinn.com
This charming plantation-style home, set in pleasant gardens near downtown Wailuku, offers a quiet retreat far from any of the island's other tourist crowds. Rooms are decorated with Hawaiian crafts, accentuating the history of the place. 10 rooms. **$$**

West Maui

The Mauian
5441 Lower Honoapi'ilani Road
Napili
Tel: 669-6205
www.mauian.com
This charming, beachfront hideaway is set right on one of West Maui's finest beaches. Rooms are outfitted with "island" décor and come standard with private lanais. All guests also receive complimentary continental breakfast every day. 44 rooms. **$$**

Napili Kai Beach Resort
5900 Lower Honoapi'ilani Road
Napili
Tel: 669-6271
www.napilikai.com
Hawaiian-style rooms characterize this old-fashioned family hotel beside the beach at lovely Napili Bay, north of Ka'anapali in West Maui. Kids love the on-site classes in hula dancing and *lei* making. The hotel also fronts a great snorkeling spot. 163 rooms. **$$**

The Ritz-Carlton, Kapalua
One Ritz-Carlton Drive
Kapalua
Tel: 669-6200
www.ritzcarlton.com
The culture of Maui is alive and well at this resort, which employs a cultural naturalist to inform guests about local history. Grown-ups love the pool and hot tubs that are open 24 hours; kids love the on-site Environmental Education Center. The property doesn't have a beach of its own, but it is next to D.T. Fleming Beach, one of the island's best. 463 rooms. **$$$$**

PRICE CATEGORIES

$ = below $100
$$ = $101–200
$$$ = $201–300
$$$$ = above $301

Condominiums

Aston at Papakea Resort
3543 Lower Honoapi'ilani Highway
Honokowai
Tel: 669-4848
www.resortquesthawaii.com
Privacy comes standard at this condo hotel, which has studio, one-, and two-bedroom units spread out among 11 low-rise buildings on 13 acres (5 hectares) of land. All guests receive complimentary swimersize, yoga, and tennis lessons. The resort is a short talk to shops nearby. **$$$**

Aston at The Whaler on Ka'anapali Beach
2481 Ka'anapali Parkway
Ka'anapali
Tel: 888-671-5310
www.whalerkaanapali.com
Located just north of Whaler's Village Shopping Center, this towering condo building offers studio, one-, and two-bedroom units – all of which come with private lanais. Room décor varies widely, but units are clean and relatively modern. **$$$**

Ka'anapali Ali'i
50 Nohea Kai Drive
Ka'anapali
Tel: 667-1400
www.kaanapalialii.com
Spacious one- and two-bedroom units characterize this property, which is located right in the heart of Ka'anapali Beach and offers amenities such as daily housekeeping, an activities desk, and a DVD lending library. Down by the beach, guests also have access to fireplaces. **$$$**

Kamaole Sands
2695 S. Kihei Road
Kihei
Tel: 800-451-5008
www.kamaolesands.com
Located across the street from its namesake beach, this property comprises a variety of one- and two-bedroom guest rooms – which all come standard with a lanai. Also on site are tennis courts and a pool. Golf nearby. **$$**

Kapalua Villas
2000 Village Road
Kapalua
Tel: 665-9170
www.kapaluavillas.com
Condominium units of varying sizes are available from this property with fairway settings flanking the golf courses at Kapalua Resort. Units themselves are elegantly furnished, and have access to a resort pool. **$$$**

Mana Kai Maui Resort
2960 S. Kihei Road
Kihei
Tel: 879-1561
www.manakaimaui.com
Lava rocks and tiki torches help enhance the old-school Hawaiian vibe at this resort, located just behind Keawakupu Beach in Kihei. Units come standard with free parking and free local calls. Downstairs the activity desk can help you plan an adventure. **$$**

Outrigger Palms at Wailea
3700 Wailea Alanui
Wailea
Tel: 879-5800
www.outrigger.com/PalmsatWailea
These one- and two-bedroom units are located atop a bluff, giving them a commanding view of Wailea Beach and the choppy waters between Maui, Kaho'olawe and Lanai. All rooms come standard with daily housekeeping, washer/dryer units and kitchens or kitchenettes. **$$$**

MOLOKAI

Ke Nani Kai
50 Kapuhi Place
Kaunakakai
Tel: 858-679-2016
www.kenanikai.com
There are 120 units at this condominium-hotel surrounded by the Kaluakoi golf course, but only some of them are available to rent.

Numerous facilities include parking, TV, swimming pool, tennis court, and more. Minimum stay of 2 nights. 35 units. **$$**

Hotel Molokai
1300 Kamehameha V Highway
Kaunakakai
Tel: 660-3408
www.hotelmolokai.com

A-frame buildings and other low-lying buildings are de rigeur at this property, arguably the biggest and most notable hotel in Kaunakakai. Rooms are basic with a Polynesian décor; they all look out on a central lawn. 53 rooms. **$$**

LANAI

Four Seasons Resort, Lanai, The Lodge at Ko'ele
One Keomoku Highway
Lanai City
Tel: 565-4000
www.fourseasons.com/koele
This resort doesn't feel Hawaiian; it is a cool mountain retreat in the uplands of Lanai. Still, it is luxurious. Rooms are outfitted with thick, comfy furniture, as well as spacious bathrooms. Outside, activities include everything from horseback riding to tennis, golf and clay-shooting. 102 rooms. **$$$$**

Four Seasons Resort Lanai, at Manele Bay
One Manele Bay Road
Lanai City
Tel: 565-2000
www.fourseasons.com/manelebay
Set on a cliff overlooking the beach at pristine Hulopo'e Bay, this property is swanky and understated at the same time. Rooms offer modern conveniences with a traditional Hawaiian spin; private lanais boast wicker furniture and plenty of space to move around. The resort also borders a marine preserve, where there is great snorkeling and stellar hiking. 236 rooms. **$$$$**

Hotel Lanai
828 Lanai Avenue
Lanai City
Tel: 565-7211

www.hotellanai.com
This cozy little inn, which dates to 1923, is the affordable way to visit Lanai, especially considering that the other two properties on island are Four Seasons. Rooms are modest and feature antique furniture and hand-sewn Hawaiian quilts. Don't forget to try the Lanai City Grill, one of the best restaurants in town. 11 rooms. **$$$**

PRICE CATEGORIES
$ = below $100
$$ = $101–200
$$$ = $201–300
$$$$ = above $301

HAWAII (BIG ISLAND)

East side

Hilo Hawaiian Hotel
71 Banyan Drive
Hilo
Tel: 935-9361
www.castleresorts.com
This Hilo Bay hotel, located just minutes from Hilo International Airport, faces Coconut Island and the open ocean. Rooms are dated but clean; each boasts high-speed internet and a private lanai. 286 rooms. **$$**

Naniloa Volcanoes Resort
93 Banyan Drive
Hilo
Tel: 969-3333
www.naniloaresort.com
Two towers comprise this resort, which looks out over Hilo Bay. Rooms come standard with lanais and sofa beds; those in the Mauna Kea tower also include complimentary high-speed internet access. 325 rooms. **$$**

Palms Cliff House
28-3514 Mamalahoa Highway
Honomu
Tel: 963-6076
www.palmscliffhouse.com
This luxurious B&B on the bluffs overlooking the Pacific has been voted best in the East Side consistently since it was built in 2000. Rooms and suites boast tropical décor, communal rooms offer a number of cozy nooks for snuggling and reading books. 8 rooms. **$$$**

Shipman House Bed & Breakfast Inn
131 Kai'ulani Street
Hilo
Tel: 934-8002
www.hilo-hawaii.com
The main house at this B&B dates back to 1899, making it one of the oldest accommodations on the island. Guests are invited to participate in a hula class every Tuesday. Daily breakfast buffet has a tropical theme (think mac-nut granola and banana muffins). 5 rooms. **$$**

Uncle Billy's Hilo Bay Hotel
87 Banyan Drive
Hilo
Tel: 961-0861
www.unclebilly.com/UB_Hilo.html
This hotel, on Hilo Bay, is a favorite for visitors who are looking for a place to crash before or after a long day at Hawaii Volcanoes National Park (a 45-minute drive away). Rooms are barebones at best; guests receive free continental breakfast. 145 rooms. **$$**

The lagoon at Hilton Waikoloa Village.

Kohala Coast

Fairmont Orchid Hawaii
One North Kaniku Drive
Kohala Coast
Tel: 885-2000
www.fairmont.com/orchid
A peaceful lagoon and beach popular among sunning sea turtles are among the attractions at this sprawling luxury resort. While standard accommodations are fine for most travelers, concierge-level rooms, which include access to all-day snacks, are exquisite. Rental bikes available. 540 rooms. **$$$$**

Hapuna Beach Prince Hotel
62-100 Kauna'oa Drive
Kohala
Tel: 880-1111
www.hapunabeachprincehotel.com
This hotel sits on one of the largest sand beaches on Hawaii Island, and all rooms face the ocean. Large rooms boast marble bathrooms and private lanais. The on-site golf course, designed by Arnold Palmer, is a favorite among locals. 411 rooms. **$$$**

Hilton Waikoloa Village
69-425 Waikoloa Beach Drive
Waikaloa
Tel: 886-1234
www.hiltonwaikoloavillage.com
Yes, there actually are dolphins in the lagoon at this 62-acre (25-hectare) mega-resort. There also are water slides, a nightly torch-lighting ceremony and a cornucopia of restaurant options. If you dislike crowds, this resort may not be for you. 1,297 rooms. **$$$**

Mauna Lani Bay Hotel & Bungalows
68-1400 Mauna Lani Drive
Kohala
Tel: 885-6622
www.maunalani.com
Guests to this classic Hawaii Island resort are greeted by an open-air lobby with cathedral ceilings, and the breathtaking architecture continues in the spacious-yet-understated guest rooms. Free cultural and educational programs provide guests with one-of-a-kind local knowledge. 343 rooms. **$$$**

Waikoloa Beach Marriott
69-275 Waikoloa Beach Drive
Waikaloa
Tel: 886-6789
www.marriotthawaii.com
Ancient fishponds, historic trails and petroglyph fields are all within a short walk from the lobby of this 15-acre (6-hectare) resort. Rooms boast Hawaiian art and private lanais. The sprawling pool complex features a sand-bottom pool for little ones. 545 rooms. **$$$**

Kona

Courtyard King Kamehameha's Kona Beach Hotel
75-5660 Palani Road
Kailua
Tel: 329-2911
www.konabeachhotel.com
A 2011 renovation rejuvenated this landmark hotel; rooms are now modern and include sliding plantation shutter screens. The hotel also added a fitness center and spa. It is an easy walk to downtown Kailua attractions. 457 rooms. **$$**

Four Seasons Resort Hualalai
72-100 Kaupulehu Drive
Kailua-Kona
Tel: 325-8000
www.fourseasons.com/hualalai
Everything at this resort revolves around bungalows; 36 of them house rooms and suites. This means everything at the resort is spread out, adding to a feeling of calm and privacy. Informative exhibits are on view at the resort's Hawaiian Interpretive Center.

Be sure to play the PGA-quality golf course. 294 rooms. **$$$$**

Holualoa Inn
76-5932 Mamalahoa Highway
Holualoa
Tel: 324-1121
www.holualoainn.com
This Kona area inn is located in a cedar home on a 30-acre (12-hectare) coffee-country estate, a few miles above Kailua Bay. Rooms boast an Asian theme, and daily breakfasts comprise a coffee, fruits, vegetables, and eggs harvested on site. 6 rooms. **$$$**

Royal Kona Resort
75-5852 Ali'i Drive
Kailua
Tel: 329-3111
www.royalkona.com
Formerly the Kona Hilton, this hotel overlooks Kailua Bay and is one of the best values in town. One highlight: the weekly *lu'au* with Polynesian entertainment. Other notable amenities: the bar, pool, and restaurant, which are right on the water. 444 rooms. **$$**

Uncle Billy's Kona Bay Hotel
75-5739 Ali'i Drive
Kailua
Tel: 329-6488
www.unclebilly.com
This hotel is all about location – it's situated in the heart of Kailua, across from Kailua Bay. Rooms include mini-refrigerators and private lanai. The hotel also has a small swimming pool. 145 rooms. **$$**

North Kohala

Hawaii Island Retreat at Ahu Pohaku Hoomaluhia
250 Maluhia Road
Hawi
Tel: 889-6336
www.hawaiiislandretreat.com
With seven yurts and a host of eco-friendly initiatives including solar- and wind-generated power, this small inn clearly emphasizes sustainability. Lavish rooms seem almost out of

place amid all the surrounding nature. All stays include complimentary breakfast. 16 units. **$$**

Kamuela Inn
65-1300 Kawaihae Road
Waimea
Tel: 800-555-8968
www.thekamuelainn.com
Set back from Kawaihae Road, this motor inn boasts picturesque gardens and a welcoming lanai with great views of Mauna Kea. Homey rooms have private baths, and all guests receive complimentary breakfast. 30 rooms. **$$**

Puakea Ranch
56-2864 Akoni Pule Highway
Hawi
Tel: 315-0805
www.puakearanch.com
Guests of this historic country estate enjoy their own private swimming pools, horseback riding, and plenty of fresh fruit and veggies to pick whenever they wish. The ranch is 10 minutes to the closest beach and about 15 minutes outside Hawi Town. Staying here is a true escape. 4 units. **$$$$**

Volcano and Captain Cook

Hale Ohia
11-3968 Hale Ohia Road
Volcano
Tel: 967-7986
www.haleohia.com
This mansion was built in the 1930s as a summer home for a wealthy Scotsman, today it has transformed into a quaint B&B and a series of cottages. Guests receive continental breakfast in their rooms each afternoon for the morning that follows. No televisions. 8 units. **$$**

Kilauea Lodge
19-3948 Old Volcano Road
Volcano
Tel: 967-7366
www.kilauealodge.com
One mile from the entrance of Hawaii Volcanoes National Park, this lodge was built as a YMCA camp in the 1930s.

Today, rooms feature antiques, rich quilts, and Hawaiian artwork. Some even boast fireplaces. Off-site cottages also are available. 16 rooms. **$$$**

Manago Hotel
82-6151 Mamalahoa Highway
Captain Cook
Tel: 323-2642
www.managohotel.com
This family-run hotel in the center of Captain Cook overlooks Kealakekua Bay. About two thirds of the hotel's rooms have private bathrooms; the rest share bathrooms. The hotel also boasts a Japanese room with tatami mats and a futon. 64 rooms. **$**

Volcano House
Crater Rim Drive
Hawaii Volcanoes National Park
Tel: 441-7750
www.hawaiivolcanohouse.com
Valued for its location inside the Hawaii Volcanoes National Park overlooking Halema'uma'u crater, this hotel reopened in 2013 after years of renovation. On certain nights, guests can see the glow of molten lava from the hotel's main lanai. 33 rooms. **$$**

Condominiums

Aston Kona by the Sea
75-6106 Ali'i Drive
Kailua
Tel: 327-2300
www.astonkonabythesearesort.com
All of the units at this condo-hotel include modern kitchens and washer/dryer machines. The nearest sandy beach is two miles away, but the pool is next to the ocean and many rooms have ocean views. **$$$**

Aston Shores at Waikoloa
69-1035 Keana Place
Waikoloa
Tel: 886-5001
www.astonhotels.com
This luxury condominium resort on Kohala Coast is located next to Waikoloa Golf Club's famed Beach Course. Rooms vary in décor, but all boast gourmet kitchens, private lanais and daily housekeeping service. Guests can reserve PlayStation3 Blu-Ray consoles for the duration of their stays. **$$$**

Outrigger Kanaloa at Kona
78-261 Manukai Street
Kailua
Tel: 322-9625
www.outrigger.com
Overlooking Keauhou Bay, this condominium is close to a championship golf course and boasts tennis courts and oceanfront swimming pools. All one- and two-bedroom units are furnished elegantly with marble kitchens and bathrooms. They also all have private lanais. **$$**

Japanese-style bathroom at Puakea Ranch.

KAUAI

East Side

Garden Island Inn
3445 Wilcox Road
Lihu'e
Tel: 245-7227
www.gardenislandinn.com
Budget-conscious travelers love this three-story hotel across the street from Kalapaki Beach and adjacent to the Marriott (and all of its restaurants). The property is a short walk from the Anchor Cove shopping center. 21 rooms. **$$**

Kauai Beach Resort
4331 Kauai Beach Drive
Lihu'e
Tel: 954-7419
www.kauaibeachresorthawaii.com
Formerly the Hilton Kauai Beach Resort, this resort is now owned by Aqua, which has upgraded in-room amenities such as televisions and shutters. Guests are welcome at the monthly wine reception in the lobby on the first Thursday of every month. 356 rooms. **$$$**

Kauai Marriott Resort on Kalapaki Beach
3610 Rice Street
Lihu'e
Tel: 245-5050
www.kauaimarriott.com
Everything is big at this beachfront resort, from the 26,000-sq ft (2,400-sq meter) swimming pool to the tropical garden, spacious guest rooms, and the view of the Haupu Ridge. The resort sits about a mile from Kauai International Airport, and a free shuttle is available. 367 rooms. **$$$**

North Shore

Hanalei Bay Resort
5380 Honoiki Road
Princeville
Tel: 826-6522
www.hanaleibayresort.com
Vistas are everything at this resort; guests are hard-pressed to avoid views of Hanalei. Rooms are casual and fun, featuring rattan furniture and island art. The upper-level pool has lava-rock waterfalls and a kid-friendly sand beach. 134 rooms. **$$$**

Hanalei Colony Resort
5-7130 Kuhio Highway
Haena
Tel: 826-6235
www.hcr.com
The only true beachfront resort on the North Shore, this 5-acre (2-hectare) property is great for its simplicity. There are no phones, TVs or stereos,

but the place does offer Wifi. There's also an art gallery, spa and restaurant on site. 48 rooms. **$$$**

St. Regis Princeville Resort
5520 Ka Huku Road
Princeville
Tel: 826-9644
www.princevillehotelhawaii.com
Little touches make a huge difference in the rooms at this North Shore gem. Among them: lighted closets, original artwork, marble bathrooms with privacy windows. The hotel is so swanky, so upscale, that it almost sticks out from the serene landscape of Hanalei Bay. 252 rooms. **$$$$**

South Shore

Grand Hyatt Kauai Resort and Spa
1571 Po'ipu Road
Koloa
Tel: 742-1234
www.grandhyattkauai.com
If a mega-resort can be understated, this property proves the point. The hotel is cut into the cliffs overlooking an undeveloped coastline, providing stellar views. Most of the rooms have ocean views. The pool area boasts both freshwater and saltwater swimming lagoons. 639 rooms. **$$$$**

Koa Kea Hotel and Resort
2251 Po'ipu Road
Koloa
Tel: 828-8888
www.koakea.com
Families are not welcome at this uber-luxurious resort, which mixes contemporary Asian touches with white, blue, and sandy tones. Because the clientele is limited, because the place is small, it has a calmer vibe than many of the bigger resorts in the area. 121 rooms. **$$$$**

Sheraton Kauai Resort
2440 Ho'onani Road
Koloa
Tel: 742-1661
www.sheraton-kauai.com
Oceanfront takes on new meaning at this resort, where crashing waves actually splash guests in the ocean wing. Elsewhere on property, three fire pits provide great places for visitors to interact. Hotel is a short walk to restaurants in Po'ipu. 405 rooms. **$$$$**

West Side

Kokee Lodge
3600 Kokee Road
Waimea
Tel: 335-6061
www.thelodgeatkokee.net

Backpackers swear by these cabins, noting that while the accommodations are austere, they're far better than tenting it on a windy night. Most cottages boast wood-burning stoves (wood is extra). On site, a small museum teaches about local animals and plants. 12 cabins. **$$**

Waimea Plantation Cottages
9400 Kaumuali'i Highway
Waimea
Tel: 338-1625
www.waimeaplantation.com
The homes of different sizes on this historic plot mix porches and plantation-era furnishings with modern kitchens and cable TV. The property also offers hammocks, a spa and a museum. Located on one of the island's black-sand beaches. 55 cottages. **$$$**

Condominiums

Kauai Coast Resort
520 Aleka Loop
Kapa'a
Tel: 822-3441
www.shellhospitality.com
Fully furnished one- and two-bedroom condo units at this Coconut Marketplace resort boast private lanais and well-equipped kitchens. Also on site: a heated pool, day spa, children's pool, restaurant, and ocean-side hot tub. **$$**

Outrigger Kiahuna Plantation
2253 Po'ipu Road
Koloa
Tel: 742-6411
www.outrigger.com
This resort represents Kauai's largest condo project, and the location – smack in the middle of the Po'ipu resort strip – is stellar. Families love the place for its swimmable beach and lawn for picnics and games. **$$**

Villas at Po'ipu Kai
2373 Ho'ohu Road
Koloa
Tel: 866-407-0249
www.villasatpoipukai.com
Two-, three-, and four-bedroom units at this Koloa-area hotel are spacious and luxurious – each unit feels more like a mansion than a condo. The resort has its own pools and also is a short walk to Brennecke Beach. **$$$$**

PRICE CATEGORIES
$ = below $100
$$ = $101–200
$$$ = $201–300
$$$$ = above $301

TRANSPORTATION · ACCOMMODATIONS · EATING OUT · ACTIVITIES · A – Z · LANGUAGE

EATING OUT

RECOMMENDED RESTAURANTS, CAFES & BARS

CHOOSING A RESTAURANT

It's easy to eat well on the Hawaiian Islands. With a multitude of good restaurants serving up a bevy of different cuisines, there are options at every price point. The chefs here enjoy experimenting, adding a little Asian to Continental, or Italian to Pacific. The results are excellent, including the popular "Pacific Rim" cuisine that has gained international respect. In addition, there are numerous ethnic cuisines to be enjoyed: Thai, Vietnamese, Korean, Chinese, and Japanese are only a few of the ones you see every day.

If you're eating breakfast or lunch, reservations aren't necessary. For dinner, however, especially in some of the busier tourist spots such as Honolulu on Oahu and Lahaina or Paia on Maui, it's always a good idea to book a table in advance by phone or on line.

Etiquette in Hawaiian restaurants is the same as it is in restaurants on the US mainland. Beach attire is generally acceptable for breakfast and lunch, but for dinner guests should spruce up a bit (read: no ballcaps or tank tops). Tipping servers also is customary; 15 percent is standard for average service; good service deserves 20 percent.

Where to eat

Hawaii restaurants span the gamut from roadside shack to swanky and formal. In between is everything from casual beachfront tiki bars to family-friendly diners and bistros. Most of the time, the best restaurants are located in central commercial areas: on rare occasions, good restaurants will stand alone. It's common to find multiple cuisines clustered in one area. The exception is Honolulu's Chinatown, which boasts a preponderance of restaurants serving Asian food.

For the best and freshest produce, explore some of the islands' farmers' markets. On Oahu, check out the **People's Open Market** in Honolulu, the Saturday market at the Kapiolani Community College on Diamond Head Road in Honolulu, and the Thursday market at Kailua Square Shopping Center in Kailua. On Maui, the **Maui Swap Meet** on Kahului Beach Road at Maui Community College is a great option. On Hawaii Island, the **Hilo Farmers' Market** is great for fresh fruit (especially papaya). And on Kauai, the **Kauai Community Market** goes off weekly on the campus of the local community college across from Grove Farm in Lihu'e.

Drinking notes

Drinking on Hawaii is almost as important as eating; with the blazing sun overhead, hydration is an essential part of life. Local water in the Hawaiian Islands is absolutely fine to drink; doing so actually benefits the environment, since bottled water only creates more trash. Many restaurants and hotels have established their own in-house water filtration systems. If you are concerned about the quality of local water, ask for filtered water when you go out.

In terms of alcoholic beverages, the Mai Tai is as much a part of the local culture as Spam, *poke* (type of raw seafood salad), and other delicacies. Perhaps the best place to experience a real tropical drink is an authentic tiki bar – an open-air establishment with South Pacific-style decor. Some of the best bars in the islands are actually "barefoot bars," meaning they are situated on the sand and the management encourages patrons to take off their shoes before partaking. One of the best of the bunch: **The Hula Grill** (2435 Ka'anapali Parkway; tel. 667-6636, www.hulagrillkaanapali.com) in Whaler's Village, on Maui.

Beer-lovers swear by some of the local brews in Hawaii, too, namely those from the **Kona Brewing Company** (75-5629 Kuakini Highway; tel. 334-2739, www.konabrewingcompany.com) in Kailua on Hawaii Island. In recent years a number of small-batch spirits producers have sprouted up on the islands. One of the best: the **Koloa Rum Company** (see page 274), in Koloa, on Kauai. Another notable player in the space is Sammy Hagar, the former frontman for Van Halen, who distills his Beach Bar Rum at a small facility outside of Makawao on Maui.

It's worth noting that the legal drinking age in Hawaii is the same that it is on the US mainland: 21.

OAHU

Honolulu

Alan Wong's Restaurant
1857 S. King Street
Tel: 949-2526
www.alanwongs.com
Chef Wong made a name for himself by taking creative and innovative approaches to traditional Island cuisine, and that's exactly what he continues to do at this restaurant, one of the best in all of Hawaii. Fans rave about the "Da Bag," which comprises clams and *kalua* pig steamed in an aluminium pouch. Reservations essential. **$$$**

Chef Mavro
1969 S. King Street
Tel: 944-4714
www.chefmavro.com
Some see chef George Mavrothalassitis as a bit eccentric; he has been known to spend hundreds of dollars to track down the freshest fish for certain dishes. The result is a French-inspired menu like none other, complete with wine pairings. Menu changes quarterly. Reservations essential. **$$$**

Little Village Noodle House
1113 Smith Street
Tel: 545-3008
www.littlevillagehawaii.com
Smack in the heart of Honolulu's Chinatown, this restaurant serves up an eclectic, pan-Chinese menu. In particular, vegetarian options abound; the dried green beans are addictive. Free parking available next door. **$**

Lucky Belly
50 N. Hotel Street
Tel: 531-1888
www.luckybelly.com
Pork lovers will adore this Modernist and upscale eatery, which elevates the swine to gastronomic heaven. Try the pork belly *bao* to start, then move on to *ramen* with pork belly, bacon,

and sausage. Meat-free salads also available. **$$**

MW Restaurant
1528 Kapiolani Boulevard
Tel: 955-6505
www.mwrestaurant.com
Local foodies cheered when this restaurant opened in October 2013. The brains behind it: Wade Ueoka and Michelle Karr-Ueoka, a husband-and-wife team from Alan Wong's, who strive to blend local seafood and produce. Try the hearty oxtail soup. Reservations recommended. **$$–$$$**

Rainbow Drive-In
3308 Kana'ina Avenue
Tel: 737-0177
www.rainbowdrivein.com
Food at this drive-in restaurant is about as authentic as Hawaiian food can get. The signature dish is the Plate Lunch, with two scoops of rice, one scoop of macaroni salad, and your choice of protein. Daily specials – particularly the beef stew – are worth sampling, too. Breakfasts here are also delicious. **$**

Sorabol
805 Ke'eaumoku Street
Tel: 947-3113
www.sorabolhawaii.com
This 24-hour eatery represents the largest Korean restaurant in the city, and is a favorite spot among late-night revelers. Traditional dishes such as *bi bim bap* and *kal bi* are above average. **$$**

Vintage Cave
1450 Ala Moana Boulevard.
Tel: 441-1744
www.vintagecave.com
Small portions and Japanese sensibility characterize the experience at this sophisticated eatery, which serves a set menu every night. Attire here is semi-formal for men and women alike. Reservations essential. **$$$**

Wai'oli Tea Room
2950 Manoa Road
Tel: 988-5800
Experiencing old-fashioned "high tea" at this tea room in the hills above Honolulu feels like stepping into someone's house, though it is run by the Salvation Army and profits go towards a local rehabilitation center. Tea is hot, goodies are fresh and delicious, and photos and clippings on the walls are like a walk down memory lane. **$–$$**

North Shore

Cholo's
62-250 Kamehameha Highway, Hale'iwa
Tel: 637-3059
www.cholos.mx
This homestyle Mexican restaurant is located in the North Shore Marketplace. The highlights are fish tacos and margaritas in giant goblets the size of small fish tanks. The place boasts authentic, colorful artwork from Mexico; most of it is for sale. **$–$$**

Ted's Bakery
59-024 Kamehameha Highway, Sunset Beach
Tel: 638-5974
www.tedsbakery.com
There's more to this North Shore hole-in-the-wall than chocolate cream pies; Ted's is a classic sandwich shop as well, serving up giant submarine sandwiches, mixed plate lunches and more. Buy an extra roll or two, sit outside and feed the local chickens. **$**

Waikiki

Arancino
255 Beach Walk
Tel: 923-5557
www.arancino.com
This is the first of four locations for the popular local Italian chain, and it's still the best. Pasta dishes such as black tiger shrimp and arugula in homemade tomato sauce are executed to perfection. Homemade desserts such as cannolis don't disappoint either. **$$–$$$**.

BLT Steak
Trump Hotel Waikiki
223 Saratoga Road
http://www.trumphotelcollection.com/waikiki

Seafood feast at Mama's Fish House, near Pa'ia.

PRICE CATEGORIES

Price categories are for a meal for one, not including alcohol:
$ = below $25
$$ = $25–50
$$$ = above $50

Tel: 683-7777
This French spin on an American steakhouse offers prime cuts of beef, fresh seafood, and a variety of side dishes. There's also a raw bar – one of the best in town. Because the Trump attracts celebrities, you might even find yourself dining with the stars. **$$$**
Duke's Canoe Club
Outrigger Waikiki Hotel
2335 Kalakaua Avenue
Tel: 922-2268
www.dukeswaikiki.com
Memorabilia on the walls of this oceanfront restaurant pays tribute to Duke Hakanamoku, the father of modern surfing. The food is pretty appealing, too; the place is known for its tasty prime rib and rotisserie chicken. Sunday brunch here is good value. **$$–$$$**
Hau Tree Lanai
New Otani Kaimana Beach Hotel
2863 Kalakaua Avenue
Tel: 921-7066
www.kaimana.com

Follow in the footsteps of author Robert Louis Stevenson as you sit under the *hau* tree at this beachside seafood restaurant. Kids will love the purple *poi* pancakes at breakfast. Breakfast and lunch only. **$$–$$$**
Michel's at the Colony Surf
Colony Surf
2895 Kalakaua Avenue
Tel: 923-6552
www.michelshawaii.com
Lovers, this is the place for you. Restaurant windows sit mere inches from the ocean. An exquisite French menu includes traditional options such as escargot and foie gras, as well as newer items that incorporate local seafood. Dinner only. Reservations essential. **$$$**
Morimoto
The Modern
1775 Ala Moana Boulevard
Tel: 943-5900
www.morimotowaikiki.com
Try the *kim chee* tofu dish made tableside at this upscale eatery from TV Iron Chef Morimoto. The restaurant

serves mostly super-fresh sushi and sashimi – largely caught in local waters the day you dine. **$$$**
Roy's Waikiki Beach
226 Lewers Street
Tel: 923-7697
www.roysrestaurant.com
This isn't Roy Yamaguchi's first restaurant in Honolulu, but it is by far the most popular. Located in the Beach Walk development, the eatery turns out Roy's signature spin on Island cuisine, blending European techniques and Asian cuisine. **$$–$$$**
Teddy's Bigger Burgers
134 Kapahulu Avenue
Tel: 926-3444
www.teddysbiggerburgers.com
Hawaiians love their comfort food, and the burgers (and shakes and fries) at Teddy's rank among the best. There are other locations around town but this is the original. It even has a place to store surfboards for customers who come in off the beach. **$**

MAUI

Lahaina and environs

Hula Grill
2435 Ka'apanali Parkway, Ka'anapali
Tel: 667-6636
www.hulagrill.com
This restaurant cranks out upscale pub food Hawaiian Style; think *pupus*, hamburgers, and workmanlike fish dishes. Perhaps the best part of the eatery is the Barefoot Bar, with its live music and drink specials during Happy Hour on weekdays. **$$–$$$**
Lahaina Grill
127 Lahainaluna Road
Tel: 667-5117
Iconic chef David Paul is no longer associated with this upscale restaurant, but the food is still

delicious. An obvious favorite is the Cake Walk, with samples of Kona lobster crab cake, Louisiana rock shrimp cake and seared *ahi* cake. Reservations essential. **$$$**
Mala Ocean Tavern
1307 Front Street
Tel: 667-9394
www.malaoceantavern.com
This tiny restaurant overlooking the Mala Ramp and Lahaina Harbor offers an eclectic menu that touches on the Mediterranean, Italy, Thailand, and the Middle East. If you can't sit on the patio, ask for a seat at the bar. **$$–$$$**
Star Noodle
286 Kupuohi Street
Tel: 667-5400

www.starnoodle.com
Disregard the location of this restaurant (it's in an industrial park); the food here is among the best on the island. Try the pan-roasted Brussels sprouts with bacon and *kim chee* purée, or the Lahaina fried soup (*fat chow fun*, pork, and bean sprouts). For a more sociable experience, sit at the communal table in the center of the restaurant. **$**

Paia

Flatbread Company
89 Hana Highway
Tel: 579-8989
www.flatbreadcompany.com
Locals line up in droves for the brick-oven pizzas made with organic ingredients from this down-home restaurant just outside of downtown Paia. Vegetarians, rejoice: there are a number of meat-free pizzas, and salads are tremendous. **$$**
Mama's Fish House
799 Poho Place, on highway near Paia
Tel: 579-8488
www.mamasfishhouse.com
It's no fluke that this has become Maui's most famous restaurant. The food – freshly caught fish from around the islands – is stellar and the beachfront view never ceases to amaze. It's also a great place to spot local celebs such as Sammy Hagar and Steven Tyler. **$$$**

Shrimp truck in Hale'iwa, North Shore of Oahu.

Milagro's Food Company
3 Baldwin Avenue
Tel: 579-8755
www.milagrosfoodcompany.com
Margaritas and Tex-Mex food are the attractions at this closet-sized eatery near the intersection of Baldwin Avenue and the Hana Highway. Most ingredients are organic; some are even grown locally. Grab a seat on the patio and watch the world walk by. **$$**

Upcountry

Casanova Italian Restaurant & Deli
1188 Makawao Avenue, Makawao
Tel: 572-0220
www.casanovamaui.com
This Makawao restaurant revolves around its pizza oven; it's an authentic dinner house and nightclub, but most guests just come for a pizza and some beer. By day, the eatery is a deli, pouring strong coffees and wrapping fat sandwiches. **$–$$**

Grandma's Coffee House
9232 Kula Highway, Kula
Tel: 878-2792
www.grandmascoffee.com
Yes, they sell coffee at this country-style restaurant on the Back Road to Hana, but the place is famous for its giant breakfast dishes and its baked goods. On weekends there is live music on the small patio (in the shade of coffee plants). **$**

Wailea

Ko
Fairmont Kea Lani
4100 Wailea Alanui Drive
Tel: 669-6299
www.fairmont.com/kea-lani-maui/dining

The menu at this upscale Asian restaurant is the only restaurant on Maui to be serving food inspired by Hawaii's sugar cane plantation era. What's more, chef Tylun Pang incorporates family recipes from his own family and families of his line cooks. Reservations essential. **$$–$$$**

Manoli's Pizza Company
100 Wailea Ike Drive
Tel: 874-7499
www.manolispizzacompany.com
Gluten-free crust is a huge hit at this brick-oven pizzeria in Wailea, as it is one of the only pizza shops on the island to offer such an option. Menu options also include traditional pizzas and a host of homemade pastas. Delivery available. **$$–$$$**

Spago
Four Seasons Resort
3900 Wailea Alanui Drive
www.fourseasons.com/maui/dining/restaurants/spago
Tel: 879-2999
Wolfgang Puck's famous restaurant translates well in Hawaii, where chefs prepare freshly caught fish every night. Dessert is a spectacle, as well, with options such as passionfruit crème brûlée. In winter, Puck himself might be working the line. Reservations essential. **$$$**

Wailuku

Saeng's Thai Cuisine
2119 W. Vineyard Street, Wailuku
Tel: 244-1567
Tucked behind a row of county buildings in Wailuku, this tiny

restaurant serves what many locals consider to be the best Thai food on Maui. One don't-miss dish: red prawn pineapple curry. **$**

West Maui

Honokowai Okazuya
3600-D Lower Honoapi'ilani Highway, Honokowai
Tel: 665-0512
Locals swear by this hole-in-the-wall restaurant, located in a Honokowai strip mall. The signature dish: mahi-mahi with lemon capers, which always comes with a scoop of macaroni salad. The restaurant has a few small tables but is designed mostly for take-away. **$**

Plantation House Restaurant
2000 Plantation Club Drive, Kapalua
Tel: 669-6299
www.theplantationhouse.com
Views of Molokai from this top-notch restaurant in the clubhouse on Kapalua's Plantation golf course are remarkable. The food is good, too; chefs incorporate local produce and products into a modern take on traditional Hawaiian cuisine. Reservations essential. **$$$**

Sansei Seafood Restaurant & Sushi Bar
600 Office Road, Kapalua
Tel: 669-6286
There is sushi on Maui, and then there's Sansei. The cult favorite serves up a variety of traditional sushi dishes, as well as new spins that incorporate ingredients such as panko-flakes, Asian shrimp cakes, and mango. Meat-based dishes are available, too. **$$–$$$**

MOLOKAI

Molokai Pizza Café
Kahuna Center,
Kaunakakai
Tel: 553-3288

In addition to serving pizza (as the name suggests), this restaurant offers a mean prime rib and surprisingly good Mexican food. The atmosphere

is casual and fun; at times, even on sparsely populated Molokai, it can actually feel lively. **$–$$**

LANAI

Dining Room
Four Seasons Resort Lanai, The Lodge at Ko'ele
1 Keomoku Highway
Tel: 565-4580
www.fourseasons.com/koele
The menu at this upscale in-lobby restaurant features a Hawaiian spin on the nature-to-table concept, incorporating as many locally grown and harvested items as possible (including meat). The multi-course

chef's tasting menu with wine pairings is a surprisingly good value. **$$$**

Nobu Lanai
Four Seasons Resort Lanai, Manele Bay
1 Manele Bay Road
Tel: 565-4580
www.noburestaurants.com/lanai
Of all the Nobu restaurants around the world, this one has the most spectacular view –of Manele Bay and the Pacific Ocean. Sushi and sashimi

here are as fresh as they come; hot items – especially steak dishes – also are worth a try. Reservations essential. **$$$**

PRICE CATEGORIES

Price categories are for a meal for one, not including alcohol:
$ = below $25
$$ = $25–50
$$$ = above $50

HAWAII (BIG ISLAND)

Hilo

Café Pesto
308 Kamehameha Avenue
Tel: 969-6640
www.cafepesto.com
Pizzas in this charming restaurant feature exotic ingredients such as gorgonzola and artichokes, while pastas and risottos incorporate fresh seafood and locally raised meats. Live music on weekends. $$

Hilo Bay Café
315 Maka'ala Street
Tel: 935-4939
www.hilobaycafe.com
Roasted eggplant-parmesan custard and Hamakua mushroom pot-pie are among the options at this vegan-friendly restaurant in a strip mall on the outskirts of Hilo. This is a favorite among locals, so be prepared to wait. $

The Seaside Restaurant & Aqua Farm
1790 Kalaniana'ole Avenue, Hilo
Tel: 935-8825
www.seasiderestaurant.com
Sure, the food here is tasty (try the fried aholehole), but the real attraction is the 30-acre (12-hectare) brackish-water fishpond outside, where the Nakagawa family raise their own fish. Reservations suggested. $$

Kailua-Kona

Beach Tree at the Four Seasons Resort Hualalai
Four Seasons Resort Hualalai
72-100 Ka'upulehu Drive, Kailua-Kona
Tel: 325-8000
www.fourseasons.com/hualalai
Waves break just beyond your table at this alfresco, modern eatery that combines cuisine from Italy and Spain. Though the atmosphere feels a bit formal, the restaurant actually is great for kids, with chalk and chalkboards for every table. $$$

Bite Me Fish Market Bar & Grill
425 Kealakehe Parkway
Tel: 327-3474
www.bitemefishmarket.com
You can't get fish much fresher than what's on offer here; the joint looks out on the boat ramp at Bite Me Fish Market in Honokohau Harbor. Sandwiches are named after fishing lures. For a real treat, order the fish tacos. $

Huggo's
75-5828 Kahakai Road
Tel: 329-1493
www.huggos.com
There aren't many fancy restaurants in Kailua, but this oceanfront eatery is the fanciest (and most expensive) of the bunch. Local seafood is the specialty here; also, try the guava-braised baby back ribs. $$$

Kona Brewing Company Pub and Brewery
75-5629 Kuakini Highway
Tel: 329-2739
www.konabrewingco.com
Every visitor to Kailua-Kona should come here and dine on the patio at least once. Never mind that the place is in an industrial part of town; the microbrews are stupendous and the Polynesian-themed menu (think pulled-pork quesadillas) is great for any occasion. $$

North Kohala

Kawaihae Seafood Bar & Grill
61-3642 Kawaihae Harbor, Kawaihae
Tel: 880-9393
www.seafoodbarandgrill.com
The building that houses this restaurant dates back to the 1850s. If you're with a big group, order off the *pupu* (appetizer) menu; if you like vegetables, the Island Salad comprises the very best of the island's produce of the day. $$

Merriman's
65-1227 Opelo Road, Waimea
Tel: 885-6822
www.merrimanshawaii.com
Renowned Hawaiian chef Peter Merriman considers this his signature restaurant, which means the food is fresh, exciting, and delicious. Try the seared *ahi* or any of the braised meats, all of which are raised locally to the restaurant's specifications. Reservations essential. $$$

Sushi Rock
55-3435 Akone Pule Highway, Hawi
Tel: 889-5900
www.sushirockrestaurant.net

At Sushi Rock in Hawi.

There's no question that this small and quirky eatery serves up some of the best sushi on the entire island. Rolls change daily and often incorporate local ingredients with a twist – beef, lamb, or another type of meat. There's also a full bar (and a lengthy cocktail list). $$

Village Burger
67-1185 Mamalahoa Highway, Waimea
Tel: 885-7319
www.villageburgerwaimea.com
Burgers from this Parker Ranch Center eatery aren't just any old hamburgers; they're locally raised, grass-fed, hormone-free hamburgers. Toppings include local bacon, local avocadoes, and local cheese. Even the ice cream for the house shakes is made in town. $

North Kona/Kohala Coast

Brown's Beach House at the Fairmont Orchid Hawaii
1 North Kaniku Drive, Kohala Coast
Tel: 885-2000
www.fairmont.com/orchid
Every restaurant on Hawaii Island serves local seafood; few do it as expertly as Browns. Consider the Keahole lobster tails cooked with lilikoi Hawaiian vanilla bean gastrique. Other dishes incorporate daikon, ginger, lavender, and different local ingredients. $$$

South Kona

The Coffee Shack
83-5799 Mamalahoa Highway, Captain Cook
Tel: 328-9555
www.coffeeshack.com
Think of this diner as a Hawaiian spin on a traditional Greasy Spoon; it's only open for lunch and dinner, but breakfasts are huge and all of the breads are homemade. Beans

for the house coffee are grown on the mountainside directly below the lanai. **$**

Manago Hotel
82-6155 Mamalahoa Highway, Captain Cook
Tel: 323-2642
www.managohotel.com
T-shirts for this throwback restaurant boast that the place has the best pork chops in town, and that's no exaggeration. Meals come with rice for the table, as well as sides such as macaroni salad and a braised tofu and veggie dish. **$–$$**

Vibrant sushi platter.

KAUAI

East Shore

Art Café Hemingway
4-1495 Kuhio Highway, Kapa'a
Tel: 822-2250
www.artcafehemingway.com
What do you get when you mix a historic building with an Eastern European menu and homage to Ernest Hemingway? This café, which also displays work from local artists. Locals rave about the food and rant about the service. **$**

Caffe Coco
4-369 Kulio Highway, Kapa'a
Tel: 822-7990
This café, in a restored plantation set back from the highway, serves up an eclectic menu that includes pot-stickers, samosas, Greek salads, fresh fish, and soups. In nice weather, try to grab a seat in the garden out back. **$$**

Hamura Saimin
2956 Kress Street, Lihu'e
Tel: 245-3271
Saimin is the big draw at this downscale diner. The dish, a Hawaiian delicacy, essentially amounts to noodle soup, and it is said to have originated here. Save room for the eatery's other specialty: passion fruit chiffon pie. No credit cards. **$**

Hanama'ulu Restaurant, Tea House, Sushi Bar, and Robatayaki
3-4291 Kuhio Highway, Hanama'ulu
Tel: 245-2511
Tearooms featuring tatami-seating are the highlight of this no-frills, pan-Asian restaurant that has added to its list of expertise over the years. Popular dishes include ginger chicken, fried shrimp, and the robatayaki, which, essentially, comprises grilled meat and fish. **$**

Restaurant Kintaro
4-370 Kuhio Highway, Wailua
Tel: 822-3341

Tatami-mat seating is available at this Japanese restaurant that is a favorite among locals. Try the Bali Hai bomb, a roll of crab and smoked salmon, baked and topped with wasabi mayonnaise. Expect long lines on weekends. **$$**

North Shore

Bar Acuda
5-5161 Kuhio Highway, Hanalei
Tel: 826-7081
www.restaurantbaracuda.com
Tapas (small plates) such as whole-roasted tomato bruschetta and Spanish chorizo with grilled apples rule the menu at this unpretentious eatery in downtown Hanalei. Grab a seat on the tiny patio to dine under the stars. **$$$**

Postcards Café
5-5075A Kuhio Highway, Hanalei
Tel: 826-1191
www.postcardscafe.com
There really are postcards adorning the walls of this Hanalei café, which caters to vegans, vegetarians and meat-eaters alike. A local favorite: taro fritters, which often appear on the menu as a special. All deserts are made without refined sugar. **$$**

Tahiti Nui Restaurant and Cocktail Lounge
5-5134 Kuhio Highway, Hanalei
Tel: 826-6277
www.thenui.com
This Polynesian-themed restaurant and bar saw a huge spike in business after its star turn in *The Descendants*, the 2011 movie with George Clooney. There's live music nightly with Hawaiian slack-key guitar on Fridays. **$$**

South Shore

Beach House
5022 Lawai Road, Koloa
Tel: 742-1424

www.the-beach-house.com
Many say this is Kauai's best seafood restaurant – the lemongrass and kaffir-lime sea scallops are a local favorite. The setting also is a stunner, especially at sunset. Vegetarian menu available. Reservations essential. **$$$**

Brennecke's Beach Broiler
2100 Ho'one Road, Poipu
Tel: 742-7588
www.brenneckes.com
Portions are huge at this casual, busy bar with windows overlooking the beach. Burgers come with a veritable pile of fries and rib racks are longer than most human forearms. If you prefer just drinks, there are two Happy Hours every day. **$$**

Casa di Amici
2360 Nalo Road, Poipu
Tel: 742-1555
www.casadiamici.com
Classical piano music on Saturday nights makes the "House of Friends" a popular romantic destination. The food certainly packs them in, too; chefs make their own sausages, and risotto dishes that incorporate island produce always impress. **$$$**

Keoki's Paradise
2360 Kiahuna Plantation Drive, Koloa
Tel: 742-7534
www.keokisparadise.com
Food is almost secondary at this raucous restaurant, which is built to look like a Polynesian boathouse and boasts live music every night. Still, the list of seafood appetizers is always a good bet after a long day on Poipu Beach. **$$**

PRICE CATEGORIES

Price categories are for a meal for one, not including alcohol:
$ = below $25
$$ = $25–50
$$$ = above $50

ACTIVITIES

ATTRACTIONS, FESTIVALS, CHILDREN'S ACTIVITIES, SHOPPING AND WATERSPORTS

THE ARTS

Art always has been an important part of Hawaiian culture, and it is thriving today. Most of the modern emphasis is actually on traditional craft: *lei*-making, basket weaving, woodcarving, and the like. A surprising number of galleries on all four of the major islands display and promote traditional art. Still, at various galleries around the islands visitors can experience modern Hawaiian art, too – paintings and sculpture that are obviously inspired by nature, but in a more abstract way. Modern crafts and decorative arts are widely available too.

Art galleries

Art galleries can be found in just about every town on every island in the State of Hawaii. Here are a handful worth special mention.

Oahu
Jeff Chang Pottery & Fine Crafts
1200 Ala Moana Boulevard, Honolulu
Tel: 591-1440
Hundreds of artists are represented at this lovely store, which peddles items made from glass and pottery.
Louis Pohl Gallery
1111 Nu'uanu Avenue, Honolulu
Tel: 521-1812
www.louispohlgallery.com
Modern art reigns supreme at this gallery, which displays the work of local as well as visiting artists.

Maui
Lahaina Printsellers Ltd.
2435 Kaanapali Parkway, Kaanapali
Tel: 667-7617
www.printsellers.com

If you're looking for original antique maps, this is the place for you. The gallery also sells prints and reproductions of works pertaining to Hawaii and the Pacific.
Martin Lawrence Galleries
790 Front Street, Lahaina
Tel: 661-1788
www.martinlawrence.com
Art icons such as Picasso, Chagall, Miro, Haring, and Warhol are on display at this uber-upscale gallery in Lahaina.
Maui Crafts Guild
69 Hana Highway, Paia
Tel: 579-9697
www.mauicraftsguild.com
This is Maui's only artist cooperative. Resident artists make everything from pottery and baskets to glass and feather art. There's usually even some flower art.
Viewpoints Gallery
3620 Baladwin Avenue, Makawao
Tel: 572-5979
www.viewpointsgallerymaui.com
Co-owned by six local artists, this gallery has paintings, sculptures, photos, ceramics, and glass.

Kauai
Galerie 103
2829 Kalanikaumaka Road, Koloa
Tel: 742-0103
www.galerie103.com
International and local artists share wall space at this modern and sparsely decorated gallery, where a lot of work focuses on environmental issues.
Kapaia Stitchery
3-3551 Kuhio Highway, Lihu'e
Tel: 245-2281
www.kapaiastitchery.com
This "gallery" displays quilt work made by hand and machine. All of the quilts (and other stitched stuff) are for sale.

Kela's Glass Gallery
4-1354 Kuhio Highway, Kapa'a
Tel: 822-4527
www.glass-art.com
Glass vases, bowls, and other items are the specialty at this exquisite gallery on the main road in Kapa'a.

Hawaii Island
Ackerman Fine Art Gallery
54-3897 Akoni Pule Highway, Kapaa'u
Tel: 889-5971
www.ackermangalleries.com
The Ackerman family uses this gallery to peddle its art; painter Gary Ackerman's daughter, Alyssa, and her husband, Ronnie, run the shop.
Eclectic Craftsman
75-5744 Alii Drive, Kailua-Kona
Tel: 334-0562
Representing 60 different local artists, this shop features local art and crafts, including woodwork, paintings, and more.
Elements Jewelry & Fine Crafts
55-3413 Akoni Pule Highway, Hawi
Tel: 889-0760
www.elementsjewelryandcrafts.com
Jewelry is the star of the show in this quirky shop – necklaces and earrings made of silver and gold. Ceramics, paintings, and prints are on display and for sale, too.
Gallery of Great Things
65-1279 Kawaihae Road, Waimea
Tel: 885-7706
www.galleryofgreatthingshawaii.com
Great "things" at this gallery include quilts, sculptures, vintage kimonos, paintings, *koa*-wood furniture, etched glassware, and feather art.
Waipio Valley Artworks
Highway 240, Kukuihaele
Tel: 775-0958
www.waipiovalleyartworks.com
Local artists made the wooden bowls,

koa furniture, paintings, and jewelry on display at this gallery near the road down to the Waipio Valley.

Performance art

All four of the major Hawaiian Islands boast a year-round schedule of theater, dance, and other forms of performance art. Here are some places visitors can experience this type of cultural spectacle.

Oahu

Hawaii Theatre Center
1130 Bethel Street, Honolulu
Tel: 528-0506
www.hawaiitheatre.org
Fresh off a $22 million renovation, this *c*.1922 theater brings in acts of all shapes and sizes – choral music, theater, dance, and more. The place has been around so long, it's nicknamed the "Pride of the Pacific."

Maui

Maui Academy of Performing Arts
81 N. Church Street, Wailuku
Tel: 244-8760
www.mauiacademy.org
This non-profit performing arts group dates back to 1974 and has been producing great shows ever since. Recent performances have included *West Side Story* and *Macbeth*, to name a few.

Maui Arts & Cultural Center
1 Cameron Way, Kahului
Tel: 242-7469
www.mauiarts.org
This facility comprises a number of different venues for live music and dance, including the Yokouchi Pavilion, the A&B Amphitheater, and the 1,200-seat Castle Theater. Also on site: the free Schaeffer International Gallery, which brings in art exhibits from all over the world.

Warren & Annabelle's
900 Front Street, Lahaina
Tel: 667-6244
www.warrenandannabelles.com
Magic, singing, and general hijinks take center stage at this quirky spin on dinner theater in downtown Lahaina.

Kauai

Kauai Community College Performing Arts Center
3-1901 Kaumualii Highway, Lihu'e
Tel: 245-8352
Kauai.hawaii.edu/pac
Set back on the island's main community college campus, this venue hosts an annual concert music series, plays, musicals, and special events.

South Pacific Dinner Show
4331 Kauai Beach Drive, Lihu'e
Tel: 346-6500
www.southpacificofkauai.com
It makes perfect sense for the Kauai Beach Resort to perform the show that shouts out to Hanalei in the song "Bali Hai." This performance, which includes a buffet dinner for audience members, has been running since 2002.

Hawaii Island

Aloha Theatre Performing Arts Company
79-7384 Mamalahoa Highway, Kainaliu
Tel: 322-9924
www.alohatheatre.com
Community theater is at its island best at this company outside of Lihu'e. Recent performances have included Broadway musicals and plays.

Volcano Art Center
19-4744 Old Volcano Road, Volcano
Tel: 967-8222
www.volcanoartcenter.org
Locals drive from all over the island for concerts and dance performances at this local art center.

Movies

The islands have dozens of theaters that screen current movies, old-time cinema, and independently produced art films. Each of the main islands has its own film festival. In addition, on Oahu, the city government sponsors Sunset on the Beach (tel: 923-1094), open-air film screenings in Queen's Surf Beach Park, across from the Honolulu Zoo. Bring a blanket or folding chairs and enjoy the show.

CHILDREN'S ACTIVITIES

Hawaii is a great destination for families with young kids, and by far the biggest attraction for kids in Hawaii is the ocean. All beaches offer free access to all visitors all the time. However, few have lifeguards, so it's important to be aware that the waves and currents can be very dangerous. Surfing and windsurfing lessons are widely available in all the major tourist areas, and snorkeling and whale-watching cruises and kayaking excursions are offered everywhere. Beyond these pastimes, there are a number of other attractions and activities geared specifically toward children.

Children's museums

Honolulu is home to Hawaii's only formal children's museum, the **Hawaii Children's Discovery Center** (111 Ohe Street; tel: 524-5437; www.discoverycenterhawaii.org; Tue–Fri 9am–1pm, Sat–Sun 10am–3pm), has four major galleries filled with interactive exhibits that cover the history of the islands, geology, and modern-day culture.

Steam trains

In the olden days, steam trains helped the sugar cane industry grow. Though most of this industry now is gone, a handful of trains remain, affording families a great opportunity to experience the islands while riding the rails.

The most popular of these is Maui's **Sugar Cane Train** (tel: 661-0800; www.sugarcanetrain.com), which runs from just beyond the Ka'anapali Resort to just outside Lahaina. Along the way, guides explain a bit about the history of sugar cane in the islands, and about the rise and fall of the Lahaina, Ka'anapali, and Pacific Railroad.

A performer blows a ceremonial conch shell to begin the Kuhio Beach Hula Show in Waikiki, Oahu.

On Kauai, visitors also can ride steam trains at **Grove Farm** (tel: 245-3202; www.grovefarm.org), and at **Kilohana** (tel: 245-5608; www. kilohanakauai.com), both in Lihu'e.

On Oahu, the **Hawaiian Railway Society** (tel: 681-5461; www. hawaiianrailway.com) operates old steam trains on a track west of old 'Ewa. The non-profit society also runs the only Hawaiian Railroad museum in the state.

Theater

Save for a number of traveling performances that stop in Honolulu every year, the only child-themed theater in the islands is on Maui, at **The Maui Theatre** (878 Front Street, Lahaina; tel. 856-7900; www. mauitheatre.com). Here, the show 'Ulalena (www.ulalena.com) depicts the Hawaiian creation myth in song and dance. The hour-long show plays out like a Cirque du Soleil performance: graceful, compelling, and fun to watch.

Water-themed attractions

Because Hawaii is surrounded by water, the islands offer many water-themed attractions geared toward kids. Oahu has **Sea Life Park** (41-202 Kalaniana'ole Highway, at Makapu'u Point; tel: 259-2500; www.sealifeparkhawaii.com; daily 10.30am–5pm), which boasts a dolphin show and offers visitors the opportunity to swim with these amazing creatures too (reservations advised). Along the Kapi'olani waterfront is the **Waikiki Aquarium** (2777 Kalakaua Avenue; tel: 923-9741; www.waquarium.org; daily 9am–4.30pm), a facility that features the greatest collection of Hawaiian fish ever assembled. Elsewhere on the island, near Kapolei, **Wet 'N' Wild Hawaii** (400 Farrington Highway; tel: 674-9283; www.wetnwildhawaii.com; June through Sept daily 10.30am–dusk, Sept through May Thu–Mon times vary) serves up a tropical spin on the traditional water park, complete with slides and splashdown zones. On Maui, don't miss the **Maui Ocean Center** (193 Maalaea Road, Wailuku; tel: 270-7000; www. mauioceancenter.com; daily 9am–5pm (July–Aug until 6pm)). A walk through the facility takes you through Hammerhead Harbor, Turtle Lagoon, and the Marine Mammal Discovery Center, which boasts a stand-out exhibit on humpback whales.

Zoos

There's only one zoo of note in the Hawaiian Islands, and that's the **Honolulu Zoo** (151 Kapahulu Avenue; tel: 971-7171; www.honoluluzoo. org; daily 9.30am–4pm). This facility boasts everything from aardvarks and elephants to the endangered *nene* bird, which is indigenous to Hawaii. The zoo is located within walking distance from most Waikiki hotels.

FESTIVALS

For such a relatively small state, Hawaii has a host of festivals throughout the year. Some are more tourist-friendly than others; those we listed here. An up-to-date calendar of events can be accessed at www. gohawaii.com.

January

Hula Bowl
War Memorial Stadium, Maui
Second or third Saturday
Annual college all-star football game spotlighting the top senior players in the nation. Held on Oahu for 51 years, the game relocated to Maui in 1998 and is played at the 24,500-seat War Memorial Stadium.

Lunar New Year
Chinatown, Honolulu
Mid- to late January
A 15-day celebration starting on the day of the second new moon after the winter solstice. Drums, firecrackers, and traditional lion dances chase bad spirits out of homes and shops, clearing the way for a *kung hee fat choi* (Prosperous New Year).

Pro Bowl
Aloha Stadium, Honolulu
Last Sunday in January
Annual all-star football game featuring the top players from the National Football League. Held on Oahu at Aloha Stadium on the Sunday between the Conference Championship games and the Super Bowl.

February

Champions Skins Game
Grand Wailea Resort, Maui
1st weekend in February
Annual two-day golf event features four golf legends. Jack Nicklaus, Arnold Palmer, Lee Trevino, and Tom Watson are among past participants. www.championsskinswailea.com

Punahou Carnival
Manoa Valley, Honolulu
Early February

Largest and most popular school carnival in the state. Attractions include fruit jams, jellies, and other homemade local foods on sale; white elephant tent; art sale; games; rides.

Great Aloha Run
Honolulu area
President's Day (3rd Monday in February)
Annual 8.2-mile (13.2km) fun run to benefit Oahu charities. Begins at Aloha Tower and finishes at Aloha Stadium. www.greataloha.com

March

Hawaii International Sport Kite Championships
Kapi'olani Park, Waikiki
Early March
Kite-flying demonstrations and competitions featuring expert kite-flyers from around the world.

Honolulu Festival
Waikiki
Mid-March
A Waikiki parade is the highlight of this series of events that highlight links between Hawaii and Japan. www. honolulufestival.com

Prince Kuhio Festival
Kauai (various locations)
Late March
The birthday of Prince Jonah Kuhio Kalaniana'ole is a state holiday. On Kauai, where he was born, the celebration spans two weeks with parties and events in multiple locations. www.princekuhio.net

April

Celebration of the Arts
The Ritz-Carlton, Kapalua, Maui
Early April
Annual festival featuring hula and chant performances, art workshops, and demonstrations.

Merrie Monarch Festival
Hilo, Hawaii Island
Mid-April
A *ho'olaule'a*, arts and crafts fair, and a parade highlight the week-long hula festival, which honors King David Kalakaua. The Merrie Monarch hula competition is considered Hawaii's finest and most prestigious. www. merriemonarchfestival.org

May

***Lei* Day**
Statewide
May 1
Hawaiians celebrate May Day island-style – dressed in cheerful, printed *mu'umu'u* and *aloha* shirts, lots of *leis* (garlands) and smiles. Students

throughout the islands – notably at elementary school level – perform multi-ethnic dances and songs in full costume.

Maui Onion Festival
Ka'anapali, Maui
Early May
Food demonstrations (featuring the famous Maui onion), entertainment, and a Maui onion cook-off highlight this festival at Whaler's Village in Ka'anapali, Maui.

World Fireknife Dancing Championships
La'ie, Oahu
Mid-May
Hosted by the Polynesian Cultural Center, this annual competition features top fireknife dancers from around the world performing amazing feats with the traditional Samoan fireknife. Tel: 293-3333; www. worldfireknife.com

Molokai Ka Hula Piko
Papohaku Beach Park, Molokai
3rd Saturday of May
Annual festival celebrating the birth of the hula on Molokai; the event includes a sunrise ceremonial, hula and music performances, arts and crafts, and food booths

Honoka'a Western Weekend and Rodeo
Honoka'a, Hawaii Island
Late May
Annual Memorial Day festival with a rodeo, parade, ethnic foods, arts and crafts, entertainment, and country dance.

June

50th State Fair
Aloha Stadium, Honolulu
Early June
The state fair for the 50th state usually boasts Hawaiian quilt-making contests, local musicians and a rainbow of ethnic dances, produce and livestock shows, food booths, carnival rides and commercial booth displays, and specially scheduled entertainment.

Pan-Pacific Festival
Honolulu
Early June
Also known as the "Matsuri in Hawaii Festival," this event celebrates the cultures of Hawaii, Japan, and the Pacific. Cultural demonstrations and entertainment take place at various sites. www.pan-pacific-festival.com

King Kamehameha Celebration
Statewide
June 11
King Kamehameha Day honors Hawaii's great king who united all the Hawaiian Islands under single rule. On Oahu events include a lei-draping ceremony at the King Kamehameha Statue in downtown Honolulu. A similar ceremony is held at the "other" Kamehameha statue in Kapa'au, on Hawaii Island.

Hawaii State Farm Fair
Kualoa Ranch, Oahu
Mid-June
Midway rides, carnival games, food booths, agricultural exhibits, and entertainment are featured at this annual fair.

Kapalua Wine & Food Festival
Kapalua, Maui
Mid-June
This three-day affair gathers winemakers and chefs from around the globe and includes seminars, demonstrations, tastings, and spectacular evening galas. www. kapaluawineandfoodfestival.com

Pu'uhonua 'O Honaunau Festival
Pu'uhonua 'O Honaunau, Hawaii Island
Late June
This week-long celebration at one of Hawaii Island's most important monuments features traditional Hawaiian games, entertainment, food, and cultural demonstrations.

July

Makawao Rodeo
Makawao, Maui
July 4
For more than 50 years, this cowboy town in Upcountry Maui has celebrated America's Independence Day with an old-school rodeo. Traditional rodeo events are complemented by traditional Hawaiian dance.

Koloa Plantation Days
Koloa, Kauai
Mid-July
This week-long festival pays tribute to Hawaii's once-thriving sugar plantations. Entertainment includes sporting events, rodeo, cooking demonstrations, and a parade. www. koloaplantationdays.com

Queen Lili'uokalani Keiki Hula Competition
Neal Blaisdell Center, Honolulu
Mid-July
This annual statewide hula competition features Hawaii's top young hula students and crowns a hula champion.

Hawaii All-Collectors Show
Honolulu
Late July
Collectors of things Hawaiian (and even non-Hawaiian) should not miss this annual end-of-July production at the Neal Blaisdell Exhibition Hall.

Leis for sale in Honolulu.

Antique coins, postcards, dolls, toys, records, aloha shirts, and more are available for sale.

Bon Odori Dance Festival
Statewide
Late July and early August
Japanese Buddhists honor deceased ancestors during this festival of lively dance. Temples throughout the islands hold these dances (around 7.30pm to midnight), and visitors are invited to join. The season ends with the Floating Lanterns Festival at the Jodo Mission in Hale'iwa, on Oahu.

August

Hawaiian International Billfish Tournament
Kailua, Hawaii Island
Early August
Giant marlin are caught during this popular annual fishing tournament. www.hibtfishing.com

Pu'ukohola Heiau Cultural Festival
South Kohola, Hawaii Island
Mid-August
This annual cultural festival features demonstrations, food tastings, arts and crafts workshops, and hula performances.

September

Aloha Festivals
Statewide
Throughout September
Hawaii's biggest festival, with statewide, month-long celebrations encompassing beautiful floral parades, street parties, special ceremonies, and community events to celebrate the spirit of aloha. www. alohafestivals.com

Maui Marathon
Maui
Mid-September

Popular with runners from around the world, the 26-mile (42km) run starts at Kahului and ends at Ka'anapali. www.mauimarathon.com

A Day at Queen Emma's Summer Palace
Honolulu
September 21
Hawaiian arts and crafts, entertainment plus food highlight this annual tribute to Hawaii's Queen Emma, held at the home she once kept outside Honolulu.

October

Ironman World Triathlon
Kailua-Kona, Hawaii Island
Early October
Hard-core athletes come from all over the world to compete in a 2.4-mile (4km) open-ocean swim, followed by a 112-mile (180km) bike ride, and a full 26-mile (42km) marathon. The event is held annually on Hawaii Island. www.ironman.com

Molokai Hoe
Molokai and Oahu
Mid-October
This open-ocean, outrigger canoe race starts at Hale o Lono Harbor on Molokai and ends at Fort DeRussy Beach in Waikiki. The first finishers are expected around noon–12.30pm. www.molokaihoe.com

Hawaii International Film Festival
Oahu
Mid-November
Acclaimed two-week festival features international films and celebrates an "East meets West" theme. Generally held on Oahu during the second week of November, followed by a week-long stint on the neighboring islands. www.hiff.org

Lahaina Halloween
Lahaina, Maui
October 31
Hawaii's biggest Halloween party takes place on Halloween night in Lahaina, Maui, with costumed parades and plenty of raucous entertainment. www.lahainahalloween.com

November

Infinity Pacific Rim Jazz Festival
Hawaii Convention Center, Honolulu
Early November
Top international jazz musicians and vocalists gather in Waikiki for a four-day jazz celebration. www.pacificrimjazzfestival.com

Kona Coffee Cultural Festival
Kailua, Hawaii Island
Early November
Week-long festivities include judging of coffee recipes, Kona coffee-farm tours, and local parade and pageantry. www.konacoffeefest.org

Mission Houses Christmas Fair
Honolulu
Late November
Annual handcrafters' fair features more than 50 of Hawaii's finest craftspeople, a special display in Honolulu's 1831 Chamberlain House, and much free entertainment.

Surfing Contests
North Shore, Oahu
November through February
Winter means big waves on Oahu's North Shore. World championship contests are scheduled each year, dates determined by the condition of the surf. Check local newspapers for day-by-day announcements.

December

Honolulu Marathon
Honolulu
Early December
Every year, thousands of dedicated runners set off from the Aloha Tower on a marathon course along Oahu's south shore. The Honolulu marathon ends at Kapi'olani Park Bandstand. www.honolulumarathon.org

Na Mele O Maui Festival
Ka'anapali Resort, Maui
Early December
In honor of the Christmas holiday, several Ka'anapali hotels participate in a celebration of Hawaiian music and dance.

Pearl Harbor Day
Oahu
December 7
In memory of those who were killed during the Japanese bombing of Oahu on December 7, 1941, a memorial service is held every year at the USS *Arizona* Memorial.

NIGHTLIFE

Generally speaking, nightlife is an afterthought in Hawaii. Because the culture revolves around beaches, because many beachgoers prefer the surf in the early morning, before the wind and waves pick up, the vast majority of Hawaiians turn in early.

Still, it is possible to find hip bars and sleek nightclubs. In all of the major tourist areas, you can find musicians in venues ranging from hotel bars to intimate clubs. Check out local newspapers, their online entertainment listings, and, on Oahu, www.nonstophonolulu.com for the latest information.

Bars

Bars in Hawaii generally come in three flavors: swanky, dive, and tiki. Attire at the latter two is casual; for the swanky spots, you'll need to wear long pants. Here are some bars worth investigating.

Oahu

Breaker's Restaurant
66-250 Kamehameha Highway, Hale'iwa
Tel: 637-9898
www.breakersnsh.com
Surfers flock to this surf-themed bar, especially after surf competitions in the neighborhood. Benji Weatherly, the owner's son, is a professional surfer.

Mai Tai Bar
1450 Ala Moana Boulevard, Honolulu
Tel: 947-2900
www.maitaibar.com
This classic Tiki bar, on the fourth floor of the Ala Moana Center, has two nightly Happy Hours and live entertainment.

Nocturna Lounge
500 Ala Moana Boulevard, Honolulu
Tel: 521-1555
www.nocturnalounge.com
This hipster hot spot has a full bar, four karaoke suites, and video game consoles with all of the most popular social gaming titles.

The Study
The Modern, Waikiki
Tel: 943-5800
www.themodernstudy.com
Speakeasies are alive and well in the Pacific Islands, and this pricey-yet-hip hot spot, with its entrance hidden behind a bookcase in the lobby, is Exhibit A.

Maui

Ambrosia Martini Lounge
1913 S. Kihei
Tel: 891-1011
www.ambrosian
Open nightly
house musi
hand-crafte
might even

Charley's
142 Hana Hi
Tel: 579-945
www.charleysr
This classic
among loca
in the wave
play reggae, house, and other types of music.

Kauai

Duke's Barefoot Bar
3610 Rice Street, Lihu'e
Tel: 246-9599

www.dukeskauai.com
Happy Hours are "Aloha Hours" at this lively beachside bar in Nawiliwili on the island's East Side. Weekend nights feature live music, as well.

Trees Lounge
440 Aleka Place; Kapa'a
Tel: 823-0600
www.treesloungekauai.com
Live music, late-night dancing characterize the scene at this off-the-beaten-path bar. Closed Sundays.

Hawaii Island

Cronie's Bar & Grill
11 Waianuenue Avenue, Hilo
Tel: 935-5158
This divey sports bar is a favorite among locals.

Mask-querade Bar
75-5660 Kopiko Street, Kailua-Kona
Tel: 329-8558
www.themask-queradebar.com
One of Hawaii Island's most popular gay bars, this hard-to-find spot books drag shows, DJs, and weekend barbecues.

Dinner cruises and lu'aus

A number of cruise companies depart from major ports on all four major islands; some, however, are better than others. On Oahu, the **Alii Kai Catamaran** (tel: 954-8652; www.aliikaicatamaran.com) is a giant ship designed to look like an ancient Polynesian vessel. On Maui, check out the **Hula Girl Dinner Cruise** (tel: 665-0344; www.sailingmaui.com), a catamaran with a VIP lounge near the captain's fly bridge. Another option: **Teralani Sailing Charters** (tel: 661-1230; www.teralani.net), which operates a number of different ships catered by a local Italian restaurant. On Hawaii Island, the "Evening on the Reef Glass Bottom Dinner Cruise," from Blue Sea Cruises (tel: 331-8875; www.blueseacruisesinc.com), is designed around dolphin-spotting and sunset.

Without question, the best and most eclectic lu'aus in the state are at the **Polynesian Cultural Center** (tel: 293-3333; www.polynesia.com) in La'ie, on Oahu. A close second: the very traditional **Old Lahaina Lu'au** (tel: 667-1998; www.oldlahainaluau.com) in downtown Lahaina, on Maui. On Hawaii Island, don't miss the **Island Breeze Lu'au** (tel: 866-482-9775; www.islandbreezeluau.com), a Polynesian revue that includes Tahitian dancing and a fireknife performance. And on Kauai, **Smith's Tropical Paradise Lu'au** (tel: 821-6895; www.smithskauai.com) takes

place in a vast, private tropical garden overlooking a lagoon ringed with torches.

Live music

Whether you're looking to hear a slack-key guitarist or a rock 'n' roll concert from an international superstar, Hawaii also is a great place for experiencing live music. Honolulu is the best place to head for, with big-name concerts at such venues as the Hawaii Theatre (see page 301); top-class nightly music at Mai Tai Bar in the Ala Moana Center (see page 306); and the Lewers Lounge at the Halekulani Hotel (see page 286). Here are some more of the best venues statewide:

Oahu

The Dragon Upstairs
1038 Nu'uanu Avenue, Honolulu
Tel: 526-1411
www.thedragonupstairs.com
Hosts live jazz performances almost every night of the week.

Hawaii Opera Theatre
777 Ward Avenue, Honolulu
Tel: 596-7372
www.hawaiiopera.org
Known around town as HOT, this organization performs all operas in original language with projected English translation.

Waikiki Shell
2805 Monsarrat Avenue, Honolulu
Tel: 768-5400
www.blaisdellcenter.com/venues/waikiki-shell
Unique outdoor stage featuring artists like Jimmy Buffet and Jack Johnson against the dramatic Diamond Head backdrop. Possibly Hawaii's best venue on a moonlit night.

Maui

George Kahumoku Jr.'s Slack Key Show
Napili Kay Beach Resort, Lahaina
Tel: 669-3858
www.slackkeyshow.com
Grammy-winner George Kahumoku Jr. invites Hawaii's most renowned slack-key musicians to join him and play every Wednesday in the Aloha Pavilion at Napili Kai. The show is incredibly intimate. And the talent is off the charts.

Kauai

Kauai Concert Association
3-1901 Kaumualii Highway, Lihu'e
Tel: 245-7464
www.kauai-concert.org
This non-profit group puts together a concert series every year at the Kauai Community College

Performing Arts Center, and they always seem to attract a big-name artist or two.

Hawaii Island

Huggo's on the Rocks
75-5828 Kahakai Road, Kailua-Kona
Tel: 329-1493
www.huggos.com
People generally end up dancing in the sand at this club, where jazz, country, and rock bands perform weekly.

SHOPPING

Shopping in the Hawaiian Islands can be an all-consuming experience; with so many malls and so many boutiques, it will be hard to see everything that is on offer. Here's an inside look at what to buy, what not to buy and where to shop when you're out and about on the various islands.

What not to buy

As with any major tourist destination, Hawaii has shops and vendors that sell items they should not be selling. One of the offending items: black coral, which is harvested from the waters between Maui and Lanai and is believed to be rare. It also pays to inquire about the origin of many items advertised as "authentic" Hawaiian; upon investigation many of these items turn out to be manufactured in China or Indonesia.

What to buy

Typically Hawaiian goods range from Polynesian kitsch tiki gods with olivine stone eyes to fine Ni'ihau shell leis that may cost as much as $2,500 for four strands.

Aloha wear

Hawaii has its own fashions, the mu'umu'u and aloha shirt. The first mu'umu'u, designed and introduced by the early missionaries, was a loose, lengthy, high-necked, long-sleeved shroud. Because of variations in its style, mu'umu'u has come to refer to just about any casual smock, long or short, made of Hawaiian print fabric. The aloha shirt was first marketed in the 1930s by a Chinese tailor in Honolulu. Mu'umu'u and aloha shirts are sold and worn everywhere. Some island occasions, such as wedding receptions and dinner parties, specify "aloha attire" as the preferred mode of dress.

TRANSPORTATION • ACCOMMODATIONS • EATING OUT • ACTIVITIES • A–Z • LANGUAGE

Antiques

The notion of "antiques" means something different in Hawaii, which has only been a state for the better part of 60 years. Most "period" pieces date back to the time of monarchy, which lasted until 1893; these pieces include jewelery, furniture, and clothes. More modern "antiques" include Hawaiiana such as Pan-Am posters, 1950s-era suitcases, and hula girl paraphernalia.

Arts and crafts

Perhaps the most famous byproduct of Hawaii's burgeoning artisan scene is the appliqué quilt. This handiwork is available in countless artisan shops across the islands. Other arts and crafts products span the gamut from hand-woven baskets to hand-sewn garments, hand-carved bowls to hand-hewn fish spears.

Books

Every island has great bookstores, though independent stores are not too many. On Oahu, check out **BookEnds** (600 Kailua Road, Kailua; tel: 261-1996), an independent shop that specializes in children's books. On Maui, visit the **Maui Friends of the Library Used Book Store** (658 Front Street, Lahaina; tel: 667-2696; www.mfol.org), with a huge section reserved for new Hawaiiana books. On Hawaii Island, check out **Kona Bay Books** (74-5487 Kaiwi Street, Kona; tel: 326-7790; www.konabaybooks.com). Finally, on Kauai, try **Talk Story Bookstore** (3785 Hanapepe Road, Hanapepe; tel: 335-6469; www.talkstorybookstore.com).

Hawaiian instruments

Popular Hawaiian hula instruments include the *ipu*, *pu'ili* (slashed percussive bamboo sticks), *'uli'uli* (a feather-topped gourd rattle filled with seeds) and *'ili'ili* (small smooth stones used like castanets in a set of four). There are also the *hano* (nose flute) and *'ukulele*. All are available at island hula supply shops and some music stores. *Ipu* are tan-colored bottle gourds that are hollowed-out and dried and used as a drum, a hula instrument, or a food and water receptacle.

Leis

There are many variations on the traditional Hawaiian *lei* (garland). The tradition of stringing and wearing the brown and black-and-white *kukui* nuts, commonly called candlenuts, is still very popular. *Koa*-seed *leis* are also appealing, but most of these are

strung in the Philippines.
Small, rare shells are washed up onto the beaches of the privately owned island of Ni'ihau, where some of the 200-plus residents will gather and string them into *leis* or necklaces. There is a beautiful range of delicate, subtle colors. The *leis* are very expensive, and found only in upscale shops, especially on Kauai.
Feathers of birds such as the pheasant and peacock are made into attractive *leis* and hat bands. In ancient Hawaii, items made of feathers were reserved for royalty and high-ranking *ali'i*.

Local produce

Plums, cherries, mangos, guavas, apricots, lemons, and limes are salted and preserved in the form of sweet-sour pickles known as "crack seed." Introduced by the Chinese, these preserves have become a favorite snack treat in Hawaii. Shops specializing in these pickled seeds can be found downtown and in major suburban shopping areas.
For a sweeter tooth, tropical fruits such as guava, *poha*, mango, passion fruit, papaya, and coconut are made into unique, luscious spreads. Macadamia nuts are delicious roasted and eaten plain or chocolate-covered, this rich nut, grown and packaged in Hawaii, is true gourmet fare.

Photographs of old Hawaii

Peer into Hawaii's past. Leaf through the photo albums at the Hawaii State Archives (364 S. King Street, Honolulu; tel: 586-0329), in the 'Iolani Palace grounds. The archives are open Mon–Fri 9am–4pm. Copies are available but generally take up to two weeks for delivery (by mail). Or visit the archives at the Bernice Pauahi Bishop Museum (tel: 847-3500), by far the largest in the state with more than 500,000 images. Here, copies are more expensive, but the choice is greater.

Plant-based products, wood, and textiles

Tapa (bark cloth), properly called *kapa*, is made into popular items – place mats, wall-hangings, bags, and hats. However, the *tapa* for sale may not be Hawaiian *kapa*, but a related fabric made in Samoa and Tonga. The art of making real Hawaiian *kapa* was lost during the 19th century, but is now enjoying a revival with a new generation of artisans. *Lauhala* (pandanus), coconut fronds, makaloa sedge, and the rootlets of the *ieie* forest vine are used to weave mats,

Kona Coffee

Hawaii's own homegrown and roasted coffee beans are produced in the Kona region of Hawaii Island, on the only commercial coffee plantations in the United States. The resulting product has been accorded a gourmet status in international coffee-drinking circles. If you're a purist, stay away from the blends, which require only 10 percent Kona beans.

baskets, bowls, hats, and more.
Monkeypod, *koa*, and *milo* are three popular island woods used in the making of furniture, *calabashes* (large ceremonial bowls), and other fine wood creations. *Koa* and rosewood are also used to make quality guitars and *'ukuleles*.

Scrimshaw

This Pacific art came into its own in the 1800s when bored sailors on whaling vessels scratched pictures on whale teeth. Nowadays, a number of non-endangered materials are used, such as fossilized walrus tusk. Maui is a good place to look at and purchase scrimshaw; it also has the richest whaling history anywhere in Hawaii.

Sea shells

Arguably one of the best souvenirs from a beach-oriented place like Hawaii, these are free and come in a seemingly infinite number of shapes and sizes. Just don't take home too many; sea life need them too.

Surfboards

Custom-made fiberglass surfboards can be adapted to your height, weight, and personal taste in design by some of the finest board shapers in the world.

Where to shop

All the Hawaiian Islands, with the exception of less-developed Molokai and Lanai, offer endless retail possibilities, from shopping centers to surf shops to small-town treasures or chic resort boutiques. Here's a look at some of the larger shopping destinations on each of the major islands.

Oahu

Ala Moana Center, one of the largest open-air malls in the world, housing about 200 stores (including more than two dozen eateries) and covering 50 acres (20 hectares) across from

Ala Moana Park in Honolulu. Free island entertainment regularly takes place on the mall's centerstage (tel: 955-9517; www.alamoanacenter. com; Mon–Sat 9.30am–9pm, Sun 10am–7pm).

Aloha Tower Marketplace, located at Pier 9 near the downtown Honolulu business district. This harborside complex features an interesting array of shops and restaurants (tel: 566-2337; www.alohatower.com; Mon–Sat 9am–9pm, Sun 9am–6pm restaurants and bars close later). The adjacent Hawaii Maritime Center celebrates Hawaii's maritime heritage.

Chinatown, an integral part of downtown Honolulu and by far the most interesting shopping area in the islands. Watch noodles being made, take your ailments to an acupuncturist's or herbal medicine shop, choose from more than 30 restaurants, or visit the shops and galleries on side streets from Hotel Street. At night, a section of Hotel Street retains its sailors-on-liberty flavor, with strip joints and bars that should not be entered alone.

DFS Galleria Waikiki, 330 Royal Hawaiian Avenue, at the corner of Kalakaua Avenue in Waikiki. The nautically themed complex, complete with a multi-level aquarium, features stores including Hermes, Cartier, Michael Kors, and Marc Jacobs (tel 931-2655; www.dfsgalleria.com; daily 9am–11pm).

Downtown Honolulu, on Bishop Street, which was named after the islands' first banker and is today the financial center of Hawaii. All the major banks are here, along with airlines, restaurants, and shops. Every Friday there are entertaining free concerts at Tamarind Park, which spotlight the best Hawaiian, contemporary and jazz musicians. Business hours are 8am–5pm.

Kahala Mall, in the Kahala residential district just east of Diamond Head and Waikiki, home of the designer pizza and a movie complex (tel: 732-7736; www.kahalamallcenter.com; openings are staggered, beginning at 8.30am, most shops close at 9pm, although the supermarkets are open 24 hours).

Kapahulu Avenue, which ends in Waikiki, offers an interesting selection of shops that feature collectible Hawaiiana approximately 1 mile (1.5km) from the beach.

King's Village, 131 Ka'iulani Avenue, behind the Hyatt Regency Waikiki Beach Resort & Spa. This rambling, made-to-look-old split-level commercial complex takes its theme from the 19th century, right down to a changing of the King's Guard every night at 6.15pm (daily 10am–11pm).

Pearlridge Center, 1005 Moanalua Road, in 'Aiea. A massive upscale mall that actually is the largest enclosed shopping space in the state (tel: 488-0981; www.pearlridgeonline. com; Mon–Sat 10am–9pm, Sun 10am–6pm).

Royal Hawaiian Shopping Center, along Kalakaua Avenue in Waikiki, offering a wide variety of shops and cafés on three levels and daily entertainment at its central courtyard (tel: 922-2299; www.royalhawaiian center.com; daily 10am–10pm).

Waikele Center, 94–790 Lumiaina Street, Exit 7 off H-1, about 15 minutes west of Honolulu. Home to 50 outlets including Calvin Klein, Ralph Lauren, and the like – discounts abound at the factory outlet shops (tel: 671-6977; www. waikelecenter.com; Mon–Sat 9am–9pm, Sun 10am–6pm).

The Ward Centers, on Auahi Street in Kakaako, near Waikiki. With Hawaii's largest multiplex (16 screens) and trendy shops and restaurants like Dave & Buster's (games and dining), the complex is a popular destination in and of itself. 135 stores, 40 restaurants (tel: 591-8411; www. wardcenters.com;.daily 10am–10pm, Sun 10am–7pm).

Maui

Kahului is the focus of Maui's urban commerce, but don't overlook the street shopping of historic Wailuku, just above Kahului, and of Makawao and Pa'ia, toward Upcountry. As nearly everybody visiting Maui stays in either the Wailea or Ka'anapali resorts, those are rich with shopping opportunities, mostly within the resorts. Lahaina lives off both shopping and eating; wander its streets to find an abundance of temptations.

Lahaina Cannery Mall, 1221 Honoapiilani Highway. West Maui's most comprehensive indoor shopping mall, north end of Lahaina (tel: 661-5304; www.lahainacannerymall. com; Mon–Sat 9.30am–9pm, Sun 9.30am–7pm).

Queen Ka'ahumanu Center, 275 Ka'ahumanu Avenue, Kahului. Maui's largest mall with over 75 shops and eateries (tel: 877-3369; www. queenkaahumanucenter.com; Mon–Sat 9.30am–9pm, Sun 10am–5pm).

The Shops at Wailea, 3750 Wailea Alanui. An elegant upgrade of the old shopping village, with dozens of shops and restaurants in a multi-level mall (tel: 877-3369; www. queenkaahumanucenter.com; daily 9.30am–9pm).

Whaler's Village, Ka'anapali Resort, West Maui. This outdoor venue includes more than 50 shops, several popular restaurants on the beach, a whaling museum and a 40ft (12-meter) sperm whale skeleton (tel: 661-4567; daily 9.30am–10pm).

Hawaii Island

The commercial centers of Hilo and Kailua are the obvious choices here. Historic downtown Hilo is small, compact and undergoing a revival, and is good for quiet walking and browsing. Kona's waterfront thrives on tourism, and the offerings range – with the emphasis on low-end souvenirs – from T-shirts and postcards to at times dubious art. The resort hotels of Kohala – Mauna Lani, Waikoloa, Mauna Kea – have what those with gold cards are looking for. Smaller towns such as Holualoa, Honoka'a, Volcano, and Waimea are great places to find artisans who exhibit work in shops and galleries. Hanapepe is the island's best destination for art.

Kings' Shops, Waikoloa Beach Resort, South Kohala. Hawaiiana exhibits throughout this shopping complex complement the nearly 40 shops and restaurants (tel: 885-8811; daily 9.30am–9.30pm).

Prince Kuhio Plaza, 111 East Puainako Street, Hilo. Largest enclosed mall on the Big Island (tel: 959-3555; www.princekuhioplaza.com; Mon–Thu 10am–8pm, Fri–Sat until 9pm, Sun until 6pm).

Kauai

In keeping with its personality, Kauai's shopping is lower-key than other islands', but pleasurable and often unique. Shopping centers are found in Lihu'e, Po'ipu, Koloa, Kapa'a, Princeville, and Hanalei on the North Shore. Shopping tends to be decentralized, with small, quality pockets of stores.

Coconut Marketplace, on the main highway, near Kapa'a. Open-air shopping mall with 70 assorted shops, a good selection of casual restaurants and a movie theater (tel: 822-3641; www.coconutmarketplace. com; Mon–Sat 9am–9pm, Sun 10am–6pm). There's also a farmers' market on Tuesday mornings.

Kilohana, Route 50, 1.5 mile (2km) north of Lihu'e. Plantation estate with high-quality retail shops, galleries, and an old sugar cane train (tel: 245-

TRANSPORTATION

ACCOMMODATIONS

EATING OUT

ACTIVITIES

A – Z

LANGUAGE

5608; www.kilohanakauai.com; daily 9.30am–9.30pm).
Kukui Grove, Highway 50, near Lihu'e. Kauai's largest mall (tel: 245-7784; www.kukuigrovecenter.com; Mon–Thu & Sat 9.30am–7pm, Fri until 9pm, Sun until 6pm).
Po'ipu Shopping Village, 2360 Kiahuna Plantation Drive. Pleasant outdoor mall with shops and restaurants. On weekends the mall also brings in live entertainment (tel: 742-2831; www.poipushoppingvillage.com; Mon–Sat 9am–9pm, Sun 10am–7pm).

SIGHTSEEING TOURS

A number of specialty tour operators offer themed sightseeing tours in and around the Hawaiian Islands. There are tours that serve just about every interest. (For more general tour operators, see page 314.)

For birders, **Field Guides** (tel: 800-728-4953; www.fieldguides.com) has a three-island, 11-day guided birdwatching trip that stops at Oahu, Kauai, and Hawaii Island. **Victor Emanuel Nature Tours** (tel: 800-328-8368; www.ventbird.com) offers two eight-night trips to the same three islands.

Road Scholar (tel: 800-454-5768; www.roadscholar.org), formerly known as Elderhostel, offers trips that look into the culture, history, and beauty of the Islands.

Hiking enthusiasts will love the five-night hiking tour to Kauai and Maui from The World Outdoors (tel: 800-488-8483; www.theworldoutdoors.com).

SPORTS

If you need a diversion from lounging on the beach or frolicking in the surf,

Surfing at Waipi'o Valley, Big Island.

Hawaii offers a sizable menu of both spectator sports and participant sports. Opportunities for the former are concentrated on Oahu, where most of the state's population is clustered. As for participant sports – you can do those just about anywhere.

Participant sports

Thanks to great weather and a nearly perfect climate, Hawaii is an ideal place to play sports oneself. Tennis is popular among locals and visitors alike and there are tennis courts in many cities and towns across the islands. Running is another common sport on the Hawaiian Islands; Maui, Oahu, Kauai, and Hawaii Island all have annual marathons (Hawaii Island also is home to the Ironman triathalon). Cycling is another sport that is popular among residents and visitors to the Islands.

Golf

Without question, the biggest participant sport in Hawaii is golf. At last count, the islands were home to more than three dozen 18-hole courses; some are public, the very best of the bunch, however, are private. Here, are some fan favorites where you can spend an afternoon with the tees.
The Challenge at Manele
1 Manele Road, Lanai City, Lanai
www.fourseasons.com
Club at Hokulia
81-6636 Pu'u Oahu Place, Kealakekua, Hawaii Island
www.hokuliaclub.com
The Experience at Koele
1 Keomoku Highway, Lanai City, Lanai
www.fourseasons.com
Gold Course at Wailea Golf Club
100 Wailea Golf Club Drive, Wailea, Maui
www.waileagolf.com

Hualalai Golf Course
100 Kalpulehu Drive, Kailua-Kona, Hawaii Island
www.hualalairesort.com
Mauna Kea Golf Course
62-100 Mauna Kea Beach Drive, Kohala Coast, Hawaii Island
www.princeresortshawaii.com
North Course at Mauna Lani Resort
68-1310 Mauna Lani Drive, Kohala Coast, Hawaii Island
www.maunalani.com
Plantation Course at Kapalua Resort
2000 Plantation Club Drive, Kapalua, Maui
www.kapalua.com/golf
Poipu Bay Golf Course
2250 Ainako Street, Koloa, Kauai
www.poipubaygolf.com
Prince Golf Course at Princeville
5-3900 Kuhio Highway, Princeville, Kauai
www.princeville.com

Spectator sports

Because of its location in the middle of the ocean, Hawaii doesn't have professional (or even semi-professional) sports teams. This means that locals' passion for the University of Hawaii college sports teams runs high. In particular, the Fighting Rainbows football team attracts huge crowds to **Aloha Stadium** in Honolulu. That stadium also is the site of the NFL's Pro Bowl, that sport's all-star game that takes place the week before the Super Bowl.

Not surprisingly, surfing is a huge spectator sport in Hawaii. Especially in winter, when the waves are cranking, fans flock to watch pros shred it up off beaches on Maui, Kauai, and Oahu. Perhaps the biggest spectator-oriented celebration of this sport is the **Vans Triple Crown of Surfing**, held on Oahu's North Shore every November and December. The three events that comprise the "triple crown" are: the Reef Hawaiian Pro in Haleiwa, the Vans World Cup of Surfing on Sunset Beach, and the Billabong Pipe Masters on Pipeline. For more information, visit www.vanstriplecrownofsurfing.com.

Outdoor activities

Hawaii is an adventure-lover's paradise, with dozens of outdoor activities available year-round. Among the activities available to visitors: cycling, mountain biking, fishing, hiking, horseback riding, paragliding, wildlife-watching, surfing, kayaking, and snorkeling. The website www.

TRANSPORTATION

gohawaii.com has great resources for outfitters who can help you try out all of these activities. Here are some top suggestions to get you started.

Adventure sports

Everything from paragliding to ziplining qualifies as adventure sports these days. Also on the list: sky diving and "flight-seeing." On Oahu, one of the most unique outfitters is **Stearman Bi-Plane Rides** (tel: 637-4461; www.stearmanbiplanerides.com), which takes thrill-seekers up in c.1941 biplanes. On Kauai, check out the Na Pali Coast from the air on a flight-seeing tour with **Wings Over Kauai** (tel: 635-0815; www.wingsoverhawaii.com). On Hawaii Island, float on an inner-tube through the irrigation ditches of old sugar cane fields with **Kohala Ditch Adventures** (tel: 889-6000; www.kohaladitchadventures.com). Finally, on Maui, fly like an eagle with Proflyght Paragliding (tel: 874-5433; www.paraglidemaui.com), which offers tandem jumps off the slopes of Mount Haleakala.

A growing number of outfitters even offer helicopter flight-seeing. Blue Hawaiian (tel: 800-745-2583; www.bluehawaiian.com) offers trips on all four of the major islands.

Birdwatching

For birders, Hawaii literally is a dream come true; the islands are home to some tropical birds found nowhere else on Earth. The best spots to see feathered friends in their natural habitats include the Na Pali Coast and Kilauea Point National Wildlife Refuge on Kauai, and the Kamakou Preserve on Molokai. The latter spot is home to the Molokai thrush and Molokai creeper, two species that only can be found on Molokai. **The Nature Conservancy** (tel: 800-628-6860; www.nature.org) offers guided birding trips throughout the year.

Cycling

It's no secret that public roads across Hawaii offer some of the most spectacular (and, at times, challenging) terrain in the US. But Hawaii is famous for another kind of cycling, as well: down the slopes of a volcano. This pastime is perhaps most popular on Maui, where a number of outfitters lead early-morning trips down the slopes of Haleakala. One of the best is **Bike Maui** (tel: 888-922-2453; www.bikemaui.com), which sells trips that include pick-up and drop-off from their store in Haiku, as well as a bike and helmet rental for the day.

Fishing

Hawaii is world-famous for big-game fishing, especially for catches taken off the Kona Coast of the Big Island. World-class fishing tournaments held there each summer draw competitive game fishermen from across the globe. One of the biggest is the Hawaii International Billfish Tournament, held every summer. For visitors who aren't competing in the tournament, outfitters offer charter boats with staff that will bait lines and clean fish you decide to keep. One outfitter to try: **Sea Wife Charters** (tel: 329-1806; www.seawifecharters.com).

Other islands offer fishing charters also depart from Lahaina and Ma'alaea on Maui, and Kewalo Basin on Oahu.

Hiking

You could hike a different trail every day for a year on the Hawaiian Islands, and probably still have a few more months' worth after that. For visitors who'd rather not go it alone, **Hawaiian Walkways** (tel: 800-457-7759; www.hawaiianwalkways.com) offers a number of guided hikes in various spots around Hawaii Island.

Horseback riding

Cowboys were brought to the Islands in the 1860s to corral a bunch of wild cattle and they never left. Today, the cowboy lifestyle remains at various ranches around the islands, and visitors can sample it first-hand on horseback rides. On Maui, **Piiholo Ranch** (tel: 270-8750; www.piiholo.com) offers two- and four-hour trips around its Upcountry ranch. On Hawaii Island, look to take a tour at **Parker Ranch** (tel: 885-7311; www.parkerranch.com), the largest in the state. On Oahu, horseback tours at **Kuoloa Ranch** (tel: 237-7321; www.kualoaranch.com) include cultural history. Finally, on Kauai, traverse river, meadow, palm garden, and mountainside on a ride with **Silver Falls Ranch** (tel: 828-6718; www.silverfallsranch.com).

Water sports

Considering Hawaii is surrounded by water, it's no surprise that the islands are a great place to engage in water sports.

Take windsurfing, for example. This sport, which adds a sail to a thick and long surfboard, is popular at Kailua Beach on Oahu and Ho'okipa Beach on Maui, and can be learned in a variety of windsurfing schools.

Kiteboarding is another sport that locals seem to love. The sport is like windsurfing, only the board is smaller (think snowboard-size), so athletes can do flips and other tricks. **Kiteboarding School of Maui** (tel: 873-0015; www.ksmaui.com), located in Kahului, was the first kiteboarding school in the world.

Diving also is incredibly popular in Hawaii. While the diving is not equal to that in Fiji or Palau, it is quite good and often unique, especially around Hawaii Island, which is too young for a decent coral reef but which has lots of interesting underwater lava formations. The waters are usually warm, although in winter a full wetsuit is recommended, and the experience of swimming with the fish is like nothing else on earth. One outfitter that serves Hanauma Bay on Oahu **Hanauma Bay Dive Tours** (tel: 256-8956 www.hanaumabaydivetours.com).

Snorkeling also is a favorite pastime in the islands. On Maui, a plethora of outfitters offer trips to places such as Molokini to snorkel; **Pride of Maui** (tel: 242-0955; www.prideofmaui.com) is among the most reputable. Just rent a snorkel set (flippers, fins, mask, snorkel) from **Snorkel Bob's** (www.snorkelbob.com) and swim out from any beach with a reef.

One other water sport worth trying is kayaking. River kayaking is limited mostly to Kauai, particularly on the Hanalei River. **Kauai Kayak** (tel: 826-9844; www.kauaikayak.com), runs trips up the Hanalei daily. Ocean kayaking is found everywhere; popular excursions include multi-day paddles along the Na Pali Coast of Kauai and the north coast of Molokai.

Whale-watching

Every winter, when the waters around Hawaii become infested with humpback whales, watching the leviathans in their natural environment becomes the No.1 priority for visitors of every age. The best place to observe these animals is Maui, and a handful of whale-watch outfitters operate out of Lahaina and Ma'alaea harbors. Ultimate Whale Watch (tel: 667-5678; www.ultimatewhalewatch.com) boasts some of the fastest boats; because the outboard inflatables are so sleek, it usually takes less than 15 minutes to get from slip to whales. Another worthwhile outfitter is the Pacific Whale Foundation (tel: 800-942-5311; www.pacificwhale.org); they operate large motor vessels off both Lahaina and Ma'alaea, and naturalists on board the vessels are generally knowledgeable.

ACCOMMODATIONS   EATING OUT   ACTIVITIES   A – Z   LANGUAGE

A – Z

A HANDY SUMMARY
OF PRACTICAL INFORMATION

A

Admission charges

The typical admission fee to museums or other public buildings in Hawaii, and also to state or county parks, is $4–5 per adult, half that for children (though the maximum age for half-price tickets can range from 12 to 17). The two national parks, Haleakala on Maui and Hawaii Volcanoes on Hawaii Island, charge $10 each, but the fee covers all passengers in a single vehicle. The only charges that will make a serious impact on your budget are likely to be those for commercial tourist attractions, and especially so on Oahu, where the very cheapest adult admission to the Polynesian Cultural Center costs $40, and an adult entrance to Sea Life Park is $30.

Animals

Hawaii is free of rabies, snakes, and poison ivy, and state officials work hard to keep it that way. Incoming animals are placed in quarantine for 120 days at the owner's expense, although recent legislation now permits dogs and cats that meet certain pre- and post-arrival requirements to be quarantined for only 30 days.

B

Budgeting for your trip

Broadly speaking, Hawaii ranks at the expensive end of American vacation destinations. Prices are generally high, as so much of what is consumed in the islands has to be shipped there from across the Pacific

or beyond. In addition, many tourists are happy to pay premium rates for a once-in-a-lifetime holiday in paradise. However, it is possible to keep costs down. The finest hotels tend to charge at least $250 per room per night, and often double that. For pretty good accommodations close to the sea, it's perfectly possible to pay $125–150 in a hotel, or perhaps $100 for a rented condo. All the islands hold significantly cheaper options too, well worth considering if you expect to spend most of your time exploring.

Only on Oahu is it realistic to think you won't need a car; typical rental rates would be $350–400 per week for a compact vehicle. Gas isn't cheap, but you won't use all that much, because you can't drive very far on such small islands. Taxi fares vary greatly from island to island, but because most of the major airports are at least 10–15 miles from major tourist destinations, plan on spending $30–50 to travel to your destination by taxi. Finally, ticket prices for bus travel vary from island to island but no transit fees exceed $3 per ride.

The perfect climate for sunbathing – in moderation.

The average visitor spends about $30 per day on food and drink; even if you buy and prepare your own meals, it's hard to go much lower than say $20 per day, while at the other end of the spectrum there are plenty of fine-dining restaurants charging $50 or more for a single meal. Average beers cost anywhere from $3 to $5 per pint; the average glass of house wine ranges from $6 to $12 (or $15 at posh restaurants).

You'll never have to pay to go on the beach and will rarely have to pay to access the islands' best hiking trails. Still, prices for most kinds of commercial activity – a snorkel- or whale-watching cruise, a bus tour, a submarine ride, a guided hike, or bike ride – also tend to be high.

C

Children

Unless otherwise specified (or unless you're heading to a bar), most places in the Hawaiian Islands are child-friendly and actually encourage families to visit together. Many restaurants have children's menus and offer young kids crayons when they sit down. Many attractions charge reduced-price admission fees for children. Also, most luxury hotels will recommend babysitting services for a (steep) fee.

Private and independent babysitting services exist on every island and many travelers use them without incident. If you opt to reserve a child-minder through this type of service, be aware of minimum fees; most will not book unless you can guarantee at least four hours of work.

Climate and weather

There are seasons in sub-tropic Hawaii, it just takes time to recognize them. Rarely does the mercury drop below 60°F (15°C), nor go higher than about 90°F (32°C). The surrounding sea and northeasterly trade winds are a natural air-conditioning system. However, when the trade winds stop, and less frequent southerly winds take over, the result is often sticky and humid.

Certain areas on each island – usually on the windward side of mountains – receive more rainfall than others. One of the wettest spots on Earth is Mount Wai'ale'ale on Kauai, which has been drenched by as much as 486ins (12,340mm) of rain in a year.

Sometimes during volcanic eruptions on the Big Island, a smoky pall lingers over the islands for several days, especially in the Kona area. Islanders call this volcanic haze "vog," or volcanic smog. People suffering from asthma or other respiratory conditions may wish to take extra precautions during "voggy" weather.

Seasons

During the dry season (April to October) most of Hawaii experiences balmy 73–88°F (23–31°C) weather and only intermittent rain. In higher places such as Upcountry and Haleakala on Maui, and Koke'e on Kauai, temperatures range from 48°F to 72°F (9–22°C). In the wet season (November to March), temperatures are cooler, ranging from 65°F to 83°F (18–28°C). It also rains more consistently during this time of year (though few rainstorms in the islands ever last for more than an hour or two). In wet season, it's a good idea to bring a jacket for cold and rainy nights. In mountainous parts of the Big Island the average temperature

Hawaii Climate Chart

Maximum temperature
Minimum temperature
— Rainfall

drops to 31°F–58°F (-1–14°C) during the winter and at night. Snow falls on Mauna Kea (and sometimes Haleakala on Maui) in the winter, so bring warm clothing if you intend to tour these areas.

While sunbathing is a common activity here, don't overdo it. Slowly create a tolerance for Hawaii's strong sunlight by taking no more than 30 minutes of direct sun exposure the first day, 40 minutes the second day, 50 minutes the third day and so on. To prevent sunburn, be sure to wear sunscreen and keep applying it – you will find instructions on use on the container.

Flash floods

In the mountain areas, intense rain can cause flash floods. If you are hiking, take care during heavy rains as flash floods can occur without warning. If a flash flood watch has been issued by the National Weather Service, be alert: flooding is possible. A warning means that flooding is imminent or already occurring. If you are in a flood-prone area, get to higher ground immediately.

Hurricanes

Hurricanes are infrequent in Hawaii, but when they do touch the islands, they generally hit hard. Take all warnings seriously. The hurricane season is from June through November. When the civil defense sirens sound, tune to local radio or television stations for emergency disaster instructions. Stay indoors during high winds, and evacuate areas that may flood. Evacuation orders by authorities must be followed at all times.

Tsunamis (tidal waves)

Earthquakes, particularly on Hawaii Island, sometimes forebode a *tsunami*, the correct term for a

seismic or tidal wave. Earthquakes elsewhere, including Alaska, can send a *tsunami* to Hawaii. They can occur with little warning or time for preparation. When a *tsunami* warning is issued, leave coastal low-lying areas immediately.

Crime and safety

Hawaii has earned a reputation for hospitality and all the good cheer that the word *aloha* implies. However, travelers should be warned that all types of crime – including burglaries, robberies, assaults, and rapes – do occur on the islands. To avoid them, follow the usual precautions as when traveling anywhere else. Use common sense. Don't carry jewelry, large amounts of cash, or other valuables. In areas far from population centers, car break-ins and beach thefts of unattended personal property are becoming common, even at popular tourist sites.

If your hotel has a safe in the room, it is advisable to use it.

Customs regulations

Travelers from the mainland United States to Hawaii are not eligible for duty-free shopping, but travelers from other nations are. There is no limit to the amount of money travelers are allowed to bring into Hawaii – or any part of the United States, for that matter – but any amount exceeding $10,000 requires a formal report with US Customs.

In order to prevent the spread of fruit flies and other hazardous plant insects and disease, no fruit, plants, or live snails from the mainland are allowed to be brought into Hawaii, and no fruit, plants, or live snails from Hawaii are allowed to be brought back to the mainland. Airline passengers must pass through inspection stations to make sure they comply with these rules.

D

Disabled travelers

Hawaii is very well geared towards meeting the needs of disabled travelers. Download detailed reports on facilities from the website of the State of Hawaii Disability and Communication Access Board (tel: 586-8121; health.hawaii.gov/dcab). Specific information on Hawaiian hotels is also available from Access–Able (www.access–able.com). Many vehicles on public transportation networks on Oahu and Maui are adapted for travelers with disabilities.

E

Emergencies

Hawaii has its own response units, and outposts of major national responders as well. In the event of emergencies, there are a number of options to call for help:
American Red Cross, tel: 734-2101
Coast Guard Search and Rescue, tel: 800-552-6458
Dental emergency service, tel: 944-8863
Fire, Police, Ambulance, tel: 911
Lifeguard Service, tel: 922-3888
Poison Center, tel: 941-4411
Sex Abuse Treatment Center, tel: 524-7273
Suicide and Crisis Center, tel: 832-3100

Embassies and consulates

There aren't many embassies in Hawaii – most of the formal diplomatic outposts are on the mainland, in Los Angeles, or in San Francisco. Still, the islands are home to a number of consulates:
Australia, tel: 524-5050
Japan, tel: 543-3111
Korea, tel: 595-6109
Philippines, tel: 595-6316
Taiwan, tel: 595-6347

Electricity

Standard US 110-120 volts, 60 cycles AC. Large hotels usually are able to provide voltage and plug converters.

Etiquette

All etiquette rules for the mainland United States apply to the Hawaiian Islands as well. In addition, it is custom in Hawaii to remove shoes before entering someone's private home. Furthermore, when addressing elderly women, it is customary to say, "Mama." Finally, it's worth noting that islanders can be lax about time, especially when going on dates and to meetings outside of strictly commercial business circles. This habit of being "fashionably late" by around 10 minutes is generally known as being on "Hawaiian time."

G

Gay and lesbian travelers

Hawaii always has been a popular spot among gay and lesbian travelers, and the destination became even more gay-friendly when the state legislature legalized same-sex marriage in 2013. Since this historic change, many accommodations have added gay-friendly packages and special deals for same-sex couples seeking to plan destination weddings. Some of the properties that were gay friendly before the new law include the Cabana at Waikiki on Oahu (www. cabana-waikiki.com), the Sunseeker Resort on Maui (www.mauisunseeker. com), and the Mahina Kai B&B on Kauai (www.mahinakai.com).

H

Health and medical care

Most of the larger hotels have a physician on call. Other medical services can be obtained at hospitals and/or clinics, which are prevalent on every island except Lanai and Molokai. At bigger hospitals, the quality of care is superb. At some of the smaller clinics and medical outposts, care may be less so. It is always prudent to take out travel insurance that covers medical issues; there is no free health care in the United States.

For prescription medicine, there are pharmacies located in most towns around the islands. In larger towns, at least one pharmacy usually is open 24 hours. Pharmacies only are necessary to fill prescriptions; all supermarkets (and many corner markets) in the United States sell a sampling of over-the-counter medications.

I

Internet

Internet access is widely available throughout Hawaii. Upscale hotels invariably offer high-speed access from guest rooms (though usually for a fee of anywhere from $10 to $15 per day), while most resorts offer free Wi-fi in their respective lobbies. Free Wi-fi also is available at most coffee shops. All state libraries and most university libraries provide free access and these days, a number of other

types of commercial enterprises – from restaurants to boutiques – also offer free Wi-fi.

M

Maps

If you are doing any serious exploring or adventuring, don't rely on the free maps distributed by hotels or rental-car agencies. By far the best maps of the Hawaiian Islands are published by the University of Hawaii, for around $5 each and are available at most island bookstores. If you need detailed hiking maps, then make a visit to the state parks office in Honolulu, or inquire at ranger stations at Haleakala or Hawaii Volcanoes national parks.

Media

Newspapers

Hawaii has a handful of island daily and weekly newspapers. On Oahu, the main daily is the *Honolulu Star-Advertiser*; this is the de facto daily for other islands as well. Neighbor islands also have their own daily newspapers, with circulation restricted to that specific island. These papers publish wire copy about state and national stories, but have the feeling of community newspapers (because their respective readerships are so small). A variety of other newspapers are published by ethnic groups, the military, religious organizations, and by the tourism and business industries. The biggest weekly in the islands is the *Honolulu Weekly*. On Maui, *Maui Time* has amassed quite a following for the way it covers entertainment news. The Associated Press maintains a bureau in Honolulu to cover both Hawaii and the areas around the Pacific.

Radio

Honolulu's listeners have some 30 radio stations to listen to; there are fewer stations elsewhere on Oahu and on other islands. Hawaii Public Radio news and fine arts can be found on KHPR 88.1 in Honolulu; KKUA 90.7 on Maui, Molokai, and Lanai; and KANO 91.1 in Hilo. Hawaii Public Radio talk and music can be found on KIPO 89.3 in Honolulu; KIPM 89.7 on Maui, Molokai and Lanai; and KIPL 89.9 on Kauai. ESPN sports radio is KKEA 1420 AM. KHUI (99.5 FM) and KINE (105.1 FM), both in Honolulu, broadcast both contemporary and traditional Hawaiian music. Listings

General store on Maui.

in the local newspapers give relevant frequencies.

Television

There are more than 10 broadcast television channels that originate in the state of Hawaii. These include channels 2 (KHON-FOX); 4 (KITV-ABC); 5 (KFVE); 9 (KGMB-CBS); 11 (KHET-PBS); and 13 (KHNL-NBC). For broadcasts originating on Oahu (in Honolulu), relay transmitters serve the neighbor islands, while private companies provide cable TV programming by subscription only. Most of the other islands have their own local access channels. The majority of moderate-to-good hotels offer cable viewing to guests, showing a vast array of channels and, in a separate facility, first-run movies.

Money

Hawaii uses standard US currency and coins in all denominations. $1 = 100 cents. All major credit cards are accepted, including American Express, Visa, MasterCard, and Discover. Most car rental companies require a credit card. Cash machines (ATMs) are everywhere, especially at banks and shopping centers; ATMs accept bank cards from the mainland (and abroad) and are accessible 24 hours a day.

Currency exchange

Currency conversion is readily available at all of the state's international airports, and at most major banks. Currency exchange is also available at most hotels, although the rate tends to be a little less favorable than at a bank. There are no street money changers in Hawaii.

O

Opening hours

Normal banking hours are Monday to Thursday 8am–4pm, and Friday 8am–6pm. Some banks are open on Saturday until noon. Typical opening hours for offices and small businesses in Hawaii are 9am or 10am until 5pm or 6pm. Shops, especially in malls and tourist areas, usually stay open later, until 10pm. One word of warning: most Hawaiians take "lunch" break around noon or 1pm. Often, instead of actually eating lunch, they are swimming or surfing at the nearest beach. Some shops and businesses are also open on Sundays.

P

Postal services

Believe it or not, normal American postal rates apply across Hawaii. From Honolulu, it costs the same price to mail a letter to New York City as it does to Maui. Stamps are sold at all post offices; most supermarkets and corner stores sell them, too. As of 2013, some ATMs even carry them. Post boxes in Hawaii look the same as they do across the mainland US – blue boxes with an arched top.

Many resort hotels will mail postcards free of charge.

Public holidays

Hawaii observes all the US national holidays, plus three state holidays – Prince Kuhio Day, Kamehameha Day, and Admission Day. On national holidays, all government offices, banks, post offices, and most businesses – except shops – close. On state holidays, local government offices and banks close, but federal offices and post offices remain open. Here are the important holidays to note:

New Year's Day: January 1
Martin Luther King Day: third Monday in January
Presidents' Day: third Monday in February
Prince Kuhio Day: March 26
Good Friday: Friday preceding Easter Sunday
Memorial Day: last Monday in May
Kamehameha Day: June 11
Independence Day: July 4
Admission Day: third Friday in August
Labor Day: first Monday in

September
Columbus Day: October 12
Veterans Day: November 11
Thanksgiving Day: fourth Thursday in November
Christmas Day: December 25

T

Tax

Hawaii does not have a state sales tax, but instead has something called a General Excise Tax, which, together with a Use Tax, means that just about every kind of transaction is assessed with a 4 percent surcharge statewide. Across the islands, some cities and counties across Hawaii add a local sales tax on top of this rate; in Oahu, for instance, all transactions include extra tax to fund a new rail system. Few destinations in Hawaii charge more than 6 percent in total tax.

Hotels, especially those in major tourist zones, are allowed to charge an occupancy tax, known as a Transient Accommodations Tax. This tax currently is 9.25 percent and is scheduled to roll back to 7.25 percent in 2015. Governor Neil Abercrombie has proposed increasing the tax to 11.25 percent before then.

Rental car customers will pay the General Excise Tax as well as a state highway surcharge ($3 per day) and a vehicle registration fee ($0.35-1.45 per day). Those who rent from an airport location (in other words, the vast majority of visitors) also must pay a customer facility charge ($4.50 per day) and an airport concession recovery tax of 11.1 percent. To put these fees into perspective, the actual cost of a rental car usually ends up being anywhere from 35 to 40 percent higher than the base price quoted.

Telephones

From the middle of the Pacific, you can dial directly to almost anywhere in the world. Because of underwater fiber-optic cables, the quality of phone calls to both Asia and North America is excellent. Cellular service is reliable as well; major carriers servicing the Hawaiian Islands include AT&T, Verizon, Sprint, and T-Mobile, and all of them sell pay-as-you-go plans for international travelers. If you prefer dialing out from a hotel, note that most hotels charge $0.75–$1 for local calls, and up to $1 per minute for long distance. If you can find public telephones (most of them have been phased out), they cost $0.35 per minute for local calls.

Area and dialing codes

The telephone area code for all the Hawaiian Islands is **808**.
Same-island calls:
dial number.
NB 800 numbers need to be preceeded by a 1 ie 1 + 800 + number.
Inter-island (direct):
1 + 808 + number.
Mainland (direct dial):
1 + area code + number.
International (direct dial):
011 + country + city + number.
Home-country direct:
Operators in some countries can be called directly from Hawaii by special toll-free 800 numbers. Call 643-1000 for a list of numbers and foreign countries where this particular service is available.

Directory assistance

Operator assistance: dial 0.
Same-island: 1 + 411.
Inter-island: 1 + 808 + 555-1212.
Mainland: 1 + area code + 555-1212.

Time zone

Hawaii is GMT-10 hours, which means it is 10 hours behind Greenwich Mean Time, two hours behind Pacific Standard Time, three hours behind Mountain Standard Time, four hours behind Central Standard Time and five hours behind Eastern Standard Time. As Hawaii does not adjust to Daylight Saving Time, these time differences grow by one hour between April and October (or, some years, November).

Tipping

Tipping for service is expected in Hawaii, as tips are considered part of a service worker's overall salary. In general, airport porters' baggage-handling fees run at roughly $1 per bag, and taxi drivers are usually tipped 10 percent in addition to about 25¢ per bag. A 15–20 percent tip at a fine restaurant is the norm, and at other eating establishments you should tip whatever you feel is fair, typically 15 percent.

Tourist information

The Hawaii Visitors and Conventions Bureau is in charge of promoting

Hawaii to the general public. While the majority of the organization's efforts focus on media and corporate tourism, the outfit does have a public-facing arm and provides visitor guides upon request (tel: 800-4-2924). It also maintains an informative website, gohawaii.com. Under the auspices of this office, each of the four largest islands has its own visitors' bureau:
Kauai, tel: 800-262-1400
Oahu, tel: 877-525-6248
Maui, tel: 800-525-6284
Hawaii Island, tel: 800-648-2441

Tour operators

Many US-based tour operators offer tours in Hawaii that are available to customers from anywhere in the world; the most useful include **Backroads** (tel: 800-462-2848; www.backroads.com), **Roberts Hawaii** (tel: 800-831-5541; www.robertshawaii.com), **Pleasant Hawaiian Holidays** (tel: 800-742-9244; www.pleasantholidays.com), the **Sierra Club** (tel: 415-977-5522; www.sierraclub.org), and **Tauck Tours** (tel: 800-788-7885; www.tauck.com).

V

Visas and passports

Details of the visa waiver scheme, under which travelers carrying passports issued by Britain, Ireland, and most European countries, as well as Australia and New Zealand, do not need visas for trips to the United States lasting less than 90 days, can be obtained from your travel agent or via http://travel.state.gov.

W

Weights and measures

Hawaii uses the imperial system of weights and measures. Metric weights and measures are rarely used.

What to bring

Hawaii is very much part of the modern US, so if you forget to bring something, you'll most likely be able to buy it there. Camera equipment and accessories are widely available in tourist areas, but there are surprisingly few bookstores or map outlets in the resorts. If you take

prescription drugs, make sure you bring sufficient for your visit and if travelling with infants, it is safest to bring the formula or baby food they are familiar with as you might not be able to find it in Hawaii.

What to wear

Although Hawaii is a sub-tropical destination, characterized at sea level by consistently comfortable temperatures, you're likely to encounter rain at some point during your stay, so you'll be glad of light, waterproof clothing or perhaps an umbrella. If you plan to venture at all higher, to areas like Maui's Upcountry, Waimea on the Big Island, or Koke'e on Kauai, you'll need something warmer too. And if you head towards the summits of the volcanoes, most notably for the dawn at Haleakala on Maui, you should be prepared for literally freezing temperatures.

All the islands hold rough volcanic terrain, so good walking shoes or hiking boots are very useful, and in many places the ocean floor can be rocky and abrasive, so reef shoes are a good idea too.

Dress is cool and casual in Honolulu and even more so beyond the city proper. Light, loose garments are suitable for the summer months. Hawaiian-print *mu'umu'u* and *aloha* shirts are practical all-round garments. Thongs, flip-flops, slippers, *zoris* – all different names for the same thing – are ideal for pacing the pavement or at the beach.

A few exclusive restaurants and nightclubs require a coat, maybe a tie, and definitely shoes, but they are the exceptions. Leather sandals and shoes are appropriate for nightlife. In most island homes, shoes are removed at the entrance.

Aloha Friday

Friday is usually greeted in the islands with *aloha* wear, where even businessmen don *aloha* shirts of bright and cheerful Hawaiian prints instead of formal suits and ties. Ladies often tuck a fragrant plumeria behind their ear, or drape a *kukui* nut or flower *lei* on their shoulders. These are appropriate accessories for their *mu'umu'u*. This is a Friday custom that has become de rigueur here, even in state, federal and business offices, and at public schools. And in most businesses, it is no longer limited to Friday only.

LANGUAGE

UNDERSTANDING THE LANGUAGE

BACKGROUND

Until the 1970s, most linguists agreed that the Hawaiian language stood little chance of survival. In the background, however, local people of all persuasions could be heard chattering in pidgin English, a hybrid island language that flits in and out of conversations like a sassy mynah bird. A typical after-work conversation between people of Hawaiian, Chinese, Japanese, Korean, Filipino, or Samoan backgrounds might include an invitation like this: "Hey, pau hana like go my hale for grind? Get plenty 'ono pupu – even pipikaula and poke in da fridge." Translation: "Hey, after work would you like to go to my house to eat? We've got plenty of tasty appetizers, even some beef jerky and raw fish marinated with seaweed in the refrigerator."

Today, pidgin continues to predominate among locals, but increasingly, true, grammatically correct Hawaiian is heard among part-Hawaiian members of many families and other individuals at social get-togethers. The startling change can be credited to a renaissance of pride in being Hawaiian and the establishment of language immersion schools (funded by the Hawaii Department of Education with assistance from the Office of Hawaiian Affairs), where all classes are taught in the native language. Today, not only children take classes to 'olelo (speak) Hawaiian, their parents do so too, in order to keep up with their multilingual kids. Even a straightforward conversation in English will be peppered with Hawaiian words that are known to all residents of the islands, and that sometimes better describe something than an equivalent word in English.

Pau hana, used in the example above, could superficially be translated as "after work." Yet, in Hawaiian it has a richer meaning and texture that, nonetheless, defies description. You have to be in the islands for a while for the subtleties to take effect.

To describe the Hawaiian language in English is problematical because it is a language of emotion, poetry, and nature-related sound and nuance. It is an ancient language that was not transliterated until after 1820, when American missionaries arbitrarily chose 12 English letters to represent the Hawaiian sounds they thought they heard. While any transliteration of one language into the letters and sounds of another isn't perfect, the Romanization of Hawaiian works well, mostly.

A language of the Pacific

For hundreds of years, the language had thrived expressively and melodically as the exclusively spoken tongue of a Polynesian people who were rich in an unwritten literature; this included complicated poetic chants detailing history, genealogies, and mythologies set to memory and passed orally from generation to generation.

Historians have not determined all of the intricacies of the development of the Hawaiian language, but a fairly clear picture has emerged regarding its relationship to other languages. Hawaiian belongs to the Austronesian (formerly called Malayo-Polynesian) language family. These were the languages spoken by seafaring peoples who settled over a broader area of the globe than was covered by any other group until the 18th and 19th centuries, when Europeans began extensively exploring beyond their known world.

Hawaii is the furthest point of Austronesian expansion to the north, with Easter Island the eastern extent and New Zealand the most southern. From these points westward, Austronesian tongues are spoken through the Pacific to Indonesia, Malaysia, the Philippines, and parts of Taiwan. The furthest western point is the island of Madagascar off the coast of Africa.

More specifically, Hawaiian is classified as a Polynesian language closely related to the language spoken in Tahiti, the Marquesas, and the surrounding island groups of the South Pacific. Early ancestors of the Hawaiian race originated from these groups, sailing their outrigger canoes from Southeast or Indo-Malay Asia around the north coast of New Guinea, through the islands of Melanesia and into Polynesia.

Variations in the core language evolved along the way, but certain words and verbal inflections continue to reveal the ancient ties between them. Instead of the Hawaiian term i'a for fish, people of Southeast Asia say ika or ikan. Instead of hale for house, they say fare, 'are, or vale. Instead of maka for eye, they say mata. Na Pali, the name for the towering cliffs in Kauai's North Shore, comes from the same root as the name of the Himalayan kingdom of Nepal.

By 1819, Calvinist Christian missionaries had succeeded in converting several adventurous Hawaiian seamen who had sailed on various trading ships to America's east coast.

The first missionaries to Hawaii knew that the Hawaiian language was a spoken language only, but they were eager to set it to writing to facilitate the translation of the Bible.

TRANSPORTATION

ACCOMMODATIONS

EATING OUT

ACTIVITIES

A – Z

LANGUAGE

By 1823, three years after their arrival, the various missionaries established the Hawaiian alphabet, although not without disputes. Some argued that the *k* sound was closer to *t*, or that the flapped *r* sound was more of an *l* sound. When the final vote was taken, *k* was adopted over the *t*, and *l* was chosen over the flapped *r*. The consonants were established as *h, k, l, m, n, p*, and *w*, while the vowel sounds were recorded as the five distinctive *a, e, i, o*, and *u* sounds of Western romance languages. These 12 letters remain the official Hawaiian alphabet today.

For some time after Westerners began settling in the islands, Hawaiian continued to be spoken and written in government, business, and social circles of the Hawaiian kingdom. For years, it was used almost exclusively in newspapers. Then, as the outside culture came to predominate, with missionary schooling widespread and Hawaii emerging as the Pacific's key port, the use of Hawaiian fell into disfavor. It was forbidden in public schools by 1896, and by the start of the 20th century, it had been replaced by English in the territorial legislature.

Many Hawaiian households suppressed the use of the language in an attempt to conform to the standards of the day, and the art of chanting, which is the oral preservation of history and genealogy, diminished. The last Hawaiian language newspaper, *Ka Hoku O Hawaii (The Star of Hawaii)*, printed in Hilo on Hawaii Island, stopped its presses in 1948. In 1992, a monthly paper called *Na Maka O Kana*, aimed at Hawaiian-language students and published by the University of Hawaii, Hilo, began to offer news about sports, movies, and other activities in the Hawaiian language.

In the 1980s, it was estimated that only 2,000 native speakers of Hawaiian – about 300 of them residents of the privately owned island of Ni'ihau – remained in Hawaii. Today, the picture has brightened considerably. In 1979, the state legislature approved funding for the Office of Hawaiian Affairs (OHA), run for and by Hawaiians for the betterment of Hawaiians. The OHA assists the Department of Education in running language-immersion schools for children from kindergarten through 12th grade. Slowly, besides a few remaining *kupuna*, or elders, who are fluent enough to teach their native tongue, a younger generation of teachers is emerging.

Pronunciation guidelines

Every letter in Hawaiian is pronounced distinctly. Vowels have just one sound: *a* sounds like *ah*, *e* like *ay* (as in hay), *i* like *ee*, *o* like *oh*, and *u* like *oo*. Likelike Highway, for example, is correctly pronounced *lee-kay lee-kay*, not *like-like*. Keep these simple rules in mind when you see signs such as Kalaniana'ole Highway or Kapi'olani. And remember, glottal stops, called *'okina*, indicate that each vowel should be pronounced distinctly.

Words and phrases

In its development, the Hawaiian language has acquired several interesting grammatical complications, as well as a pronunciation system known for its complex vowel combinations and small number of consonants. The Hawaiian alphabet has eight consonants including the *'okina*. Each of the letters in this bunch is roughly similar in pronunciation to their equivalent letter symbols in English, with the exception of *w*.

h *hula* (Hawaiian dance)
k *kai* (sea)
l *lani* (heaven)
m *manu* (bird)
n *niho* (tooth)
p *pua* (flower)
w *wa'a* (canoe)

In Hawaiian, the letter *w* varies in pronunciation between a *w* and *v* sound. To English speakers, *w* often sounds like a *v* after a stressed vowel, as in the place name Hale'iwa. At the beginning of a word or after an unstressed vowel, *w* sounds like an English *w* as in the place names Waikiki and Wahiawa.

The five Hawaiian vowels come in both short and long duration forms. Pronunciation of vowels is similar to Spanish or Japanese: no sloppy or lazy sounds as found in English.

a as in father *nana* (look)
e as in hay *nene* (goose)
i as in beet *wiwi* (skinny)
o as in boat *lolo* (feeble mind)
u as in boot *pupu* (snack)

If you would like more *kokua* (help) with Hawaiian language, refer to three excellent books on the subject: *Spoken Hawaiian*, by Samuel Elbert; *Let's Speak Hawaiian*, by Dorothy Kahananui and A. Anthony; and *The Hawaiian Dictionary*, by Samuel Elbert and Mary Kawena Pukui.

Word list

ali'i **ancient Hawaiian royalty, nobility**
aloha **love, greeting, farewell**
'Ewa **toward 'Ewa**
hana hou **one more time, encore**

The 'okina

Two symbols can be added to Hawaiian words to assist pronunciation: a glottal stop ('), called an *'okina*, and a macron, which is a horizontal line over a vowel, indicating it is drawn out. *Insight Guide: Hawaii* uses the *'okina*, but not the macron. The *'okina*, which gives a "hard edge" to a vowel or separates two adjoining vowels with distinct sounds, is necessary for basic pronunciation in normal conversation; the macron offers a more subtle pronunciation.

All place names in this guide that need them use a glottal stop, with three exceptions: Hawaii, Oahu and Kauai, also written as Hawai'i, O'ahu, Kaua'i. But the non-glottal spellings are so common and ubiquitous that most cartographers delete the glottal stop for these islands. Two islands requiring glottal stops for pronunciation are Ni'ihau *(nee ee how)* and Kaho'olawe *(kah ho o lah vay)*. We use these forms.

haole **technically all foreigners, now refers mainly to people of Caucasian ancestry**
hapa **half, part**
hapa-haole **part-Caucasian**
heiau **traditional Hawaiian place of worship, a temple**
ho'olaule'a **celebration, party**
imu **underground cooking oven**
kama'aina **island-born or longtime resident of Hawaii**
kanaka **man, person, especially a native Hawaiian**
kane **man**
keiki **child, children**
kokua **help, assistance**
lanai **porch, balcony, veranda**
lauhala **pandanus leaf, for weaving**
lu'au **traditional feast**
mahalo **thank you**
makai **toward the ocean**
malihini **newcomer or visitor to the islands**
mana **spiritual power**
mauka **toward the mountains**
mauna **mountain**
'ohana **family**
'ono **delicious, tasty**
pali **cliff, precipice**
paniolo **cowboy**
pau **finished, completed**
pau hana **end of work**
poi **food paste made from taro roots**
puka **hole, opening**
pupu **hors d'oeuvre**
shaka **an island hand greeting**
wahine **woman**

FURTHER READING

NON-FICTION

The Art of the Hula by Allan Seiden. Richly illustrated history of Hawaii's nature dance.

The Betrayal of Lili'uokalani by Helena G. Allen. All-important biography of Hawaii's last queen.

The Death of William Gooch by Greg Dening. Focusing on the murder of three British seamen on Oahu in 1792.

Diamond Head, Hawaii's Icon by Allan Seiden. A comprehensive look at Hawaii's renowned landmark.

Discovery by Bishop Museum Press. A superb collection of essays and photographs addressing ancient, contemporary, and future Hawaii.

Exalted Sits the Chief by Ross Cordy. An archeologist's view of Hawaiian history.

From Fishponds to Warships – An Illustrated History of Pearl Harbor by Allan Seiden. The full story, from geology and natural history to the war and the present day.

Haleakala: A History of the Maui Mountain by Jill Engledow. A look at the science of how Haleakala was formed, as well as the people who live there today.

Hawaii 1959–89 by Gavan Daws. A thorough history of Hawaii's first 30 years of statehood.

Hawaii: The Royal Legacy by Allan Seiden. The illustrated story of Hawaii's chiefs and Kings.

Hawaii's Birds by Hawaii Audubon Society. A local birdwatcher's bible.

Hawaii's Story by Hawaii's Queen by Queen Lili'uokalani. The memoirs of Hawaii's first and only reigning queen.

Hawaiian Dictionary by Mary Kawena Pukui and Samuel H. Elbert. The definitive reference on Hawaiian vocabulary.

Hawaiian Hiking Trails by Craig Chisholm. A must for backpackers and nature-seekers.

Hawaiian Legends by William Hyde Rice. Attractive reprint of a 1923 classic, with new photos by Boone Morrison.

Hawaiian Music and Musicians by George S. Kanahele. Hawaii's musical heritage.

Hawaiian Mythology by Martha Warren Beckwith. Definitive and comprehensive.

Hawaiian Son: The Life and Music of Eddie Kamae by James Houston with Eddie Kamae. The illuminating biography of the 'ukulele-playing co-founder of the Sons of Hawaii makes a great introduction to Hawaiian music.

Hawaiian Yesterdays by Ray Jerome Baker, with text by Ronn Ronck. A wonderful collection of historic photos by Hawaii's pioneer cameraman.

Honor Killing by David Stannard. The gripping real-life story of a crime that exposed Hawaii's underlying racial tensions in the 1930s.

History Makers of Hawaii by A. Grove Day. A biographical dictionary of the people who shaped Hawaii from ancient times to the present.

Kaho'olawe: Na Leo O Kanaloa by Wayne Levin, Rowland B. Reeve,

Send Us Your Thoughts

We do our best to ensure the information in our books is as accurate and up-to-date as possible. The books are updated on a regular basis using local contacts, who painstakingly add, amend and correct as required. However, some details (such as telephone numbers and opening times) are liable to change, and we are ultimately reliant on our readers to put us in the picture.

We welcome your feedback, especially your experience of using the book "on the road". Maybe we recommended a hotel that you liked (or another that you didn't), or you came across a great bar or new attraction we missed.

We will acknowledge all contributions, and we'll offer an Insight Guide to the best letters received.

Please write to us at:
**Insight Guides
PO Box 7910
London SE1 1WE**
Or email us at:
insight@apaguide.co.uk

Franco Salmoiraghi, and David Ulrich. Images of the Forbidden Island of Kaho'olawe.

Ka Poe'e Kahiko, the People of Old by Samuel Manaiakalani Kamakau. Important memoirs by a 19th-century Hawaiian historian.

Mark Twain's Letters from Hawaii by Mark Twain. Twain's look at Hawaii in the 1860s.

Na Leo I Ka Makani: Voices on the Wind by Palani Vaughan. A pictorial look at early Hawaii.

Oceanwatcher, An Above-Water Guide to Hawaii's Marine Animals by Susan Scott.

Pau Hana by Ronald Takaki. A history of plantation life.

The Price of Paradise Volumes 1 and 2, edited by Randall W. Roth. A collection of essays highlighting important issues in contemporary Hawaii.

Volcanoes in the Sea by Gordon A. MacDonald. A historical and scientific look at Hawaii's spectacular volcanoes.

A Voyage to the Pacific Ocean, 1776–1780 by Captain James Cook and James King. Official account of Cook's discovery of Hawaii.

Waikiki Beachboy by Grady Timmons. A colorful history of Waikiki's famed beachboy era.

FICTION

The Descendants by Kaui Hart Hemmings. The novel that inspired the motion picture of the same name; about death, family bonding, and land ownership in Hawaii.

Fluke: Or I Know Why the Winged Whale Sings by Christopher Moore. This laugh-out-loud novel is based on humpback whale researchers who still conduct work off the coast of Maui every winter.

From Here to Eternity by James Jones. The novel that spawned a movie (and, in 2013, a musical); tells the story of military life on Oahu leading up to D-Day in 1941.

Shark Dialogues by Kiana Davenport. A historic novel of 20th-century Hawaii.

CREDITS

Photo Credits

123RF 141B, 147B
Alamy 92, 93, 95
AWL Images 14/15, 190
Corbis 36, 39, 40, 48
Dreamstime 4BR, 153, 161, 178, 255BR
Fairmont Hotels 231
FLPA 165
Fotolia 160
Getty Images 52, 53, 78, 130
Hawaii Tourism Authority 232T, 272T, 273T, 274T, 276T
Hawaii Tourism Authority/Daeja Faris 77
Hawaii Tourism Authority/Dana Edmunds 198BL
Hawaii Tourism Authority/Kirk Lee Aeder 113T
Hawaii Tourism Authority/Pierce M Myers Photography 69TR
Hawaii Tourism Authority/Tor Johnson 60, 68/69T, 69BR, 82, 83, 84BL, 84/85T, 84BR, 85ML, 85BR, 86, 88, 119, 120, 193B, 195B, 227, 252, 273B, 277, 294, 299
Hawaii Tourism Japan 68BL, 69ML, 207
iStock 5BL, 25L, 35, 91, 137, 140,

182, 198/199T, 198BR, 199ML, 199BR, 243, 248, 255BL, 255TR, 317
Kobal 94
Leonardo 195T, 196
Library of Congress 38, 43, 44, 46, 50, 254BR
Photoshot 246
Press Association Images 254/255T
Robert Harding 28
Starwood Hotels & Resorts 131
Steven Greaves/Apa Publications 1, 2/3, 4BL, 4M, 4MR, 5TR, 5ML, 5MR, 5BR, 5TL, 6BR, 6M, 6BL, 7BR, 7ML, 7T, 8T, 8B, 9B, 9T, 10/11, 12/13, 16, 17T, 17B, 18, 19, 20, 21, 22, 23, 24, 25R, 54, 55, 56/57, 59, 61, 62, 63, 64, 65, 66, 67, 68BR, 69BL, 70, 71, 72, 73, 74, 75, 76, 80, 81, 85TR, 85BL, 87, 89, 90, 96/97, 98/99, 100/101, 102, 103T, 103B, 106, 107T, 107B, 110, 111, 118T, 118B, 122, 123, 124B, 125, 126, 128T, 129B, 135, 136, 139, 143B, 144, 145, 148, 149, 151, 152, 154, 155B, 155T, 156, 157, 158, 159, 162B, 162T, 163,

164, 166/167, 168, 169, 172, 173, 174, 175, 176, 177, 179B, 179T, 180, 181, 183, 184, 185, 186, 187, 188, 189B, 189T, 191, 192, 193T, 194, 197, 199TR, 199BL, 200/201, 202, 203, 204, 205T, 205B, 208, 209, 210, 211, 212/213, 215, 216B, 216T, 217, 218/219, 220, 221T, 221B, 224, 225, 226B, 226T, 228, 229, 230T, 230B, 232B, 233, 234, 235, 236, 237, 238, 239, 241, 242, 244/245, 247, 249, 250, 251, 253, 255ML, 256/257, 258, 259T, 259B, 262, 263, 264T, 264B, 265T, 265B, 266, 267, 268, 269, 270, 271, 272B, 274B, 275, 276B, 278, 280, 281, 282, 283, 284, 291, 292, 295, 296, 298, 300, 301, 303, 308, 310T, 313, 315
SuperStock 254BL
Tim Thompson/Apa Publications 58, 112, 113B, 115, 116, 117T, 117B, 121, 128B, 129T, 134, 138, 141T, 142T, 142B, 143T, 146T, 146B, 147T, 150, 285, 287, 310B
Public domain 26B, 26T, 27, 29, 30, 31, 32, 33, 34, 37, 41, 42, 45, 47, 49, 51, 79, 124T

Cover Credits

Front cover: Maui island, *4Corners Images*
Back cover: (top) surf Oahu, *Dreamstime*; (middle) traditional Samoa dance, *Dreamstime*
Front flap: (from top) Akaka Falls;

Keahi a Kawelo; Keahi a Kawelo; windy Road to Hana *All Steven Greaves/Apa Publications*
Spine: Tiki, Statue, *Steven Greaves/ Apa Publications*

Insight Guide Credits

Distribution

UK
Dorling Kindersley Ltd
A Penguin Group company
80 Strand, London, WC2R 0RL
sales@uk.dk.com

United States
Ingram Publisher Services
1 Ingram Boulevard, PO Box 3006,
La Vergne, TN 37086-1986
ips@ingramcontent.com

Australia and New Zealand
Woodslane
10 Apollo St, Warriewood,
NSW 2102, Australia
info@woodslane.com.au

Worldwide
Apa Publications GmbH & Co. Verlag
KG (Singapore branch)
7030 Ang Mo Kio Avenue 5
08-65 Northstar @ AMK
Singapore 569880
apasin@singnet.com.sg

Printing
CTPS-China
© 2014 Apa Publications (UK) Ltd
All Rights Reserved
First Edition 1988
Thirteenth Edition 2014

www.insightguides.com

Project Editor
Sarah Clark
Series Manager
Rachel Lawrence
Author
Matt Villano
Picture Editor/Art Editor
Tom Smyth/Shahid Mahmood
Map Production
Original cartography Original
Cartography, updated by
Apa Cartography Department
Production
Tynan Dean and Rebeka Davies

Contributors

This edition was commissioned by **Sarah Clark** and updated by **Matt Villano**, who got married in Hawaii in 2004 and has visited many times since. He considers the islands to be his personal 'Happy Place,' especially during humpback whale season. Contributors to previous editions include **Joyce Akamine**, **Kekuni Blaisdell**, **Joan Conrow**, **Betty Fullard-Leo**, **Jerry Hopkins**, **Alberta de Jetley**, **Larry Lindsey Kimura**, **Leonard Lueras**, **Ronn Ronck**, **Susan Scott**, **Lance Tominaga**, **Greg Ward**, **Marty Wentzel**, and **Paul Wood**. The text was edited by **Naomi Peck**, proofread by **Leonie Wilding** and indexed by **Penny Phenix**. **Steven Greaves Photography** would like to thank Jacque, James, Nikole, Koa, George, Kika and Jimmy.

About Insight Guides

Insight Guides have more than 40 years' experience of publishing high-quality, visual travel guides. We produce 400 full-colour titles, in both print and digital form, covering more than 200 destinations across the globe, in a variety of formats to meet your different needs.
  Insight Guides are written by local authors who use their on-the-ground experience to provide the very latest information; their local expertise is evident in the extensive historical and cultural background features. All the reviews in **Insight Guides** are independent; we strive to maintain an impartial view. Our reviews are carefully selected to guide you to the best places to stay and eat, so you can be confident that when we say a restaurant or hotel is special, we really mean it.

Legend

City maps

	Freeway/Highway/Motorway
	Divided Highway
	Main Roads
	Minor Roads
	Pedestrian Roads
	Steps
	Footpath
	Railway
	Funicular Railway
	Cable Car
	Tunnel
	City Wall
	Important Building
	Built Up Area
	Other Land
	Transport Hub
	Park
	Pedestrian Area
	Bus Station
❶	Tourist Information
✉	Main Post Office
✝	Cathedral/Church
☾	Mosque
✡	Synagogue
⚊	Statue/Monument
⚲	Beach
✈	Airport

Regional maps

	Freeway/Highway/Motorway (with junction)
	Freeway/Highway/Motorway (under construction)
	Divided Highway
	Main Road
	Secondary Road
	Minor Road
	Track
	Footpath
	International Boundary
	State/Province Boundary
	National Park/Reserve
	Marine Park
	Ferry Route
	Marshland/Swamp
	Glacier	Salt Lake
✈	Airport/Airfield
∴	Ancient Site
⊖	Border Control
	Cable Car
	Castle/Castle Ruins
∩	Cave
	Chateau/Stately Home
✝	Church/Church Ruins
	Crater
	Lighthouse
▲	Mountain Peak
★	Place of Interest
	Viewpoint

INDEX

Main references are in bold type

A

accommodations **284**. *See also* camping
bed-and-breakfasts 284
cabin rentals 268
condominiums 288, 290, 292, 293
home exchanges and farm stays 285
hotel chains 284
resorts 53, 154, 159, 163, 169, 180, 229, 230
vacation rentals 285
activities 8, 71, **300**. *See also* by name
admission charges 310
Adventure Lanai Ecocenter 217
adventure sports 309
'Aiea 160
'Aikanaka 157
air travel 9, 280
Hawaii Island 280
history of 52
inter-island flights 281
Kauai 280
Maui 280
Molokai and Lanai 280
Oahu 280
'Akaka Falls 9, 237, 240
Alaka'i Swamp 259, 267
'Alau Island 195
'Alekoko Fishpond 274
Ali'i Kula Lavender Farm 187
Ali'iloa, Bill Lincoln 81
aloha 17
Aloha Friday 314
Aloha Stadium 159
Aloha Stadium Swap Meet 160
amusement and water parks
Hawaiian Waters Adventure Park (Ko 'Olina) 163
Wet 'N' Wild Hawaii (Oahu) 302
'Anaeho'omalu 230
animals 310. *See* wildlife
Apaka, Alfred 80
aquaculture 89, 153, 208
aquariums and zoo
Honolulu Zoo (Waikiki) 131, 302
Maui Ocean Center (Ma'alaea) 175, 302
Sea Life Park (Makapu'u Point) 147, 302
Waikiki Aquarium (Waikiki) 131, 302
art and crafts 34, 275
courses 272
featherwork 34
jewelry 34
shopping for 306
textiles 34
art galleries. *See* museums and galleries
arts and entertainment 301
astronomy 29, 30, 239

Keck Observatory (Hawaii Island) 242
Onizuka Astronomy Complex (Hawaii Island) 243
Au'au Channel 73
'Au'au Channel 178, 169
Aulani 163

B

Baldwin, Dwight 179
Barking Sands 267
bars 304
baseball 159
beaches 7, 9, 21, 301
access 54
Hawaii Island 231, 240, 251, 252
Kauai 259, 264, 265, 267, 274
Lanai 217
Maui 169, 180, 181, 182, 186, 193, 194, 195
Molokai 207, 210
Oahu 107, 144, 146, 149, 152, 163, 164
Waikiki 123
Beamer, Keola 81, 82
Beamer, Mahi 81
Bellows Air Force Station 147
Berger, Heinrich 78
bicycling 71, 188, **281**, 309
Biggers, Earl Derr 62, 128
The Adventures of Charlie Chan 62
Bingham, Hiram 42, 114
Bird, Isabella 238
bird life 23, 165, 173, 263, 268
albatrosses 164
goony birds 165
honeycreepers 259
moa (wild Hawaiian chickens) 268
mynahs 198
nene (Hawaiian Goose) 25, 244
birdwatching 309
Bishop, Charles Reed 135
Black Rock 180
boat trips and cruises 283, **305**
Hawaii Island 221, 228
Kane'ohe Bay 151
Kauai 266
Molokai 205
Oahu 128
bodyboarding 73, 146, 147, 164, 195
bodyboardng 274
Boiling Pots 239
Brennecke's Beach 274
Bronte, Emory 208
Brotman, Charles 82
Brower, Kenneth 29
Brown, William 114
Buck, Sir Peter 31
Vikings of the Pacific 31
business hours. *See* opening hours

bus travel 9, 282
Hawaii Island 282
Kauai 282
Maui 282
Oahu 282

C

camping 285
Kauai 267
Lanai 217
Maui 188, 193, 194, 195
Molokai 207, 210
national and state parks 285
canoeing, outrigger 75
Cape Kumukahi 245
Captain Cook (town) 227, 292, 298. *See also* Cook, James
car rental 281, 282. *See also* driving
restricted routes 196, 242
Carrere, Tia 82
Cartwright, Alexander Joy, Jr. 136
cathedrals
Our Lady of Peace (Honolulu) 117
St Andrew's (Honolulu) 117
caves 193, 194
Kaneana (Oahu) 164
Kazumura Cave (Hawaii Island) 249
Cazimero brothers 81
Central Oahu 159
Chain of Craters Road 250
Chang Apana 62
children 310
activities 301
Choy, Sam 89
churches
Holy Ghost (Waiakoa) 187
Huialoha (Maui) 189
Ka'ahumanu Congregational (Wailuku) 174
Kalua'aha 208
Kaulanapueo (Huelo) 192
Kawaiaha'o (Honolulu) 114
Moku'aikaua (Kailua) 221, 227
Our Lady of Sorrows (Kalua'aha) 208
Palapala Ho'omau (Kipahulu) 196
Siloama (Kalawao) 207
St Benedict's Painted Church (Hawaii Island) 228
St Gabriel's (Wailua) 193
St Joseph's (Kaupo) 189
St Peter and Paul (Waimea Bay) 155
St Philomena's (Kalawao) 207
Cleveland, President Grover 47
cliff-diving 181
climate and weather 21, 311
Clinton, President Bill 55
clothing 314
cocoa 228
Coconut Coast 273
coffee 221, **227**, 229, 306

Cook, James 31, 34, 35, 185, 228, 259, 271, 276
coral reefs 21
cowboys 90, 187, 233
crafts. See art and crafts
crime and safety 163, 311
Crosby, Bing 80
Crouching Lion. See Kauhi
cruise ships 121, 238, 271, **281**
culture and society 32, 61
customs regulations 311

D

Damien, Father 205, 206, 208
dance. See music and dance
de La Pérouse, Jean-François 183
Diamond Head 144
Dillingham Airfield 156
disabled travelers 311
diving and snorkeling 8, 9, 21, 73, 75, 301, 309
  Kauai 265
  Lanai 214, 217
  Maui 181, 183
  Ni'ihau 277
  Oahu 146, 151
Dole, James D. 49, 161, 215
Dole, Sanford 47, 49, 161
driving 145, 282, **283**. See also car rental
  Hana Highway 191, 192
  in Honolulu 125

E

East Shore (Kauai) 299
eating out 9, 294. See also food and drink, restaurants
  food trucks 174
economy 17, 43, 53, 169
ecosystems 19, 21, 22, 251
Edgar, Thomas 38
Eisenhower, President Dwight D. 143
electricity 312
Ellison, Larry 55, 95, 215
embassies and consulates 312
emergencies 312
Emma, Queen 44, 45
environmental issues 24
  extinction of native species 24
  Great Pacific Garbage Patch 25
etiquette 312
  in restaurants 294
'Ewa 107

F

Fagan, Paul 194
ferries 283
festivals and events
  Buffalo's Longboard Contest (Makaha) 164
  calendar of events 302
  Feast Day of Santa Cruz 64
  Fiesta Filipina 64
  Hale'iwa Festival (Hale'iwa) 156
  Hale'iwa Taro Festival (Hale'iwa) 156

Hawaiian International Billfish Tournament (Hawaii Island) 74, 227
  Honolulu Marathon 129
  Ironman World Championship (Kailua) 228
  Ka Hula Piko Festival (Maunaloa) 83
  Lanai Film Festival 95
  Makawao Rodeo (Makawao) 187
  Maui Film Festival 95
  Merrie Monarch Festival (Hilo) 83, 239
  Molokai Ka Hula Piko festival (Molokai) 210
  Molokai-to-Oahu outrigger canoe race (Hale o Lono) 209
  Na Mele O Maui Song Contest and Hula Festival (Ka'anapali) 83
  Oiwi Film Festival 95
  Prince Albert Hula Festival (Princeville) 83
  Prince Lot Hula Festival (Moanalua Gardens) 83, 159
  Queen Lili'uokalani Keiki Hula festival 83
  rodeo (Makawao) 74
  toronagashi festival (Hale'iwa) 156
  Triple Crown of Surfing (Oahu) 308
Triple Crown of Surfing (Oahu) 157
film and television 93
  50 First Dates 95
  Baraka 95
  Bird of Paradise 94
  Blue Crush 95, 163
  Blue Hawaii 94
  Fantasy Island 94
  Forgetting Sarah Marshall 95
  From Here to Eternity 94
  Girls! Girls! Girls! 94
  Hawaii 164
  Hawaii Five-O 95
  Jurassic Park 95, 264
  Just Go With It 95
  Lost 94, 149, 151
  Magnum P.I. 95
  North Shore 95
  Outbreak 93
  Pearl Harbor 95
  Pirates of the Caribbean 94
    At World's End 95
  Planet of the Apes 95
  Raiders of the Lost Ark 264
  Six Days, Seven Nights 94
  South Pacific 94, 263, 264, 265
  The Descendants 94
  The Devil at 4 O'Clock 95
  The Hunger Games, Catching Fire 94
  The Tempest 95
  Tora! Tora! Tora! 161
  Voodoo Island 94
  Waikiki Wedding 94
  Waterworld 95
fishing 175, 309
  deep-sea 74
  deep-sea fishing 271
  game fishing 227

fishponds 150, 151, 208, 210, 230, 274
flora. See plant life
folklore. See mythology and legends
food and drink 87, 294
  fish and shellfish 89
  Hawaii Regional Cuisine 88
  Koloa Rum Company 294
  Koloa Rum Company (Koloa) 274
  Kona Brewing Company 294
  local produce 89, 306
  malasadas 174
  Maui food scene 182
  plate lunch 90
  shave ice 90, 156
  shopping for 194
  Spam 90
  Tedeschi Winery 187
food trucks 174
football 159
forests 22, 149. See also rainforests
Fornander, Abraham 31
  An Account of the Polynesian Race: Its Origins and Migrations 32
further reading 317

G

Garden of the Gods 9, 71, 215, 217
gardens. See parks and gardens
Gates, Bill 215
gay and lesbian travelers 312
geography and geology 19, 203, 221, 266. See also volcanoes
Gilliom, Amy Hanaiali'i 81
golf 162, 163, **308**
  Hawaii Island 229, 231
  Kauai 264, 273
  Maui 169, 180, 181, 182
government and politics 44, 46, 47, 50, 51, 64
Grant, President Ulysses S. 45
Gregg, John 275
Gregg, Robert 275

H

Ha'ena 265
Ha'iku 192
Halawa Bay 209
Halawa Valley 9, 207, 209
Haleakala 169, 185, 188
Haleakala National Park 188, 191, 195
Hale'iwa 9, 155, 295
  Hale'iwa Jodo Mission 156
Halema'uma'u 255
Halona Blowhole 146
Hamakua Coast 221, 234, 240, 241
Hamoa Beach 195
Hana 194
  Hana Cultural Center & Museum 194
  Hana Ranch 194
  Ka'uiki Hill 194
  Travaasa Hana 194

Hana Airport 193
Hana Airport 280
Hana Coast 191
Hana Highway 191, 193
Hanakapi'ai 266
Hanakoa 266
Hanalei 264, 299
Hanalei Bay 264
Hanama'ulu 299
Hanama'ulu 271
Hanapepe 9
Hanapepe Town 271, 275
Hanauma Bay 73, 146
handicrafts. See art and crafts
Hansen's Disease exiles 203, 205, 206
Hapa 82
Hapuna Beach State Park 231
Hau'ula 152
Hawaiian Islands National Wildlife Refuge 165
Hawaiian Volcano Observatory 248
Hawaii Island 17, 19, 38, 55, 103, 307. See also individual place names
  accommodations 291
  eating out 298
Hawai'i Kai 146
Hawaii Ocean Science and Technology (HOST) Park 229
Hawaii Tropical Botanical Garden 240
Hawaii Volcanoes National Park 221, 247, 292
Hawaii Water Sports Center 146
Hawi 9, 234, 292, 298
Healing Stones 160
health and medical care 312
Helm, Raiatea 81
heritage railways 301
  Grove Farm (Lihu'e) 302
  Hawaiian Railway Society ('Ewa) 138, 302
  Kilohana (Lihu'e) 302
  Lahaina Ka'anapali Railroad (Ka'anapali) 180
  Sugar Cane Train (Maui) 301
Hi'ilawe Falls 241
hiking 7, 9, 71, 309
  Hawaii Island 234, 240, 242, 244, 247, 250, 252
  Honolulu 140
  Kalalau Trail 71
  Kalalau Trail (Kauai) 263, 266
  Kauai 259, 266, 268
  Kukui Trail (Kauai) 268
  Lanai 215, 216, 217
  Mahana Ridge Trail 72
  Maui 181, 188, 192, 193, 194, 195, 196
  Molokai 205, 207, 209
  Munro Trail 75
  Oahu 144, 146, 152, 159
  Pepe'opae Trail (Molokai) 205
Hilo 50, 221, 237
  accommodations 291
  Banyan Drive 239
  East Hawaii Cultural Center Gallery 239

eating out 298
Hawaii Tropical Botanical Garden 237
  history 238
  'Imiloa Astronomy Center 239
  Kaiko'o 238
  Lili'uokalani Gardens 239
  Lyman Mission House and Museum 239
  Mauna Loa Macadamia Nut Factory and Visitor Center 238
  Pacific Tsunami Museum 239
  Waianuenue Avenue 238
Hilo Bay 237
Hilo International Airport 280
Hindu Monastery 273
historical sites
  Kalaupapa National Historical Park (Molokai) 206
historic sites. See also temples
  Kalaupapa National Historical Park (Molokai) 71, 205
  Kaloko-Honokohau National Historical Park (Hawaii Island) 229
  Lapakahi State Historical Park (Hawaii Island) 68
  Mauna Kea adze quarry (Hawaii Island) 242
  Pu'uhonua O Honaunau 33
  Pu'uhonua 'O Honaunau National Historical Park (Hawaii Island) 68, 228
  Pu'ukohola Heiau National Historic Site (Hawaii Island) 231
history 8, 17
  20th century 49
  monarchy 41
  Polynesians, arrival of 29
  statehood 51
  US annexation 47
  World War II 50, 142, 161, 183
hitchhiking 282
Ho, Don 80
Hokule'a, voyages of 30
Holualoa 226
Honaunau Bay 228
Honoka'a 237, 241
Honokohau 181
Honokowai 181, 297
Honoli'i 240
Honolua/Mokule'ia Marine Preserve 181
Honolulu 53, 103, 107. See also Waikiki
  accommodations 286
  Aina Moana State Recreation Area 121
  Ala Moana Beach Park 121
  Ala Moana Boulevard 120
  Ala Moana Shopping Center 121
  Ala Wai Canal 121
  Ala Wai Yacht Harbor 121
  Aloha Tower 120, 121
  Bernice Pauahi Bishop Museum 135
  Bishop Square 118
  Bishop Street 118
  Boat Days 121

Cathedral of Our Lady of Peace 117
  Chinatown 119
  Coronation Stand 112
  East–West Center 141
  eating out 295
  Foster Botanical Gardens 120
  Hawaii Children's Discovery Center 301
  Hawaii State Art Museum 117
  Hawaii State Library 115
  Hawaii Theatre Center 118, 301
  Honolulu Hale 115
  Honpa Hongwanji Mission 138
  Hotel Street 119
  'Iolani Barracks 112
  'Iolani Palace 111
  Judiciary Building 113
  Kawaiaha'o Church 114
  Kewalo Basin 121
  King Kamehameha the Great Statue 114
  Kuan Yin Temple 119
  Likeke Hale 114
  Lyon Arboretum 141
  Magic Island 121
  Manoa Falls 141
  Manoa Valley 141
  Maunakea Marketplace 119
  Mission Houses 114
  National Memorial Cemetery of the Pacific 139
  Neal S. Blaisdell Center 121
  Nu'uanu 138
  Nu'uanu Pali Lookout 139
  Nu'uanu Stream 119
  Oahu Cemetery 136
  Oahu Market 119
  Prince Kuhio Kalaniana'ole Federal Building 120
  Punchbowl Crater 139
  Pu'u 'Ualaka'a State Park 140
  Queen Emma's Summer Palace 137
  Royal Burial Ground and Tomb 112
  Royal Mausoleum 137
  sculpture of Father Damien 116
  shopping 121
  Soto Zen Mission of Hawaii 138
  Spalding House 140
  St Andrew's Cathedral 117
  State Capitol Building 115
  statue of Queen Lili'uokalan 116
  Sunset on the Beach 301
  Tantalus 140
  University of Hawaii 141
  Waipuhia Valley Falls 138
  Ward Center 121
  Ward Warehouse 121
  Washington Place 117
Honolulu International Airport 280
Honomanu 192
Honomu 240
Ho'okio Gulch 217
Ho-olehua Airport 204
Ho'olehua Airport 280
horseback riding 74, 309
  Hawaii Island 234, 242

Maui 187, 196
Oahu 151
hotels. See accommodations
hot springs 245
Hualalai 20, 225
Hualalai Resort 229
Huelo 192
    Kaulanapueo church 192
Huialoha 196
Huialoha Church 189
Hui Ohana 81
Hulopo'e 214
Hulopo'e Bay 216

I

'Iao Needle 9, 175
'Iao Valley 174
    Hawaii Nature Center 174
    Kepaniwai Heritage Gardens 174
'Iao Valley State Park 175
'Ili 'ili 'opae Heiau 68
internet 312
irrigation 193

J

James Campbell National Wildlife
    Refuge 153
jet-skiing 151
Johnson, Jack 82
Josting, Edward 259

K

Ka'ahumanu 42
Ka'ahumanu, Queen 194
Ka'ala, Mount 164
Ka'anapali 290, 296
    accommodations 288
Ka'anapali 180
    Ka'anapali Beach 55
    Ka'anapali Resort 180
    Whaler's Village 180
    Whaler's Village Museum 180
Ka'apana, Ledward and Nedward
    81
Ka'ena Point 156, 164, 165
Kahakuloa 181
Kahala 131, 145
Kahalu'u Beach Park 72
Kahana 181
Kahana Bay 152
Kahanamoku, Duke 124, **130**
Kahanu Gardens 68, 194
Kahe Point 163
Kaho'olawe 17, 103, 169, 183
Kahuku 153
Kahului 50, **173**, 174
    Kanaha Pond State Wildlife
        Sanctuary 173
    Maui Arts and Cultural Center
        173, 301
Kahului Airport 280
Kahuna Falls 240
Kaiaka Bay 156
Kailua 149, 221, 225, **226**, 292,
    298. See also Kona
    accommodations 291
    Ahu'ena 226

'Ahu'ena Heiau 221
Hulihe'e Palace 221, 227
Kailua Beach Park 149
Kamakahonu 226
Moku'aikaua Church 221, 227
Kailua Bay 149, 226
Kainaliu
    Aloha Theatre Performing Arts
        Company 301
Kaiser, Henry J. 146
Kaiwio Pele 195
Ka Lae 221, **229**, 251
Kalahaku Overlook 188
Kalaheo 274
Kalakaua, King David 45, 79, 83
Kalalau Trail 71, 263, 266
Kalalau Valley 267
Kalalau Valley Lookout 268
Kalalea Heiau 252
Kalama, Benny 80
Kalanikaula 209
Kalapaki 271
Kalapaki Beach 271
Kalapana 250
Kalaupapa National Historical
    Park 71, 205, 206
Kalaupapa Overlook 206
Kalaupapa Peninsula 206
Kalaupapa Rare Adventure 207
Kalawao 207
    Siloama Church 207
    St Philomena's church 207
Kaleikini, Danny 80
Kaliuwa'a Falls 152
Kaloko-Honokohau National
    Historical Park 229
Kalua'aha 208
    Kalua'aha Church 208
    Our Lady of Sorrows Church 208
Kamae, Eddie 80
Kamahualele 31
Kamakau, Samuel M. 31, 38
Kamakawiwo'ole, Skippy and
    Israel 81
Kamakilo Village 273
Kamalo 208
Kamehameha II 42, 114
Kamehameha III 42, 114, 187
Kamehameha IV 44
Kamehameha, Lot 45
Kamehameha the Great 41, 114,
    208, 226, 231
    birthplace of 233
    statue 234
Kamehameha V 45, 77, 204, 277
Kamoa Wind Farm 251
Kamokila Hawaiian Village 93
Kamuela. See Waimea
Kanaka'ole, Edith 81
Kane'aki 68
Kaneana 164
Kane'ohe 150
    Byodo-In Temple 150
    He'eia Fishpond 150
    Senator Fong's Plantation and
        Gardens 151
    Valley of the Temples Memorial
        Park 150
Kane'ohe Bay 150
Kanepu'u 217

Kanepu'u Preserve 75
Kapa'a 293, 299
Kapa'a 271, 273
Kapa'au 234
    Kamehameha the Great statue
        234
    Kohala Tong Wo Society 232
Kapalua 176, 289, 297
    Kapalua Resort 181
Kapalua-West Maui Airport 280
Kapi'olani 43
Kapolei 287
Kapuaiwa Coconut Grove 204
Ka'u 247
Kauai 17, 37, 53, 103, 199. See
    also individual place names
    accommodations 293
    eating out 299
    shopping 307
Ka'u Desert 251
Ka'u District 252
Kauhako 204
Kauikeaouli 42
Kaulakahi Channel 277
Ka Ule o Nanahoa 206
Kaumahina State Wayside 192
Kaumakaiwa 82
Kaumalapau Harbor 216
Kaunakakai 9, 204, 297
Kaunolu 216
Kaunolu Bay 216
Kaupo 189, 196
    St Joseph's Church 189
Kaupo Gap 189, 196
Kaupo Ranch 196
Kawaihae 233, 298
Kawela 208
Kawelo 157
kayaking 8, 75, 183, 301, 309
    Kauai 266
Kazumura Cave 249
Kealaikahiki 31
Kealakekua Bay 35, 39, 228
Keale, Moe 81
Kealohi Point, 150
Ke'anae 192
    Ke'anae Arboretum 192
Ke'anae Peninsula 192
Keauokalani, Kepelino 31
Keawa'ula Bay 164
Keawe, Auntie Genoa 81
Keck Observatory 242
Ke'e Beach 265
Keokea 187
Keomuku 217
Keopuolani, Queen 176
Keoua 41
Kepuhi Bay 210
Kihei 182, 289
Kilauea 20, 19, 103, 245, **247**,
    263
    Crater Rim Drive 248
    eruptions 245, 247
    Halema'uma'u Crater 248
    Kilauea Iki Crater 249
    Kilauea Visitor Center 247
    Thomas A. Jaggar Museum 248
Kilauea Point National Wildlife
    Refuge 264
Kina'u 43

Kipahulu 196
Kipahulu Sugar Mill (Kipahulu) 196
Palapala Ho'omau Church 196
Kipahulu Valley 196, 199
Kipuka 'Ainahou Nene Sanctuary 244
Kipuka Pua'ulu 251
kiteboarding 309
Kohala 20, 221, 225, 291
Pu'u Kohala 41
Kohala Coast 291
Kohala Ditch 234
Kohala Mountains 233
Kohala Tong Wo Society 232
Kohumoku, George, Jr. 82
Koke'e 259, 268
Iliau Nature Loop 268
Koke'e Lodge 268
Koke'e Museum 268
Koki Beach 195
Koko Head 71, 146
Kolekole Pass 161
Koloa 274, 293, 299
Koloa Rum Company 274, 294
Komohana 169
Kona 221, 225, 291, 298. See also Kailua
Kona International Airport 225
Kona Village Resort 229
Kona International Airport 280
Ko'olau Mountains 135
Ko'olau Mountains 149
Ko 'Olina 107
Hawaiian Waters Adventure Park 163
Ko' Olina 159
Ko 'Olina Resort 163
Kualapu'u 205
Molokai Museum and Cultural Center 205
R.W. Meyer Sugar Mill 205
Kualoa Ranch 151
Kualoa Regional Park 151
Kuau 289
Ku'ilioloa Heiau 163
Kukuiho'olua 153
Kukui Trail 268
Kula 187, 297
Kure Atoll 19, 21

L

Lahaina 72, 114, 169
accommodatiions 288
Baldwin Home 179
Banyan Tree 177
eating out 296
Front Street 177
Hale Pa'ahao 179
Hale Pa'i 180
Jodo Mission Buddhist Cultural Park 179
Lahainaluna High School 179
Malu'uluolele Park 179
Pioneer Inn 177
Warren & Annabelle's 301
Wo Hing Society Temple 179
La'ie 152
Mormon Temple 152

Polynesian Cultural Center 152, 305
La'ie Point 153
Lake Wai'au 242
Lanai 17, 55, 61, 75, 103, 169. See also individual place names
accommodations 290
eating out 297
Lanai Airport 280
Lanai City 9, 214, 216
Hotel Lanai 216, 290
Lana'ihale 217
Lanaihale 75
land ownership 43, 54
language 17, 43
Lapakahi State Historical Park 68, 233
La Pérouse Bay 183, 187
Laulima Farm stand 194
Laupaho'eho'e 241
Laupaho'eho'e Train Museum 241
Laupaho'eho'e Natural Area Reserve 241
Lava Tree State Monument 245
lava tubes 249
Lawa'i Kai 275
Ledyard, John 39
Lee, Kui 80
Leeward Islands 165
legends. See mythology and legends
leis 84, 228, 306
leprosy colony. See Hansen's Disease exiles
Liholiho 42
Liholiho, Alexander 44
Lihu'e 293, 299
Lihu'e 259, 271
Grove Farm Homestead & Sugar Plantation Museum 272
Kauai Community College Performing Arts Center 301
Kauai Museum 272
South Pacific Dinner Show 301
Lihu'e Airport 280
Lili'uokalani, Queen 46, 117, 147
statue (Honolulu) 116
Lili'uokalani, Queen 79, 81
Limahuli 265
Lindbergh, Charles 196
Lingle, Linda 55
literature 31
mele 31
Lo'ihi 19, 250
London, Jack 205
The Cruise of the Snark 205
lu'aus 91, 305
Lumaha'i 265
Lunalilo, King William 45, 114

M

Ma'alaea 175
Maui Ocean Center 175, 302
macadamia nuts 238, 241
Machado, Lena 81
Makaha 163
Makaha Sons of Ni'ihau 81
Makaha Valley 164
Kane'aki Heiau 164

Makanalua Peninsula 206
Makapu'u Beach Park 146
Makapu'u Point 147
Sea Life Park 147
Makawao 9, 74, 186, 187, 297
Pi'iholo Ranch 187
Makena 182, 289
Makua Beach 164
Malo, David 31, 32
Manele Bay 214
Manele Boat Harbor 217
maps 312
Marcos, Ferdinand and Imelda 140
marijuana 231, 245
marine conservation districts 23
Hulopo'e Bay (Lanai) 217
Kealakekua Bay (Hawaii Island) 228
markets
Aloha Stadium Swap Meet 160
farmers' markets 294
Hana 194
Hanalei 264
Kauai 264
Mars, Bruno 82
Maui 17, 38, 53, 103. See also individual place names
accommodations 288
eating out 296
shopping 307
Mauiaki 251
Mauna Kamakou 204
Mauna Kea 20, 237, 239, **242**, 254
Mauna Kea Beach Hotel 231
Mauna Lani Resort 230
Maunaloa 210
Mauna Loa (Hawaii Island) 20, 75, 227, 239, **244**, 247
eruptions 239, 244
Mauna Loa (Molokai) 204
Mauna Ulu 249
Maunawili 147
Mavrothalassitis, George 89
McAllister, J. Gilbert 163
McKinley, President William 47
McNamara, Garrett 73
media 312
Melville, Herman 177
Menehune Ditch 274
Merriman, Peter 89
Michener, James 206
Hawaii 206
Midway Islands 165
Miloli'i 228
missionaries 42
Moanalua Gardens 159
Moanalua Valley 159
Mokoli'i 151
Mokualai 153
Moku'aweoweo 244
Moku Ho'oniki 209
Mokulau 196
Mokule'ia Polo Farm 156
Moli'j Fishpond 151
Molokai 17, 21, 59, 103, 169, 199. See also individual place names
accommodations 290
eating out 297

Molokai Ranch 210
Molokini 183
Molokini Atoll 21, 73
money matters 313
budgeting for your trip 310
money-saving tips 9
tax 313
Mo'okini Heiau 233
Mo'oula Falls 209
movies. See film and television
movie theaters 301
Munro Trail 75, 217
Murdock, David 215
museums and galleries 7
Alexander & Baldwin Sugar
Museum (Pu'unene) 175
Bailey House (Wailuku) 174
Baldwin Home (Lahaina) 179
Bernice Pauahi Bishop Museum
(Honolulu) 135
commercial art and craft galleries
300
East Hawaii Cultural Center
Gallery (Hilo) 239
Grove Farm Homestead & Sugar
Plantation Museum (Lihu'e)
272
Hana Cultural Center & Museum
(Hana) 194
Hawaii Children's Discovery
Center (Honolulu) 301
Hawaii Nature Center ('Iao Valley)
174
Hawaii State Art Museum
(Honolulu) 117
Hulihe'e Palace (Kailua) 227
'Imiloa Astronomy Center (Hilo)
239
Kauai Museum (Lihu'e) 272
Koke'e Museum (Koke'e) 268
Laupaho'eho'e Train Museum
(Laupaho'eho'e) 241
Lyman Mission House and
Museum (Hilo) 239
Maui Arts and Cultural Center
(Kahului) 173
Mission Houses (Honolulu) 114
Molokai Museum and Cultural
Center (Kualapu'u) 205
Pacific Tsunami Museum (Hilo)
239
Parker Ranch Museum and Visitor
Center (Waimea) 233
Spalding House (Honolulu) 140
Thomas A. Jaggar Museum
(Kilauea) 248
Tropic Lightning Museum
(Schofield Barracks) 160
US Army Museum (Waikiki) 128
USS Bowfin Submarine Museum
& Park (Pearl Harbor) 142
West Kauai Technology & Visitor
Center (Waimea) 276
Whaler's Village Museum
(Ka'anapali) 180
Wo Hing Society Temple (Lahaina)
179
music and dance 77
Aloha 'Oe 79, 147
hula 43, 79, **82**, 210, 239

live music venues 305
musical instruments 78, 306
slack key style 78
ukuleles 67
mythology and legends 17, 162,
194, 209, 250, 265
gnomes 31
Kamohoali'i 164
Kauhi 152
Maui 185, 240
menehune 274
Pehe and Makakehau 216
Pele 195, 225
Poli'ahu 242
sacred stones 124

N

Na'alehu 251
Nahiku 193
Na Leo Pilimehana 81
Na Palapalai 81
Na Pali 265
Na Pali Coast 71, 103, 263
**Na Pali Coast State Wilderness
Park** 266
Napili 181, 289
national and state parks 23
camping 285
Haleakala National Park (Maui)
188, 191, 195
Hapuna Beach State Park (Hawaii
Island) 231
Hawaii Volcanoes National Park
(Hawaii Island) 221, **247**
'Iao Valley State Park (Maui) 175
Na Pali Coast State Wilderness
Park (Kauai) 266
Pala'au State Park (Molokai) 205
Polihale State Park (Kauai) 267
Pua'a Ka'a State Park (Maui) 193
Pu'u 'Ualaka'a State Park
(Honolulu) 140
Russian Fort Elizabeth (Waimea)
276
Wai'anapanapa State Park (Maui)
193
Wailuku River State Park (Hawaii
Island) 239
**national historical parks and
sites**. See historic sites
**National Tropical Botanical
Garden** 265, 275
nature reserves 23
Alaka'i Swamp (Kauai) 259, 267
Hawaiian Islands National Wildlife
Refuge (Oahu) 165
Honolua/Mokule'ia Marine
Preserve (Maui) 181
James Campbell National Wildlife
Refuge (Oahu) 153
Ka'ena Point (Oahu) 164
Kamakou Preserve (Molokai)
205
Kanaha Pond State Wildlife
Sanctuary (Kahului) 173
Kanepu'u Preserve (Lanai) 75
Kilauea Point National Wildlife
Refuge (Kauai) 264
Kipahulu Valley (Maui) 196, 199

Kipuka 'Ainahou Nene Sanctuary
(Hawaii Island) 244
Kipuka Pua'ulu (Hawaii Island)
251
Laupaho'eho'e Natural Area
Reserve (Hawaii Island) 241
Waimea Valley (Oahu) 155
Nawiliwili 50
Nawiliwili Harbor 271
Neighbor Islands 53
newspapers 312
nightlife 226, 304
Ni'ihau 17, 37, 59, 103, 267, 272,
277
Niuli'i 234
North Kohala 221, 233, 292, 298
North Kona 229
North Shore (Kauai) 293, 299
North Shore (Oahu) 107, 286, 295
**Northwestern Hawaiian Islands
Marine National Monument**
165
Nu'uanu Pali Lookout 9

O

Oahu 17, 37, 50, 55, 103. See
also individual place names
accommodations 286
eating out 295
shopping 306
Obama, President Barack 55, 90,
149, 150
obsidian 226
off-roading 74, 215
Munro Trail 217
Ohe'o Gulch 191, 195
Olomana 147
Oneali'i Park (Royal Sands) 207
Onizuka Astronomy Complex 243
Onomea Bay 240
Opaeka'a Falls 273
opening hours 313
orientation 283

P

Pa'auhau 241
Pa'auilo 241
paddleboarding 73, 266
Pahinui, Gabby 80, 147
Pahoa 245
Pa'ia 186
Ho'okipa Beach 186
Mantokuji Mission 186
Paia 289
eating out 296
Pailolo Channel 209
Pala'au State Park 205
Palawai 216
Palawai Basin 216
Papa'aloa 241
Papa Ii, John 31
Papa'ikou 240
Papakolea Green Sand Beach
252
Papohaku Beach Camp 210
paragliding 75
parasailing 146
Parker, John Palmer 232

parks and gardens
Ala Moana Beach Park (Honolulu) 121
Foster Botanical Gardens (Honolulu) 120
Hawaii Tropical Botanical Garden (Hawaii Island) 240
Hawaii Tropical Botanical Garden (Hilo) 237
Kahanu Gardens 68
Kahanu Gardens (Maui) 194
Kapi'olani Park (Waikiki) 129
Kaumahina State Wayside (Maui) 192
Ke'anae Arboretum (Ke'anae) 192
Kepaniwai Heritage Gardens ('Iao Valley) 174
Kualoa Regional Park (Oahu) 151
Lili'uokalani Gardens (Hilo) 239
Lyon Arboretum (Honolulu) 141
Malu'uluolele Park (Lahaina) 179
Moanalua Gardens (Oahu) 159
National Tropical Botanical Garden (Kauai) 265, 275
Sacred Falls Park (Oahu) 152
Senator Fong's Plantation and Gardens (Kane'ohe) 151
Valley of the Temples Memorial Park (Kane'ohe) 150
Wahiawa Botanical Garden (Wahiawa) 161
Waimea Valley (Oahu) 155
Pauoa Bay 230
Pava'o, Dennis 81
Peahi 72
Pearl City 160
Pearl Harbor 46, 47, 103, 107
Hickam Air Force Base 143
USS Arizona Memorial 142, 143
USS Bowfin Submarine Museum & Park 142
USS Missouri 143
World War II 50, 142
Pearl Harbor 141
people 17, 274
Caucasians 66
Chinese 61, 232
ethnic diversity 44
Filipinos 64
indigenous Hawaiians 59, 204
Japanese 62, 238
Koreans 64
Marquesans 30
Mormon community 152, 215
Samoans 66
Tahitians 30
Pepe'ekeo 240
Pepe'opae Trail 205
petroglyphs 69, 159, 230
Puako petroglyph field 230
pets 310
Pi'ilanihale Heiau 68, 194
Pi'ilani Highway 195
pineapples 49, 159, 161, 173, 215
Dole Plantation 161
plant life 19, **22**, 23, 198, 263, 265

Cook Island pine 215
kukui trees 209
silverswords 23, 188
Pohakuloa 244
Po'ipu 271, 273
Poipu 299
Poipu Beach 72
Polihale State Park 267
Polihua Beach 215
politics. See government and politics
polo 156
Pololu Valley Lookout 234
postal services 313
Preis, Alfred 142, 143
Presley, Elvis 121, 142, 146
Princeville 263, **264**, 293
Pua'a Ka'a State Park 193
Puako 69
Puako petroglyph field 230
public holidays 313
Pukalani 186
Puna 238, 245
Punalu'u Beach 251
Puohokamoa Falls 192
Pu'uhonua 'O Honaunau National Historical Park 33, 68, 228
Pu'u Keka'a. See Black Rock
Pu'ukohola Heiau National Historic Site 68, 231
Pu'u Kukui 175
Pu'unene 175
Alexander & Baldwin Sugar Museum 175
Pu'u O Hoku Ranch 209
Pu'u O Mahuka 68
Pu'uomahuka Heiau State Monument 155
Pu'u 'Ula'ula 188
Pu'u Wa'awa'a 226
Pu'uwai 277
Pyle, Ernest Taylor (Ernie) 139

Q

Queen's Medical Center 44

R

Radford, Arthur 143
radio 312
rail travel. See heritage railways
Rainbow Falls 239
rainforests 22, 23, 107, 135, 191, 204, 247
Reichel, Keali'i 82
religion 33
Christianity 43
Polynesian deities 35
sacred sites 161
traditional beliefs 60, 156
restaurants 9, 294. See also eating out, food and drink
Rhee, Dr Syngman 65
Rice, William Harrison 272
Rice, William Hyde 272
Robinson Keith and Bruce 277
Rowan, Chad 147
Royal Hawaiian Band 78
royal stones 69

S

Sacred Falls Park 152
Saddle Road 242
salt ponds 275
Sandalwood Boat 205
Sandwich Islands 37
Sandy Beach 146
Schofield Barracks 160
Tropic Lightning Museum 160
Science City 188
sea travel 281, 283. See also cruise ships
Sheffer, Dr Anton 276
Shimabukuro, Jake 82
Shipwreck Beach 75, 217
shopping 305
what to buy 305
Simeon, Sheldon 89
skydiving 156
Smith, Ernest 208
snorkeling. See diving and snorkeling
society. See culture and society
Sons of Hawaii 80
South Kohala 55, 230
South Kona 227
South Maui 181
South Point. See Ka Lae
South Shore (Kauai) 293, 299
sports 308. See also by name
sports venues 308. See also sports by name
Aloha Stadium (Oahu) 159, 308
Mokule'ia Polo Farm 156
The Ice Palace (Oahu) 160
Spouting Horn 274
Stadium Mall 160
state parks. See national and state parks
St Benedict's Painted Church 228
Steaming Bluff (Sulfur Banks) 248
Stevens, John B. 47
sugar 44, 46, 49, 173, 193, 240, 271, 274
Alexander & Baldwin Sugar Museum (Pu'unene) 175
R.W. Meyer Sugar Mill (Kualapu'u) 205
sumo wrestling 66, 147
Sunday Manoa 81
Sunset Beach 295
Sun Yatsen 62, 232
surfing 6, 9, **72**, 124, **157**, 175
Hawaii Island 240
Kauai 263, 264
Maui 181, 196
Oahu 107, 154, 164
surfboards, shopping for 306
tuition 72, 157, 301
Sweetheart Rock 216
swimming. See also beaches
Hawaii Island 231
Lanai 217
Maui 192, 193, 195
with dolphins 230

T

Tantalus, Mount 140
taro 192, 193
tattoos 34
tax 313
taxis 283
Tedeschi Winery 187
telephones 313
television 313. See also film and television
temples 33, 155, 228
  'Ahu'ena Heiau (Kailua) 221
  Ahu'ena (Kailua) 226
  Byodo-In (Kane'ohe) 150
  'Ili 'ili 'opae Heiau (Molokai) 68
  Kadavul (Kauai) 273
  Kalalea Heiau (Hawaii Island) 252
  Kaloko-Honokohau (Hawaii Island) 229
  Kane'aki Heiau (Makaha Valley) 164
  Kane'aki (Oahu) 68
  Ku'ililoa Heiau (Oahu) 163
  Laka heiau (Molokai) 210
  Mantokuji Mission (Pa'ia) 186
  Mo'okini Heiau (Hawaii Island) 233
  Mormon Temple (La'ie) 150
  Pi'ilanihale Heiau (Maui) 68, 194
  Poli'ahu Heiau (Kauai) 273
  Pu'uhonua 'O Honaunau (Hawaii Island) 228
  Pu'ukohola Heiau (Hawaii Island) 231
  Pu'ukohola Heiau National Historic Site (Hawaii Island) 68
  Pu'u O Mahuka (Oahu) 68
  San Marga Iraivan (Kauai) 273
  Valley of the Temples Memorial Park (Kane'ohe) 150
  Wo Hing Society Temple (Lahaina) 179
theaters and concert venues 305
  Aloha Theatre Performing Arts Company (Kainaliu) 301
  Hawaii Theatre Center (Honolulu) 118, 301
  Kauai Community College Performing Arts Center (Lihu'e) 301
  Maui Academy of Performing Arts (Wailuku) 301
  Maui Arts and Cultural Center (Kahului) 173, 301
  Neal S. Blaisdell Center (Honolulu) 121
  Polynesian Cultural Center (La'ie) 152
  South Pacific Dinner Show (Lihu'e) 301
  The Maui Theatre (Lahaina) 302
  Volcano Art Center (Volcano) 301
  Warren & Annabelle's (Lahaina) 301
Thiebaut, Daniel 89
Thurston Lava Tube 249
tiki bars 294
tipping 294, 314
tourism 52, 53
tourist information 314

tour operators 314
tours
  helicopter tours 151, 205, 221, 266, 277
  Molokai rainforest 204
  sightseeing tours 308
trains. See heritage railways
transportation 9, 280
tsunamis 229, 238, 242, 311
  Pacific Tsunami Museum (Hilo) 239
Tunnels Beach 263, 264
Turtle Bay Resort 154, 286
Twain, Mark 177, 185, 206

U

'Ulupalakua Ranch 187
'Umi, King 243
Upcountry 186, 297
'Upolu Point 233

V

Vancouver, George 31, 155
Vaughan, Palani 81
visas and passports 314
Volcano 250, 292
  Volcano Art Center 250, 301
  Volcano House 250
volcanoes 6, 19, 17
  eruptions 248, 249
  Haleakala (Maui) 169, 185, 188
  Halema'uma'u (Hawaii Island) 255
  Hawaiian Volcano Observatory (Hawaii Island) 248
  Hualalai (Hawaii Island) 20, 225
  Kaiwio Pele (Maui) 195
  Kauhako (Molokai) 204
  Kilauea (Hawaii Island) 19, 20, 103, 245, 247
  Kohala (Hawaii Island) 20
  Komohana (Maui) 169
  Mauna Kamakou (Molokai) 204
  Mauna Kea (Hawaii Island) 20, 237, 239, 242, 254
  Mauna Loa (Hawaii Island) 20, 75, 227, 244, 239, 247
  Mauna Loa (Molokai) 204
  Mauna Ulu (Hawaii Island) 249
  Palawai (Lanai) 216
  Pu'u Kukui (Maui) 175
  Pu'u Wa'awa'a (Hawaii Island) 226
von Kotzebue, Otto 31

W

Waha'ula 250
Wahiawa 160, 161
  birth stones of Kukaniloko 161
  Dole Plantation 161
  Wahiawa Botanical Garden 161
Waiakoa 187
  Church of the Holy Ghost 187
Wai'ale'ale 259
Waialua 209
Wai'anae 107
Wai'anae Coast 162

Wai'anapanapa State Park 193
Waihe'e, John 54
Waikaloa 291
Waikiki 52, 55, 107, 121
  accommodations 125, 286, 288
  Atlantis Submarines 128
  eating out 295
  Halekulani hotel 127, 286
  Hawaii Convention Center 125
  Hilton Hawaiian Village 128, 286
  Honolulu Zoo 131, 302
  Kaimana Beach 131
  Kapi'olani Park 129
  Moana Surfrider Hotel 126, 286
  Queen's Surf Beach 129
  Royal Hawaiian Hotel 127, 287
  Sans Souci 124
  Statue of Duke Kahanamoku 124
  Stones of Kapaemahu 124
  Trump International Hotel Waikiki 128, 287
  US Army Museum 128
  Waikiki Aquarium 302
  Waikiki Trolley 282
  War Memorial Natatorium 129, 131
Waikiki Beach 72, 103
Waikolu Lookout 205
Wailea 55, 182, 289, 297
Wailua 193, 273, 299
  Fern Grotto 273
  St Gabriel's Church 193
Wailua Falls 195
Wailua River 273
Wailuku 173, 174, 181, 289, 297
  Bailey House 174
  Ka'ahumanu Congregational Church 174
  Maui Academy of Performing Arts 301
Wailuku River 237
Wailuku River State Park 239
Waimanalo 144, 147
Waimanalo Beach 147
Waimanu Valley 242
Waimea 37, 221, 232, 275, 292, 293, 298
  Parker Ranch 232
  Parker Ranch Museum and Visitor Center 233
  Russian Fort Elizabeth State Park 276
  West Kauai Technology & Visitor Center 276
Waimea Bay 154
  St Peter and Paul Church 155
Waimea Canyon 9, 103, 263, 267
Waimea-Kohala Airport 280
Waimea River 267, 268
Waimea Town 271
Waimea Valley 155
Waimoku Falls 196
Waipahu 160, 162
  Hawaii Plantation Village 162
Waipi'o Valley 75, 237, 241, 243
Waipouli 271, 273
walking 282. See also hiking
waterfalls 264
  'Akaka Falls (Hawaii Island) 9, 237, 240